D1737018

THE EMERGENCE OF THE ARMENIAN DIOCESE OF NEW JULFA IN THE SEVENTEENTH CENTURY

University of Pennsylvania
Armenian Texts and Studies

Series Editor
MICHAEL E. STONE

Number 14
THE EMERGENCE OF THE ARMENIAN DIOCESE
OF NEW JULFA
IN THE SEVENTEENTH CENTURY
by
Vazken S. Ghougassian

THE EMERGENCE OF THE ARMENIAN DIOCESE OF NEW JULFA IN THE SEVENTEENTH CENTURY

by

Vazken S. Ghougassian

Scholars Press
Atlanta, Georgia

THE EMERGENCE OF THE ARMENIAN DIOCESE
OF NEW JULFA
IN THE SEVENTEENTH CENTURY

by
Vazken S. Ghougassian

© 1998
University of Pennsylvania
Armenian Texts and Studies

Library of Congress Cataloging in Publication Data

Ghougassian, Vazken S.
    The emergence of the Armenian Diocese of New Julfa in the
seventeenth century / by Vazken S. Ghougassian.
      p.   cm. — (University of Pennsylvania Armenian texts and
studies ; no. 14)
    Based on the author's thesis (doctoral)—Columbia University, 1995
    Includes bibliographical references and index.
    ISBN 0-7885-0438-X (hardcover : alk. paper)
    1. Armenian Church. Diocese of New Julfa—History. 2. Işfahān
(Iran)—Church history.   I. title. II. Series.
BX124.5.I7G48 1998
281'.62'095595—dc21   98-2669
                              CIP

Printed in the United States of America
on acid-free paper

This publication was made possible by a generous grant

from the

Dolores Zohrab Liebmann Fund.

To His Holiness
Karekin I
Katʿołikos of All Armenians

TABLE OF CONTENTS

Illustrations

Maps

PREFACE

The journey of the present work, from its beginnings to its conclusion has lasted–due to lengthy interruptions and other occupational disadvantages–for almost eighteen years.

After completing my graduate studies at Columbia University, in April 1979, I returned to Lebanon, to begin an administrative and academic career at the Armenian Katolikosate of Cilicia and its Theological Seminary. Soon after, I started preliminary research for my Ph.D. dissertation. However, due to a hectic work schedule and various types of hardship, largely caused by the long lasting Lebanese civil war, my research was often interrupted, and by 1982, it was completely halted.

Following the kind advice of Prof. Nina G. Garsoïan and with the support of His Holiness Karekin II, then Katolikos of Cilicia, in January 1989, I returned to New York and resumed my research, amid full time administrative duties at the Prelacy of the Armenian Apostolic Church of America. The present work is a thoroughly revised version of that dissertation, which was defended in April 1995.

In bringing this work to its conclusion, I am greatly indebted to numerous individuals and institutions for their support, advice, encouragement, and active participation. I would like to thank them all. My special thanks go to H.H. Karekin I, now Katolikos of All Armenians and Archbishop Mesrob Ashjian for their many years of active support and encouragement.

I am much indebted to Archbishop Koriwn Babian, Mr. Levon G. Minasean and the Diocesan Council of New Julfa, who provided me with most of the archival materials utilized in this work. At the State Manuscript Library –the *Matenadaran*– of Armenia, Prof. Hakob Papazyan—a great scholar of Armenian and Iranian studies, who passed away a few weeks ago— and the late Nicholas Gevorgyan helped me in the most difficult task of reading and translating the Persian royal decrees.

I would like to express my special gratitude to Prof. Nina G. Garsoïan, for teaching me the art of scholarship and guiding me through the entire course of this work, even after her retirement from Columbia University.

I thank Rev. Dr. Krikor Maksoudian, Director of the Krikor and Clara Zohrab Information Center and Prof. Hamid Dabashi of Columbia University for their valuable comments and suggestions; Prof. Robert H. Hewsen of Rowan College for his professional help in drawing two maps for this publication; Dr. Linda Rose of New York for her editorial skills and linguistic contribution; and Dr. Armen Haghnazarian of Aachen, Germany, for his contribution of five original photos.

Special thanks are due to Prof. Michael E. Stone of Hebrew University and the University of Pennsylvania Armenian Texts and Studies Series Editor for his editorial advice and approval of the present publication; and Mr. Suren D. Fesjian, Co-Trustee of the Dolores Zohrab Liebman Fund Publications Program, for the generous grant which made this publication possible.

I owe much to my sister Seta Ghougassian for her professional assistance in typesetting this work; my wife, Houri, whose constant support and encouragement helped me endure all kinds of difficulties while bringing this work to a conclusion; and my six years old son, Varant, for being able to adapt to my work schedule during the past few years. Finally I thank my two colleagues: Mrs. Iris Papazian and Mrs. Varteny Koulian for their assistance in various capacities.

Translation and Transliteration

Whenever possible, the English translations of Persian sources and western travel accounts are used and properly acknowledged in this work. The translation of all Armenian sources and most of French travel and missionary accounts are my own. For the translation of Persian royal decrees, I have partly consulted the work of Yarutiwn Tēr Yovhaneanč.

For easy reading purposes, the more familiar form of certain names and titles, including New Julfa, Isfahan, *Shah*, *Khan*, *Agha* and *Khwaja* are used. For the transliteration of Armenian names and words the Hubschman Meillet Benveniste system has been adopted. The Persian words are transliterated according to the system used in the *Encyclopaedia Iranica*. A special attempt has been made to follow the same system, as much as possible, for the transliteration of Persian geographical names and words discovered in the Armenian sources.

INTRODUCTION

The year 2005 will mark the 400th anniversary of the establishment of New Julfa, a small town on the right bank of river Zayenderud, adjacent to the Safavid Capital of Isfahan. Until the mid-twentieth century, this town was inhabited exclusively by Armenians. Even now, the Armenian community of New Julfa, numbering seven thousand souls, is the oldest, and one of the most active Armenian communities in the diaspora. The All Saviour's Monastery and thirteen surviving parish churches, all of which were built in the seventeenth century, along with three schools and a number of social, medical, charitable, cultural and youth institutions established during the last one hundred years, operate in full capacity, serving the spiritual, cultural and social needs of the community.

During the past three hundred and ninety two years, as a religious minority in Muslim Iran, the Armenians of New Julfa faced different religious, political, economic, social and cultural conditions. For several decades in the seventeenth century, they enjoyed a glorious period, in terms of limited internal autonomy, religious freedom and economic prosperity. During this period they laid the foundations of a strong religious institution, the diocesan entity, which was centered in the All Saviour's monastery. This entity served as a source of spiritual guidance and ethnic solidarity not only for the local community but also for all the Armenians scattered in central parts of Iran. It also strengthened their resolve to maintain their identity despite long periods of hardship in a foreign land.

Thereafter, for the greater part of the eighteenth and nineteenth centuries, due to political instability and several military operations in Iran, as well as constant pressures and occasional persecutions against the non-Muslim minorities, the Armenians of New Julfa and other parts of Iran faced tremendous hardships and periods of confusion and total chaos. Many fled the country and relocated primarily in India and Russia. But as expatriates, especially those who settled in India, they continued to be loyal to the All Saviour's Monastery, and formed small but very active communities under the jurisdiction of the diocese of New Julfa.[1] Primarily through their financial support, the All Saviour's monastery was able to continue its religious and cultural mission and help the Armenians of Iran maintain their churches, their ethnic and religious identity, their cultural heritage and survive as the largest non-Muslim minority of Iran.

Scholars have so far treated the Armenian community of New Julfa primarily as a trade settlement which, in the seventeenth century, played an important role in the international trade between the Far East, Iran and Europe, accumulated great wealth and financed the construction of the All Saviour's monastery and more than thirty parish churches, where, for a few decades, the Armenian arts and culture flourished. They have mostly ignored the fact that the Armenian community of New Julfa was only one component, albeit an important one, of a much larger diocesan entity. Little attempt has been made to study the diocesan structure of the Armenian Church in Iran and its religious and administrative role in the life of the local Armenian communities.

Indeed, the task of studying the history of the diocese of New Julfa, particularly of its geographical, demographic, social and administrative setting, based on the available sources is made particularly difficult by their simultaneous extensiveness and the scanty information they actually contain concerning these aspects of the history of the diocese. Also, as will be seen in the following chapter, these sources are largely unpublished, untranslated and sometimes even not collected systematically, as is the case of tombstone inscriptions.

For a long time, the exploration of the sources for the history of the Armenian communities of Iran were carried out by a few individuals. First and the most distinguished among them was Yarutiwn Tēr Yovhaneanc, who in mid-nineteenth century served as secretary of All

---

[1] Since late seventeenth century, the primates of New Julfa used to assign pastors for the small Armenian communities of India and the Far East. In the eighteenth century, the diocese of New Julfa was gradually renamed *Iranahndkastani tem* (diocese of Iran and India) to better express the jurisducictional sphere of the diocese.

Saviour's monastery between 1851 and 1871. He compiled two volumes[2] on the basis of material gathered at first hand, mainly from the archives of the monastery, certain Armenian historians, and the available manuscript colophons and inscriptions of New Julfa churches and cemetery.

Despite the undeniable value of his work, Tēr Yovhaneanċ was not able to utilize several important Armenian sources, which were published only after his death in 1871. Nor was he able to utilize the accounts of Western travelers and Catholic missionaries, probably due to his lack of knowledge of Western languages. Furthermore, the work published posthumously may have been left incomplete by the author and the publishers allowed numerous errors, (primarily in numbers, dates and footnotes) to creep into the work.

Since the late 1960's and early 1970's, new opportunities have been created for scholarly research on New Julfa. Between 1968 and 1972, The Calouste Gulbenkian Foundation of Lisbon, Portugal sponsored the publications of an architectural survey on the Armenian churches of New Julfa by John Carswell[3] and the two-volume catalogue of manuscripts of the All Saviour's monastery by S. Tēr Awetisean and L.G. Minasean.[4] During the same period the Italian Institute for the Middle and the Far East (IsMEO) and the Italian Cultural Institute of Teheran started architectural surveys and some restoration work on churches and old houses of New Julfa. In 1971, a new museum with a rich collection of various types of items preserved in the monastery, or collected from churches, old houses or individuals, was inaugurated. The same year, Bishop Karekin Sarkissian, the newly elected primate of the diocese of New Julfa, initiated a number of new projects which created a new impetus for cultural activities and scholarly work in New Julfa. Sirarpie Der Nersessian, a great authority in Armenian and Byzantine arts, was asked by the bishop to study the miniatures of the manuscript collection of the All Saviour's monastery. Arpag Mekhitarian, the curator of the Islamic Department of the Royal Museum of Art and History in Brussels, Belgium was invited to New Julfa to photograph the manuscripts for the proposed study.[5] L.G. Minasean was entrusted with the task of classifying and cataloguing the

---

2 Patmuťiwn Nor Ĵuɫayu or yAspahan, New Julfa, 1880-81.
3 Carswell J., New Julfa, Oxford 1968.
4 Printed in Vienna 1970-2.
5 The study and the photographs were later published under the title *Armenian Miniatures from Isfahan*, Brussels 1984.

archives of the monastery. I was invited from Lebanon to reorganize the seventy years old library of the monastery, which included a very valuable collection of almost twenty thousand volumes.

During my tenure of three years (1971-1974) at the library of New Julfa, I had an unique opportunity to do extensive reading and get acquainted with the historical past of the Armenian community of New Julfa. More importantly, however, I was able to visit many times all the thirteen surviving churches, the few old houses and the historical cemetery of New Julfa. Furthermore, I occasionally visited several old Armenian villages in the districts of P̌eria and Čhar Mahal (Geandiman and J̌łaxor) and in some of the villages of P̌eria observed the traditional lifestyle and the customs of the Armenian villagers. These visual experiences broadened my interests, enhanced my knowledge and made me realize how limited in scope was the available literature on the matter.

Following my graduation from Columbia University in 1979, I once again focused my attention on the history of the Armenian communities of Iran, in search for a possible topic for my Ph.D. dissertation. By then, the first two volumes of the seventeenth century Armenian manuscript colophons had been published,[6] covering the period between 1600 and 1640. But more importantly, L.G. Minasean had completed the basic classification and cataloguing of the archives of the all Saviour's Monastery and had published a preliminary catalogue.[7] A revised and more detailed catalogue of the archives was published in 1983.[8] Upon my written request, Bishop Goriwn Babian of New Julfa and L.G. Minasean kindly provided me with copies of more than three hundred documents from the archives. With such a treasure in my hands, I could hardly think of any other possible field for research.

To a certain degree, the documents in my possession were a randomly selection, because, due to the difficulties beyond my control, I was not able to go back to Iran and make my own selections in the archives of the monastery. Furthermore, both the preliminary and the revised catalogues of the archives did not include itemized lists for every single document in the collection. Most of the documents were grouped under separate files and were classified according to their subject, chronological order and geographical relevance. Only the pontifical encyclicals and the royal decrees were numbered and listed as

---

[6] Hakobyan V., Hovhanisyan A., *ŽĒ Dari Hayeren J̌eragreri Hišatakaranner*, vols I-II, Erevan 1974-8.

[7] Minasean L.G., *Diwan N. J̌ułayi S. Amenap̌rkič̣ Vanḱi*, New Julfa 1976.

[8] _____, *Diwan S. Amenap̌rkič̣ Vanḱi*, New Julfa 1983.

individual items in the published catalogue. Therefore, along with my written request to the diocesan authorities of New Julfa, I presented a general list of documents, primarily guided by the titles in the published catalogues and with the aim of securing as many documents as possible, from the seventeenth and early eighteenth centuries. Fortunately, most of the documents I obtained from New Julfa proved to be very useful and many of them were unpublished.

A substantial part of the documents in my possession comprised encyclicals, letters, petitions, and decrees pertinent to the religious and administrative rights of the diocese of New Julfa, a long lasting jurisdictional conflict between the Katʻolikate of Ējmiacin and the All Saviour's Monastery, the religious policies of the Safavid kings towards the Armenian community of New Julfa and the Catholic missionary activities among the Armenians of Iran. They also included scanty information on geographical, demographic, social and administrative setting, as well as other aspects of the history of the diocese of New Julfa.

Many of these documents were utilized and partly published by Y. Tēr Yovhaneanč,[9] who, as a compiler, does not seem to have studied most of them in depth, in order to evaluate their informational content and present clear conclusions on certain issues related to the diocese of New Julfa. Even after the publication of Tēr Yovhaneanč's work, these documents did not attract much attention among Armenian scholars. Consequently, important aspects in the history of New Julfa remained unexplored.

The aim of this study is to explore and bring to light the geographical and demographic distribution of the Armenian refugees in Iran, their social composition, their civil and religious administrative setting, their treatment by the Safavid state, the formation and the emergence of the diocese of New Julfa, its relations with the Katʻolikate of Ējmiacin, its reaction to Catholic missionary activities among the Armenians of Iran and its cultural legacy. The English translation of twenty-two original Armenian and Persian documents will be presented in the Appendix. The translated documents, most of which still remain unpublished, are selected for their direct relevance to the policies of the Safavid Kings towards the Armenians of New Julfa, the jurisdictional conflict between Ējmiacin and New Julfa and Catholic missionary activities in Armenia and Iran.

The present study will cover the first one hundred and twenty years in the history of the Armenian diocese of New Julfa. This time

---

9 *Patmutʻiwn Nor Ĵulayu*, vols. I-II.

frame is determined by the mass deportation of Armenians to Iran in 1604 and the Afghan occupation of Isfahan in 1722, which at least economically devastated New Julfa and caused a large migration to India, Russia and other countries.

The diocese of New Julfa was created in 1605 for the religious administration of the local Armenian community, which was exclusively composed of merchants. But within two decades, its jurisdiction was expanded over other Armenian communities of Iran and it emerged as one of the most prosperous and influential Sees of the seventeenth century Armenian Church. It maintained its prominence and played an important role in the religious, administrative and cultural life of the Armenian Church and people for almost a century, until the Afghan occupation of Isfahan and the fall of the Safavid Kingdom. Therefore, this study will attempt to explore the historical past of that diocese and fill an important gap in the seventeenth century history of the Armenian Church.

CHAPTER ONE

A GENERAL SURVEY OF SOURCES

The available sources on the history of the Armenian diocese of New Julfa fall into three main categories: archival materials, published Armenian sources, including narrative histories, chronicles, colophons and inscriptions, and accounts of western travelers and catholic missionaries.

Archival Materials: The main and hitherto little consulted body of evidence is to be found in the various unpublished collections of Armenian archives. The most important collection of archival materials belongs to All Saviour's Armenian Monastery of New Julfa, which for the last three hundred and ninety two years has served continuously as the spiritual and administrative center of the diocese. The collection includes decrees, encyclicals, official correspondence, pastoral or circular letters, public announcements, appeals, petitions, birth, marriage and death registers, land deeds, trade agreements and ledgers, inventories of churches, individual agreements, wills, etc. Even so, the present collection of archives of All Saviour's Monastery is not as large and rich as one would expect from such an important center which is almost four hundred years old. There is no doubt that on certain occasions in the past, due to invasions, lootings and mainly carelessness, a great many of the documents, together with manuscripts and printed books perished. In his letter of September 21, 1785, addressed to a certain *Paron* [1] Mkrtum in Astrakhan, Bishop Mkrtič, the primate of New Julfa (1769-1787) writes as follows:

---

[1] Sir, mister.

Your primate Yovsep *Vardapet*[2] has written to us twice, requesting a few books. His Eminence thinks that Julfa still is the place, where you can find any book you want. You must have heard that during the rule of Azadkhan[3] the books were bought by the *at'ar-s*[4] and the gun powder makers of the city, [paying] 300 *dinar-s*[5] per *litr*[6].[7]

As already mentioned, Yarutiwn Tēr Yovhaneanč was the first and until recently, the only individual who conducted extensive research in the archives and published many documents. In 1850 he found the archives as "piles of papers, covered with dust in the remote corners"[8] of the monastery. The conditions of the archives remained almost unchanged until 1972, when a project for their preservation and classification was initiated, as I explained in my introduction.

The second most important Armenian collection of archives for the study of the history of the New Julfa diocese are the Armenian Patriarchal archives transferred to the state collection of manuscripts or *Matenadaran* of Erevan in the Republic of Armenia. They include decrees, encyclicals, official correspondence between the Holy See of Ējmiacin and the diocese of New Julfa, circular letters, petitions, etc. Surprisingly, the documents related to the diocese of New Julfa are not great in number and are mostly original or even duplicate copies of documents which can also be found in the archives of All Saviour's Monastery. Therefore they add, regrettably little new material.[9] Hakob D. P̌ap̌azyan, a great scholar and one of the few experts on Irano-Armenian relations, has published many documents from the *Matenadaran* collection during the past forty years. His publication of *The Persian Documents of Matenadaran*, contained in three volumes,[10] is a

---

[2] Theologian. A title given to highly educated celibate priests.

[3] An Afghan chieftain from Khorasan, who occupied Isfahan first in 1748 and later 1753-55.

[4] Grocer or spice seller.

[5] 10,000 *dinars* were equal to one *toman*.

[6] Weight unit called *Man* in Persian sources. The Tabriz *Man* which was adopted in the state accounts was approximately 3 kgs. Another kind of *Man*, known as "Ajamstana litr" was commonly used by the people. It was the equivalent of 6 kgs. See Xačikyan L.S., P̌ap̌azyan H.D., *Hovhannes Tēr Davtyan Ĵulayec̆u Hašvetumarǝ*, Erevan 1984, pg. 391.

[7] Tēr Yovhaneanč Y., vol. II, pg. 16.

[8] Ibid, vol. I, pg. 3.

[9] In July 1989, I spent two weeks at the *Matenadaran*. Most of the documents that I saw and which could be useful for this study, were copies of documents which I had already obtained from the collection of All Saviour's Monastery. I was able to find only three original documents at *Matenadaran*, to be utilized in this study.

[10] *Decrees*, 2 vols., *Land Deeds*, 1 vol.

great contribution to the study of the history of Armenia and the neighbouring countries between fourteenth and seventeenth centuries. However, for the study of the seventeenth century Armenian communities in Iran, they contain very little and only indirect information.

The third Armenian collection of archives which should be taken into consideration for the history of the Armenian communities in Iran and India, are the private archives of Dr. Caro Owen Minassian acquired in 1972 by The University of California, Los Angeles (UCLA). They include decrees, individual correspondence, land deeds, trade agreements and ledgers, wills, public announcements, etc. The great majority of the documents date from the late eighteenth and nineteenth centuries. Seventeenth and early eighteenth century documents are unfortunately very scarce. Insofar as can be judged at present, since it has not yet been classified or catalogued, this collection seems ultimately more useful for the history of Armenian communities in India than for those in Persia.[11]

The Safavid royal archives, as well as numerous western state[12] and church collections, including the archives of the Propaganda Fide in Rome should certainly serve to complete the picture of the history of the diocese of New Julfa. But at least for the time being, all the collections of archives are beyond my reach, and the present work must therefore be largely based on the Armenian archival materials.

Armenian Published Sources: The Armenian published sources include seventeenth and eighteenth century Armenian histories, chronicles, manuscript colophons and inscriptions, including epitaphs.

The first and the only Armenian chronicler to witness the forced deportation of the Armenians in 1604 was Augustin Baječi, a catholic Armenian bishop, who described the events in passing, in the initial section of his Itinerary to Europe.[13]

Chronologically, the second valuable source is the *Chronicle* of Grigor Daranałči (1576-1643). The author was a well educated man and

---

[11] In January 1990, I spent one week at UCLA, studying this collection.

[12] State archives in Russia, France, Holland, Italy, Great Britain, Portugal and some other European countries include ample information on the trade of New Julfa Armenian merchants, therefore, they are important for the economic history of the Armenian people. Such archives have been partly studied by scholars interested in the economic history of the New Julfa Armenian community.

[13] "Čanaparhorduťiwn Yewropa", in *Notark Matenagruťean Hayoč*, St. Petersburg, 1884. See also "*Itineraire du très Révérand Frère Augustin Badje'tsi, Evêque Arménien de Nakhidchevan, de l'ordre des Frère-Precheurs, à travers l'Europe*", tr. by M. Brosset, *Journal Asiatique*, 1837, pp. 209-245, 401-421.

an active participant in church affairs of the time. He travelled extensively between Eastern and Western Armenia, Jerusalem, Cyprus, Constantinople, Crimea and Rodosto. His *Chronicle*[14] covers a period of forty five years (1595-1640). It is a valuable eye witness account of religious and political affairs of the time, under Ottoman and Safavid rules.

The most important historian for the period is Aŕaḱel Dawrižeći. Born in Tabriz at the end of the sixteenth century, Dawrižeći studied in Ējmiacin under Kaŕołikos P̌ilippos [Philip] (1633-1655). Later, as a patriarchal legate, he travelled extensively, visiting many Armenian communities in the Ottoman Empire and the Safavid Kingdom.

At the urging of Kaŕołikos P̌ilippos, Dawrižeći wrote a contemporary history of the Armenian people,[15] covering the first six decades of the seventeenth century, for much of which he was an eyewitness. He presented detailed accounts of wars between the Safavids and the Ottomans, mass deportation of Armenians to Iran, the situation of the Armenian church both in Armenia and in other Armenian communities abroad, cultural affairs, religious persecutions and the martyrdom of many individual Armenians for their Christian faith. In his opinion, chronology was "the foundation on which history had to be build."[16] Therefore, he tried to provide an accurate chronology for all the events presented in his work.

As a monk educated in a purely religious environment, Dawrižeći could not be an impartial historian. His opinion is not uniform throughout the work, particularly towards Shah 'Abbas the Great and the Safavids in general. But his accounts are mostly confirmed by documentary evidence, which make his work a fairly trustworthy source.

Another chronicler is Zaḱaria Aguleći, a merchant who travelled constantly between India, Iran, the Ottoman Empire and Europe. During these travels, he kept a valuable *Diary*[17] for thirty four years (1647-1681) in which he registered every type of information: descriptions of places, events, social issues, meetings with local people, feasts, church services, local customs, market values of goods, etc. In his introduction, he stated very clearly that he witnessed everything he has

---

[14] *Žamanakagrutiwn Grigor Vardapeti Kamałećwoy kam Daranałćwoy*, Jerusalem, 1915.
[15] *Girk' Patmut'eanć*, first published in Amsterdam, 1669. Second and third editions: *Patmut'iwn Aŕaḱel Vardapeti Dawrižećwoy*, Vałaršapat 1884 and 1896. Basically the third edition is utilized for this study.
[16] Ibid, 1896, pg. 3.
[17] *Zaḱaria Aguleću Oragrutyunə*, Erevan, 1938.

registered, and whenever necessary, he has double checked his information with at least three or four different people.[18]

The second contemporary historian is Zaḱaria *Sarkawag* [the Deacon] Ḱanaḱerc̆i (1627-1700). His work[19] covers the entire seventeenth century, particularly presenting the situation in Eastern, that is to say Persian Armenia. As an eyewitness, Zaḱaria provides valuable information on the history of the Armenian Church in the second half of the seventeenth century.

Petros di Sargis Gilanentz, an early eighteenth century Armenian chronicler, narrated the Afghan occupation of Isfahan and the fall of Safavid kingdom.[20] He obtained the greater part of his information from Joseph Apisalaimian, who was delegated by Gardane, the French Ambassador in Isfahan, to negotiate with the Afghan leader Mahmud, for the protection of French nationals and interests in Isfahan. Joseph was in Farahabad with Mahmud when Shah Sultan Husayn came to surrender his crown.[21] Gilanentz presented a detailed description of the siege of Isfahan, the Afghan occupation of New Julfa and the miserable conditions created for the church and people of New Julfa.

The most important historian from the eighteenth century is Xac̆atur J̌uɫayec̆i. His *History of Persia*[22] is far broader in scope, starting with the fourth century and ending in 1779. Besides the history of Persia, he presents valuable information related to the history of Armenian people, particularly in the eighteenth century. To be sure, his work is not a primary source for the period under study, but is valuable since he has gathered his information from earlier written sources and well informed people.

To these may be added the hitherto unpublished history of Step̆anos Erēc̆,[23] a native of P̆eria[24] and a contemporary of Xac̆atur J̌uɫayec̆i. The author was a humble priest, who compiled a history, using whatever information was available to him, without analyzing the accuracy of his sources; and, his work must consequently be utilized

---

[18] Ibid, pg. 5-6.

[19] Zaḱaria Sarkawag, *Patmagru̇n̄wn*, Vaɫaršapat, 1870.

[20] *The Chronicle of Petros di Sarkis Gilanentz concerning the Afghan Invasion of Persia in 1722*, tr. by Caro O. Minassian, Lisbon 1959. Original Armenian text in *Krunk* monthly, Tbilisi, Feb.-March, 1863. Russian translation by K. Patkanov (Patkanean), St. Petersburg, 1870.

[21] Lockhart L., *The Fall of the Safavi Dynasty and the Afghan occupation of Persia*, Cambridge, 1958, pg. 506.

[22] Xac̆atur J̌uɫayec̆i, *Patmutiwn Parsic̆* Vaɫaršapat, 1905.

[23] *Hangitagirk;*, ms. # 654 in the collection of All Saviour's Monastery.

[24] District of Faridan, 90 miles to the west of Isfahan.

with caution, nevertheless, it provides information on the seventeenth and eighteenth century events related to the Armenian communities of New Julfa and P'eria not available elsewhere.

Finally, a number of seventeenth and eighteenth century chronicles of lesser importance contain some complementary information concerning the period under study. Among these are: Dawit̔ Bałišeči, Isahak *Vardapet*, Simēon Erewanči and several anonymous chroniclers.[25]

Seventeenth century colophons of Armenian manuscripts[26] and printed books,[27] especially those copied or printed in New Julfa or commissioned and sponsored by New Julfa merchants, are of major importance for our purpose. They provide brief, but important information on the lives and works of prominent clerics and wealthy families, the School of All Saviour's Monastery, the activities of Catholic missionaries and special events of historical importance.

Finally, among the Armenian sources, the inscriptions of churches, old houses and the epitaphs of cemeteries are of primary importance for their chronological accuracy, geographical information and terminology, to identify the social rank and occupation of individual clerics, donors, merchants and artisans. To this date, only the inscriptions of churches and some tombstones in New Julfa Cemetery have been partly studied or utilized,[28] while tens of thousands of inscriptions in the New Julfa Cemetery and more than one hundred towns and villages, previously inhabited by Armenians, are not studied and may soon disappear due to natural causes and local lack of interest.

Western Sources: The final body of evidence complementing the Armenian material is to be found in the accounts of Western travelers and Catholic Missionaries. In the course of the seventeenth century, diplomatic and trade relations between Iran and Europe developed greatly. Shah 'Abbas' ultimate goal was to recover Persian territories, occupied by the Ottomans, the prime enemy of the Safavids. He desperately tried to form an alliance with the European states hostile to

[25] Ałaneanč Giwt, *Diwan Hayoč Patmutean*, vols. I-X, Tbilisi, 1893-1912.
Ališan Ł., *Ayrarat*, Venice, 1890.
_____, *Hayapatum*, Venice, 1901.
Hakobyan V., *Manr Žamanakagrutyunner*, vols. I-II, Erevan, 1951-56.
[26] _____, Hovhanisyan A., *ŽĒ Dari Hayeren Jeṁgreri Hišatakaranner*, vols. I-III, Erevan, 1974-1984.
Also printed catalogues of Armenian manuscripts in general.
[27] Oskanyan N., Korkotyan Ḱ, Savalyan A., *Hay Girk'ə 1512-1800 Tvakannerin*, Erevan, 1988.
[28] Tēr Yovhaneanč Y., vols. I-II.
Carswell J., New Julfa.
Minasean L.G., *Nor Ĵulayi Gerezmanatunə*, New Julfa, 1985.

the Ottomans by sending emissaries to the popes of Rome and European courts.[29] In addition, he was most concerned with the economic development of his realm; therefore, he succeeded in establishing trade between Iran and the West. As a result, travel between Iran and Europe became very common and numerous diplomatic, trade and religious missions were established in Isfahan, Shiraz and other cities of Iran.

Records and correspondence of the English East India Company, the Dutch East India Company, the French diplomatic mission of Isfahan, the Augustinian, Carmelite, Dominican, Capuchin, and Jesuit missions are important sources for the study of political, economic, religious and social history of seventeenth century Iran in general. Westerners, temporarily stationed in Iran as agents of European trade companies or Catholic missionaries, could understandably be biased in the assessment of their surroundings in an Eastern and non-Christian country. But without their reports, our knowledge of the economic and religious affairs of the Safavid Iran would have been very limited. The records and the correspondence of trade companies and Catholic missions are mostly unpublished and are preserved in collections of archives in various European cities.[30] Some of these archival materials are studied by only a limited number of scholars,[31] who are mainly focused on the trade between Europe and the East or the work of the Catholic missionaries in the East. Regrettably, I had no means of consulting any unpublished material in the western collections of archives.

Besides general correspondence, individual travelers, diplomats, tradesmen, missionaries and explorers have recorded ample information concerning their itineraries, their personal experiences, their meetings with local officials and people in general, their observations and impressions of political and economic situation, official policies, major events, sites, local customs and the daily life of the local inhabitants. From the beginning of Shah 'Abbas' reign (1588) to the Afghan occupation and the fall of Safavid kingdom (1722), at least seventy travelers kept records of their journeys to or through Iran.[32]

---

[29] Savory R., *Iran Under the Safavids*, Cambridge, 1980, pg. 109.

[30] For partial description of various collections of archives, see Lockhart L., pp. 531-542.
Among published archival materials, for our study the most valuable work: *A Chronicle of the Carmelites in Persia and the Papal Mission of the XVIIth and XVIIIth Centuries*, vols. I-II, London, 1939.

[31] Among few others, I can mention the names of R.W. Ferrier, Robert Gulbenkian, Ina Baghdiantz McCabe, C.A. Frazee and P.A. Rabbath.

[32] See the list: Vartoogian J.C., *The Image of Armenia in European Travel Accounts of the 17th Century*, Ph.D. dissertation, Columbia University, 1974, pp. 275-277.

Most of the seventy travelers do provide information about Armenians in Iran in general and the Armenian community of New Julfa in particular. Both tradesmen and missionaries came into close contact with Armenian merchants, clerics and the general population. While in Iran, most of them settled among the Armenians of New Julfa, and observed the trade activities and lifestyle of the Armenians, their customs, churches, religious traditions and ceremonies, administrative setting and their relations with the Safavid court. For our study, the most lengthy and valuable information can be obtained from the works of the following travelers: Antonio de Gouvea (1598)[33], Pietro della Valle (1618), Garcia de Silva y Figueroa (1618), Jean-Baptiste Tavernier (1633), Adam Olearius (1636), Gabriel de Chinon (c.1640), Rafael du Mans (1644), Alexander de Rhodes (1648), Jean de Thevenot (1664), André Daulier-Deslandes (1664), John Chardin (1666), Jan Struys (1670), John Fryer (1677), Jacques Villotte (1689), Joseph Pitton de Tournefort (1701), Cornelis de Bruyn (1703), and Tadeusz Juda Krusinski (1708).

Some of these authors, such as John Chardin and Rafael du Mans, spent years in Iran; therefore, they should not be considered as ordinary travelers, but as residents in Iran. They had learned Persian, were familiar with the local customs and had close relations with the Safavid court and the Armenian community of New Julfa. As such, they were very well informed on the contemporary affairs of the Safavid kingdom. Tavernier and Chardin were Protestants, and compared to other travelers, who were mostly Catholics, they were more objective and less prejudiced in dealing with non-Catholic Armenians.

Scholars differ considerably in their evaluation of travelers' accounts. According to Bernard Lewis, the travelers are usually ignorant, prejudiced and unreliable:

> For the general reader they supply, so he believes, the superior knowledge and consequent superior wisdom of the man (or woman) who has been there and met them and knows ... For 'expert' of various kinds, who wish to specialize on the Middle East without actually having to learn a Middle Eastern language, they offer the comforting appearance of inside information, a primary source for the historian, a field report for the social scientist, a first-hand informant for the political analyst.[34]

Yet, V. Minorsky emphasizes the value and the credibility of western travelers:

---

[33] The dates after each name indicates the traveller's first arrival in Persia.

[34] Lewis B., "Some English Travelers in the East", *Middle Eastern Studies*, IV, 3 (April, 1968), pg. 296.

Our most detailed and trustworthy intelligence on the internal structure
of the Safavid kingdom has been derived from European travellers and
residents in Persia.[35]

Certainly one cannot ignore the importance of western travelers in
Middle Eastern studies, especially in the history of Safavid Iran, since
the contemporary Persian sources are very limited in number and
content. However, in the light of the scholarly disagreements as to their
worth, we must exercise considerable caution in dealing with such
travel accounts.

[35] *Tadhkirat Al-Muluk*, tr. by V. Minorsky, London, 1943, pg. 6.

CHAPTER TWO

THE PRESENCE OF ARMENIANS IN IRAN AND THE FORCED MIGRATION UNDER SHAH 'ABBAS I

Since the time of the Achamenid rule in Iran (VI-III centuries B.C.) Armenia has very often been ruled by or fallen under the political, military, administrative, social and economic influence of its powerful neighbor in the South-east. Travel between the two countries was very common. Armenian princes and soldiers often traveled to or served in various parts of Iran, especially during the Sasanid period (III-VII centuries A.D.).[1] Throughout the centuries, Iran has been a familiar market for the Armenian tradesmen.[2]

According to the Armenian hisotorians Pawstos Biwzandaći[3] and Movsēs Xorenaći,[4] in the fourth century, the Sasanian King Šapuhr II took thousands of prisoners from Armenia and settled them in the Khuzistan region of Iran. No record has been kept on the fate of the Armenian prisoners settled in Khuzistan. Most probably they perished or were assimilated by the native Iranians.

Between the eleventh and the fifteenth centuries, under Seljukid, Mongol and other Turkic domination, forced deportation and

---

[1] Information provided in the works of the following Armenian historians: Pawstos Biwzand, Łazar Parpeći, Movsēs Xorenaći and Sebēos.

[2] Manandyan H., *The Trade and Cities of Armenia in Relation to Ancient World Trade*, N.G. Garsoian (tr.), Lisbon, 1965.

[3] Pawstos Biwzandaćwoy Patmutiwn Hayoć, Venice 1933, pp. 178-180.

[4] Movsēs Xorenaći, Patmutiwn Hayoć, Venice, 1865, pg. 223.

enslavement of Armenians were common practices. According to Aristakēs Lastivertċi[5] and Matťēos Urhayeċi[6] between 1048 and 1070, the Seljuks constantly invaded Armenia and took a great number of Armenian prisoners to Iran. Kirakos Ganjakeċi described his own ordeal of 1236-7 when, together with his teacher Vanakan *Vardapet* and other classmates, he was taken captive to Iran by the Mongols.[7] A number of fourteenth and fifteenth century Armenian chronicles and manuscript colophons mention similar cases of deportations and slavery of Armenians to Iran, carried out by the Mongol and the Turkmen invaders of Armenia.[8]

We have no information on the fate of the Armenians transferred to the central parts of Iran between the eleventh and fourteenth centuries. But the presence of Armenian communities in the northern regions of Iran, namely in Tabriz, Sultaniyya, Salmas, Urmiya, Maragha, Rasht and Ray were noted by western travelers between the fourteenth and sixteenth centuries.[9]

In Tabriz, two Armenian churches named Surb Astuacacin (Holy Mother of God), and Saint Sargis were in existence as early as 1334.[10] Two Armenian manuscripts copied in the said churches in 1336 and 1342[11] also mention the names of bishops or primates, indicating a diocesan structure for the area. However, it is not clear if Tabriz formed a separate diocese or was simply under the jurisdiction of the Bishop of Saint Ťaddē Monastery, one of the oldest and most sacred sites for the Armenian Christianity, located over 100 miles to the north of Tabriz.

Sultaniyya, more than two hundred miles to the south of Tabriz, was the center of Catholic Unitors in Persia. In 1318, Pope John XXII had declared Sultaniyya an archbishopric and had entrusted the See to the Dominican missionaries, who were established in the area two decades earlier.[12] The Armenian Church also was present in Sultaniyya, as evidenced by scanty information in the Armenian sources. In a manuscript colophon dated 1338 and written in Sultaniyya by Mxiťar

[5] *Patmuťiwn Aristakesi Lastivertaċwoy*, Erevan, 1963, pp. 67-101.
[6] *Patmuťiwn Matťeosi Urhayeċwoy*, Jerusalem, 1869, pp. 121, 140, 162, 175.
[7] Kirakos Ganjakeċi, *Patmuťiwn Hayoċ*, Erevan, 1961, pg. 234.
[8] Xaċikyan, L., *ŽD Dari Hayeren Jeragreri Hišatakaranner*, Erevan, 1950.
_____., *ŽE Dari Hayeren Jeragreri Hišatakaranner*, vols. I-III, Erevan, 1955-67.
Hakobyan, V.A., *Manr Žamanakagruťyunner*, vol. I-II.
[9] Hakobyan, H. (tr.) *Ułegruťyunner*, vol I, Erevan, 1932, pp. 60, 121, 126, 213, 230, 313, etc.
[10] Xaċikyan, L., *ŽD Dari ... Hišatakaranner*, pg. 264.
[11] Ibid, pp. 282, 331.
[12] Frazee, C.A., "The Catholic Missions to Azerbaijan and Nakhichevan," *Diakonia*, vol 9, #3, New York, 1974, pg. 253.

Anedi, a well-known Armenian chronicler, the names of Bishop Sargis and Bishop Grigor as primates of the region are mentioned. In addition, the names of seven priests and several deacons at the local Armenian church are listed.[13] Another manuscript copied at the same church in 1341 confirms the names of the two bishops.[14]

In Rasht, Ašot Abrahamyan mentions the presence of Surb Yakob Armenian church. He cites a manuscript copied by Tēr Vardan, the pastor of the said church in 1496.[15] I attempted but could not locate the said manuscript in the collection of *Matenadaran* of Erevan. Obviously, Abrahamyan's reference, as appears in his book, is not correct.

Undoubtedly Armenian refugees and tradesmen had reached and were settled in central and southern parts of Iran, especially in areas like Isfahan and Shiraz, centuries before the forced deportations of Armenians carried by Shah 'Abbas in 1604-5. Isfahan was known to Armenians from very early times and is mentioned in various Armenian sources between XI and XIII centuries.[16] In 1090, Katolikos Barsel Anedi accompanied by a delegation of Armenian clergy and noblemen, traveled to Persia, met the Seljuk ruler Melikshah, whose main headquarters was in Isfahan, and obtained a Royal decree exempting the Armenian church from heavy taxes.[17]

In XV-XVII century Armenian sources, Isfahan was commonly known as Šōš, being mistakenly identified with the ancient city of Shush or Shushan. An Armenian manuscript colophon, dated 1461 and quoted by Aṙakel Dawrižedi, stated: "...Isfahan, which is the city of Šōš, where the prophet Daniel had the vision."[18]

The earliest actual records on the presence of an Armenian community in Isfahan are from the second half of the sixteenth century. According to Yarutiwn Tēr Yovhaneand, some tombstones in the Armenian cemetery of New Julfa are dated 1550-1,[19] which prove the presence of an Armenian community in the area at least fifty-five years

---

[13] Xačikyan, L., *ŽD Dari Hišatakaranner*, pp. 307-312.

[14] Ibid, pp. 328, 406.

[15] Abrahamyan, A.G., *Hamarot Urvagic Hay Gaḷtavayreri Patmutťyan*, vol. I, pg. 246.

[16] See the works of Mattēos Urhayedi pg. 301, Kirakos Ganjakedi pp. 180, 234.

[17] *Mattēos Urhayedi*, pg. 290.
Samuel Anedi, *Hawakmunk i Groc Patmagrac*, Vaḷaršapat, 1893, pg. 117.

[18] Aṙakel Dawrižedi, pg. 420. - «... Ասպահան, որ է Շոշ բաղաք, յոր մարգարէն Դանիէլ զտեսիլն տեսաւ». See also Daniel, VIII, 1-3.

[19] Tēr Yovhaneand simply states that the tombstones are dated Ռ (1000) according to the Armenian calendar. If that specific date applies to all the tombstones in question, one tends to doubt the accuracy of the inscriptions and think of the possibility that one or more letters needed to specify the units or decimal numbers of the dates that are missing in the inscriptions.

before the actual establishment of New Julfa.[20] Tēr Yovhaneanč also presents the Armenian translation of an edict dated 1593[21] and issued by Shah 'Abbas the Great in favor of an Armenian merchant named *Khwaja Nazar.*[22]

During the last decade of the sixteenth century, due to persecutions, physical insecurity and the general confusion caused by the Jalali rebellion against the Ottomans, a considerable number of Armenians fled to Iran. According to Aṙakʿel Dawriževi, the following Armenian notables and communities sought refuge in Isfahan, under the protective care of Shah 'Abbas the Great.

> Armenians from Aluankʿ[23] Saruxan *Beg* and his brother Nazar from the village of Oskanapat, Oḷlan *Kešiš* and his brother Lalabēk from the village of Haṫerkʿ, Jalal *Beg* and his nephews from Xačen, *Melikʿ* Suǰum from Dizak, *Melikʿ* Pʿašik from the village of Kʿočiz, *Melikʿ* Babē from the village of Bridis, Bishop Melkʿisēṫ from the village of Melikʿzatay in upper Zakam, *Melikʿ* Haykaz from the village Xanacax in Kʿštaḷs region. Also the entire inhabitants of four villages from the region of Dizak emigrated to Persia and the Shah settled them in Isfahan. In addition, three quarters of the people of Dašt from the province of Goḷṫn near Agulis emigrated to Persia and the Shah settled them also in Isfahan.[24]

Apparently some of the Armenian *meliks*[25] resided in Isfahan only for a very short period of time and having obtained special privileges from Shah 'Abbas, and taking advantage of the restoration of peace,

---

[20] Tēr Yovhaneanč Y., vol. I. pg. 158, vol. II, pp. 282-3.

[21] The edict is dated *Jumada Al-Aula* 1001, which corresponds to February 3-March 4, 1593. Apparently, due to a miscalculation Tēr Yovhaneanč has concluded that *Jumada Al-Aula* 1001 corresponds to the Christian year 1580. (See Ibid. vol. I, pg. 158).

[22] Aršak Alpoyačean and some other Armenian scholars have confused that person with the famous *Khwaja* Nazar of the seventeenth century, who served as *Kalantar* of New Julfa and died in 1636 at the age of 52, as indicated in his tombstone inscription. Therefore, in 1593, the future *khwaja* Nazar was only nine years old and certainly not in a position to receive an edict from the Shah. (See Alpoyačean A., *Patmutʿiwn Hay Gaḷṫakanutean* , vol. III, Cairo, 1961, pg. 192.

[23] Karabagh.

[24] Aṙakʿel Dawriževi, pg. 16. «իսկ յաշխարհէն Աղուանից՝ եւ յազգէն հայոց զնախին Սարուխան Բէկն եւ իւր եղբայր Նազարդ ի յՈսկանապատ գեղջէ. Oղլան քէշիշն եւ իւր եղբայր Լալաբէկին ի Հաթերք գեղջէ: Ջալալ բէկն իւր եղբօր որդւովքն ի խաչէնայ: Մէլիք Սուջումն ի Դիզակայ. Մէլիք փաշիկն ի Քոչիզ գեղջէ. Մէլիք Բաբէն ի Բրիտիս գեղջէ. Մէլիքսէթ եպիսկոպոսն ի վերին Զակամայ ի Մէլիքզատայ գեղջէ. Մէլիք Հայկազն ի Քշտաղս երկրէն ի Խանածախ գեղջէ: Այլեւ չորս գեղ ի Դիզակա երկրէն միաբանողյն չուեցին եւ գնացին յերկիրն Պարսից, եւ շահն բնակեցոյց զնոսա ի քաղաքն Ասպահան: Այլեւ երեք մասն ի ժողովրդոց՝ Դաշտ կոչեցեալ տեղին՝ որ է ի գաւառն ի Գողթաց՝ մերձ յԱգուլիս՝ գնացին յերկիրն Պարսից, եւ շահն զնոսա եւս բնակեցոյց ի քաղաքն Ասպահան:»

[25] Noblemen, village chieftains. See Hewsen R.H., "The Meliks of Eastern Armenia," *Revue des Etudes Arméniennes*, N.S., vol. IX, 1972, pp. 285-329.

returned to their native regions under the Iranian domination. The colophon of a manuscript dated 1606 and belonging to *Melik̈* Haykaz states that the *Melik̈* fled from the Ottoman persecutions, reached Isfahan, expressed loyalty to Shah 'Abbas and was granted the lordship of Ǩaštał region[26] with the right to collect the taxes and the tithe according to his own judgment.[27] In 1609 and 1620 two decrees were issued by Shah 'Abbas in favor of *Melik̈* Haykaz.[28] *Melik̈* Suǰum of Dizak and *Melik̈* Ṗašik of Ǩočiz are also listed among those who returned to their native lands after the withdrawal of the Ottomans from the area.[29]

Based on the available data, it is hard to conclude that by the end of the sixteenth century the Armenians of Isfahan were numerous enough to form a separate religious community, at least with a place of worship and clerics serving their spiritual needs.[30] The settelement of Bishop Melk̈isēt of Melik̈zatay village and possibly other Armenian clergy in Isfahan, as indicated by Dawrižeči, could certainly facilitate the establishment of a church and the organization of a community around it, but we have no trace of any Armenian Church in Isfahan, before the deliberate and artificial creation of the Armenian community of New Julfa by Shah 'Abbas I in 1605.

The situation of the Armenians was radically altered with the establishment of the Safavid Kingdom in Iran in 1501, bringing about a period of one and a quarter century of wars with the Ottoman Empire, beginning with the battle of Chaldiran (1514) and ending with the Treaty of Zuhab (1639).[31]

Armenia being divided between the Ottoman Empire and the Safavid Kingdom was the main battlefield during most of these wars. Armenians were subjugated to all kinds of hardship by the invading or retreating armies. Towns and villages were devastated and looted, people were massacred, thousands were deported or taken away in slavery[32] and the economy was in total shambles. Thus, in 1514, after the battle of Chaldiran, three thousand Armenian artisans were

---

[26] Part of the province of Siwnik̈, presently the area of Lačin.

[27] Hakobyan V., *Žē Dari Hišatakaranner*, vol. I, pg. 207.

[28] P̌aṗazyan H. D., *Matenadarani Parskeren Hrovartakner∂*, vol. II., pp. 89-90, 99-100.

[29] Ibid. pg. 33.

[30] In Alpoyačean's opinion (Vol. III, pg. 156), the mosques of Harun Velayat and Emamzadeh Ismail in Isfahan were originally Armenian churches. Alpoyačean does not provide convincing evidence to justify his theory.

[31] The wars were waged respectively in the following years: 1514-15, 1533-35, 1548-49, 1553-55, 1578-88, 1603-7, 1610-11, 1616-18, 1623-26, 1629-33, 1635-39.

[32] Ibrahim Pechevi, *Tarihi Pechevi*, A.X. Safrastyan, *Ṫurk̈akan Ałbyurner∂ Hayastani, Hayeri ev Andrkovkasi myus Žołovurdneri Masin*, vol. 1, Erevan, 1961, pp. 27-59. Hakobyan V.A., *Manr Žamanakagrut'yunner*, vol. II, pp. 227-231.

deported by the Ottomans and sent to Constantinople.[33] Between 1540 and 1553, during the Safavid campaigns in the Caucasus, thousands of Georgian, Circasian and Armenian prisoners, mostly women and children, were sent to Iran in slavery.[34] The scorched earth policy adopted by the Safavid Shah Tahmasp was still more devastating for Armenia. "The frontier areas of Azarbayjan through which invading Ottoman armies had to pass were systematically laid waste."[35] In his *Tazkireh*[36] Shah Tahmasp justifies that policy in the following words:

> When I was informed that the *Kondkar*[37] had arrived in Sivas, where he would wait for three weeks until the camels were fed, I called into my presence the elders, the leaders and the *Kadkhuda*-s[38] of the surrounding areas and informed them that I had ordered my soldiers to burn and destroy all the grain and the harvest in the area, during their retreat before the advancing Turkish army ... We burnt and destroyed the grain and shut off the water sources in those areas. It is obvious to every clever man, that the act of war is like a gamble. No matter by what means it is necessary to defeat the enemy. According to Ali, 'the warfare is fraud'. During the war you may flee, you may cheat, but you must not give any chance to your enemy.[39]

A similar military strategy was adopted by the Ottomans. According to the Ottoman historian, Ibrahim Pechevi, in 1554, during the invasion of Erevan, Karabagh and Naxčawan, "To the length of four-five days journey, all villages, towns, fields and constructions were destroyed to such a degree that there was no trace of constructions and life."[40]

With the peace treaty of Amasya in 1555, hostilities between the Ottomans and the Safavids were halted for more than twenty years. But the war resumed in 1578 and in 1585 the Ottomans occupied Tabriz.[41]

Immediately after his ascension to the Safavid throne, Shah 'Abbas I signed a peace treaty with the Ottomans in 1589-90 and ceded to them Tabriz and the territories dependent thereon in Azerbaijan, Karabagh together with Ganja, Shirvan, Georgia, Luristan, parts of Kurdistan and

---

[33] Čamčean M., *Hayoč Patmuťiwn*, vol. III, Venice, 1786, pg. 511.

[34] Savory R., *Iran Under the Safavids*, pg. 64.

[35] Ibid. p. 58.

[36] *Tazkireye Shah Tahmasp*, Calcutta, 1912. Cited by H. D. Paṗazyan.

[37] Ottoman Sultan.

[38] Headman of a village.

[39] Paṗazyan H.D., *Matenadarani Parskeren Hrovartaknerə*, vol. II, pg. 8.

[40] Safrastyan A.X., *Turkakan Ałbyurnerə* ... vol. I, pg.34.

[41] *The Cambridge History of Iran*, vol. 6, Cambridge 1986, pp. 257-8.

Mesopotamia.[42] Having secured the kingdom against the Ottoman threat, the young Shah focused his attention on the restoration of internal security, the reorganization of the army and the economic development of the country.

For the greater part of the sixteenth century, Safavid society was basically divided between two main races, the *Qizilbash*[43] Turkmen tribes and the Persians. The *Qizilbash* tribes constituted the backbone of the Safavid army; therefore, their chiefs were dominant in the state affairs of Iran. They were also responsible for internal struggles and conspiracies, especially when the Safavid kings were in a weak position or there was a crisis of succession. The Persians were basically entrusted with administrative tasks. Constant tensions between the Persians and the *Qizilbash* Turks caused great anxieties for the Safavid kings.[44]

In order to balance the influence of the *Qizilbash* and the Persian elements, in the latter part of his reign, Shah Tahmasp had introduced a "third force" into the state, namely, the Georgians, Circassians and Armenians, who were brought from the Caucasus as prisoners, were converted to Islam and were employed as *ghulams* (slaves) of the Shah.[45] Shah 'Abbas I "gave official recognition to these 'third force' elements by making the *ghulamani khassayi sharifa* (slaves of the royal household) an important part of both the civil and military administration."[46]

Since the army inherited by Shah 'Abbas mainly composed of *Qizilbash* horsemen loyal to their own chiefs, he considerably reduced the number of the tribal contingents and created a new standing army of 37,000 men, basically recruited from his Caucasian *ghulams* and Iranian elements. He greatly increased the use of firearms by creating a corps of musketeers (*Tufangchiyan*) and an artillery corps (*Tupchiyan*), in addition to *ghulam* regiments armed with muskets.[47]

While the Safavid Kingdom was emerging from more than a decade long weak and unstable situation, the Ottomans were occupied with external and internal problems. By the turn of the seventeenth century, eastern regions of the Ottoman Empire, swept by major rebellions, were devastated and plundered. Heavy taxation, religious persecution and physical insecurity had forced many inhabitants, including Armenian, Georgian and Kurdish feudal lords and common people to flee from

---

[42] Ibid, pg. 266.
[43] Literally meaning red heads, a reference to their red turbans.
[44] Savory, R. *Iran Under the Safavids*, pp. 77, 184-5.
[45] Ibid. pg. 78.
[46] Ibid. pg. 65.
[47] *The Cambridge History of Iran*, vol. 6, pp. 264-266.

their native lands and seek refuge in the Safavid Kingdom.[48] Numerous appeals were made to Shah 'Abbas by Kurdish chieftains, Georgian princes and Armenian clergy seeking the Shah's protection against the Ottoman and Jalali[49] extortions.[50] The Armenian Coadjutor Kaťolikos Melkiseť, accompanied by two bishops, traveled to Isfahan and personally urged Shah 'Abbas to recapture the territories ceded to the Ottomans.[51]

In 1603, Gazi *Beg* Kord, the Lord of Salmas rebelled against 'Ali *Pasha*, the Ottoman *Beglarbeg*[52] of Tabriz and sent word to Shah 'Abbas, urging him to recapture Tabriz "while the Ottoman commander was absent from the city, campaigning against the Kurds."[53] Shah 'Abbas having already decided to deal with the Ottomans, used this golden opportunity and rapidly marched towards Tabriz and captured the city on October 21, 1603.[54] Soon after, the Shah captured Naxčawan and headed towards Erevan.

On his way to Erevan, the Shah passed through Julfa, a town of Armenian merchants located on the left bank of the river Arax. He was enthusiastically received by the local inhabitants. In a procession, the Shah was led to the house of *Khwaja* Xačik, passing through decorated and carpeted streets. For three days he was hosted by the Armenian merchants and was presented with trays full of gold coins. The Shah was greatly impressed by the wealth and the economic success of the Armenian merchants.[55]

In December 1603 Shah 'Abbas advanced towards Erevan, and after a six-months siege, on June 8, 1604, he occupied the city.[56] Meanwhile, Safavid army units commanded by various *Khans* had made several forays into Karabagh, Kars, Van, Arjiš, Manzikert, Khnus, Bergri, Basen and Erzrum and had deported tens of thousands of people, mainly Armenians, to Iran.[57]

---

[48] Aťaǩel Dawriẑeči, pp. 15-17.
[49] Anti-Ottoman rebels who had swept accross Asia Minor between 1596 and 1610. See Zulalyan M.K., *Ĵalalineri Šaržumə ev Hay Žoɬovrdi Vičake Osmanyan Kaysruťyan Meĵ,* Erevan, 1966, pp. 143-166.
[50] Aťaǩel Dawriẑeči, pp. 15-16.
[51] Ibid. pg. 17.
[52] Governor General, A Safavid title.
[53] Eskandar Beg Monshi, *History of Shah 'Abbas the Great,* R.M. Savory (tr.), vol. II, Colorado, 1978, pg. 827.
[54] Sykes, P., *A History of Persia,* vol. II, London, 1951, pg. 178.
[55] Aťaǩel Dawriẑeči, pp. 24-25.
[56] Eskandar Beg Monshi, *History,* vol. II, pg. 846.
[57] Aťaǩel Dawriẑeči, pp. 33-35.

In the summer of 1604, the Ottomans started a counter-offensive against the Safavids. Shah 'Abbas decided to avoid a direct confrontation with such a large Ottoman army. Instead, he preferred to retreat and adopt the traditional scorched earth policy. He ordered his troops to deport immediately all the inhabitants of the province known as *Chukhuri Sa'd*[58] to Iran and "burn the crops and pastures, with the object of denying supplies to the Ottomans for a period of several days as they marched through that region."[59]

In addition to being a military strategy, Shah 'Abbas' decision to deport such a large number of people to Iran was also based on economic considerations. The Armenians as traders, artisans or farmers would greatly help develop the Iranian economy. Furthermore, as *Zimmi*[60] subjects of the Shah, they would pay *Jizya*,[61] which would increase the royal revenues.

The Shah's orders were carried out promptly and in a matter of a few days the retreating Safavid troops deported hundreds of thousands of Armenians from Kars, Širakavan, Kałzuan, Alaškert, Aparan, Lori, Ałbak, Hamzačiman, ŠarapXana, Erevan, Ełegnaĵor, Naxčawan, and other towns or villages, burnt and destroyed the vacated towns and hastily pushed the deported people to move into Iran, before the arrival of the Ottoman army.[62]

According to Aṙakel Dawriẑeći, the forced deportation of the Armenians was carried out in the month of *Nawasard*, 1054[63] which corresponds to October 21-November 19, 1604 of the Roman (Gregorian) calendar. That was the time of the year when cold weather, heavy rains and muddy roads would make traveling very difficult, especially when, due to the general confusion and the limitation of time, transportation as well as basic provisions for the road had not been secured in advance.

---

[58] The central parts of Armenia, mainly the province of Ayrarat. The name *Chukhuri Sa'd*—literally meaning the ditch of Sa'd—has derived from the name of Amir Sa'd, the chieftain of Sa'dlu tribe, who dominated the area in late fourteenth and early fifteenth centuries. See *History of Armenia*, ASSR Academy of Sciences, vol. IV, Erevan, 1972, pg. 57.

[59] Eskandar Beg Monshi, *History*, vol. II, pg. 857.

[60] Non-Muslim (mainly Christian and Jewish) inhabitants of territories conquered by Muslims, who were eligible for certain private and public rights as long as they were loyal to the state and paid a special poll tax. See Fattal A., *Le Status Légal des Non-Musulmans en Pays d'Islam*, Beirut 1958, pg. 72-73.

[61] Poll-tax paid by non-Muslims as a price for their *Zimmi* status. See Ibid., p. 264.

[62] Aṙakel Dawriẑeći, pp. 52-53.
Hakobyan V., *ŽĒ Dari Hišatakaranner*, vol. I, pp. 129-130, 181-182, 196, 285-291, 411-412, etc.

[63] Ibid. pg. 40. The date and time of the deportation is confirmed also by many other contemporary sources who simply mention Autumn of 1604.

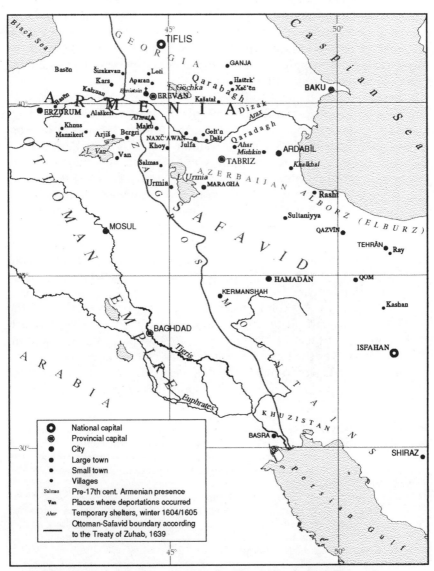

1. Armenian Deportations to Iran in the Seventeenth Century

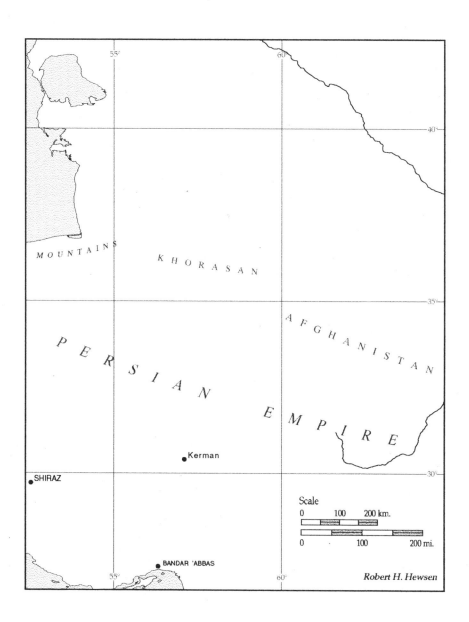

MOUNTAINS

KHORASAN

AFGHANISTAN

PERSIAN EMPIRE

Kerman

SHIRAZ

BANDAR 'ABBAS

Scale

0   100   200 km.

0   100   200 mi.

Robert H. Hewsen

Antonio de Gouvea, the Augustinian missionary, who also served as Spanish Ambassador to the Court of Shah 'Abbas, described the suffering of the deported people in the following words:

> The lamentations, the tears and the confusion of these poor migrants were such that they could have moved the hearts of the cruellest men. No one was allowed to stay behind and yet no one was equipped to undertake such a journey. There were many women whose poor husbands had perished while digging trenches and setting barricades. Each of these women was surrounded by five or six children too old to be carried and too young to be made to traverse such great distances on foot... If we were to take into consideration only those villages which were destroyed and evacuated, the estimated number of the deportees would reach 60,000 families...[64]

The Safavid troops were still in the vicinity of Erevan occupied with deporting as many people as possible, when news reached Shah 'Abbas that the Ottomans were already in Kars. The Shah issued new orders urging his troops to retreat all the way south to the right bank of river Arax, taking with them the mass of uprooted people.

Crossing the river Arax was a difficult and dangerous task for the deportees. The river was deep and overflowing its banks at that time of year. Very few boats or rafts were available. The Ottomans had almost caught up with the retreating Safavids, who had to cross the river after the deportees. According to Aṙakʿel Dawriẓečʿi:

> The cruel Persian troops were pushing the people into the river ... some people were able to get hold of the edges of boats or rafts, the tails of horses, oxen and buffaloes. Others were able to swim. But those who were unable to swim and were weak, especially the elderly men and women, boys and girls and little children were driven by the river ... those who were able to cross the river survived, but many drowned.[65]

Augustin Baječʿi, a survivor of that terrible ordeal, described his own experience as follows:

> We reached the river Arax, a very wide river which could not be crossed without a boat. They dumped all the people in the river with no boats or animals. Some survived and others were driven away by the water ... Too

---

[64] Gouvea, Antonio de. *Relation des Grandes Guerres ...* Rouen, 1646, pg. 354.

[65] *Aṙakʿel Dawriẓečʿi*, pp. 43-44, «Եւ անողորմ զօրացն Պարսից վարեալ զժողովուրդն լՆռւթն ի գետն... ոմանք ի նոցանէ կալեալ զեզերս նաւացն, եւ ոմանք զտոհոցն, եւ ոմանք զագիս ձիոց եւ զեզւանց, եւ զգոմշ2ոց, եւ ոմանք իրրովի լողեալք անցանէին։ Եւ որք անճմուտք էին լողելոյ եւ անզօրք, ծերք եւ պառաւունք, տղայք եւ աղջկունք, եւ մատաղ մանկնիք... գետն առեալ տանէր զնոսա եւ թեւլտ անցին, որք անցինն, այլ բազմ֊ք այնք էին՝ որք ֆեղձմամբ շրոյն մեռանն:»

many people drowned. I, the sinful person, was about to drown when I managed to get hold of the tail of a buffalo and was saved by the will of God.[66]

Immediately after crossing the river, the deportees were forced to make their way through mountainous and difficult roads to escape the Ottomans. Very harsh road and weather conditions as well as other hardships and brutalities claimed a great number of lives. According to Augustin Baječi:

> On our way, those who remained behind were killed. Many of them suffered due to the cold weather, illness, starvation and hardship ... in the mornings, after nightly rests, many were left behind dead or very sick. On our way, many women abandoned their infants due to their weakness.[67]

By the beginning of the winter, the people had already crossed the Karadagh mountains. It was impossible to move any further; therefore, they were sheltered in Khalkhal, Ahar, Mishkin and the surrounding areas.[68] In the spring of 1605, they were moved once again and distributed to different parts of Iran, mainly Gilan, Mazandaran, Kashan, Qazvin, Shiraz, Hamadan, Isfahan and its neighboring districts of Linjan, Alinjan, Geandiman, Jlaxor, Peria and Burwari.[69]

The Armenian merchants of Julfa, a community of two thousand families, were the only people fairly well treated during the mass deportations. Before being forced to leave their homes, they were granted a three-day grace period to prepare for the road and were allowed to take with them their movable belongings. Horses and camels were provided for their transportation. At the time of their departure, the Safavid forces demolished the town to prevent the inhabitants from returning and reestablishing themselves in the area. During the winter of 1605 the people of Julfa were sheltered in the city of Tabriz and in the spring they were transported to Isfahan, where they were granted a

66 "Čanaparhorduti'iwn Yewropa" in Notark Matenagruťaan Hayoč, pg. 6. «եկաք ราաաք ի գետն, որ կոչի Արասատպ, խիստ մեծ, որ մարդ առանց նաւի չէ կարիլ անցնիլ: Ամենայն ժողովրդորդ լցին ի մէջն առանց նաւի եւ առանց տաւարի, որն որ անցաւ, որն որ ջորն տարաւ ... շատումնք ի գետ խեղդեցան: Ես մեղատոլ այլ գետն կու տանէր. մեկ չամ2ի աքի ընկաւ ձեռս, Աստուծով դու եկի:»

67 Ibid. pg. 9. «ի Čանապարհն որ երթայինք, այն ինչ լետ մնայր՝ սպանէին: ... շատն ի ս). ในสงชนต์ ธูมชนต์ กูก ห และ ยานสาน สาน สาน สาน สาน สาน สาน สาน สาน สา
որ իջևէաք, ի վաղն ելնեաք բազում մեռեալք մնային իջևանքն եւ բազում հիւանդք: ... Ի Čանապարհն բազում կանայք ղնէին իրեանց ստնդեայ տղայքն ի վայր երթայն վասն տկարութեան:»

68 Aŕakel Dawriżeči, pg. 46.

69 Ibid. pg. 46.

large parcel of land on the right bank of the river Zayandarud and were allowed to immediately build the town of New Julfa.[70]

With the mass deportation carried out in such a large geographical area, Shah 'Abbas succeeded in his military strategy. The Ottoman army led by Çighala-Zade Sinan Pasha, passed through devastated lands and reached the river Arax exhausted. Unable to advance any further and faced with harsh weather conditions, the Ottomans were forced to return to Van for the winter. The following year Shah 'Abbas waged successful battles against the Ottomans and scored important victories. By 1607 the Ottomans were completely "expelled from Iranian territory as defined by the Treaty of Amasya in 1555."[71]

In 1605, 1608 and 1618 during new campaigns against the Ottomans, Shah 'Abbas continued to deport thousands of people from different parts of Armenia to transfer them to Iran,[72] thus completing the establishment of a very large Armenian community in Iran.

The total number of Armenians deported to Iran by Shah 'Abbas is not clear. Various estimates are presented in the sources. Arak̕el Dawriẑeči, the most important Armenian source of the time, provides only partial numbers and offers the following quantitative, but vague description for the mass deportation of 1604:

> The width of the area filled with the deportees extended from the slopes of the Garni mountains to the banks of the river Arax—so you can estimate the length of the area accordingly. I personally would say that it was a full day's journey, although elsewhere I have seen written estimates of five days' journey.[73]

Dawriẑeči also states that half of the Armenians deported to Iran were settled in Farahabad (Mazandaran), and the other half were settled in the city of Isfahan and its neighboring areas.[74]

According to Armenian manuscript colophons, written in Isfahan in 1605[75] and 1607[76] by scribes who had witnessed and experienced the hardship of the migration, thousands of innocent people were killed and 300,000 were deported to Iran in 1604-5. Georgian sources put the

---

[70] Ibid. pp. 57-64.
[71] Savory R., pg. 87.
[72] Aṙak̕el Dawriẑeči, pp. 148, 455.
[73] Ibid. pg. 40. «Ի սատրրունէ լերանցն Գառնւոյ մինչ ի յեզրն Երասխայ մեծի գետոյն, լայնութիւնն էր բանակին․ իսկ զերկայնութիւնն դովիմբ կշռեաց դու, բայց ես ասեմ ատր մնչ ճանապարհ. եւ յայլոր տեսի՛ որ հինգ ատր ճանապարհ էին գրեալ:»
[74] Ibid. pg. 148.
[75] Hakobyan V., Ž̄Ē Dari Hišatakaranner, vol. I, pg. 182-183.
[76] Tēr Awetisean S., Čučak Jeṙngrač ... vol. I, pg. 152.

number at 80,000 families or more than 400,000 souls.[77]

As already cited, Antonio de Gouvea estimated the number 60,000 families or more than 300,000 souls.[78] John Chardin,[79] Raphael du Mans,[80] Jean-Baptiste Tavernier[81] and Joseph Pitton de Tournefort[82] state that 30,000 Armenian families were taken to Gilan-Mazandaran area by Shah 'Abbas.

According to Eskandar Beg Monshi, first, three thousand Armenian families or some twenty thousand souls were taken captive from Kars region and were transferred to Iraq to embrace Islam in *Qizilbash* custody.[83] Later, all the inhabitants of Erevan and Naxčawan regions were deported. Only a few people escaped deportation by hiding in mountain defiles and remote spots.[84]

All the above-listed estimates may somehow be confirmed. If the 30,000 families settled in the Gilan-Mazandaran area represent half the number of the total migrants who arrived Iran as Dawrižeči indicates, then another 30,000 families must have been scattered throughout Iran, mainly in Isfahan and the surrounding districts. That confirms the information provided by Antonio de Gouvea.

Between seventeenth and nineteenth centuries, under normal living conditions, an average family included 6-7 souls.[85] But during wars or forced migrations, that figure could have changed. Assuming that 25% of the Armenian deportees who, unable to withstand the harsh winter weather and to fight off the various diseases, which are common in such situations, could have perished on the road, we can easily conclude that, in 1604-5 alone, almost 400,000 people were deported by Shah 'Abbas from Armenia, and 300,000 of them survived and reached Iran, as indicated by the two Armenian scribes. Furthermore, as suggested by Dawrižeči, thousands of people were deported from Armenia between 1605 and 1618.[86] That brings the total number of deportees to well over 400,000 souls.

With the deportation of the people from Armenia, Shah 'Abbas

---

[77] Danelyan, L.G., "Hayeri Brnagałt'n Iran 17-rd Darum," Lraber, 1969, #8(315), pg. 72.
[78] Antonio de Gouvea, pg. 354.
[79] *Voyages du Chevlaier Chardin, en Perse, et Autres Lieux de l'Orient...*, Amsterdam 1735, vol. III, pg. 7.
[80] Raphael Du Mans, *L'estat de la Perse en 1660*, Paris, 1890, pg. 183.
[81] *The Six Travels of John Baptista Tavernier, Baron of Aubonne, through Turkey and Persia to the Indies, during the space of Forty Years....* London 1684, vol. I, pg. 16.
[82] Joseph Pitton de Tournefort, *A Voyage into the Levant*, vol. III, London 1741, pg. 228.
[83] Eskandar Beg Monshi, vol. II. pg. 857.
[84] Ibid. pg. 859.
[85] Tēr Yovhaneanč Y., vol. II, pp. 312-16.
[86] Ałakel Dawrižeči, pp. 148, 455.

successfully completed his military objective against the Ottomans. Taking advantage of the winter when the deportees were temporarily sheltered in Northern Iran, he would carefully plan their distribution in different parts of Iran, according to his own economic agenda.

CHAPTER THREE

THE CREATION OF ARMENIAN SETTLEMENTS IN CENTRAL IRAN

The forced deportations of Armenians in 1604 and their settlement throughout Iran was to give birth to one of the largest and most populous dioceses of the Armenian Church. In this chapter, based primarily on archival materials, as well as Armenian and Western published sources, we will attempt to present a general survey of the geographic and demographic distribution of the seventeenth century Armenians in central Iran and their social composition.

Isfahan and New Julfa

Isfahan, as the capital of the kingdom and being located on the international trade roads, was the center of economic life of Iran; therefore, from among the refugees Shah 'Abbas selected the most qualified people, especially tradesmen and artisans, and had them settled in and around Isfahan, so that they might contribute to the economic prosperity of the kingdom.

In 1605, a few thousand Armenian families were brought to Isfahan, including the two thousand families from Julfa, mostly merchants and skilled artisans who were provided with lands on the right bank of river Zayandarud and were encouraged to build their own town of New Julfa, isolated from the local Iranian people.[1] The rest of the Armenians brought to Isfahan were mostly artisans and were selected from the refugees gathered in Tabriz from Erevan, Naxčawan, Dašt, and many

[1] Aṙakel Dawrižeći, pg. 63.

other cities and towns of Armenia. They were settled in the following central quarters of Isfahan itself: Erevančis in Takhtē Gharaja and Baghat, Daštečis in Shamsabad and the rest in Torskan near Narenqala (the citadel) and Sheikh Shaban.[2]

Coexistence between Muslim Persians and Christian Armenians proved to be very difficult. Due to religious conflicts and differences in lifestyle and social habits, tensions were always high between the two communities.[3] The erection of churches, the sound of church bells, the outdoor religious processions and the common use of wine by the Armenians had annoyed the Muslim population of the city. Their constant and decades-long complaints to the Royal Court ultimately resulted in the deportation of the Armenians from Isfahan and their transfer to the plain of Marnan[4] on the southwestern edge of New Julfa, between 1655 and 1659.[5] Thus the small town of New Julfa doubled in size and population.

In the early decades of the seventeenth century, New Julfa was a small town of 2000 families[6] or 10,000 souls.[7] According to Chardin, in late 1660's the population of New Julfa had grown to 3400-3500 families, or 30,000 souls.[8] Ten years later, in 1677 John Fryer provided the following information on the population of New Julfa:

> Here inhabit not only Armenians but the Ancient Gabers[9] who remain here with their tribes, with some Mechanick French (as Jewellers, Gunsmiths, and Watchmakers); and some few Musslemen, as spies rather than inmates. Of the Armenian Christians, here are more than six thousand families, besides an innumerable company of dispersed husbandmen in the villages, following their patriarch in the same Faith. [10]

---

[2] Ibid, pp. 450-1. In some sources, the name Sheikh Shaban is replaced by the Armenian name Nor Šinik or Noraśen, and the name Shamsabad by Dašt. An Armenian manuscript colophon written in Isfahan in 1628, states: "... the present book of sermons was copied by Gaspar Ereč... at the gate of the city of Isfahan, in the village of Nor Šinik, which previously was known as Sheikh Shaban ..." («զրեգա պարոզ գիրքս ձեռամբ Գասպար իրիցոս... ի յերկիրն Րասպանան, ի դրաշ քաղաքին, ի գիւղն Նոր Շինիկ, որ առաջ Շիշապական կոչէին...»). Hakobyan V., ŽĒ Dari Hišatakaranner, vol. II, pg. 307. See also vol. I, pp. 564, 667, vol. III, pg. 425.

[3] Ařakel Dawrižeči, pp. 448, 453-4.

[4] Hakobyan V., ŽĒ Dari Hišatakaranner, vol. III, pg. 846.

[5] Ařakel Dawrižeči, pp.450-7.

[6] A chronicle of the Carmelites in Persia, vol. I, pg. 130.

[7] Herbert, Sir Thomas. Some Years Travels into Diverse Parts of Africa and Asia the Great, London 1677, pg. 169.

[8] Chardin, Jean. vol. II, pg. 107.

[9] Zoroastrians.

[10] Fryer, John. A New Account of East India and Persia, being Nine Years Travels, 1672-1681, vol. II, London 1898, pp. 252-3.

Cornelis de Bruyn, who visited Isfahan in 1701, presented the following description of New Julfa:

> The town or suburb of Julpha is divided into several parts, and particularly into the old and new colony. The old one, which they call Soeg-ga [šukay–market] is inhabited by the principal merchants; and they say their ancestors came thither from several parts, and even from the frontiers of Turkey, in the reign of Abbas the Great, and that this prince assigned them certain lands for their support ... New Julpha is higher up and subdivided into several districts, (1) that of Gaif-rabaet [Gawrapat] or of Koets, inhabited by stone cutters who work for buildings and tombs; (2) that of Tabriese [Dawrež] full of weavers and artificers in stuffs, among whom are some Frenchmen; (3) that of Toest or of Samsha-baet (Shams Abad) which belongs to the old colony, and is inhabited by merchants and artificers; (4) that of Eriwan, full of common people; (5, 6 and 7) are called Nagt-siewaen [Naxčawan] Siachsa-baen [Sheikh Shaban] and Kasket-sie [Gaskečis]; these are inhabited by the same and all these people are called after the district they live in, without any other distinction. Old Julfa is much larger than all the other districts put together, and contains nearly two thousand families, of which are those of some of the most wealthy and most considerable merchants.[11]

Seventeenth century Armenian sources do not provide estimates or numbers on the total Armenian population of New Julfa. Stepannos Ereč who started writing his History in 1787, stated that in the seventeenth century 12,000 Armenian families used to live in New Julfa.[12] Based on oral tradition and the information provided by Stepannos Ereč, Yarutiwn Tēr Yovhaneanč accepted the theory of the 12,000 families.[13] Others followed suit without realizing that 12,000 families could mean more than 70,000 souls, enough to fully populate a large town.

The seventeenth century New Julfa was a small town built on a small area of 233 hectares or 575 acres,[14] which could not accommodate more than three thousand five hundred houses.[15] The larger part of the town, built in the beginning of the seventeenth century, was inhabited by two thousand families, who were provided with larger parcels of land. The remaining and much smaller part of the town, built in the late 1650's, could hardly accommodate more than one thousand five hundred houses, despite the fact that the houses in this part of the town

---

[11] Bruyn, Cornelis de. *Travels into Muscovy, Persia and Part of the East Indies*, London 1737, pp. 225-6.

[12] Manuscript #654, in the collection of All Saviour's Monastery, New Julfa.

[13] Tēr Yovhaneanč, Y., vol. I, pg. 44.

[14] Karapetian K., *Isfahan, New Julfa: The Houses of the Aremenians*, pg. XXIV.

[15] In J.G. Hananean's opinion, the land capacity of New Julfa was enough for a maximum of 2600-3000 houses. See *"Nor Ĵulayi Bnakčuǔwnə Sksbič minčew Mer Orerð"*, *Nor Azdarar*, Calcutta, 1951, p. 12-3.

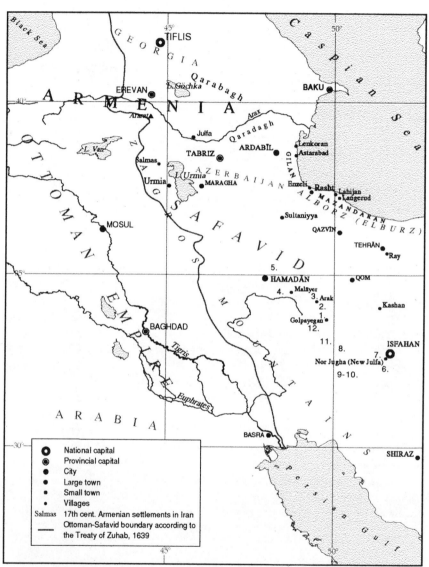

2. Armenian Settlements in Iran in the Seventeenth Century

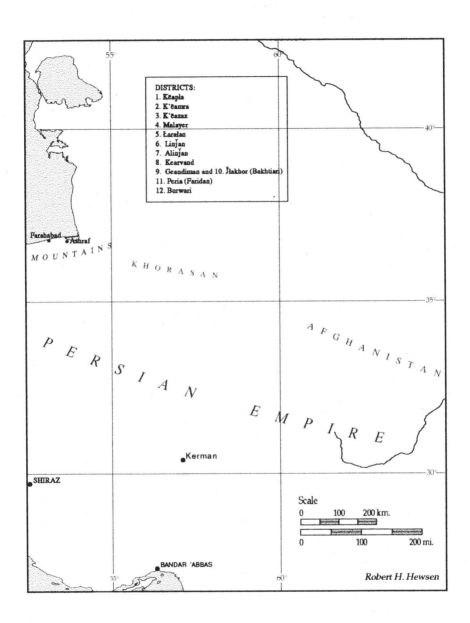

DISTRICTS:
1. Kčapla
2. K'čamra
3. K'čazaz
4. Malayer
5. Łarałan
6. Linjan
7. Alinjan
8. Kearvand
9. Geandiman and 10. Jłakhor (Bakhtiari)
11. Peria (Faridan)
12. Burwari

Farahabad Ashraf

MOUNTAINS

KHORASAN

PERSIAN

AFGHANISTAN

EMPIRE

Kerman

SHIRAZ

Scale

0   100   200 km.

0   100   200 mi.

BANDAR 'ABBAS

Robert H. Hewsen

were built on smaller parcels of land. According to a recent topographic survey made by K. Karapetian in nine houses from the seventeenth century, the average ground floor construction of a house covered a surface area of 300 sq. metres.[16] If 35% of a given parcel of land was used for construction, then each house would have occupied an average of 875 sq. metres. Assuming that the surveyed constructions were mostly larger houses and bringing the size of an average parcel of land down to 650 sq. metres, the whole town could have been divided into 3580 units. Therefore, it is reasonable to conclude that in the second half of the seventeenth century, the Armenian population of New Julfa was approximately 3500 families or a maximum of 25,000-30,000 souls, as confirmed by Chardin.

Small Armenian communities were scattered in some villages in the immediate vicinity of Isfahan and New Julfa. The existence of Armenian churches is mentioned at least in the following four villages: Šaxasoron,[17] Govdēh Zayenderud[18] Dowlatabad[19] and Yarewan.[20] No further information is available on these communities.

Rural Settlements in the Seven Districts to the West of Isfahan

Tens of thousands of refugees from rural areas of Armenia were brought to central Iran and were settled in more than one hundred villages[21] scattered between Isfahan and Sultanabad (Arak), and administratively divided into the following seven small districts:

Linǰan - The region of Linǰan is located ten miles to the southwest of Isfahan, in the vicinity of the present day Falavarjan. In the seventeenth century, it included at least seventeen villages inhabited by Armenians. Among them, Tēr Yovhaneanč has listed only the following eleven villages: Ḱearḱēn, Ṗarťan, Zudan, J̌uzdan, Ḱalisan, Ṗēlard, Buruzard, Sēmsan, Xunsarēḱ, Mirgiwn and Ḱealē Masih.[22] Taking his information from Sheikh Jaberi Ansari, L.G. Minasean adds the name of the village of Vardan.[23]

---

[16] Karapetian K., pp. 69-312.
[17] Hakobyan V., ŽĒ Dari Hišatakaranner, vol. III, pg. 91.
[18] Ibid. pg. 959.
[19] Ibid. pg. 845.
[20] Ibid. vol. II, pg. 400.
[21] Most of the scholars, including H. Aŕaḱelean, A. Alpoyačean, A. Abrahamyan and N.Y. Goroyeanč have simply followed Tēr Yovhaneanč in limiting the number of the seventeenth century Armenian villages in central Iran to 73. L.G. Minasean has listed 81 villages.
[22] Tēr Yovhaneanč, Y., vol. I, pg. 32, vol. II, pg. 295.
[23] Minasean L.G., Patmuťiwn Ṗeriayi Hayeri, Antelias, 1971, pg. 469.

The fragment of a public petition, most probably circulated in 1693 or 1697 to express loyalty to the diocese of New Julfa, lists the following five additional Armenian villages of Linjan: Ḱarťman,[24] Fundroy, Kuhē kalaman, Zuvali and Susan,[25] thus raising the total number of the seventeenth century Armenian villages of Linjan to seventeen.

Alinjan - Approximately thirteen miles to the west of Isfahan, Alinjan is adjacent to Linjan. Only the following seven villages inhabited by Armenians are known from this region: Bondard, Zazran, Mēmēd, Mšałbur (Shahabad), P̌idan, Karuj and Kap̌ašan.[26]

Kearvand - The region of Kearvand is situated sixty miles to the west of Isfahan. Information on the seventeenth century Armenian population of this region is very limited. Based on Armenian manuscript colophons, epitaphs and late eighteenth and early nineteenth century sources, it is possible to trace the presence of Armenians in the following seven villages: Alwar, Dowlatabad, Iškiran, Hovčun, Madarshah, Nerḱin Ḱrder, Verin Ḱrder.[27]

Geandiman and Jłaxor - The districts of Geandiman and Jłaxor, presently known as Čhar Mahal, are situated approximately seventy miles to the southwest of Isfahan, in the vicinity of Shahr Kord. From their initial settlement in this area in the early seventeenth century to their final departure in 1946,[28] the Armenians have constantly moved within the area, often abandoning a well-established village and moving elsewhere to build a new one. The presence of Armenians in this area between 1605 and 1950 can be traced in more than forty villages. Tombstones with Armenian inscriptions can still be found in most of the villages.

Among the Armenian settlements of Geandiman and Jłaxor in the seventeenth century, Tēr Yovhaneanč has identified only the following six villages: Ahmadabad, Sirak, Kišnikan, Livasian, Frntikan and Ziwrikan.[29] Based on manuscript colophons,[30] tombstone inscriptions[31]

---

[24] At least two Armenian manuscripts copied in K'art'man in the first half of the seventeenth century have survived. Hakobyan V., *Žē Dari Hišatakaranner*, vol. I, pg. 32, vol. III, pg. 813.

[25] Archives of All Saviour's Monastery, hereafter AASM, (Cab. 1, file 30b).

[26] Tēr Yovhaneanč, Y., vol. I, pg. 32. Also, the public Petition in AASM (cab. 1, File 30b).

[27] Minasean L.G., *Patmuťiwn P̌eriayi Hayeri*, pp. 471-478. These villages are not mentioned by Tēr Yovhaneanč.

[28] In 1946 most of the Armenian villagers of the area migrated to Armenia. The rest moved to Tehran, New Julfa and other cities in Iran.

[29] Tēr Yovhaneanč, Y., vol. I, pg. 32.

[30] Hakobyan V., *Žē Dari Hišatakaranner*, vol. I, pg. 412.

[31] Andreasean V., *Čarmahal Gawar*, New Julfa, 1977, pp. 25-52.

and certain documents in the archives of All Saviour's Monastery of New Julfa,[32] I was able to trace the names of the following six additional Armenian villages of this area in the seventeenth century: Vastikan,[33] Katak, Kulukert, Šalomzar, Bĵkert and Abasabad.

Ṗeria - The province of Ṗeria corresponds to the present-day region of Daran and Akhora, ninety five miles to the west of Isfahan. At present Ṗeria is the only rural area in Iran where a small number of Armenians continue to live in some villages established in early seventeenth century, when thousands of Armenian and Georgian[34] refugees settled there.

The history of Armenians in Ṗeria is relatively better known thanks to the efforts of L.G. Minasean, who has brought to light many sources, especially archival materials, manuscript colophons, inscriptions and oral traditions.[35]

In the region of Ṗeria, Minasean has listed fifty-eight old and new villages inhabited by Armenians in the course of 350 years (1606-1956),[36] including the following twenty nine villages from the seventeenth century. Hazarĵarib, Azgol, Mēvrstan, Mēydanak, Ałča, Ṗnstan, Boloran, Daškēšan, Verin Khuygan, Sangbaran, Khunk or Khnkirana, Šahbua, Šuriškan or Shirshagun, Milakert, Ťang Halvayi, Nerḱin Khuygan, Ťalbulał, Bēku or Bekri, Eskandariłuza, Mułan, Mukēli Geł, Eskandaria, Sangerd, Marzi Draz, Ałama, Gušxarad, Ĵamin, Darbni Geł or Namakert and Daramara.[37]

Burwari - To the north west of Ṗeria, in the vicinity of the present day Golpayegan lies the district of Burwari, a region most heavily populated by Armenians in the seventeenth century and almost ignored by all scholars of Iranian-Armenian studies.

Y. Tēr Yovhaneanč has simply compiled and presented a list of twenty two Armenian villages in the district of Burwari.[38] Most scholars have accepted the list as presented by Y. Tēr Yovhaneanč. However, L.G. Minasean has identified two of the listed villages: Mēvrstan and Azgol as part of the district of Ṗeria.[39] The remaining twenty villages of

---

[32] A public petition of 1693 signed by the Armenians of Geandiman, expressing their loyalty to the Diocese of New Julfa, in AASM (Cab. 5, File 30b, Doc. #2. Also documents in Cab. 4, File #232)

[33] Mentioned also by Aṙaḱel Dawriẑeči, pg. 418.

[34] At least ten villages in the vicinity of Daran and Akhora are still inhabited by people of Georgian origin, who have lost their language and are converted to Islam.

[35] Patmuťiwn Ṗeriayi Hayeri, and many articles in varioius Armenian periodicals.

[36] Ibid. pp. 220-1.

[37] Ibid. pp. 219-335.

[38] Tēr Yovhaneanč, Y., vol. I, pg. 32-33.

[39] Minasean L.G., Patmuťiwn Ṗeriayi Hayeri, pg. 29.

the seventeenth century Burwari listed by Tēr Yovhaneanč are: Čamxəsu, Jašun, Čēšmē Ṗara, K̆avarza, Anavš, Verin Čarbal, Nerk̆in Čarbal, Jłagurk, Bork̆ok̆, Łasumava, Janxoš, Ṗarmišan, Šavrava, T̆ark̆u, Ṗarčis, Ṗahra, Khosrowabad, Dēynov, Gulbahar and Hmaya.

Surprisingly, Tēr Yovhaneanč has ignored a very valuable document in compiling his list, despite the fact that he has included the Armenian translation of the said document,—an edict issued by Shah Sulayman in 1671—, in the second volume of his own work.[40] According to this document, new taxes, totalling 424 *tomans* were imposed on the Armenian churches of New Julfa, Ṗeria and Burwari. All the churches with their due taxes are listed in this document. For P'eria and Burwari the names of the villages are used for the respective church or community. Under Burwari, twenty nine villages are mentioned, fourteen of which are included in the list of villages compiled by Tēr Yovhaneanč. The remaining fifteen villages are: Ḥrahil, K̆aškriz, Juli Zang, Čaylua, Ṗiralē, Karmšan, Muratxani, Sēviriči, Jani, Halfarunak̆, Šahbulal, Jhanak, Čartal, Šarifa, and K̆ərt.[41]

A second version of the same tax list, dated 1675 and preserved in the archives of All Saviour's Monastery,[42] includes 30 villages under Burwari, 15 of which appear in the list compiled by Tēr Yovhaneanč.

My own research, on a public petition from the Armenians of Burwari and P'eria dated 1693,[43] has identified the names of two additional villages in Burwari: Šarharun and Xmst̆an, bringing the total of the seventeenth century Armenian villages of Burwari to thirty seven, a much greater number, compared to the Armenian villages of the time in other districts.

The discovery of the names of thirty two villages not known to or considered by scholars in this field, leads us to believe that further research, especially on site studies of tombstone inscriptions, can greatly increase the present list of one hundred and thirteen villages inhabited by Armenians in the seventeenth century, in the immediate vicinity of Isfahan, and, the districts of Linjan, Alinjan, Kearvand, Ṗeria, Burwari, Geandiman and Jłaxor, and can shed new light on the history of the Armenian communities of that rural areas.

The earliest available demographic data on the Armenians of Ṗeria,

---

[40] Tēr Yovhaneanč, Y., vol. II, pp. 239-242.
[41] While in 1675 the villages of Šarifa, Čartal and K̆ərt̆ are clearly listed under the district of Burwari, two centuries later, in 1856, in the statistical records of the diocese of New Julfa, they are listed as part of the district of K̆eaṗla, to the north of Burwari. See Tēr Yovhaneanč, Y., vol. II, pg. 313.
[42] AASM (Cab. 1, File #36).
[43] See Appendix I, doc. #17.

Burwari, Geandiman and Ĵłaxor is from 1856, when in the four districts[44] only thirty five Armenian villages were in existence, with a total population of 10,082 souls or 1583 families.[45] According to these figures, the average population of a village was forty five families or 288 souls.

This statistical calculation can not be applied to the seventeenth century Armenian villages of the area, since they were greatly decreased in number and population by the mid-nineteenth century. According to Stepanos Ereć, in the seventeenth century the village of Hazarĵarib alone included 600 families,[46] while in the statistics of 1856 the number of the families in the same village were reduced to ninety nine.[47] Likewise, by mid-nineteenth century the Armenian population of New Julfa,[48] Shiraz[49] and other areas of Iran were decreased by almost the same proportion. Therefore, it is logical to assume that the average Armenian population of the seventeenth century villages was at least 80-100 families or 550-650 souls, which brings the total number of Armenians in these districts to more than 10,000 families, or 65,000-70,000 souls.

Hamadan and the Surrounding Districts

The existence of a considerable Armenian community in Hamadan is evident in the seventeenth century sources. A letter by Dawit and Stepanos Ĵułayeći addressed to the people of Hamadan in 1683 mentioned three parish priests serving the community of Hamadan.[50] If we consider each priest assigned to the spiritual service of at least sixty families, then it is possible to estimate the Armenian community of Hamadan as close to 200 families, or more than 1200 souls.[51]

In the 1856 statistical records of the diocese of New Julfa, the five districts of Ḱeapla, Ḱeamra, Ḱeazaz, Malayer and Łarałan in the vicinity of Hamadan and Arak are listed with a total number of 910 Armenian

---

[44] Due to religious persecutions, heavy taxation, looting and destruction of villages by invading armies, especially under Agha Mohamed Khan Qajar in 1780; by the end of the eighteenth century there were no Armenians in the disctricts of Linĵan, Alinĵan and Kearvand. Tēr Yovhaneanć, Y., vol. I, pp. 374-5.

[45] Ibid., vol. II, pp. 296-313.

[46] Ibid. vol. II, pg. 304.

[47] Ibid. vol. II. pg. 300.

[48] By mid 1850's, the total Armenian population of New Julfa was reduced to 2641 souls. Ibid., vol. II, pp. 278-281.

[49] In 1856, there were only seven Armenian families in Shiraz out of the 500 families settled there in 1605. Ibid. vol. II. pg. 316.

[50] AASM (cabine 5, drawer 6, file 27Ž, #1).

[51] In the 1856 statistical records of the diocese of New Julfa, 40 families or 235 souls are registered in the city of Hamadan. Tēr Yovhaneanć, Y., vol. II, pg. 315.

families or 5449 souls, scattered in thirty six villages.[52]

In the seventeenth century Armenian sources, no reference was made to these five districts. Unlike the districts of Linjan, Alinjan, Geandiman, Jɫaxor, Ṗeria and Burwari, they were not mentioned in the encyclicals issued by the Kaṫolikoi of Ejmiacin. In the archives of All Saviour's Monastery, the earliest available correspondence related to these districts are from the late eighteenth and early nineteenth centuries.[53] No attempt has been made by any scholar to study the inscriptions of the Armenian tombstones in these districts, with the aim of establishing the earliest period of Armenian presence in these areas.

The statistical records of the diocese of New Julfa in 1856 listed the following villages inhabited by Armenians:[54]

Ќeaṕla. To the north of Burwari, between Golpayegan and Arak. The villages of Ortačiman, Ṫoxmar, Muɫan, Ahmadabad or Caruki Ɫala, Hoseinava, Hajiava, Ṗrčstan, Ќamian, Zarna, Abasabad, Baɫmovdi, Mazra, Čarṫal, Šarafava and Ќərt.[55]

Ќeamra. Between Ќeaṕla and Arak. The village of Davudabad, Ќeandlner, Lilihan, Saќi and Ɫorčibaši.

Ќeazaz. To the southwest of Arak. The villages of Ambarṫa, Ɫalayšex, Dilisawa, Azna, Ќealawa, Umbrian, Marand, Golzar and Seyduna.

Malayer. To the southeast of Hamadan. The villages of Anuaš, Ɫasumabad and Dyečuna.

Ɫaraɫan. To the northeast of Hamadan. The villages of Čarhad, Čanaɫči, Lar, and Čambar.[56]

Certainly at least some of these villages, like Čartaɫ, Šarifa and Ќərt in the district of Ќeaṕla were inhabited by Armenians in the seventeenth century. The majority of the remaining villages of these districts were probably established or inhabited by Armenians, following the four years (1785-1788) military campaigns of Agha Mohammed Khan Qajar in the vicinity of Isfahan, when the Armenian villages of Linjan, Kearvand and Ṗeria were repeatedly plundered and the inhabitants

---

[52] Ibid. pp. 313-315.
[53] Minasean L.G., *Diwan S. Amenapŕkič Vanќi*, pp. 32-54.
[54] Ter Yovhaneanć, Y., vol. II, pp. 313-315.
[55] As already indicated, these last three villages were mentioned as part of Burwari in the seventeenth century. See pg. 41, note #41.
[56] In late nineteenth century, N.Y. Goroyeanć mentions two additional villages: Engiɫala and Bargušat, with twenty Armenian families in each. See *Parskastani Hayerə,* Tehran, 1968, pp. 325-6.

were deported or taken into captivity.[57]   But due to the lack of sources, for the time being no final conclusions can be made.

Gilan and Mazandaran

Situated on the western and southern shores of the Caspian Sea, the provinces of Gilan and Mazandaran were the center of Iranian silk production. Before the reign of Shah 'Abbas this region was neglected, and due to its very humid climatic conditions and the marshy topography, it was lightly populated. Malaria and other diseases originating from the marshlands would not give much chance of survival for the inhabitants.

Shah 'Abbas the Great, whose mother was from Mazandaran,[58] demonstrated a special interest in the development of the region, primarily because silk was the backbone of the Iranian economy and the main commodity for export to Europe. He constructed a stone causeway along the marshy littoral of the Caspian Sea and two winter palaces: Ashraf and Farahabad. He spent every winter in the region, especially in Farahabad, which in fact served as a sort of second capital.[59]

The refugees forcefully deported from their ancestral lands and brought to Iran were an easy source of manpower for Shah 'Abbas who was in great need of labour for his construction projects and the cultivation of silk. He settled half of the entire Armenian refugees in Gilan and Mazandaran,[60] especially in Lenkoran, Rasht, Enzeli, Lahijan, Langerud, Astarabad, Salian, Kismē, Farahabad and the surrounding villages.[61] The Shah gave special orders to *Rahdars*[62] to prevent anyone from fleeing the region. Special travel permits were issued only to individuals who could present a good reason for their travel and had a family member to leave behind, insuring his return to the region.[63]

Jean Baptiste Tavernier, Raphael du Mans and Jean Chardin, the three most renowned travelers of the seventeenth century to Iran, provide some information on the number and the fate of the Armenians in Gilan and Mazandaran. Tavernier, who has made six lengthy voyages to Iran between 1633 and 1668, reports:

He [Shah 'Abbas] sent above 27000 families of Armenians into Guilan,

---

[57] Tēr Yovhaneanč, Y., vol. I, pp. 340-377.
[58] Chardin, Jean. vol. III, pg. 7.
[59] Savory R., pp. 96-100.
[60] Aṙakel Dawrižeči, pg. 148.
[61] Alaneanč G., *Diwan Hayoč Patmuṫean*, Book A-B, Tbilisi, 1893, pp. 801-2.
Simēon Erewanči, *Jambr*, Vałaršapat, 1873, pg. 48.
[62] Road patrols.
[63] Aṙakel Dawrižeči, pg. 456-7.

whence the silks came; and where the harshness of the climate killed abundance of those poor people, that were accustomed to a milder air.[64]

Rafael du Mans, a well informed Capuchin missionary who lived in Isfahan for 52 years (1644-1696) and authored a valuable work on the state of Iran in 1660, stresses the unhealthy climate of Gilan and Mazandaran and adds:

Finally, this is a land which devours its inhabitants, as happened in the case of the 30,000 Armenian families transported there by Shah 'Abbas. At present, we can barely count 1200 families there, and their number is getting reduced to nothing on a daily basis, as I was told by their Bishop Isaac Vardapet...[65]

Chardin, who first visited Iran in 1666, provides the following valuable information:

This country of Mazenderan was almost grown a desert, by reason of the bad air, before Abas the Great's time: but that prince, a mighty conqueror, and a vast politican, transported thither a prodigious number of people from Armenia, and Georgia, as well to depopulate those countries where the Turks came every year to encamp and make war against them, as because he believed that soil to be of more significance and importance, seeing among other things, that the silkworms bred very kindly, and came to perfection in those parts. His mother, who was of Mazenderan, which might of consequence be called his native country inasmuch as it produced the person who gave him his being, solicited him on the other hand, to people again and place, to which he owed his birth. He transported thither a thousand families of Christians, imagining that they would be very fruitful and increase there mightily: it is, say'd he, a perfect right country for the Christians; it abounds with wine and Hog's-flesh, two things which they will trafick with their brothers the Muscovites, by the Caspian Sea. Abas caus'd towns to be built, and magnificent palaces to be erected, in several places of that country, and all this to encourage the increase of the colony; but the malignity of the air was so cross to his designs and projects, though laid and carried on with the utmost care and diligence, that when I was at Mazenderan with the court about forty years ago, the number of Christians was reduced to four hundred families, from the thirty thousand that were there at first, as I was very credibly informed. The Bishop of Ferackbad a good old Armenian Prelate, who was well enough acquainted with the country, told me frequently, that if it was not for the fertility of the soil, which draws the neighboring people thither, the whole country would be left like a desert, by reason of the unwholesomeness of the air.[66]

---

[64] Tavernier, John Baptiste. vol. I, pg. 16.

[65] Raphael du Mans, pg. 183.

[66] Chardin, John. vol. III, pg. 7. English translation of the passage taken from Chardin's *Travels in Persia*, Dover publications, New York, 1988, pg. 132.

By mid 1670 the number of Armenians in the Gilan-Mazandaran area was reduced to two hundred families. In an encyclical dated 1676, Katołikos Yakob Julayeċi states the following:

> We have heard from our forefathers that eleven thousand Armenian families were taken to Farahabad, and now there are less than two hundred families in the entire Farahabad region.[67]

The unhealthy climate was the main but not the only cause for the very sharp decline of the Armenian population in Gilan and Mazandaran. Persecutions and forced conversions to Islam took their toll, specially from poor people, who could not afford to pay high taxes to preserve their faith and ethnic identity.[68] On the other hand, many people were able to flee and settle elsewhere, specially in territories under Russian rule.[69] By 1723, no Armenians were left in Gilan and Mazandaran, when the Russians, under Peter the Great, occupied the area.[70]

Other Cities

Seventeenth and eighteenth century Armenian sources and western travelers acknowledge the presence of Armenian communities in some other cities of Iran, particularly in Qazvin and Shiraz.

Qazvin, the capital city of Iran in the sixteenth century was an important trade center, located on the crossroads between Isfahan, Tabriz, Farahabad and Hamadan. All the Armenian refugees had passed through Qazvin in the early seventeenth century before being settled in different parts of Iran.[71] Some of the refugees, mainly tradesmen and artisans, settled in Qazvin. According to André Daulier-Deslandes, who visited Iran in 1664, "a great number" of Armenians were living in Qazvin.[72] For the same period, Chardin estimates only forty Armenian families in Qazvin.[73]

The Armenian community of Shiraz was much larger in the early seventeenth century. According to Aṙakel Dawriżeċi, on the request of Allahverdi Khan, Governor-General of Fars, Shah 'Abbas ordered the

---

[67] Appendix I., doc. #13.

[68] Papazyan, H., "Sefyan Irani Asimilyatorakan K̇ałak̇akanutʿyan Harċi Šurjə", *Banber Matenadarani*, #3, Erevan 1956, pg. 87.

[69] Goroyeanċ N.Y., pg. 306.

[70] Arakelean H., *Parskastani Hayerə, Nranċ Anċealə, Nerkan ew Apagan*, Vienna, 1911, pg. 92.

[71] Aṙakel Dawriżeċi, pp. 63, 442-4.

[72] Deslandes, André Daulier. *Les Beautez de la Perse*, Paris, 1673, pg. 17.

[73] Chardin, Jean. vol. I, pg. 272

settlement of five hundred Armenian families in Shiraz.[74] Apparently by the second half of the seventeenth century the number of Armenians in Shiraz was greatly decreased. John Chardin,[75] André Daulier-Deslandes,[76] and other western travelers who visited Shiraz after 1660, acknowledge the presence of only a small Armenian community in the city.

Among other places, the cities of Kashan, Qom, Kerman and Ardabil are listed as part of the diocese of New Julfa by Zakaria *Sarkawag*[77] and Katolikos Siméon Erewanči.[78] Western travelers also mention the presence of Armenians in Kashan,[79] but no information is available on the size and occupation of the Armenian communities in these four cities.

In addition to all the provinces, cities and villages listed in this chapter, there were undoubtedly many other places in Iran partly inhabited by Armenians. As André Daulier-Deslandes,[80] and other western travelers confirm, Armenians used to live everywhere in Iran in the seventeenth century. The central community was undoubtedly the newly created town of New Julfa, but it was only one component of the much more widely scattered communities.

Social Classes

Encyclicals issued by Katolikoi of Ějmiacin during the second half of the seventeenth century, other archival materials, manuscript colophons and epitaphs enable us to have a general picture of the social classes and ranks within the Armenians of Iran in the seventeenth century.

At first glance, two major social groups, the upper and lower classes, can be immediately identified. In the upper or dominant class, the following social ranks and titles can be classified:

1- The religious hierarchy, including the Katolikos, the primate, bishops, monks and parish priests.

2- The nobility, basically a small group of the most prominent families of Julfa. The heads of these families are distinguished with the

---

[74] Atakel Dawriženi, pg. 46.

[75] Chardin, Jean. vol. II, pg. 206.

[76] Deslandes, André Daulier. pg. 68.

[77] Zakaria *Sarkawag*, vol. I, pp. 14-20.

[78] *Siměon Katulikosi Yišatakaranə*, pp. 801-802.

[79] Deslandes, André Daulier. pg. 18.

[80] Ibid., pg. 18.

titles *Isxan* (prince) or *Melik*,[81]*Bek* (Lord) and *Ala* or *Paron* (sir). They are referred to as *azat*[82] (gentry), *ordik azatac*[83] (sons of the gentry), *azatacin*[84] (of gentle birth), *payazat*[85] (of noble descent), *azatazarm*[86] or *payazatazarm*[87] (of gentle origin), *aznuatohm*[88] (of noble family), *azgawn Mec*[89] (of a great family) or *azgawn azat Julayeci*[90] (of a gentle family from Julfa). The honorific *khwaja* (honorable), is largely used by the male members of these families.

In the present state of our knowledge, it is not possible to trace the social origin or the genealogy of these noble families. The epitaphs in the famous cemetery of Old Julfa would undoubtedly provide some clues in that respect. But until now, they have not been sufficiently well studied and being located in Naxčawan, present day Azerbaijan, remain inaccessible to scholarship.

In the opinion of Hagop Pap̀azyan, the noble families in question must have been the descendants of some of the old princely houses of Eastern Armenia, who lost their power mainly under the Mongol and Turkmen rules in the fourteenth and fifteenth centuries. Most of their lands were either confiscated in the name of *Beyt Al-Mal*[91] Islamic institution, or donated to monasteries to avoid confiscation. Before the mid-sixteenth century, they had gradually moved to Julfa and turned to trade.[92]

3- The wealthy (*Dowlatawork*).[93] Wealthy people, including the nobility, who had acquired properties, abundant goods and treasures, through successful trade operations. Among Armenian merchants in general, they are distinguished for being *Goyiwk Zelun*[94] (with abundant possessions). Probably they were the owners of trade companies, who employed many smaller merchants.

---

[81] A title introduced in the fourteenth century to replace the old Armenian princely titles and to designate the few surviving members of the old Armenian nobility. See Hewsen R.H., "The Meliks of Eastern Armenia," pg. 293.

[82] AASM, Encyclical of Kat̀olikos Pilip̀os, 1652.

[83] Hakobyan V., *Žē Dari Hišatakaranner*, Vol. I, p. 206.

[84] Ibid., pg. 206.

[85] Minasean L.G. *Nor Julayi Gerezmanatunə*, pg. 35.

[86] Appendix I, doc. #18.

[87] AASM, Encyclical of Kat̀olikos Pilip̀os , 1652.

[88] Appendix I, doc. #18.

[89] Minasean L.G. *Nor Julayi Gerezmanatunə*, pg. 40.

[90] Tēr Yovhaneanč Y., vol. I, pg. 50.

[91] Public treasury. According to an old Islamic law, a Christian was not entitled to large properties. If he refused to convert to Islam, his estate could be declared *Beyt Al-Mal* property.

[92] ASSR Academy, *History of Armenia*, vol. IV, pg. 247-248.

[93] From the Persian word *Dowlat*, meaning wealth.

[94] AASM, Encyclicals of Kat̀olikoi Eliazar and Nahapet.

4- The merchants in general (*Vačařmkan k̓*). Hundreds of Armenian merchants, great or small, who were involved in local and international trade, and in a relatively very short period of time, became dominant in the Iranian and international markets. In the encyclicals of the Katołikoi they are praised for being *imastun*[95] (wise), *xohem*[96] (prudent) and *Hančareł*[97] (ingenious).

5- Skilled men of arts and crafts. Usually called *Usta*[98] or *varpet*[99] (master) and categorized as *Vayel čagorc*[100] (fine craftsman) and *gełečkarar*[101] (practitioner of fine arts). This group includes master painters, manuscript illuminators, sculptors, goldsmiths, silversmiths, and other prestigious occupations. Some of them were employed in the royal workshops, while others worked independently or were affiliated with workshops established in New Julfa.[102]

In the lower class, the following three main groups can be identified:

1- Common artisans (*Arhestawor k̓*). Shoemakers, stone cutters, blacksmiths, candle makers, carpenters and people of many other occupations formed the lower class of the urban population. The tombstones of thousands of Armenian artisans in the cemetery of new Julfa depict the occupation of the deceased, thus providing a general picture of the many types of occupations of seventeenth-century Armenian artisans.

2- Agricultural labourers and husbandmen (*erkragorc k̓* and *Mšak k̓*). The rural population, who lived and worked on lands belonging to the state (*divani* or *khalisē*), the royal household (*khassa* or *khasseyē sharifē*), religious institutions (*vaqf* or *mowqufat*) or individual landowners (*arbabi* or *mulk̓*).[103] They were not allowed to move out of the village or the district where they were registered to live, work and pay taxes. Any peasant who fled to another region could be forced to return, if traced within twelve years.[104] In the encyclicals, they are characterized as

---

[95] AASM, Encyclical of Katołikos Nahapet, 1697.
[96] Appendix I. doc. #18.
[97] AASM, Encyclical of Katołikos Nahapet, 1697.
[98] From the Persian word *Ostad* (master).
[99] The most famous Armenian painter in New Julfa was *varpet* Minas. See *Ařakel Dawrižeči*, pg. 409.
[100] AASM, Encyclical of Katołikos Nahapet, 1695.
[101] AASM, Encyclical of Katołikos Nahapet, 1697.
[102] Łazaryan M., *Hay Kerparvestə XVII-XVIII Darerum*, Erevan, 1974, pg. 51.
[103] Lambton A.K.S., *Landlord and Peasant in Persia*, London, 1969, pp. 108-112.
[104] P̓ap̓azyan H.D., "Rayat̓neri Iravakan Azatut̓yan Harcə...", *Ējer Hay Žołowrdi Patmut̓ean ew Banasirut̓ean*, Erevan, 1971. pg. 127.

ašxataser[105] (hard working), *ardaravastak*[106] (those who earn honestly) and * k̆rtnaj̆an*[107] (one who toiled on swet.)

3- Servants (*Carayk̆* or *tulk̆*). Almost nothing is known about the class of servants or slave workers who were owned by the nobility. They appear to be very limited in number. As for their ethnic origin, Father John Taddeus, a Carmelite missionary, reports the following from Isfahan in 1608:

> It appears to us that great results could be gained in this country if there were a college for Armenian, Georgian, Circassian and Persian boys, who might be purchased out of many offered for sale if we were to bring them up among us ... and the king of Persia would not interfere with such work, because it is the habit here that the slave must take the religion of his master.[108]

In the Armenian sources, we only find the following three minor references on the status of the servants:

a) According to Aṙak̆el Dawrižeči, individual Christians who converted to Islam were eligible to inherit the properties of their deceased Christian relatives. Sometimes they were even able to take custody of the children and the servants of the deceased.[109]

b) In his two wills dated 1652 and 1659 respectively, *Khwaja* Połos Velijaneanč presents a detailed list of his belongings, including houses, vineyards, shops, animals and six *arcat̆agin carayk̆* (servants purchased with silver or money). He grants freedom to his servants after his death.[110]

c) In his will dated 1693, a certain *Khwaja* P̆anos bequeaths one *toman* to each of his three servants, granting them freedom after his death.[111]

The upper class of Armenian society, including clerics, noblemen, merchants and skilled craftsmen were mainly settled in New Julfa. It may be reasonable to suppose that within the limits of new Julfa community, they formed a majority. However, these two thousand wealthy families were only a small segment of the total Armenian population of Iran. The absolute majority, scattered in rural areas, belonged to the lower class of the society.

---

[105] Appendix I., doc. #18.
[106] AASM, Encyclical of Kat̆ołikos Nahapet, 1695.
[107] AASM, Encyclical of Kat̆ołikos Nahapet, 1697.
[108] A Chronicle of the Carmelites in Persia, vol. II, pg. 165.
[109] Aṙak̆el Dawrižeči, pp. 67-68.
[110] Tēr Yovhaneanč Y., vol. I, pp. 130-2.
[111] AASM, *Khwaja* P̆anos, *Ktak*, 1693.

Fig. 1 The Cathedral of All Saviour's Monastery

QUARTIERS

A Dervazeh-i Nô au Nord Ouest 500 maisons habitées
B Der Decht 700 maisons Musulmanes et 40 Juives
C Hussein-abad 900 maisons Musulmanes et 30 Juives
D Gaoudi-Maksoud-Beg
E Djoubareh 250 maisons Musulmanes et 50 Juives
F Bid-abad 1350 maisons Musulmanes
G Derkouchk ou Der-i-Mesdjid-i-Hakim 700 maisons Musulmanes
H Nimaver 200 maisons Musulmanes
I Meidan-i-Kohneh 350 maisons Musulmanes
J Meidan-i-mil ou Seid-Ahmedioun 500 maisons Musulmanes
K Mahalleh-i-No ou Bagh-i-Mourad 500 maisons Musulmanes
L Mahalleh-i-Baghat 350 maisons Musulmanes
M Kiarroun 300 maisons habitées, le restant en ruine
N Loumban et celui de Tcharsou-i-chiraziha 600 maisons habitées et 400 ruinées
O Chems-abad
P Abbas-abad il est completement ruiné; il contenait 1200 maisons
Q Tcherkh-ab. 50 maisons habitées et 1200 ruinées
R Pa-Kalaa 200 maisons habitées les autres en ruines
S Talvaskoun ou Telli-Oustoukhan 300 maisons habitées et 1000 ruinées
T Khadjou 250 maisons habitées et 1000 ruinées
U Djamala-Koula 350 maisons habitées

FAUBOURGS

V Djoulfa
X Marnoun
Y Sitchoun
Z Husein-abad

PORTES

1 Tcharbagh
2 Khadjou
3 Dervazeh-Zilleh

4 Kiarroun
5 Séid-Ahmedioun
6 Djoubareh
7 Tokhtchi
8 Derdecht
9 Kiarroun, Nord-Ouest
10 Bid-abad
11 Djouhouzan
12 Sipoulek
13 Marnoun

PONTS

14 Marnoun
15 Allah-Verdi-Khan
16 Aqueduc
17 Hassan-Beg, ou Baba-Rokn-ed-din
18 La vieille Mosquée ou Mosquée de Vendredi
19 Plusieurs Mosquées
20 Citadelle
21 Meidan-i chac ou place Royale
22 Mesdjid-i-chah
23 Mosquée du Cheikh-Loft-oullah
24 Ali-Kapou la grande Porte
25 Nagàreh-khaneh
– ou tribune de l'Orchestre
26 Coupole du Bazar des Tailleurs
27 Bazar des Chaudronniers
28 Bains Publics
29 Petit Palais Tcharbagh
30 Palais Tchehel-Soutoun
– dit des 40 Colonnes
31 Palais Narendjistan
– ou de l'Orangerie
32 Pavillon Hecht Behecht
– ou des Huit-Paradis
33 Grand Bazar et Caravanserail
– du Medreceh-i-chah
34 Medreceh-i-chah-Sultan-Hussein
35 Caravanserail
36 Tcharbagh Grande Avenue
37 Divers Pavillons
38 Aiineh-Khaneh Pavillon des miroirs
39 Palais du Chah
40 Eglises Armeniennes
41 Evèche Armenien
42 Eglise Catholique
43 Palais de l'Ambassade Française en 1840
44 Canaux d'irrigations

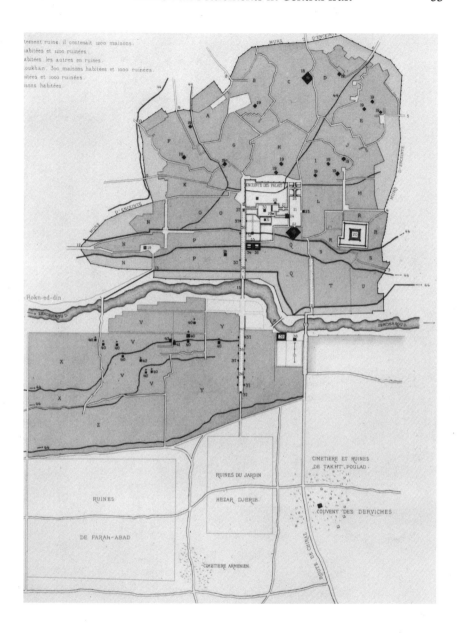

Map 3. General Plan of Isfahan by Pascal Coste (1840-41), Monuments Modernes de la Perse, Paris, 1867. Art and Architecture Collection, Miriam and Ira D. Wallach division of Art, Prints and Photographs, the New York Public Library, Astor, Lenox and Tilden Foundations.

Fig. 2 Surb Beťłehēm (left), Surb Yakob (center) and Surb Astuacacin (right) churches as viewed from All Saviour's Monastery.

CHAPTER FOUR

THE TREATMENT OF ARMENIANS
BY THE SAFAVIDS AND
THE PRIVILEGED STATUS OF NEW JULFA

Iranian society under the Safavids was largely a mosaic of ethnic, linguistic and religious groups. Ethnically speaking the two dominant elements were the Persians and the Turks. In addition, Arabs, Kurds, Afghans, Armenians, Georgians, Jews and some other ethnic groups were numerous enough to present separate entities in the Safavid state. The common use of Persian, Turkish, Arabic, Armenian, Georgian and Hebrew and several dialects derived mainly from Persian and Turkish was a major factor for social disintegration.

The *Ithna 'Ashari*[1] form of Shi'ism was proclaimed the official state religion by Shah Ismail in 1501. The Persians and the majority of Turkic elements were Shi'ite, while the Kurds, the Afghans and part of the Arabs were adherents of Sunni Islam and mostly inhabited on the Eastern and Western borders of Iran. The non-Muslim group of Iranian society included the Jews, the Zoroastrians and the Christians, namely the Armenians, Georgians and Assyrians.

In their ethnic and religious policies, most of the Safavid rulers were concerned with the social stability as well as the political and economic interests of the country. But from the very beginning they had established a theocratic Shi'ite state, by claiming to be the representatives on earth of the 12th *Imam* or Mahdi,[2] a system which could not be favourable for the non-Shi'ite subjects of the state.

[1] "Twelver", a reference for the 12th *Imam* of Shi'ism.
[2] Savory R., pg. 27.

In order to secure social stability, the prime task of the Safavid rulers was to deal with the centuries-old opposition between the Persian and Turkic elements in the country. In V. Minorsky's definition:

> Like oil and water, the Turcomans and the Persians did not mix freely and the dual character of the population profoundly affected both the military and the civil administration of Persia.[3]

The proclamation of Shi'ism as the State religion distinguished Iran from the rest of the Muslim world, specially the Sunni Ottoman Empire, the prime enemy of the Safavid state. The traditional Shi'ite animosity against the Sunni Muslims was encouraged by the Safavids, since the Sunnis, mostly living in areas bordering the Ottoman Empire, were suspected as sympathisers of the Ottomans and were harshly persecuted.[4]

In their treatment of the non-Muslims, including the Christians, Jews and Zoroastrians, the Safavid rulers varied as they were more or less influenced by the fanaticism of the Shi'ite 'Ulama[5] and masses. However, Shah 'Abbas I (1588-1629) and his two immediate successors: Shah Safi (1629-1642) and Shah 'Abbas II (1642-1666) were relatively more tolerant towards certain non-Muslim groups, specially the Armenian community of New Julfa and Catholic missionaries operating in Iran, mainly due to economic and political considerations.

In his assessment of the Safavid religious policies, Vartan Gregorian states:

> The policies of the Safavids towards non-Shi'ite Muslims and non-Muslims fluctuated but basically can be summarized as: violent theoretical opposition towards Sunnis coupled with a narrow intolerance and periodic persecution of Zoroastrians and Jews, and a relatively benevolent attitude towards and a comparatively less harsh treatment of Armenians and Georgians.[6]

---

[3] *Tadhkirat Al-Muluk*, pg. 188. As we have already seen in Ch. II, pg. 23 during the last decades of the sixteenth century, Shah Tahmasp and later Shah 'Abbas I introduced a "third force" into the state by employing a large number of *Ghulams* (slaves) of Georgian, Armenian and Circassian origin and creating a new class of royal slaves to balance the influence of the opposing Turkmen and Persian elements of the military and administrative affairs of the state.

[4] Savory, R., pg. 30.

[5] Theologians.

[6] Gregorian V., *"Minorities of Isfahan: The Armenian Community of Isfahan 1587-1722,"* *"Iranian Studies, vol. VII, #3-4, (Summer-Autumn, 1974),* pg. 654.

Many scholars, including Laurence Lockhart,[7] Roger Savory,[8] John Carswell,[9] George Bournoutian[10] and Vartan Gregorian[11] over emphasize the "religious freedom" and the "special privileges" granted to the Armenians by Shah 'Abbas I and his successors. They all reach that conclusion simply by focusing their attention on the small community of Armenian merchants of New Julfa. Vartan Gregorian in trying to justify that approach, states:

> The Safavid policy and attitudes towards the non-Muslim elements of Persia can be best observed in their capital of Isfahan, where in addition to the Ithna 'Ashari Muslims, we encounter organized communities of non-Muslims, Jews who were located in Jubarah, a special quarter of the city, Zoroastrians who were located on the south side of Zayandah Rud ... and the Armenians who were settled in New Julfa, a suburb of Isfahan.[12]

As noted in the previous chapter, the Armenian community of New Julfa was only a small segment of the total Armenian population of Iran. Therefore, the conditions of other Armenian communities, especially those in rural areas, also should be considered, before reaching a general conclusion on the treatment of Armenians by the Safavid state.

Writing in the mid-seventeenth century, when New Julfa had reached the peak of its prosperity, Aṙakel Dawriẑeći presents the following summary of the treatment of New Julfa Armenians by Shah 'Abbas I:

> Shah 'Abbas was a generous, wise and provident man who found different ways and means to keep the Armenians in Iran, who, otherwise would not remain in the country. First, the Shah expressed his love and respect towards the Armenians, especially towards the people of New Julfa, whose leader was Khwaja Safar ... Very often the Shah used to visit their homes and eat and drink with them without any discern, albeit the Persian custom of discrimination against the Christians. The shah also used to invite them to his own home and banquets, and used to honor them in the presence of high officials at the Royal Court. He also instructed his ministers to follow suite. Second, the taxes paid by the Christians to the Royal Court were lowered to the limit of their liking. Third, during conflicts between

---

[7] *The Fall of the Safavid Dynasty* , pg. 74.
[8] *Iran under the Safavids*, pg. 174.
[9] *New Julfa: The Armenian Churches and Other Buildings,* pp. 6-7.
[10] *"The Armenian Community of Isfahan in the Seventeenth Century," The Armenian Review*, vol, XXIV, #4, (Winter, 1971), pg. 35.
[11] The Armenian community of Isfahan, pg. 654.
[12] Ibid. pg. 656.

Christians and Muslims and in judicial cases of greater or lesser importance, the Shah used to justify the Christians and condemn the Muslims. Fourth, when he brought the Christians to Isfahan and the neighboring villages, he deported Muslims from their own homes and places and distributed the homes and lands to the Christians. Fifth, he voluntarily permitted the construction of churches everywhere, including in Julfa, the villages, and even in the citadel.[13] He even encouraged the Christians to build churches. On the days of major Christian feasts, such as the Easter, the Ascension and others, he used to come to the churches and share the joy of the Christians. Sixth, the Christians enjoyed freedom of worship and observance of their traditions, including ringing church bells and performing the ceremony of the blessing of water in the presence of large crowds and the Shah himself, who rejoiced attending the ceremony.[14] Funeral processions with openly displayed crosses and loudly sung hymns proceeded towards the cemetery, passing through the markets of the city. No Persian would dare to insult or curse the mourners ... The Shah made the Christians so confident that, in the bazaar and in other public places the Christians and the Muslims would fight and curse each other as equals, without any fear.

The Persians were offended and their religious teachers and leaders had complained to the Shah, saying, 'Why do you allow the Christians to be daring? Or why are you not forcing them to turn from their false religion to the true religion of Muhammad?

Feeling their pain, the shah had revealed to them his policy, saying:

Do not be offended or blame me for the little and frivolous love I express for them. After spending fortunes, with great efforts and many plots I was able to transfer them to this country, not for their own sake, but for our own benefit, so that our country may develop and our nation may grow.[15]

In the quoted passage, Shah 'Abbas I is praised for his generosity

---

[13] By 1620, ten Armenian churches were built in New Julfa and two more in the city of Isfahan. *A Chronicle of the Carmelites* , vol. I, pg. 245. Pietro Della Valle, *Les Fameux Voyages de Pietro della Valle,* Paris, 1663, vol. III, pg. 102. See a complete list of the churches in Appendix II.

[14] The water blessing ceremony on the banks of river Zayenderud was held annually on January 6, on the day of Christmas/Epiphany of the Armenian Church. Detailed descriptions of the processions towards the river, the actual performance of the ceremony and the participation of Shah 'Abbas are recorded by various sources, including:

A Chronicle of the Carmelites , vol. I, pg. 245.

Pietro della Valle., vol. III, pp. 100-113.

Hakobyan V., *ŽĒ Dari Hišatakaranner,* vol. I, pp. 257-8.

L'Ambassade de D.G. de Silva y Figueroa en Perse., Paris, 1667, pp. 282-6.

[15] Aṛakʻel Dawrižeċi, pp. 64-66.

towards the Armenians of New Julfa. However, in other chapters of Dawrižeći's work, he is pictured as a cruel ruler and a persecutor of Christians, as will be seen later.

In the seventeenth century, the Armenians were the largest non-Muslim community in Iran. According to Islamic law, they were considered *Zimmi* and in principle their public and personal rights, including their freedom of worship were supposed to be protected by the state, as long as they were loyal to the Muslim state and were paying a special poll tax called *Jizya* or *Kharaj*.[16]

According to Chardin, under Shah 'Abbas I the *Jizya* collected from the Armenians of New Julfa was very low, totalling only 9000 francs (180 *tomans*). Under Shah Safi (1629-1642), these taxes were increased to 13000 francs (260 *tomans*).[17] Adam Olearius, who visited Iran in 1637, estimates 100,000 Armenian men paying two *Reichsthales* per head as *Jizya*.[18] Later, Raphaël du Mans states that the *Jizya* or *Kharaj* imposed on the Jews and Armenians of Iran was one *mithqal*[19] of gold per head of each adult male.[20] According to Jean de Thévenot, in 1664, the Armenians of New Julfa alone were paying 500 *tomans* each year to the king.[21] A royal decree issued by Shah Sulayman in 1683, fixed the annual taxes in the amount of 580 *tomans* paid to the state by the Armenian community of New Julfa.[22]

Indeed the Armenian merchants of New Julfa, a community of not more than two thousand families, were well protected by law and enjoyed special treatment by Shah 'Abbas I and his two immediate successors, who appreciated the economic talents of the Armenians and made every effort to secure their services for the economic development of the Safavid state. During their deportation from Armenia the Armenian merchants were allowed to take with them their movable belongings, including their available savings.[23] Upon their arrival in Isfahan, they were granted lands on the northern edge of the city across the river Zayenderud, where they immediately built beautiful mansions and churches, erecting the cross on the domes of the newly built

---

[16] *Tadhkirat Al-Muluk*, pg. 180.
Fattal A., pp. 72-74.
[17] Chardin, Jean. vol. II, pg. 109.
[18] *Tadhkirat Al-Muluk*, pg. 179. According to Minorsky, 1 *Reichsthaler* was equal up to 4 *Abbasis* or 4/50 *Tomans*.
[19] One *mithqal* is equal to 4.69 grams.
[20] Rafaël du Mans, pg. 46.
[21] *The travels of M. de Thévenot into the Levant*, London, 1687, Book II, pg. 111.
[22] *Tadhkirat Al-Muluk*, pg. 180.
[23] Grigor Daranałći, pg. 39.

churches.[24] Among all the Christians in the Middle East, living under Islamic rules, they had the advantage of being entitled to private lands and properties.[25]

The Armenian merchants of New Julfa enjoyed a high social status. They were classified among the upper class of the Iranian society and the most prominent among them were called *Khwaja*, a title given to men distinguished by their wealth, services, virtues and intellect.[26] In administrative matters, they were granted a semi-autonomous status.

New Julfa was considered the right and property of the Queen Mother,[27] who was entitled to receive all the taxes collected in New Julfa on behalf of the king.[28] The Armenian merchants of New Julfa were placed under her protection. Most of them had established shops and warehouses in a large *caravanserai*,[29] built and owned by the Queen Mother and located at the north end of the *Maydan*,[30] in the *Qaysariy'a* or Royal Bazaar of Isfahan.[31] The close relationship with the Queen Mother provided the Armenian merchants with access to the Royal Court and a privileged status. Some of them became advisors[32] to the Shah in economic affairs and actively participated in trade negotiations between the Safavid Kingdom and European countries.[33]

The Armenians living in the city of Isfahan were placed under the jurisdiction of *Naqqash-Bashi*, the head of King's painters, who, during the reign of Shah 'Abbas II (1642-1666) happened to be an Armenian named Yakobjan.[34] The rest of the Armenian communities living in

[24] Aṛakʻel Dawrižeci, pp. 63-64.

[25] Tavernier J.B., vol. I, pg. 159.

[26] P. Bedik, *Cehil Sutun*, Vienna 1678, pg. 456.

[27] Bruyn, Cornelis De. *Travels* , pg. 324.

Fryer, John. *Travels into Persia*, vol. II, pg. 258.

It is interesting to note that, under Ottoman occupation, Old Julfa was considered the property of the Sultan's mother. See Ališan Ł., *Sisakan*, Venice, 1893, pg. 411.

[28] Chardin, Jean. vol. II, pg. 109.

[29] Places where goods were received, weighed, assessed and stored.

[30] City square.

[31] Bruyn, Cornelis De, pg. 253.

Tavernier , J.B., vol. I, pp. 152-3.

[32] Tēr Yovhaneanć Y., vol. I, pg. 48.

[33] Bayburtyan V.A., "Nor Jułayi Vačarakanutiwnə ew Arewmtaewropakan Kapitali Tntesakan Egspansian Iranum," *Patmabanasirakan Handes,*, Erevan, 1966, # 3, pg. 207.

[34] According to Tavernier, Yakobjan was a genius of mechanical art and the author of many inventions. He had introduced the printing art into Iran. Although it was unusual for a non-Muslim to hold such a high office in a Muslim state, but thanks to his genius he was able to survive in the office for a long time. See *Les Six Voyages en Turquie & en Perse*, Paris, 1930, pg. 225.

Yakobjan is also mentioned in various Armenian sources and documents in AASM. He was the main assistant to Xačatur Kesaraci in printing the *Book of Psalms* in 1638. See the colophon in Oskanyan N., p.22.

different parts of Iran, along with non-Armenian local population, were under the administrative jurisdiction of various ministers, governors or local officials.[35]

Under the Safavids the chief civil administrator of internal community affairs was the *Kalantar* appointed by the King or selected by the people and confirmed by the King. V. Minorsky defines the duties of the *Kalantar* as follows:

> The *Kalantar* appointed the *Katkhudas*, contributed to the repartition of taxes among the guilds, formulated the desiderata of the latter, protected the *ra'iyyat* (peasants, or rather lower classes, etc.)[36]

Jean Baptiste Tavernier describes the office of the *Kalantar* of Julfa as follows:

> The king names whom he pleases among the Armenians to be their chief and to govern them under royal authority. He is called *Kelanter*, and it is he who is their judge in the differences that can occur among them and who taxes them to make them the Sum they need to pay to the King every year.[37]

The *Kalantar* of New Julfa was selected from among the most prominent Armenian merchants. For more than half a century (1605-1660?) all the *Kalantars* were selected from the members of a single family known as Šahixasenḱ or Safrazeanḱ. They were the descendants of the famous *Khwaja* Xačik, the head of the Armenian community in old Julfa, who organized the memorable reception for Shah 'Abbas in 1603.[38]

Following the death of *Khwaja* Haykaz in the early 1660's, the *Kalantars* of New Julfa were selected from different families and very often due to internal conflicts, were subject to replacement.[39] Stepanos Dašteči, a late seventeenth and early eighteenth century Armenian Catholic poet, who was an ardent opponent of the Armenian Orthodox Church, criticises the community leadership of New Julfa for plotting against and dethroning barely installed *Kalantars*.[40]

Referring to the first *Kalantar* of New Julfa, Aṙakel Dawriẓeči states: "*Khwaja* Safar was the leader of the Armenians of New Julfa and all the Armenians living in the Kingdom of Persia."[41]

---

[35] *Tadhkirat Al-Muluk*, pp. 110-158.

[36] Ibid. pg. 148.

[37] Tavernier , vol. I, pg. 159.

[38] Aṙakel Dawriẓeči, pg. 25.

[39] See Appendix IV .

[40] Simonean S., *Norayayt Taḷasač Mə Step'anos Dašteči*, Beirut, 1981, pg. 44.

[41] Aṙakel Dawriẓeči, pg. 186.

Without mentioning his source and probably based on Dawriẑeǒi's statement, Vartan Gregorian concludes:

> The Armenian *Kalantar* of New Julfa had jurisdiction over the Armenians in the vicinity of Isfahan. He selected the headmen of each village and collected taxes on behalf of the Shah.[42]

The prominence and the influence of New Julfa *Kalantar* may not be disputed, but his direct "jurisdiction over the Armenians in the vicinity of Isfahan" is questionable, since the Armenian communities of Peria, Burwari and possibly other districts had their own *Kalantars*,[43] and Yacobjan, the Armenian *Naqqash-Baši* is commonly referred to as the leader of Erewanǒis, a major faction of the Armenian community of Isfahan, who, in 1655 were deported from the city and were settled in New Julfa.[44] Therefore, we may conclude that the administrative jurisdiction of the *Kalantar* of New Julfa was limited to his own town.

Besides the *Kalantar*, the presence of a *Darugha* in the administration of New Julfa is mentioned by several western travelers. In his description of the Armenian celebration of the Feast of Epiphany/ Christmas and the ceremony of water blessing at river Zayenderud in 1619, Garcia de Silva Y Figueroa mentions the presence of the *Darugha*, "Or the civil and criminal judge of the town [la ville]"[45] at the ceremony. Figueroa's statement is vague and his word "la ville" may apply both to the city of Isfahan and the town of New Julfa. According to Jean de Thévenot, who was in Isfahan in 1664, the Armenians of New Julfa

> Address themselves to this *Kelonter* in all their affairs and controversies and it is he that taxes them for raising the five hundred *tomans* which they yearly pay the King. But besides the *Kelonter* they have anothr royal officer who is *Deroga*, for judging their criminal affairs.[46]

Jan Struys, the Dutch traveler who passed through Isfahan in 1671, is obviously confused when stating that the Armenians of New Julfa "have a Gouvernour of their own which they call *Daruga* who must bring up 200 *Tumain* yearly contribution to the King."[47] As we already

---

[42] Gregorian V., pg. 666.

[43] See the names of *Kalantar* Meliǩ of Peria and *Kalantar* Zaǩaria of Burwari in Appendix I, Doc. #17.

[44] Aɾaǩel Dawriẑeǒi, pg. 451.

Hakobyan V., *ŽĒ Dari Hišatakaranner*, vol. III, pg. 595.

[45] Figueroa, Garcia de Silva Y, pp. 285-6 "Le Daroga, ou Juge Civil et Criminel de la Ville."

[46] *The Travels of M. de Thévenot into the Levant*, Book II, pg. 111.

[47] *The Voyages and Travels of Jan Struys*, vol. III, pg. 322.

saw, it was the duty of the *Kalantar* to secure the payment of taxes, which were much higher than the 200 *tomans* estimated by Struys.

John Chardin, who travelled to Isfahan three times between 1666 and 1676 and spent several years in the Safavid capital, provides the following information:

> Their proper magistrates are: A *Daruga*, or particular governor, a *Vizir* or recipient [of taxes] who are always Mohametans; and a *Kalantar*, who is like a provost or Mayor, [selected] from among the leadership of their nation, without whom the governor or the vizir can not take any action.[48]

In a poem, Stepanos Dašteci also indicates that the *Darugha* of New Julfa is Muslim and he blames the Armenian community leadership for having sided with the Muslim *Darugha* against the Armenian *Kalantar*. In his words: "They have pushed the *Kalantar* aside, joining their voices with the Kurd[49] *Darugha*, whom they bring in the hamlet with great fanfare."[50]

The *Tadhkirat Al-Muluk* defines the duties of *Darugha* as follows:

> The Darugha of Isfahan is under (*Juz'*) The Divan-begi. His duty is to guard the town inside and outside, so that no one may commit outrages (*khilaf-i hisab*) and oppression or start brawls (*niza'*); the Darugha prohibits whatever is against the Sharia't, such as courtesans, wine, gambling, etc., in order that no one may acquire such habits. But [if somebody commits these faults], the Darugha punishes him, prevents him from continuing and exacts for the guilty fines proportionate to their offences...

> It was a custom to attach (*tabini*) to the Darugha [representatives of] the Departments of the Qurchis, Ghulams, Aqayan, Musketeers and Artillery men, who served as the Darugha thought best. In the way which he considers appropriate or necessary, he appoints them to each of the wards of Isfahan, under the direction of one of them whom they call *Sar-dasta*. Day and night, they remain in that ward and guard it and watch over it, in order that no one should commit any act of opression, or an outrage or anything contrary to the Shari'at. They

---

[48] Chardin, Jean. vol. II, pg. 110. "...Leurs propres magistrats qui sont un *Daroga*, ou Gouverneur particulier, un *Vizir*, ou receveur, qui sont toujours Mahometans, et un *Calanter*, qui est comme un Prévot ou un Maire, qui est pris du corps de leur Nation, et sans lequel le Gouverneur ni le Vizir ne peuvent agir."

[49] In colloquial Armenian, the words "k̇urd" or "T'urk̇" were used to denote a Muslim.

[50] *Stepanos Dašteci Norahayt Talasac̓ Me Stepanos Dašteci*, Simonean S. (publ.), Beirut, 1981, pg. 44. «Քալանդարն են որել դեզն, բոլոր դարուղի ճեւն այ ձեզն, դարոյ գոռնով բերեն շեզն»:

report to the Darugha whatever happens in the ward, and the Darugha investigates and establishes the facts and calls [the guilty] to account.[51]

In his commentary on the quoted passages of the *Tadhkirat al-Muluk*, V. Minorsky concludes that "the *Darugha* of Isfahan was the appointed prefect of police with some judicial attributions."[52] He also notes that in the manuscript of *Zubdat Al-Tavarikh* by Muhammad Muhsin, the titles *Darugha Va Hakim*, "darugha and governor" are joined together.[53]

Based on these sources, particularly the description of the duties of the *Darugha* and the system of his operation as presented in the *Tadhkirat Al-Muluk*, the existence of a special *Darugha* for New Julfa remains doubtful. The *Darugha* was a judge for criminal affairs (Figueroa and Thévenot) and/or a police prefect with judicial power (*Tadhkirat Al-Muluk*). He was a Muslim and an outsider, compared to the Armenian *Kalantar* of New Julfa who was an insider (Chardin, Dašteći). The *Darugha* of Isfahan was to guard the entire town, mainly through subordinates appointed by him to each of the wards of the city. New Julfa could be considered part of the city of Isfahan, therefore, it is logical to assume that a *Darugha* was not permanently stationed in New Julfa and only serious criminal cases were brought to the attention of the *Darugha* of Isfahan. This assumption may be justified by the following information provided by Cornelis De Bruyn, who visited Isfahan in 1701:

> [The Armenians of New Julfa] have their own Kalentar, as they call him, that is, their burgomaster, or chief magistrate, and others, whom they call Betgoedaes [sic] that is to say, heads, or chief superintendents over their respective districts, who act as judges, and pass final sentence in all common causes; but such cases as one of great importance are reserved for the decision either of his majesty himself, or some of his council of state, and after their final sentence, indeed, they are carried into execution by the before mentioned Kalentar, and heads of the districts.[54]

Under the administrative jurisdiction of each *Kalantar*, a number of *Kadkhudas*[55] were in charge of the internal affairs of a village or a ward. Their main responsibility was to secure the timely payment of taxes expected from their area and solving minor problems between local

---

[51] *Tadhkirat -Al-Muluk*, pg. 82.
[52] Ibid., pg. 149.
[53] Ibid., pg. 149.
[54] Bruyn, Cornelis De. *Travels* pg. 324.
[55] Headman, head of a village, warden.

inhabitants. They were selected by the people and approved by the *Kalantar*.[56] All the Armenian villages located between Isfahan and Hamadan had their own *Kadkhudas*.

New Julfa was constructed on a special plan. The main avenue named after the famous *Khwaja* Nazar, the second *Kalantar* of New Julfa crossed the town from east to west. Ten parallel streets crossing Nazar Avenue from north to south, formed twenty quarters or wards (*Tasnak*)[57] in the town. Each ward was headed by a warden (*Tasnakawag*)[58] or a headman (*Tanuter*), selected from the most prominent merchant family of the ward.[59] Compared to village *Kadkhudas*, the warden or headman of New Julfa were more influential and played a greater role in the internal affairs of their ward. In addition, they played an important role in the administration of the whole town. They had formed a council which was mainly concerned with the internal affairs of the town[60] and the economy, specially in the field of international trade.[61] In the second half of the seventeenth century the *Kalantar* of new Julfa was simply the first among equals and was often ousted or replaced by the collective efforts of the headmen and the primate.[62]

In 1673 Grigor Lusikov, an Armenian merchant from New Julfa successfully concluded a second trade agreement between the Kingdom of Russia and the Armenian merchants of New Julfa. During his negotiations with the Russians, Lusikov presented his credentials in a Persian petition dated 1671 and signed and sealed by the *Kalantar* and the heads of twenty two Armenian trade companies from New Julfa. Most of the names of the trade companies correspond to the names of the *Tasnaks* of New Julfa. In the document the signatories are referred to as "*ɟnker Awagner*" (fellow elders), "*Łekavar anjinḱ*" (leaders), "*Hayeriɕ lavaguynnerə*" (the best of the Armenians), and the heads of "*Kupaneḱn*" (the companies), which confirm the existence of a sort of collective

---

[56] *Tadkhirat Al-Muluk*, pg. 81.
[57] Ten. One of the ten wards or blocks formed on each side of the Nazar Avenue.
[58] Headman or leader of a *Tasnak*.
[59] Tēr Yovhaneanɕ has compiled two separate lists of 18th century *Tasnaks* of New Julfa. See vol. I, pp. 40-42.
[60] Any major conflict, specially financial disputes between Armenian merchants or families would be brought to their attention and would be solved through their arbitration. Even conflicts between new Julfa Armenian merchants operating abroad were often presented to their judgment. Records of many such cases are preserved in the archives of All Saviour's Monastery. In the encyclicals of the kaɬołikoi, they are praised as *irawasēr* (truth loving) and *ardaradat* (one who judges equitably).
[61] Xaɕikyan Š.L., *Nor Ĵuɬayi Hay Vaɕarakanut'yunə*, pp. 27-28.
[62] See the list of New Julfa *Kalantars* in Appendix IV.

leadership in New Julfa.[63]

In the said petition, the name of Astuacatur Miriťenč, the *Kalantar* of New Julfa is placed on the top of the list. The remaining names are listed in the order of prominence of the families, starting with Šahixasenḱ, the descendants of the famous *Khwaja* Safar, Nazar and Sarfraz, the first three *Kalantars* of New Julfa and followed by the families of Šaxaťunenḱ, Šahrimanenḱ, Ťopčenḱ and others. The nineteenth name in the list is Yakobjan *Ustabaši*. Š.L. Xačikyan has particularly focused on that title and has concluded that, next to the *kalantar*, the *Ustabaši* (master of artisans) was the highest ranking official in the internal administration of New Julfa Armenian community.[64] Xačikyan has failed to realize that, Yakobjan was the leader of Erewančis and for many years, the official *Naqqash-Baši* (master of royal painters) of the Safavid Court,[65] therefore, the title of *Ustabaši* was probably granted to him for his personal merit alone, and we have no indication that there was such a permanent position in the administration of the New Julfa Armenian community.

Pre-Safavid Iran mainly served as a country of transit between the Far East and Europe. But due to the efforts of Shah 'Abbas I the Iranian economy developed greatly, the country became the main producer and exporter of raw silk, a very valuable commodity in the seventeenth century, and an important center for international trade.[66] The marshlands of Gilan and Mazandaran on the western and southern shores of Caspian Sea were the main production centers of the Iranian raw silk. Shah 'Abbas spent the winters in the region, personally supervising the production of silk which was a royal monopoly[67] and a very important source of revenue for the King.

For the expansion of local and international trade, Shah 'Abbas reorganized the Iranian Customs Services, established the *Rahdar* system,[68] a special security force for the safety of the trade roads in Iran, and built carvanserais and bridges on many roads used for trade caravans.[69] Between 1602 and 1622 he occupied the island of Bahrain, captured the port of Gambrun (renamed Bandar 'Abbas) and the island

---

[63] Xačikyan Š.L., Ibid., pp. 27-28.

[64] Ibid., pg. 36.

[65] See pg. 60.

[66] Bayani K., *Les Relations de L'Iran avec L'Europe Occidentale à l'Epoque Safavide*, Paris, 1937, pg. 223.

[67] Savory R., pp. 96-100.

[68] Ṗaṗazyan V.H., "*Arewtrakan Čanaparhneri Paštpanutiwnə Sefean Petuťyunum XVII Darum*," *Patma-Banasirakan Handes*, 1986, #4, pg. 160.

[69] Chardin, Jean. vol. III, pg. 55.

of Hurmuz in the Persian Gulf, expelled the Portuguese from the area, and established full control on a very important international trade route.[70] In order to secure the military assistance of the British Navy against the Portuguese, in 1617 Shah 'Abbas I granted special trade privileges to the English East India Company, including the monopoly of exporting the Iranian raw silk to Europe.[71] But since the British preferred to pay in kind rather than in gold for the raw silk, soon they lost their monopoly. In 1618 the raw silk exporting monopoly was auctioned and the Armenian merchants of New Julfa outbid all other contenders and won the exporting monopoly by paying fifty gold *tomans* for thirty-six bales of raw silk.[72]

Shah 'Abbas I kept the trade under royal control.[73] The Armenian merchants were mostly his trade agents.[74] But following his death in 1629, royal control of trade gradually diminished,[75] and the Armenian merchants, being freed from royal patronage, organized and expanded their trade activities independently. Soon they established commercial networks throughout Iran, India, Russia, Italy, Holland, France, England and many other European countries.[76] They dominated the international trade of Iran, thanks to their commercial skills and religious-social adaptability to European life. According to Chardin,

> In Turkey the Christians and Jews carry on the main foreign trade, and in Persia the Christians and Indian Gentiles. As to the Persians, they trade with their own countrymen, one province with another, and most of them trade with the Indians. The Armenians manage alone the whole European trade, the reason whereof is, because the Mohametans cannot strictly observe their religion among the Christians, with relation to the outward purity it requires of them.[77]

In the seventeenth century the British, the Dutch and the French East India companies had established agencies in many places along the trade routes between Europe and India. All of them had concluded trade agreements with the Safavid Kingdom and were in competition against each other to gain greater dominance of the international trade. The Armenian merchants of New Julfa, trading in the same markets

---

[70] Savory R., pp. 115-117.
[71] Ibid. pg. 104.
[72] Bayburtyan V.A., *Nor Juɫayi Vačarakanutiwnə*, pg. 220.
[73] Ferrier R.W., *The Armenians and the East India Company*, pg. 44.
[74] Leo, *Xoĵayakan Kapitalə*, pg. 67.
[75] Ferrier R.W., *The Armenians and the East India Company*, pg. 41.
[76] Ibid, pg. 44.
[77] Chardin, Jean. vol. III, pg. 122.

faced similar competition[78] but were able to survive the challenge of the great European Trade companies. John Fryer, a late seventeenth century English traveler-merchant provides the following reasons for the success of the Armenian merchants of New Julfa.

> The Armenians being skilled in all the intricacies and subtilties of trade at home, and travelling with these into the remotest kingdoms, became by their own industry, and by being factors of their own kindreds honesty, the wealthiest men, being expert at bargains wherever they came, evading thereby brokeredge, and studying all the arts of thrift, will travel for fifty shillings, where we cannot for fifty <u>thousands</u>; setting out with a stock of hard eggs and a *metarrah* of wine, which will last them from Spahan to the port, riding on a mean beast, which they sell or ship off for advance, their only expense being horse meat; travelling with no attendants, their mattress serving at once for horse cloth, and them to lye on; they are a kind of privateers in trade, no purchase, no pay; they enter the theatre of commerce by means of some benefactor, whose money they adventure upon, and on return, a quarter part of the grain is their own; from wuch beginnings do they raise sometimes great fortunes for themselves and masters.[79]

Indeed, the Armenian merchants of New Julfa reached the remotest countries of the world. A seventeenth century Armenian lay educator, Kostand *Varžapet*[80] who established a business school in New Julfa for the education of children and wrote a curriculum entitled *Ašxarhažołov*,[81] (General Collection or Encyclopedia), discusses the basic rules of trade and presents the currencies, weights and measures used in different countries. He also presents a detailed list of countries and cities, where Armenian merchants of New Julfa used to trade. The list includes more than one hundred countries and towns in the Far East, Central Asia, Russia, the Near East, North Africa and Europe. It also includes *"Yengiduni Erkirn"* (the New World), which is obviously a reference to America.[82]

The Merchants of New Julfa were engaged in trading all kinds of commodities. From Iran they exported raw silk, rosewater, woven carpets, dried fruits, golden and silver cloths, dyes, salt, precious stones, cotton and silk fabric, dyed cloths and fine wool. From India and the Far East they exported white and dyed fabric, rice, sugar, coffee, tea, all

---

[78] Ferrier R. W., *The Armenians and the East India Company*, pg. 44.
[79] John Fryer, vol. II, pg. 249.
[80] The father of Kaťołikos Ałeksandr J̌ułayeċi (1706-1715). See Tēr Awetisean S., vol. I, pg. 752. Also another written statement by Kaťołikos Ałeksandr in AASM.
[81] Manuscript #5994 in the *Matenadaran* of Erevan.
[82] Tēr Yovhaneanċ Y., vol. I, pp. 159-160.

kinds of spices, ivory, coconut oil, red and white sandalwood and jewels. From Europe they exported mirrors, glasses, crystal, chandeliers, watches, cotton fabric, woollen cloths and gold and silver coinage.[83]

The journey by land or by sea between the Far East and Europe with many stops in different countries and towns, to sell, buy or exchange goods would last for many years and was a very hard and often dangerous task. Most of the merchants of New Julfa spent their entire lives travelling and trading being away from their homes for many long years.

Grigor Daranałci, the well known Armenian chronicler of the seventeenth century, strongly condemns the merchants of New Julfa who leave their homes as young men and spend the rest of their lives traveling and trading for the sake of profit, ignoring their wives and families who wait for their return, sometimes for as many as thirty years.[84]

In the seventeenth and eighteenth centuries, hundreds of Armenian men from New Julfa were engaged in the international trade. Most of them started as trade agents of some twenty prominent and wealthy Armenian merchant families.[85] They were provided with goods and high interest loans or were simply entitled to a portion of profits made on the Capital provided to them by their masters. Thanks to their talents and many years of very hard work, they were able to advance and accumulate their own wealth. The following case is a typical example of a successful Armenian merchant: In 1719, Step'annos Hayrapetean was provided with 600 tomans by Agha Šafraz, Agha Ēmniaz and Agha Grigor,[86] on the condition that the profit generated from 470 tomans be given to the three Aghas and the profit made from the remaining 130 tomans be kept by Stepannos. For ten years Stepanos traveled and traded between Isfahan, Erzerum, Livorno, Izmir, Baghdad and Surat. In 1729 he settled his accounts, showing a net profit of 36,804 tomans, or an annual growth of more than 50%.[87]

The preferential treatment enjoyed by the Armenian merchants under Shah 'Abbas I and his two immediate successors can be explained by the fact that profits made by them remained in Persia while the European trade companies operating in Iran, namely the British, the

---

[83] Bayani K., pp. 47-49.

[84] Grigor Daranałci, pp. 459-460.

[85] The Xaldarean family alone employed twenty seven merchants. See the list in Tēr Yovhaneanć Y., vol. I, pg. 162.

[86] Members of Ťarxanean or Khwaja Minasean family. See Tēr Yovhaneanć Y., vol. I, pg. 145.

[87] Ibid. vol. I, pg. 161.

Dutch and the French East India Companies transferred the proceeds of their transactions out of the country.[88] Money brought into Iran by the Armenian merchants benefited the royal treasury, the state economy and the Armenian community of New Julfa for the greater part of the seventeenth century. The merchants of New Julfa maintained their homes and trade bases in Isfahan, as long as they were reasonably well treated by the Safavid state.

Contrary to the fair treatment enjoyed by the inhabitants of New Julfa, the Armenian artisans, common laborers and farmers who formed the absolute majority of the Iranian Armenian community and were scattered throughout Iran, faced physical, social, economic and religious hardship. They were uprooted from their ancestral homes, transferred to foreign lands and made a minority in a Muslim country, subject to anti-Christian bias. Being settled out of New Julfa, the center of the Armenian community life in Iran, they were mostly ignored by Armenian and Western contemporary sources. Their situation can be studied based only on fragmentary and sometimes indirect information.

As already described in the previous two chapters, the deportation of the Armenians from their ancestral lands and their transportation to Iran was carried out in the harshest possible way, when tens of thousands of people perished due to the hardships of the journey. The remnants of the deportees were sent to different parts of Iran, mostly to Gilan, Mazandaran and the rural areas between Isfahan, Hamadan and Shiraz. In Gilan and Mazandaran, thirty thousand Armenian families were settled[89] and were mostly employed by the Shah for the production of silk. Their departure from the area was strictly forbidden.[90] Due to the harshness of the climate, disease-stricken environmental conditions and hard labor, thousands of them perished in a very short period of time.[91] Others, heavily burdened by taxes imposed on Christians and persecuted, converted to Islam.[92] Few were able to escape by sea and reach northern territories under Russian rule.[93]

---

[88] *Tadhkirat Al-Muluk*, pg. 20.
[89] Aŕakel Dawrižeći, pg. 148.
Tavernier, J.B. vol. I, pg. 16.
Du Mans, Raphael. pg. 183.
Chardin, Jean. vol. III, pg. 7.
[90] Aŕakel Dawrižeći, pp. 456-7.
[91] Tavernier, J.B. vol. I, pg. 16.
Chardin, Jean. vol. III, pg. 7.
Eskander Beg Monshi, vol. II, pg. 1182.
[92] Papazyan, H., "*Sefyan Irani Asimilyatorakan Kalakakanutyan Harci Šurjə*," pg. 87.
[93] Goroyanč, N.Y., pg. 306.

By 1675, less than two hundred Armenian families were left in the whole area.[94]

While a relatively small group of Armenian artisans in Isfahan were employed by royal workshops and enjoyed certain privileges and comfort, the great majority of working class Armenians, minor artisans and peasants scattered in the city and rural areas between Isfahan, Hamadan and Shiraz were subject to different levels and types of hardship. They did not possess lands and properties. The peasants were settled on lands belonging to the State (*divani* or *khalise*), the royal household (*khassa* or *khassaye sharife*), religious institutions (*vaqf* or *mowqufat*) or individual landowners (*arbabi* or *mulk*),[95] and were employed as agricultural laborers.

Sources of the Safavid period have not recorded details of the system or systems guiding the relations between laborers and landowners and the partition of the harvest. V. Minorsky assumes that the traditional formula of '*avamil-i Panjgana* "must have influenced Persian practice at all times."[96] According to that formula, five factors: land, water, seeds, oxen, and labor are responsible for agricultural produce, therefore, distribution of the harvest between the landowner and the laborer must be carried out in proportion to their responsibility for the said factors. Landowners normally provided land, water and sometimes even seeds and oxen. The peasant received 1/5 of the total agricultural produce for his labor.[97] The formula of '*avamil-i panjgana* was a general principle and not a clear-cut order. Its practical application was modified by circumstances and the portion of harvest reserved for the supplier of each of the listed five factors could be different and largely dependent on regional customs and conditions imposed by the landowners.[98]

According to Jean Chardin, in the mid 17th century, lands around Isfahan were mostly reserved for growing vegetables and were rented

---

[94] See Appendix I, doc. #13.

[95] *The Cambridge History of Iran*, vol. 6, pg. 499-524.

Lambton, A.K.S., pp. 108-112.

AASR Academy, *History of Armenia*, vol. IV, pp. 247-274.

[96] *Tadhkirat Al-Muluk*, pg. 22.

[97] Ibid. pg. 22.

[98] As late as 1950, when 95% of cultivable lands of Iran were still owned by the state, the religious institutions and rich landlords and 85% of the peasants lived and worked on those lands, the formula of '*avamil-i panjgana* was in force. See Eganyan H.M. "*Hoḷayin Rentan Žamanakakič Iranakan Gyuḷum,*" *Arevelagitakan Žoḷovacu*, vol. I, Erevan, 1960, pp. 39-75.

for 30 ecus (0.66 *toman*) per *jarib*.[99] In cases of crop-sharing agreements, the landowner provided all or half the manure and water, the peasant worked the land, sowed the seed, paid the additional expenses of cultivation and harvested the crop. After deducting the seed, the landowner generally was entitled to one third of the harvest.[100] According to E. Kaempfer, in the neighborhood of Isfahan, if the Shah provided the seed and water and the peasant oxen, manure, labor and additional servitude, the peasant received one-third of the harvest. On rice, millet, cotton, beans, fenugreek, melon and pumpkin, the share of the peasant, even if he provided all the costs of cultivation, was two fifths.[101]

In theory, the king was the sole owner of all lands in the kingdom,[102] therefore, villagers cultivating state, religious or private lands, were obliged to pay one-fifth of their total income or harvest to the state as *bahre* or *bahracheh divani* (interest or state share).[103] The collections were carried out very systematically by *tiuldar*-s, who would normally impose on villagers additional charges for their own services.[104] The peasants were not allowed to move out of the village or the district where they were registered to live, work and pay taxes. Any peasant who succeeded in fleeing to another region, if traced within a time limit of twelve years, could be forced to return to his original place of living.[105]

Throughout the Safavid Kingdom, the class of *ra'iyyat* living in rural or urban areas, were subject to various types of unpaid services, duties and taxes, generally known as *hukuki divani* or *takalif-i divani*.[106] The most common mandatory and unpaid services were known by the names *bigar* and *shikar*. *Bigar* denoted *corvée* services of all kinds, including agricultural labor, participation in the construction of roads,

---

[99] A surface measure varying from 400 sq. metres, (478.4 sq. yds) to 1450 sq. metres (1744.2 sq. yds), depending on the regional customs, the location of land, the farming practice, irrigation facilities and the amount of seed sown per parcel of land. See Lambton A.K.S., pg. 407.
[100] *Tadhkirat Al-Muluk*, pg. 22.
Lambton A.K.S., pg. 127.
[101] *Tadhkirat Al-Muluk* pg. 22.
Lambton A.K.S., pg. 127.
[102] Lambton, A.K.S., pg. 105.
[103] Avdalbegyan T̕., "*Bahran U Mulk̠ə XVII-XVIII Durerum*", *Hayagitakan Hetazotut'yunner*, Erevan, 1969, pp. 414-440.
[104] ASSR Academy of Sciences, *History of Armenia,* vol. IV, pg. 270.
[105] P̕ap̕azyan, H.D., "*Rayat'neri Iravakan Azatutyan Harčə,*" *Ejer Hay Žoɫowrdi Patmuťyan ew Banasiruťean,* Erevan, 1971, pp. 127-136.
[106] Ibid. pp. 127-132.

water canals, fortresses, etc. *Shikar* applied mainly to unpaid services for the King. The duties of the *ra'iyyat* also included free labor during natural disasters (*avariz*) and accommodation of travelling officials and their entire retinues whom they were required to provide with mounts (*ulat*), guides (*ulam*) and provisions (*sursat*). They were also burdened with special taxes during the King's travel in the area (*safari*), the Vezir's tax (*rasm al-vizarat*), the tax for the chief religious judge (*rasm al-sudur*), the tax for the *Darugha* (*rasum-i darughegi*) and many other obligations towards the King and State officials.[107]

The Armenian artisans and peasants, unlike their Muslim counterparts, were additionally burdened by the poll tax or *Jizya*, to secure their freedom of worship. For their manual skills, the Armenian artisans were called upon more frequently to perform unpaid services for the King and the state.[108]

During the last two decades of his rule, Shah 'Abbas I used every opportunity to force his Christian subjects convert to Islam, sparing only the merchant community of New Julfa, who were useful for his economic programs. In pursuit of his religious goal, the Shah employed economic, physical and legal means of pressure. According to Eskandar Beg Monshi, the historiographer of Shah 'Abbas and the chief secretary at the Safvid court, the first group of Armenians who fell victim to the Shah's religious appetite were three thousand refugee families or some twenty thousand souls, who, in 1604, were taken captive from Kars region and were transferred to Iraq to embrace Islam in Qizilbash custody.[109]

Religious persecutions against two other groups of Armenians in Isfahan is recorded by contemporary Armenian and western sources. According to Aṙakel Dawrižeċi, in 1608, Shah 'Abbas I provided a three-year loan of 400 *tomans* to two groups of Armenian immigrants newly settled in Isfahan and headed by two *Meliks*: Yovsēṗ Łarabaš and Murat Łərxealan. By 1613, when these immigrants failed to pay their debts, they were persecuted and offered the option of converting to Islam or selling their children to the King. The price for a male child was set at four *tomans* and the price for a female child at three *tomans*.[110]

Wealthy Armenians from New Julfa and Catholic missionaries

---

[107] *The Cambridge History of Iran*, vol. 6, pp. 552-3. For a complete list of taxes and tax-related terminology, see ASSR Academy, *History of Armenia*, vol. IV, pp. 270-273.
[108] *The Cambridge History of Iran*, vol. 6, pp. 552-3.
[109] Eskandar Beg Monshi, vol. II, pg. 857.
[110] Aṙakel Dawrižeċi, pp. 148-162.
Xačatur Ĵulayeċi, pp. 126-127.

stationed in Isfahan, contributed large sums to ransom the miserable immigrants.[111] An individual Armenian named *Usta* Martiros, claims credit for having saved more than three hundred souls.[112] According to the Chronicle of the Carmelites:

> Mgr. de Govea (Bp of Cyrene and visitor of the Armenian Church)[113] contributed 1,000 ducats, the Carmelites 400 gold reals: with the money got together by the principal Armenians several thousand tomans were collected and taken to the wazir. But that part of the money subscribed by the missionaries was sent back with the sacrastic comment that the Shah was astonished that once more Mgr. de Govea should have made so bold as to meddle in the sovereign's dealings with his own vassals ... 300 households apostatized, the apostates being released from their debts.[114]

In 1621, Shah 'Abbas ordered massive religious persecutions against the Armenian peasants in the districts of Peria and Burwari. According to Eskandar Beg Monshi:

> The Shah decreed that those Armenians and other Christians who had been settled in Faridan, on the borders of Baktiari territory and had been given agricultural land there, should be invited to become Muslims. Life in this world is fraught with vicissitudes and the Shah was concerned lest, in a period when the authority of the Central government was weak, these Christians, if they preserved their present status as *zemmis*, might be subjected to attack by the neighboring Lor tribes (who are naturally given to causing injurity and mischief) and their women and children carried off into captivity. In the areas in which these Christians groups resided, it was the Shah's purpose that the places of worship which they had built should become mosques, and the muezzin's call should be heard in them, so that these Christians might assume the guise of Muslims, and their future status accordingly be assured.
>
> The Seyyed Emir Abu'l Ma'ali Natanzi, the royal *majles-nevis*, was entrusted with the task of ensuring their conversion... Some five thousand people embraced Islam, all Bibles and other Christian devotional material were collected, and taken away from the priests.[115]

---

[111] Aṙakʿel Dawrižeči, pg. 154.
[112] Hakobyan V., *ŽĒ Dari Hišatakaranner*, vol. I, pg. 570.
Tēr Yovhaneanč Y., vol. I, pp. 67-68.
[113] Antonio de Gouvea.
[114] *A Chronicle of the Carmelites* , vol. I, pp. 206-207.
[115] Eskandar Beg Monshi, vol. II, pg. 1181-2.

Aṙakʿel Dawrižeći presents a more detailed account of the same events. According to him, Shah 'Abbas came to P̌eria and in the village of Darbin[116] encountered the local Armenian priest, Tēr Awetis and tried to convert him to Islam. Being rebuffed, he struck the priest on the head and ordered his guards to circumcise the injured priest on the spot. Then the Shah ordered the *Vazir* and *Shaykh* Mir Abdullah to force all the Armenians of P̌eria and Burwari convert to Islam and have them circumcised. For two years, soldiers and hundreds of Muslim clerics terrorized the Armenian villagers of P̌eria and Burwari, converted the churches to mosques, confiscated and destroyed the books and the liturgical vessels belonging to the churches and the priests, and forcefully circumcised people. To assure loyalty, each circumcised Armenian priest was given forty sheep. Many petitions were presented to the Shah begging his mercy. In 1924, the Shah finally agreed to stop the religious persecutions, in return of 1000 *tomans* of additional taxes payable each year to the royal treasury by the Armenian villagers.[117] According to the colophon of a manuscript Bible copied in Isfahan in 1628, the persecutions were carried out in forty Armenian villages. The Shah was paid a total of 2000 *tomans* to change his orders. An additional fee of 200 *tomans* was paid to a Persian official, who negotiated with the Shah on behalf of the Armenians.[118]

The last and one of the most cruel acts of Shah 'Abbas I against the Christians of Iran was carried out shortly before his death in 1629. He issued an edict,[119] introducing the old Shi'ite law of Imam Ja'far,[120] according to which any *Zimmi* individual who apostatized and became *jadid al-Islam*[121] was entitled to inherit "possession of the property of all his relatives, up to the seventh generation."[122]

By adopting the law of Imam Ja'far, Shah 'Abbas paved the way for Muslims to encourage opportunist non-Muslim individuals convert to Islam and then support their claims of inheritance rights. Often faked documents or Muslim witnesses were introduced to prove blood relationship between a deceased person and an apostate. Not only were properties confiscated, but the children and the servants of the deceased were also taken into custody by the apostate.[123]

---

116 The present-day village of Namakert in P̌eria.
117 Aṙakʿel Dawrižeći, pp. 163-170.
118 Hakobyan V., *Žē Dari Hišatakaranner*, vol. II, pp. 318-9.
119 The promulgation of the edict is reported in the *Chronicle of the Carmelites*, vol. I, pg. 288. I have not seen the text of the edict.
120 A ninth century Shi'ite theologian, jurist.
121 Newly convert to Islam.
122 *A Chronicle of the Carmelites*, vol. I, pg. 288.
123 Aṙakʿel Dawrižeći, pp. 67-8.

Following the Shah's edict, many Christians, Jews and Zoroastrians were forced to become Muslim in order to protect their properties against the claims of the apostates. According to contemporary western sources, by mid-seventeenth century, more than fifty thousand Christians, mostly Georgians and Armenians were converted to Islam in the vicinity of Isfahan.[124]

The economic success of a group of Armenian merchants from New Julfa, their social status, prominence in community affairs and financial support to their church and culture, have overshadowed the difficult situation in which the majority of the Armenians of Iran lived and in which many of them perished. The preferential treatment of the Armenian merchants by Safavid rulers in the first half of the seventeenth century was totally conditioned by economic considerations. As long as the merchants were treated well and were prosperous, the community of New Julfa would flourish.

---

[124] *A Chronicle of the Carmelites*, vol. I, pg. 288.
Du Mans, Raphael, pp. 46-47.
Tavernier, J.B., vol. I, pg. 16.

Fig. 3 Stones of Ējmiacin at Surb Gēworg Church

Fig. 4 Early 18th century Armenian house in New Julfa.

Fig. 5 Details of ceiling decoration of 18th C. house.

Fig. 6 Details of wall decoration of 18th C. house.

Fig. 7 An Armenian village house in Boloran, P̌eria, 1977.

Fig. 8 Chafting the wheat in Peria, 1977.

Fig. 9 A centuries-old cart in Peria.

Fig. 10 & 11 Tombstones of a musician and a watch maker at New Julfa cemetery, reproduced by late Abraham Gurgenian.

CHAPTER FIVE

THE EMERGENCE OF THE DIOCESE OF NEW JULFA

The birth of the diocese of New Julfa is directly linked to the forced migration of Armenians to Iran and the establishment of the town of New Julfa in 1605. Until then, not a single Armenian church can be traced in central and southern parts of Iran, including Isfahan, where, as we have seen, a small Armenian community was established in the second half of the sixteenth century.[1]

During the mass deportations of 1604, hundreds of Armenian clerics, including Katʻolikos Dawitʻ, bishops, monks and priests were forced to abandon their monasteries and churches in eastern Armenia and move to Iran with the rest of the deported people. They were numerous enough to satisfy the spiritual needs of all Armenian refugees in Iran or to perform adequately all the pastoral services in a large diocese. According to an Armenian scribe named Xačatur Kʻahanay (priest), in 1607, more than two hundred Armenian priests participated in the celebration of Christmas/Epiphany and the ceremony of water blessing at the river Zayenderud, which flows between Isfahan and New Julfa.[2]

According to Islamic law, Armenians as a Christian community, were entitled to freedom of worship in Iran, as long as they were loyal to the State and were paying the special poll tax called *Jizya*. Therefore, in principal, they had to be permitted to build their own churches and

---

[1] See pg. 19.
[2] Hakobyan V., *ŽĒ Dari Hišatakaranner*, vol. I, pg. 259.

establish their religious institutions. Shah 'Abbas I, whose principal goals were the economic development of his country and the creation of an alliance with western powers against the Ottoman Empire, made special efforts to please the Armenian merchants and the Pope of Rome, by encouraging the Armenians of New Julfa with full religious freedom and permitting the establishment of Catholic missionary orders in Iran. The Shah's policy was best demonstrated in the following episode:

In 1614 Shah 'Abbas I issued a decree to make the "Armenian priests, clerics, elders, leaders and people living in the Royal Capital of Isfahan hold their heads high, due to the special attention paid to them by our great Kingdom."[3] He announced his decision to build for the Armenians "a large, magnificent, high and elegantly adorned church in the capital, which will serve for them as a place of worship and where they may pray according to their tradition and rules."[4] The construction of such a cathedral would also have pleased Rome and the Western Christian states, with whom there existed "friendly relationships" and the Shah was prepared to "send a messenger to the Holy Pope of Rome and ask him to send a Christian priest as cleric to the Capital of Isfahan to pray in the said church so that people may learn."[5]

In order to make the new Cathedral a sacred place for the Armenians, the Shah ordered the Cathedral of Ējmiacin in Armenia dismantled and its sacred stones transported to Isfahan for the construction of the new Cathedral. 'Ali-vazir of Isfahan, Moheb 'Ali Beg, the tutor of the princes and leaders of the Armenian community of New Julfa were entrusted with the task of receiving the sacred stones of Ējmiacin and supervising the construction of the new cathedral in Baghzereŝk, a garden on the eastern edge of New Julfa.[6] The Shah's orders were carried out promptly. In a first shipment, fifteen large stones, taken mainly from the altar and the four corners of the cathedral of Ējmiacin, together with the sacred relics of St. Gregory the Illuminator, a manuscript Bible in a golden box and a silver cross were transported to Isfahan in 1615.[7]

The Armenian community of New Julfa could not be pleased with the Shah's plan, because it clearly favored the Catholic church and if

---

3 See Appendix I, Doc. #2.
4 Ibid.
5 Ibid.
6 Ibid.
7 Aṙaḱel Dawriẑeći, pp. 211-212.
In a manuscript colophon dated 1615, Mesrop Xizanći, the most famous manuscript illuminator of New Julfa, puts the number of stones brought from Ējmiacin at 12. (See Hakobyan V., ẐĒ Dari Hiŝatakaranner, vol. I, pg. 570.

fully implemented, it would have caused total destruction of the Cathedral of Ējmiacin. Due to the efforts of *Khwaja* Nazar, one of the most prominent Armenian merchants of New Julfa and a close person to the Safavid court, the project was abandoned by the Shah and the Cathedral of Ējmiacin was saved from total destruction.[8] The sacred stones already brought from Ējmiacin, were later placed at the St. Geworg church[9] of New Julfa, where they still serve as a site of worship. The relics of St. Gregory the Illuminator were returned to Ējmiacin in 1638 by Kakolikos Pilippos.[10]

There exists no evidence for the participation of Shah 'Abbas I in the construction of any other Armenian Church in Isfahan. But probably his initiatives for the cathedral project, his close relationship with the Armenian merchants and the architectural style of the Armenian churches of New Julfa, especially the onion-shaped domes, which were very similar to the domes of Persian mosques, gave birth to an oral tradition among the Persians, attributing the construction of many Armenian churches to Shah 'Abbas. Indeed, "the construction of the great double domes, with an inner and an outer shell to achieve the onion-shape profile" suggests cooperation between Armenian and Persian craftsmen,[11] but they were not necessarily employed by the Shah.

Without mentioning his source, but probably based on the oral traditions, Robert Savory simply states: "... the Shah even donated funds for the decoration of St. Joseph's Cathedral, which was constructed in 1605."[12] According to the inscriptions on the facade and the internal walls of St. Joseph Cathedral (All Saviour's Monastery), and many other contemporary Armenian sources, the cathedral was constructed between 1655 and 1664 through the efforts of Bishop Dawit, and the generous donations of the Armenian community. The interior decoration of the cathedral was sponsored by *Khwaja* Awetik.[13] Therefore, Shah 'Abbas could not have donated funds for the decoration of a church built more than thirty years after his death.

According to the *Chronicle of the Carmelites* and the Italian traveler Pietro Della Valle, who visited Isfahan between 1617 and 1619, twelve years after their deportation to Iran, the Armenians had already built ten

---

[8] Aŕaḱel Dawriẑeḓi, pg. 210.

[9] Commonly known also as Xojenḓ church, for being built by *Khwaja* Nazar.

[10] Aŕaḱeli Dawriẑeḓi, pg. 34.

[11] Carswell, J. *"New Julfa and the Safavid Image of the Armenians," The Armenian Image in History and Literature*, Malibu, 1981, pg. 90.

[12] Savory, R., pg. 174.

[13] Tēr Yovhaneanḓ Y., vol. II, pp. 1-5.

churches in New Julfa and two more in the city of Isfahan.[14] The information provided by the Carmelite missionaries and Della Valle is confirmed by a new and more complete list of churches of New Julfa, which I was able to compile during my research.[15] Several clerics were affiliated with each church. A manuscript colophon dated 1610, lists the names of eight parish priests and a total of twenty seven clergymen as "members of the religious order" of St. Geworg church,[16] which was built by *Khwaja* Nazar.[17] Another manuscript colophon dated 1634, lists the names of twelve priests, serving Surb Amenap̕rkič̆ (All Saviour's), one of the two Armenian churches of T̕orskan, a quarter in the city of Isfahan.[18]

According to the thesis of Yaruṫiwn Tēr Yovhaneanč̆, in 1604, at the time of the forced migration of the Armenians, the Archbishop of Old Julfa was Mesrop, who moved, together with his people, to New Julfa and continued to serve in the same capacity at least until 1613.[19] But contemporary Armenian and western sources do not support the assertion of Tēr Yovhaneanč̆. The earliest reference to Mesrop, the Archbishop of New Julfa, is found in the colophon of a manuscript Bible copied in Isfahan in 1608,[20] while, few years earlier, at least until 1602, the Archbishop of Old Julfa was Yovsēp̕.[21] Furthermore, according to a vague statement made by Father Diego de Santa Ana, an Augustinian missionary stationed in Isfahan, in 1607, the See of New Julfa was divided between two bishops.[22] In addition to the unnamed two bishops of New Julfa, Father Diego also records the presence of Kaṫoḷilos Dawiṫ and at least six other Armenian bishops in Isfahan.[23] Therefore, it is logical to conclude that Archbishop Mesrop assumed full control of the

---

[14] *A Chronicle of the Carmelites*, vol. I, pg. 245.
Della Valle, Pietro. *Les Fameux Voyages*, vol. III, pg. 102.
[15] See Appendix II.
[16] Hakobyan V., *Ž̌Ē Dari Hišatakaranner*, Vol. I, pp. 360-361.
[17] The exact construction date of the church is not known. Based on an inscription on the altar of the church, but not necessarily related to the construction of the church, Tēr Yovhaneanč̆ has concluded that the church was built in 1611. (vol. II, pg. 180.) The altar of the church was reconstructed and some of the stones brought from Ēĵmiacin in 1614, were used in the reconstruction, therefore, a vague inscription on a pillar of a reconstructed altar can not serve as conclusive evidence for the construction date of the church, specially, when the existence of the church is acknowledged in the above quoted manuscript colophon, dated 1610.
[18] Hakobyan V., *Ž̌Ē Dari Hišatakaranner*, Vol. II, pg. 562.
[19] Tēr Yovhaneanč̆, vol. II, pg. 21.
[20] Hakobyan V., *Ž̌Ē Dari Hišatakaranner*, Vol. I, pg. 328.
[21] Ibid., vol. II, pg. 76.
[22] Gulbenkian R.B., *Hay-Portugalakan Haraberutyunner*, Erevan, 1986, pg. 181.
[23] Ibid., pg. 180.

diocese of New Julfa only after 1607 and that his tenure lasted much longer than Tēr Yovhaneanč' thought, because as late as 1622, he was still the Archbishop of New Julfa,[24] and according to his epitaph in the cemetary of New Julfa, he died in 1626.[25]

In contemporary Armenian manuscript colophons, Archbishop Mesrop is often mentioned simply as "*aṁjnord* (primate) of our village of New Julfa."[26] Only once, in a colophon dated 1610, he is mentioned as "patriarch, chief supervising bishop of this province, in the city of Šoš, which is Isfahan, the capital of Persia."[27] Therefore, it is obvious that the jurisdiction of the primate of New Julfa, during the tenure of Mesrob, was limited to the newly established small town of New Julfa and some parts of the city of Isfahan, where people from the diocese of Old Julfa were settled. Archbishop Mesrop, the spiritual head of the people of Julfa was simply maintaining the traditional rights and jurisdiction of the primate of Old Julfa over a new and much limited geographical area.

It should be noted that the remaining and geographically much larger Armenian communities of Iran were not part of the diocese of New Julfa, at least for the first two or three decades of the seventeenth century. No information is available on the administrative structure of the churches in those communities. Most probably, in some places, high ranking clerics were in charge of local churches, without any particular diocesan office or administrative title. Furthermore, Kaťolikos Dawiť and his coadjutor Melkiseť, who were also refugees in Iran for the greater part of this period,[28] could have partly filled the administrative vacuum, and being eager to avail themselves of every possible opportunity for their personal benefit, they may have simply declared those areas as *Teruni Temk* (Pontifical domains).[29]

The year 1627 marked a turning point in the history of the Armenian Church. Movsēs Siwneči, known also as Xotananči or Tatewači, supported by the Armenian *khwajas* of New Julfa, was able to obtain a royal decree from Shah 'Abbas, confirming his position as Sacristan of Ējmiacin and granting him full authority in the internal

---

[24] Hakobyan V., *ŽĒ Dari Hišatakaranner*, Vol. II, pg. 77.

[25] Minasean L.G., *Nor Ĵułayi Gerezmanatunə*, pg. 30.

[26] Hakobyan V., *ŽĒ Dari Hišatakaranner*, Vol. I, pg. 328, 338, 541, 738.

[27] Ibid., vol. I, pg. 360. «Պատրիարք եւ վերադիտող եւ այցելու այսմ Ганаանգի ի Շահ քաղաքի, որ է Ասպահան, որ է մայրաքաղաք Պարսկստանի».

[28] Aṙakel Dawrižeči, pp. 202-219.

[29] See the encyclical of Kaťolikos Yakob Ĵułayeči, in Appendix I, doc. #13.
As will be discussed in the following chapter, during the second half of the seventeenth century, the Kaťolikoi of Ējmiacin desperately tried to reestablish their rights in those areas.

affairs of the Holy See.[30] Movsēs Siwneći was one of the most educated, highly respected and pious Armenian clergymen of his time. In 1603, he joined Kaťołikos Srapion Urhayeći and travelled with him to western Armenia, when Srapion was forced to leave eastern Armenia, fleeing Persian persecutions. After the death of Srapion in 1605, for several years Movsēs Siwneći studied under Grigor Kesaraći, the Arachbishop of Caesarea and a great teacher. As a student and preacher, Movsēs spent more than ten years in Asia Minor, Egypt and Jerusalem, before returning to eastern Armenia, where he established schools in various monasteries and gathered hundreds of students around him.[31]

Movsēs Siwneći was consecrated bishop by Kaťołikos Melkiseť in early 1623 and was asked by the Kaťołikos to join him in blessing the Chrism in Ējmiacin.[32] Armenian *khwajas* from New Julfa who had attended this ceremony and were greatly impressed by Movsēs Siwneći, invited him to Isfahan. Movsēs accepted the invitation, and accompanied by Xačatur Kesaraći, his senior disciple, travelled for the first time to Isfahan and spent a few months in the city and the neighbouring districts, preaching, consoling the people and strengthening their faith.[33] Before returning to Armenia, Movsēs Siwneći helped elevate his disciple Xačatur Kesaraći as bishop of the diocese of New Julfa.[34]

Following the escape of Kaťołikos Sahak Gařneći to Ottoman territories in 1627, Movsēs Siwneći gained unanimous support from Armenian clergy and laity to assume the responsibility of heading the Church.[35] In late 1628, he travelled again to Isfahan and with the moral and financial support of the Armenian community of New Julfa,[36] in August 1629, he was able to obtain a royal decree, recognising him as

---

[30] See the text of the decree in Papazyan, H.D., *Matenadarani Parskeren Hrovartaknerə*, vol. I, book II, pp. 104, 333-334, 500-501. According to a manuscript colophon dated 1631, Movsēs Siwneći met Shah 'Abbas I in Farahabad (Mazandaran). Hakobyan V., *ŽĒ Dari Hišatakaranner*, Vol. II, pg. 426.

[31] In a lengthy manuscript colophon dated 1631, scribe Łukas, a student of Movsēs Siwneći, presents a detailed biography of his teacher and estimates eight hundred monks in eastern Armenia closely associated with him. Hakobyan V., *ŽĒ Dari Hišatakaranner*, Vol. II, pp. 423-432.

[32] According to M. Ormanean's calculations, the blessing of the Chrism was held in April 10, 1623. *Azgapatum*, vol. II, Beirut, 1960, pg. 2365.

[33] Arakel Dawrižeći, pp. 296-7.

[34] Hakobyan V., *ŽĒ Dari Hišatakaranner*, Vol. II, pp. 175. "*Patmutiwn Kenač Oskanay Vardapeti Erewančwoy Tpagroħ Groys ev Ayloč*", Arakel Dawrižeći, *Girk Patmuteanč*, Amsterdam, 1669, pg. 629.

[35] Arakel Dawrižeći, pp. 296-7.

[36] Ibid., pp. 309-11.

the spiritual head of the Armenian people and exempting the Church from all kinds of taxes, including a yearly payment of one hundred *tomans*[37] which was imposed on Kat'olikos Melk'iset' by Shah 'Abbas I in 1617.[38]

The selection of Katolikos Movsēs was a major historical event for the Armenian church. For the first time since 1441, a Katolikos was being elevated with general public consent.[39] As a highly educated person, devoted servant of the church and a spiritual and moral authority, he would be able to revitalise not only the Holy See of Ējmiacin , but also the Armenian Church in general. The diocese of New Julfa, being financially supported by wealthy Armenian merchants and headed by Xačatur Kesaraci, another prominent figure and a close associate of Movsēs Siwneci, would soon emerge as one of the largest and most important spiritual, administrative and cultural entities of the seventeenth century Armenian Church.

The scanty information provided by seventeenth century sources on the life and services of Xačatur Kesaraci, the central figure in the history of the diocese of New Julfa, has not been utilised efficiently in Armenian scholarship. Most scholars have simply repeated Yarutiwn Tēr Yovhaneanc's very brief and imprecise presentation of Kesaraci's biography or have added little in trying to reconstruct and bring his image to light.

Xačatur was born in Caesarea, Asia Minor, in 1590.[40] According to the information provided in several manuscript colophons, he was a student of Movsēst Siwneci,[41] probably from his early youth (1611-1614), when Movsēs was serving in the region of Caesarea.[42] As a native of Caesarea, Xačatur could have also studied under Grigor Kesaraci, the Archbishop of Caesarea and a famous teacher, to whom he later dedicated a poem.[43] In 1616 Xačatur Kesaraci was a priest at St. Makar Armenian Monastery of Cyprus, when Grigor Daranalci, the well known seventeenth century Armenian chronicler visited Cyprus and

---

[37] See the text of the royal decree in P'ap'azyan, H.D., *Matenadarani Parskeren Hrovartaknera*, vol. I, book II, pp. 104-6, 334-6, 502-3.

[38] Ibid., pp. 93-4, 323-4, 485-7.
Also, Aṙak'el Dawrižeci, pp. 218-9.

[39] Ormanean, M., vol. II, pp. 2102-2401.

[40] According to the inscription on his tombstone beneath the altar of the Cathedral of New Julfa, he died in 1646 at the age of 56.

[41] Hakobyan V., *ŽĒ Dari Hišatakaranner*, Vol. II, pp. 175, 854, vol. III, pg. 921.

[42] Ormanean, M., vol. II, pp. 2309-2311.

[43] Tēr Yovhaneanc , vol. II, pg. 22-24.

resided at the monastery for a whole year.[44] During that time Xačatur presumably studied under Daranałči, since a few years later, in 1623, Daranałči recorded a meeting with his "student", Xačatur Kesarači in Constantinople.[45]

Sometime after 1617, Xačatur Kesarači must have moved to eastern Armenia to join Movsēs Siwneči, who, as we have mentioned, had established new schools in various monasteries. He must have remained with Movsēs for a number of years, since he was identified as one of the senior student-assistants and the right hand man of Movsēs.[46] His presence in Constantinople in 1623, as reported by Daranałči, could have been only for a very short period of time, since in the same year, he accompanied Movsēs Siwneči to Isfahan, received the title *Vardapet* and became the bishop of New Julfa.[47]

According to the inscription on his tombstone, Xačatur was *"eresnameay"* (thirty years old) when he became bishop of New Julfa, and died in 1646, at the age of fifty six.[48] Based on that information alone, and accepting the term *"Eresnameay"* as a mathematically calculated exact age, Y. Tēr Yovhaneanč has concluded that Xačatur's tenure in New Julfa started in 1620.[49] Obviously, in this case the term *"eresnameay"* refers to an approximate age, since a number of contemporary sources clearly indicate that Xačatur's selection as bishop of New Julfa was a direct result of Movsēs Siwneči's visit to the area in 1623. [50] More importantly, as indicated earlier, as late as 1622, Mesrop was still mentioned as Archbishop of New Julfa.[51]

Kesarači's tenure in New Julfa is clearly divided into two periods. For the first period, 1623-1629, the sources, mostly manuscript colophons, provide only fragmented information on his activities. They commonly praise him as a saintly figure, a great teacher, a doctor of the Church, (*eramec vardapet*),[52] a great preacher and a very talented writer,

---

[44] Grigor Daranałči, pg. 183.

[45] Ibid., pg. 425.

[46] Hakobyan V., *Žē Dari Hišatakaranner*, Vol. II, pp. 175, 854,; vol. III, pg. 921.

[47] Ibid., vol. II, pg. 175. The seal of Xačatur *Vardapet* is dated ՌՀԲ, which corresponds to 1623. See Minasean L. G. , *Spahani Hayoč Temi Arajnordnera*, pg. 34.

[48] Tēr Yovhaneanč, vol. II, pg. 24.

[49] Hakobyan V., *Žē Dari Hišatakaranner*, Vol. II, pg. 77.

[50] Ibid., vol. II, pg. 175.
Oskan Erewanči, "*Patmutiwn Kenač Oskanay Vardapeti Erewančwoy ...*", p. 629.

[51] Hakobyan V., Ibid., Vol. II, pg. 77.

[52] *Trimegistus*. A title used for exceptionally great thinkers. In the Armenian literature that title is first used for Hermes, a second century Apostolic father. Later, it is commonly used for the fourteenth century great theologian Grigor Tatewači.

scribe, painter and singer.[53] They do not provide specific information on his personal initiatives and achievements. According to Oskan Erewanći, Xačatur Kesarači, following his election, introduced many reforms, established church orders and schools and educated many people in religious literature.[54] Nevertheless, Kesarači during the first period of his rule, can be credited with at least the following achievements :

- In the very first year of his tenure, the nunnery of St. Katarinē (Catherine) was established in New Julfa. According to an official document which was preserved in the convent, the establishment of the nunnery was initiated by Movsēs Siwneči and the construction costs were donated by *Khwaja* Ełnazar.[55] But undoubtedly, the construction of a whole convent, which included a church and living quarters for at least thirty nuns, could not be accomplished during the few months visit of Movsēs. Therefore, Kesarači must have supervised the actual construction and the establishment of the convent.

- According to a manuscript colophon dated 1629, Kesarači "gathered many students, built hermitages and established schools."[56] The colophon does not specify the places and the number of the schools. But it seems reasonable to assume that Kesarači built new facilities at the All Saviour's Monastery to house a monastic school which later became a very important center of higher education. Probably he also established other schools at various local churches.

-Another major achievement during this period was the construction of the church of Holy Bethlehem, the largest, most beautiful and richly decorated church of New Julfa, which was built in 1628 with the donation of a single merchant, *Khwaja* Petros Vēlijanean.[57]

As already indicated, Kaťołikos Movsēs Siwneči was in Isfahan, for the greater part of 1629, where he obtained a royal decree exempting the Church from taxes and confirming his election as head of the Armenian Church. Returning to Ējmiacin during the fall of the same year, Kaťołikos Movsēs must have taken with him Xačatur Kesarači, since few months later Kesarači was sent with his disciple Simeon Jułayeči to Lwow in Poland as Pontifical legate, so as to settle a dispute between Nikol Ťorosovič, the young and controversial bishop of the

---

[53] Ibid., vol. II, pp. 100, 136, 138, 301, 307, 336, 430.
[54] *"Patmuti'wn Kenac'Oskanay Vardapeti Erewanec'woy ..."*, pg. 629.
[55] Tēr Yovhaneanč, vol. II, pg. 236.
[56] Hakobyan V., *ŽĒ Dari Hišatakaranner*, Vol. II, pg. 336.
[57] Tēr Yovhaneanč, vol. II, pp. 173-174.

Armenians of Poland and his community.[58] The mediation efforts of Kesaraći in Lwow unfortunately proved to be fruitless, as Nikol Ťorosovič converted to Catholicism. Xačatur Kesaraći and Simeon Julayeći were forced to return in early 1631 to Ejmiacin,[59] and remained there several months to study with Melkiseť Vžaneći, the best known Armenian teacher of liberal arts, and to remedy the inferiority they had felt during their theological, philosophical and grammatical disputation with Catholic missionaries in Lwow.[60]

In the absence of Xačatur Kesaraći, the Diocese of New Julfa was headed first by Pōłos Tiwrikeći[61] and later by Zakaria *Vardapet*.[62] In late 1631, following a formal request made by a delegation representing the leadership of New Julfa community, Kaťołikos Movsēs reappointed Xačatur Kesaraći to the diocese of New Julfa. Accompanied by his two disciples: Simeon Julayeći and Oskan Erewanći, Xačatur immediately returned to Isfahan,[63] to begin his second period of tenure, which would last until his death in 1646.

Armenian manuscript colophons written after Kesaraći's return to New Julfa, commonly refer to him as archbishop[64] and "primate of the famous capital and all the districts of the province of Isfahan."[65] They indicate a clear promotion in rank and greater administrative authority granted to Kesaraći. In his encyclical dated 1659 and addressed to the Armenian communities of Burwari and Peria, Kaťołikos Yakob Julayeći states:

> After your deportation from the old country to this country—as you
> well know—you were under the direct jurisdiction of Kaťołikoi Dawiť

---

[58] Aťakel Dawrižeći, pp. 371-372. According to the inscription on his tombstone, Kesaraći occupied the diocesan seat of New Julfa at the age thirty and remained there until his death at the age fifty six. Y. Tēr Yovhaneanč has interpreted that information literally and has concluded that in 1630 Kesaraći was in New Julfa and was never sent to "Greece" (Europe) as Pontifical legate. (vol. II, pp. 24-25).

[59] Aťakel Dawrižeći, pp. 377-379.

[60] Ibid., pp. 397-399.

[61] A disciple of both Movsēs Siwneći and Xačatur Kesaraći. See his manuscript colophons in Hakobyan V., *ŽĒ Dari Hišatakaranner*, Vol. II, pp. 95, 138.

[62] Both Pōłos *Vardapet* Tiwrikeći and Zakaria *Vardapet* are not known to Tēr Yovhaneanč or any other scholar occupied with the study of New Julfa. The information is provided in an encyclical issued by Kaťołikos Yakob Julayeći (see Appendix I, doc. #13). From the words of Kaťołikos Yakob, one may get the impression that Pōłos *Vardapet* Tiwrikeći, who succeeded Xačatur Kesaraći in the diocese of New Julfa, was already in charge of the churches around Isfahan. Therefore, his jurisdiction was simply expanded to include New Julfa.

[63] "*Patmuťiwn Kenač Oskanay Vardapeti Erewanečwoy ...*", pg. 633.

[64] Hakobyan V., *ŽĒ Dari Hišatakaranner*, Vol. II, pp. 419, 449, 491, 623.

[65] Ibid., pp. 419, 449, 680, 711.

and Melkiset until the time of Katolikos Movsēs. Due to the shortage of primates, Katolikos Movsēs temporarily placed you under the jurisdiction of Xačatur *Vardapet*, until the time, when by the Divine grace, the number of clerics would increase.[66]

As will be discussed in the following chapter, Katolikos Yakob's statement may be biased, but it clearly indicates that the jurisdiction of the Archbishop of New Julfa was extended over the rest of the Armenian communities of Iran during the rule of Katolikos Movsēs (1629-1632) and Xačatur Kesarači. That could have happened only in 1631.[67] Therefore, in his second term, Xačatur Kesarači was assuming the spiritual leadership of a very large diocese, which had already gained much influence, due to its being headquartered in the Safavid capital and financially supported by wealthy Armenian merchants.

The new and united diocese included all the Armenian communities settled between Isfahan, Hamadan, Qazvin, and Shiraz.[68] The remnants of the Armenian settlements in Gilan-Mazandaran region on the shores of the Caspian Sea were somehow affiliated with the All Saviour's Monastery,[69] but were not necessarily under the direct administrative jurisdiction of the Archbishop of New Julfa, at least in the 1660's.[70] Later, in the seventeenth and early eighteenth centuries, when Armenian merchants from New Julfa settled on the shores of the Persian Gulf, particularly in Basra and Bushehr, and in different towns of India

---

[66] See Appendix I, doc. #11.

[67] During the first period of Xačatur's tenure in New Julfa (1623-1629), Movsēs was not the head of the Church and was not empowered to make jurisdictional changes in the dioceses. At the time of his elevation to the Holy See in 1629, he had delegated Xačatur, his confidant to Poland. Therefore, it seems reasonable to assume that when he reappointed Xačatur in 1631 to the diocese of New Julfa, he also granted him jurisdiction over other communities in Iran.

[68] Encyclicals, letters, birth and death registers, inventories of Churches and other documents related to all these areas and preserved in the archives of All Saviour's Monastery, justify this conclusion. The inclusion of Qazvin in the diocese of New Julfa is confirmed by a manuscript colophon dated 1634. See Hakobyan V., *ŽĒ Dari Hišatakaranner*,vol. II, pg. 533.

[69] The religious order of All Saviour's Monastery included members of Farahabad (Mazandaran) origin.

[70] The communities of Gilan-Mazandaran had their own bishop (Chardin, vol. III, pg. 7, Du Mans, pg. 183), possibly a suffragan bishop appointed either by the Katolikos of Ējmiacin, or the primate of New Julfa. In the eighteenth century, the area is clearly listed as a *teruni tem* (pontifical domain) in the official documents of Ējmiacin. (Simeon Erewanči, *Jambr*, pg. 48). However, by mid-nineteenth century, Gilan-Mazandaran were part of the diocese of New Julfa. (Tēr Yovhaneanč, vol. II, pp. 107-8. Also *Kanonadrutiwn Parska-Hndkastani Temi Hayoc Azgayin Sahmanadrutean*, New Julfa, 1909, pg. 3.

and Java, new Armenian communities were formed under the spiritual jurisdiction of the Archbishop of New Julfa, thus turning the diocese into a geographically very large religious entity.[71]

The new diocese, which until 1631 was simply the religious institution of a small and privileged merchant community, would now serve the spiritual needs of well over one hundred thousand faithful of different social ranks and classes. A network of more than one hundred parish churches was established throughout the diocese under Xačatur Kesarači. By 1634, in New Julfa and Isfahan alone, more than twenty churches were in service.[72] Several parish priests headed by a senior pastor (*awagereč*) and assisted by a number of junior priests (*p̌okr Erēčk̆*) were assigned to each church.[73] The physical and financial management of churches, including maintenance of buildings, general income (*gelur*) and expenditure were largely entrusted to lay trustees (*erespox*), who were selected from the well respected members of the community and appointed to their posts by the primate.[74] High ranking clerics, bishops and monks, were mainly accommodated at the All Saviour's Monastery of New Julfa and occasionally were assigned to pastoral and educational duties in the regions.

Financially, the Church was supported by the following three main sources:

a) Individual donations and wills. Money and properties were mostly donated or bequeathed by wealthy individuals or families to All Saviour's monastery. Copies of hundreds of wills or receipts for donations are preserved in the archives of the monastery. Most of the donations involved a house, a parcel of land, a certain amount of cash or liturgical vestments and vessels.

b) Land incomes. Under the Islamic *Vaqf* law, the churches were entitled to own lands, which they could cultivate through laborers or by entering into crop sharing agreements with peasants. In the archives of All Saviour's monastery, a great number of land titles are preserved.

---

[71] Tēr Yovhaneanč, vol. II, pp. 96-114.

[72] See the list of churches in Appendix II.

[73] Hakobyan V., *ŽĒ Dari Hišatakaranner*, Vol. I, pp. 360-361, vol. II, pp. 106, 562. Also, the encyclical of Katolikos Aleksandr, dated June 12, 1709. AASM, cab. 5, dr. 3, file # 27/d.

[74] The *erespoxk̆s* are often mentioned in the encyclicals of the Katolikoi and the pastoral letters of New Julfa primates. They are always praised as *Hawatarim* (faithful) and *Barepašton* (pious) individuals. An undated letter by Bishop Dawit and Stepanos *Vardapet*, addressed to the church of Hamadan, lists the names of thirteen *eresp'oxs* serving a single church with a senior pastor (*awagereč*) and two other priests. (AASM, cab. 5, dr. 6, #1).

c) Taxes and customary gifts collected from the people. This right was based on the tradition going back to early fourth century, when Christianity was declared the state religion in Armenia, the church inherited the estates of centuries old Armenian pagan temples and emerged as an important secular institution, entitled to secure incomes from lands and taxes collected from the people. The *Book of Canons* of the Armenian Church, which was first compiled by Kat'oĺikos Yovhannēs Ojneĉi early in the eight century, included several canons or articles on taxes (*Turk̬*) and dues (*hask̬*) payable to the Church and clergy. Some of these canons are attributed to Armenian and non-Armenian early Church fathers, while others are adopted in later centuries.[75]

In the seventeenth and eighteenth century encyclicals and pastoral letters, many types of taxes, dues and customary gifts payable to the Kat'oĺikoi, the bishops, the monasteries and local priests and churches are listed. Some of them can be traced in the *Book of Canons*, (IV-VII centuries), while others appear to be adopted in later centuries, including some which possibly originated as local customs and gradually developed into generally accepted practice. By the seventeenth century, when the diocese of New Julfa was created, the people were heavily burdened by financial obligations towards the Church. The most complete and detailed lists of taxes, dues and gifts can be found in the encyclicals of Kat'oĺikoi Yakob Juĺayeĉi[76] (1655-1680), Nahapet Edesaĉi[77] (1691-1705), Yakob Šamaxeĉi (1759-1763) and Simeon Erewanĉi[78] (1763-1780).

The dues and taxes collected on behalf of the Kat'oĺikos or the Holy See were:

Nuirakut'iwn. Dues collected by special legates (*nuirak*), visiting the dioceses once in every three years and distributing the Chrism. Every person and family had to contribute according to their ability.

Žamuĉ and *ganjanak*. Regular plate collections for the Holy See, held at local churches.

K̆aṙasnikn or *K̆aṙasniĉ*. A regular church tax, representing 1/40 of an individual's income.

Tnakan. A tax paid by every household.

Ktak, Xostmunk̬ and *Hogebažin*. Wealthy individuals in general, encouraged by their bishop or pastor, were exptected to bequeath (*ktak*) or pledge (*xostmunk̬*) substantial amounts to the Holy See and/or local

---

[75] Hakobyan V., *Kanonagirk' Hayoĉ*, vol. I-II, Erevan, 1964-1971.
[76] See Appendix I, doc. #11.
[77] See Appendix I, doc. #15.
[78] Leo, *Hay Žoĺovrdi Patmutyun*, vol. III, book 1, pp. 134-136.

monasteries and churches of their choice. These were customary donations, payable only after death in the form of *Hogebažin* (lit. the soul's share) for the salvation of the departed soul.[79]

Yišatakk̃. Special gifts, including crosses, censors, chalices, liturgical vestments, candles, oil, icons, books, money, etc. usually donated in memory of a deceased person. This was a very old custom noted in various ways in the *Book of Canons*.

All the above listed categories of taxes, dues and gifts, except *nuirakut'iwn*, were applicable on the diocesan level as well. In addition, the bishops were entitled to the following incomes:

Ptłi. A portion of each household's agricultural and animal products, given to the bishop, the monastery or the local priest. This was a very old and customary church tax, established as early as sixth century.[80]

Srbadram. A cash payment by city dwellers, who did not have agricultural products.

Kołoput. A special tax paid to the bishops for the cost of their vestments.[81]

Knk̃adram. A fee payable for the anointment, following baptism.

Harsanič. A tax payable at the time of marriage. This tax is also known as *Ałoramasn* (the share of the episcopal seat) or *Vank̃amasn* (the share of the monastery).

Hark Eričaglxoy. A tax paid annually, by parish priests to the bishop. According to an encyclical issued by Step̃anos J̌ułayeči, the Archbishop of New Julfa, the taxes collected from the parish priests were allocated to poor churches, burdened by heavy taxes.[82]

---

[79] After the death of a certain *Khwaja* Mirza, less than three *tomans* were paid to the Holy See for his *Hogebažin*. In a letter dated December 24, 1719, Kat̃ołikos Astuacatur complained to Archbishop Movsēs of New Julfa, saying: "The *Hogebažin* of late *Khwaja* Mirza ought to be more and befitting to his wealth. He had promised three *tomans*, but even that amount is not available." («Հոգաբաժին հոգի խօսք Միրզի հոգեբաժանին, որում իր ոգիարբին լայեր, այլ աւելի պարտ է լինել. Գ թումանն խօստցալ է, qwin tiu n2 գոյ») AASM, cab. 5, dr. 3, file # 27/d. In an encyclical dated June 12, 1709, Kat̃ołikos Ałeksandr J̌ułayeči acknowledged the receipt of 55 *tomans*, bequeathed to the Holy See by Khwaja Grigor, son of Sargis Erewanči, who had died in India. As part of his *hogebažin*, an additional 100 *tomans* were distributed to 23 churches and monasteries in Armenia and New Julfa. AASM, cab. 5, dr. 3, file #27/d.

[80] Hakobyan V., *Kanonagirk̃ Hayoč*, vol. I, pp. 194, 376, 384-5, 397, 401, 478-483; vol. II, pp. 115, 319, 336, 345, 361, 380.

[81] ASSR Academy of Sciences, *History of Armenia*, Vol. IV, pg. 274.

Manandyan H.A., "Nyut̃er Hin Hayastani Tntesakan Kyank̃i Patmut̃yan," *Erker*, vol. IV, Erevan, 1981, pp. 134-170.

[82] Tēr Yovhaneanč̃, vol. I, pg. 31.

The bishops were also entitled to receive special payments or taxes (*tuk'*) from church trustees, beadles, warden, heads of villages (*gzrac*), adulterers and those who suffer sudden death, unable to take the last communion.[83]

Priests were mainly entitled to customary gifts for performing the holy sacraments or other services, including: engagement ceremony, holy matrimony, baptism, funerals, requiem services, blessing of homes, blessing of tombstones, etc.

Most of the taxes, dues and gifts to the Holy See were paid in cash. The bishops and the priests were paid in cash or in kind. The amounts and the quantities of the payments were mostly based on the ability (*ast kareac*) of each individual or family.[84] The priests and the church trustees were responsible for all the collections in the parishes, while it was the duty of the bishop and the pontifical legate to secure the safe transfer of the collected dues to the Holy See.

The Katolikoi of Ejmiacin and the primates of the diocese of New Julfa were officially permitted to collect taxes from their faithful, since both of them were confirmed in their positions by royal decrees and were given robes of honour (*khelat*) by the Shah. Local Persian officials who often interfered in the tax collection rights of the church, were occasionally disciplined by royal decrees.[85] In addition to their spiritual and financial rights, the primates were granted authority in forming community courts at the churches, where all kinds of internal and non-criminal cases could be tried and settled, according to the rites and traditions of the Armenian Church.[86]

Special juries, composed of the clergy and the lay leadership of each community, particularly the *erespoxk*, would deal with all kinds of civil cases or disputes, including moral offences, inheritance disputes, family problems, divorce cases, labour issues, etc., provided that both sides in a given case were members of the community.[87] They were also empowered to notarise power of attorney documents, wills, marriages

---

[83] In his encyclical, Katolikos Nahapet claims most of the above listed taxes, dues and customary gifts, including those, to which only the primates were entitled. See Appendix I, doc. #15.

[84] Leo, *Hay Žolovrdi Patmutyun*, vol. III, book 1, pp. 134-136.

[85] See Appendix I, doc. # 6, 9.

[86] Ibid., doc. 6, 9. In the old system of Armenia, the office of *Mec Dataworutwn* (supreme justice) was the right of the Katolikos. On the diocesan level, the primates were entitled to play the role of regional justices.

[87] Any case between an Armenian and a Muslim would automatically go to the Muslim court. (See the decree of Shah 'Abbas II in Papazyan H.D., *Matenadarani Parskeren Hrovartaknera*, vol. I, Book II, pp. 145-146, 373-374, 558-560.) Criminal cases had to be refered to the *Darugha* of Isfahan, as discussed in the previous chapter.

and all kinds of agreements.[88] The most serious judicial cases, involving priests or lay leaders were brought to the attention of the bishop, the *Kalantar* and the council of wardens (*tanuterḱ*) of New Julfa. Most probably, the juries were guided by the *Book of Canons*,[89] the traditions of the church and the *Datastanagirḱ* (Code) of Mxiṫar Goš, a thirteenth century Armenian teacher, author and jurist.[90]

Under Xačatur Kesarači, All Saviour's Monastery, the administrative headquarters of the diocese of New Julfa, became a center of higher education, literature, scriptoria, printing and painting, as will be illustrated in the chapter on the cultural legacy of New Julfa. Meanwhile, the Diocese of New Julfa emerged as one of the most powerful and influential sees of the Armenian Church. This favourable situation was checked for a time by the untimely death of Xačatur Kesarači at the age of fifty six in 1646. His death seems to have created a temporary vacuum of leadership and possibly a serious division and confusion, within the monastic community of All Saviour's Monastery.

Dawiṫ Ĵuɫayeči, one of Kesarači's closest assistants, seems to have been the best qualified candidate among the monks at the All Saviour's Monastery, to succeed Kesarači. According to a manuscript colophon dated 1686 and written by Aɫekšandr Ĵuɫayeči, the future kaṫoɫikos of Ējmiacin, Dawiṫ had reluctantly agreed to Kesarači's wish and had promised to succeed him as primate. However, for five years after Kesarači's death, Dawiṫ declined to assume the leadership of the diocese, because of his humility. Finally, pressured by Kaṫoɫikos Pilippos and the community of New Julfa, he occupied the episcopal seat of New Julfa.[91] Influenced by his great admiration for his teacher however, Aɫekšandr Ĵuɫayeči seems to have presented an apology, that simplified the situation rather than a factual description of the actual events. Other sources seem to indicate that the diocesan office remained in fact vacant for six years (1646-1652), due to internal conflicts at the All Saviour's Monastery and the presence of three contenders for the office.

A manuscript colophon dated 1647 mentions Bishop Yakob

---

[88] Any document had to be notarised by at least two clerics, who would usually put their seals on the upper left side of the document. Hundreds of samples of such documents can be found in the archives of All Saviour's Monastery.

[89] The oldest complete manuscript of *The Book of Canons* of the Armenian Church, dated 1098, has survived in the collection of All Saviour's Monastery of New Julfa (#131). Hakobyan V., *Kanonagirḱ Hayoć*, vol. I, pp. LIX-LXI.

[90] The fact that several manuscripts of the *Datastanagirḱ* were copied in New Julfa in the seventeenth century, indicates the demand and the use of the book by the community of New Julfa. See the list of manuscripts in Mxiṫar Goš, *Girḱ Datastani*, Erevan, 1975, pp. 109-113.

[91] Tēr Awetisean S., *Čučak Jeragrać*, vol. I, pp. 750-751.

Julayeći (the future kaťolikos of Ējmiacin 1655-1680) as primate of New Julfa.[92] Another colophon dated 1648 clearly states that Bishop Yakob succeeded Xačatur Kesarači in the diocesan office.[93] However, a third colophon also dated 1648, mentions Dawiť *Vardapet* as primate of New Julfa.[94] For the following two years, 1649-50, the office of the primate is attributed to either Yakob'[95] or Dawiť.[96] Yet, a colophon dated 1650, mentions the name of Simeon *Vardapet* Julayeći and Dawiť *Vardapet* as co-bishops.[97] Finally, all the manuscript colophons dated 1651, acknowledge only Simeon Julayeći as Archbishop of New Julfa.[98]

Simeon and Dawiť had been the two senior students of Xačatur Kesarači, who in 1641, bestowed upon them the title of *vardapet*.[99] In 1642/3 Simeon had left New Julfa and moved to Ējmiacin, where he served as a teacher.[100] Later, he was appointed bishop of Garni and was serving in that capacity at least until April 28, 1648,[101] two years after Kesarači's death. Meanwhile, Dawiť remained in New Julfa and continually served as a very close assistant to Kesarači.[102] In recognition to his superior education and knowledge, he was honored with *"mec gawazan"* (the great staff) by Kesarači.[103] The third contender, Yakob Julayeći, another senior student of Kesarači and possibly older than Dawiť, is not mentioned by the contemporary sources as having served in any capacity under Kesarači. It is only after 1652 that he emerges as an ambitious man of great administrative abilities, first as vicar and later as Kaťolikos of Ējmiacin. On the basis of the information of the colophons, therefore, it seems reasonable to presume that, Yacob attempted to take over the administrative office of the diocese at the death of Kesarači, but that he faced a strong resistance from the supporters of Dawiť. As a result of this conflict between Yakob and Dawiť, Simeon was then invited, or volunteered, to return to New Julfa

---

[92] Hakobyan V., *ŽĒ Dari Hišatakaranner*, Vol. III, pg. 252.

[93] Ibid., pg. 313.

[94] Ibid., pg. 311.

[95] Ibid., pp. 385-410.

[96] Ibid., pp. 347.

[97] Ibid., pg. 391.

[98] Ibid., pp. 441, 452, 468.

[99] *Haranć Varḳ*, New Julfa, 1641, pg. 704.

[100] Hakobyan V., *ŽĒ Dari Hišatakaranner*, Vol. III, pg. 5.

[101] Ibid., pg. 279.

[102] Tēr Awetisean S., *Čučak Jeragrač*, vol. I, pg. 5.

[103] Ibid., pg. 751. In the tradition of the Armenian Church, the staff (*Gawazan*) with two snake heads symbolised wisdom or higher knowledge. Monks with higher education were given the title of *vardapet* and the staff by their teachers. The highest degree of education was the great staff (*mec Gawazan*).

to help ease the tension. Indeed Simeon's temporary presence[104] in New Julfa seems to have resolved the conflict. By 1651, Yakob had moved to Ējmiacin, and was serving as vicar to the Katolikos.[105] In 1652, when Katolikos Pilippos had travelled to Jerusalem, he invited Dawit to meet him in the Holy City, consecrated him bishop,[106] and officially appointed him primate of New Julfa with a special encyclical issued for the occasion.[107]

The elevation of Dawit to the diocesan seat of New Julfa and his very long tenure gave a new boost to the prosperity of the Armenian Church in Iran. Under the leadership of Dawit (1652-1683) and his three disciple-successors: Stepanos Julayeci (1683-1696), Aleksandr Julayeci (1697-1706) and Movsēs Julayeci (1707-1725), All Saviour's Monastery played a crucial role in the religious, administrative and cultural life of the late seventeenth and early eighteenth century Armenian Church.

In 1647,[108] long before he was officially installed as bishop, Dawit had already assumed full control of the school at All Saviour's Monastery. Thanks to his enormous knowledge, great dedication and exemplary character, in the course of three decades he educated and trained a new generation[109] of monks, more than forty[110] in number, who were distinguished by their learning and the leading role they played in the defence of the Armenian Christian faith against Muslim and Catholic pressures and encroachments. Three students of Dawit: Stepanos Julayeci, Aleksandr Julayeci and Astuacatur Hamatanci later became katolikoi of Ējmiacin.

The first decade of Dawits primacy was marked by large scale construction activities. In 1655, he undertook the huge task of completely rebuilding the All Saviour's Monastery,[111] which until then was a modest compound, built in the early years of the seventeenth

---

[104] After 1652, Simeon Julayeci returned to his diocese in Armenia. A manuscript colophon, dated 1654, locates Simeon Julayeci at All Saviour's Monastery, in the valley of Garni. (See Tēr Awetisean S., Ibid., pp. 766-767). In February 1657, Simeon died in Tokat, lesser Armenia, during his travels in the Ottoman territories as legate of Ējmiacin. Mirzayan H., Simeon Julayeci, pg. 71.

[105] Hakobyan V., ŽĒ Dari Hišatakaranner, Vol. III, pp. 481, 500, 526.

[106] Ibid., pp. 526, 586.

[107] See Appendix I, doc. #10.

[108] In a manuscript colophon dated 1662, Dawit's most senior student, Stepanos Julayeci testifies that he was admitted to the school in 1647. Tēr Awetisean S., pg. 5.

[109] Ibid., pg. 5.

[110] Mirzoyan H., Patmutiwn Parsic, pg. 220.

[111] Inscription on the Western entrance of the Cathedral. Tēr Yovhaneanc, vol. II, pg. 3.

century.[112] On a two acre parcel of land[113] the cathedral of St. Joseph of Arimathea and new living quarters for the growing number of monks were built. High walls were erected around the compound to isolate the monastery from the outside world. The construction, totally financed by the Armenian community of New Julfa, was completed in 1664.[114]

The construction of the Monastery coincided with the deportation of Armenians from the city of Isfahan and their resettlement on the southwestern edge of New Julfa between 1655 and 1659.[115] In order to satisfy the spiritual needs of the new settlers, at least six new churches were built between 1658 and 1666, increasing the number of churches in New Julfa alone to 24.[116] While the reconstruction of All Saviour's Monastery was only half way through, in 1659,[117] Dawit' entrusted his assistant, Stepanos *Vardapet* Julayeci, with the task of building a new monastery around the church of St. Astuacacin (*Theotokos*- the God bearer)[118] of Hazarjarib (P'eria) for the spiritual and educational needs of the Armenians living in the districts of P'eria and Burwari.[119] According to an inscription at the monastery, the construction was completed in 1668.[120]

By 1660, the diocese of New Julfa had reached the highest stage of its religious, economic and cultural prosperity. The favourable treatment of Armenians by Shah Safi and Shah 'Abbas II, the economic prosperity of the Armenian merchants of New Julfa, the revival of Ējmiacin under katolikoi Movsēs and P'ilippos and the great personal merits of the two successive primates: Xacatur Kesaraci and Dawit' Julayeci had created an ideal environment for the growth of the Church in Iran.

This situation would change drastically after 1660, and the diocese of New Julfa would face a new period marked by internal and external conflicts. Between 1660 and 1725, due to political and economic pressures and serious challenges from the katolikoi of Ējmiacin and Catholic missionaries, the internal life of the diocese would be greatly affected and the bishops of New Julfa would be involved in bitter struggles with both, as will be seen in the following two chapters.

---

[112] Tēr Awetisean S., pg. 5.

[113] Tēr Yovhaneanc, vol. II, pg. 6.

[114] Tēr Awetisean S., pg. 5.

[115] Arakel Dawrizeci, pp. 450-457.

[116] See the list of the churches in Appendix II.

[117] Tēr Awetisean S., pg. 522.

[118] The church dedicated to the Holy Virgin Mary is first mentioned in a manuscript colophon dated 1651. *Žē Dari Hisatakaranner*, Vol. III, pp. 468.

[119] Minasean L.G., *Patmuti'wn Periayi Hayeri*, pp. 45-48.

[120] Ibid., pg. 50. The monastery was destroyed few years later, as will be seen in the following chpter.

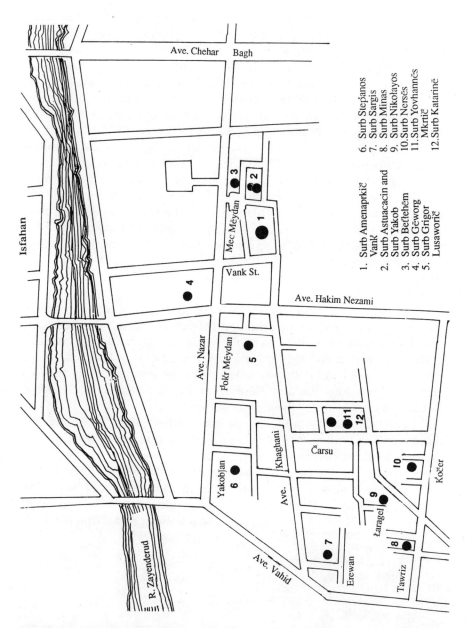

Map 4. Present day New Julfa and surviving Armenian churches, based on a sketch map in *Nor/Djulfa*, Documents of Armenian Architecture, Vol. 21, OEMME publ., Venice, 1992.

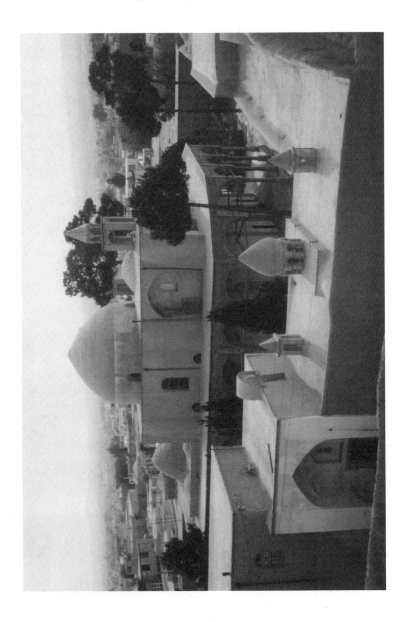

Fig. 12 General view of Surb Astuacacin and Surb Yakob (foreground) churches, New Julfa.

Fig. 13. One of the two entrances of All Saviour's Cathedral.

Fig. 14. Entrance of Surb Katarineanḋ chapel.

CHAPTER SIX

RELATIONS BETWEEN THE KAŤOłIKATE OF ĒJMIACIN AND THE DIOCESE OF NEW JULFA IN THE SECOND HALF OF THE SEVENTEENTH CENTURY

As we have just seen, between 1629 and 1655, that is to say during the tenure of Kaťolikoi Movsēs Siwneċi and P'ilippos Ałbakeċi and under the primacy of Xaċatur Kesaraċi, the diocese of New Julfa had emerged as one of the most important sees of the Armenian Church. All Saviour's monastery, the diocesan headquarters, which was located near the Safavid capital, was privileged to serve as the main bridge of communications, between the Safavid State and the Armenian Church. The financial and moral support of wealthy merchants and the mutual trust and cooperation between the kaťolikoi of ĒJmiacin and Xaċatur Kesaraċi, had secured a unique position for the diocese of New Julfa, so that in the second half of the century, it was considered equal in authority with the Armenian Patriarchate of Constantinople,[1] and was in a position to play an important role in the general affairs of the Armenian Church.

At this point the relations between the Kaťolikate of ĒJmiacin and the diocese of New Julfa entered a very difficult phase and gradually

---

[1] The election of a new Kaťolikos was conditioned by the approval of the Armenians of Constantinople and New Julfa. See "Kondak Ktakaranaċ Tearn Aleksandri Jułayeċwoy Kaťułikosi Amenayn Hayoċ", *Azgaser Araratean*, Calcuta, 1848, #12, pg. 92. Simeon Erewanċi, *Jambr*, pg. 59. Appendix I, doc. #16.

worsened during the pontificate of Kaťolikos Yakob Julayeči (1655-1680), a native of New Julfa. As noted before,[2] Yakob had been one of the main contenders of the see of New Julfa, following the death of Xačatur Kesarači (1646), and an important protogonist in the conflict, which left the see of New Julfa vacant for six years, until the official confirmation of Dawiť Julayeči in 1652. Yakob had left New Julfa in 1650/1, possibly under pressure. Consequently, his relationship with the majority of the leadership of New Julfa, including Dawit' Julayeči, the new primate, could not be good. In 1655, only two weeks after the death of Kaťolikos Pilippos, when, according to Aleksandr Julayeči, the news of the death had not even reached closer cities such as Erzerum and Tabriz, Yakob Julayeči succeeded in having himself elected and anointed kaťolikos of Ějmiacin, with the support of few clerics and laymen.[3] As a result, his election did not provoke much enthusiasm in New Julfa. On the contrary, it must have created opposition, which explains the bitter relations between Yakob Julayeči and the diocese of New Julfa.

The first sign of conflict between the Kaťolikos and the diocese of New Julfa appeared in 1659. Kaťolikos Yakob travelled to Isfahan late in 1658, with the dual purpose of visiting his faithful and obtaining official confirmation for his office from the Safavid court.[4] He spent two years[5] in New Julfa and the neighboring areas. In February 1659, he was able to obtain a royal decree from Shah 'Abbas II.[6] Kaťolikos Yakob must have been disappointed with the reception he found in New Julfa, where Bishop Dawiť, his former rival, was in charge of the church. Probably he did not find the kind of financial support he would expect from his native community. Therefore, in order to weaken the opposition and bring the church of New Julfa under control, he decided to divide the diocese into smaller units, headed by clerics of his choice.

On August 26, 1659, he issued an encyclical, addressed to the people of Burwari and Peria, declaring them a separate diocese, independent from New Julfa. In his encyclical, the kaťolikos argued:

> After your deportation from the old country... you were under the direct jurisdiction of Kaťolikoi Dawiť and Melkiseť until the time of Kaťolikos Movsēs. But due to the shortage of primates, Kaťolikos Movsēs temporarily placed you under the jurisdiction of Xačatur *Vardapet*, until the time, when by Divine grace the number of clerics would increase.

[2] pp 98-100.
[3] "*Kondak Ktakaranač Tearn Aleksandri julayečvoy* , pg. 93.
[4] Aŕakel Dawrižeči, pp. 196.
[5] "*Ktak Yakobay Kaťolikosi Julayečvoy*," *Patma-Banasirakan Handes*, 1966 #4, pg. 182.
[6] See the text of the decree, in Appendix I, doc. #5.

Now ... monasteries have been established everywhere and primates have been appointed. ... also a monastery is established among you.

From now on, non-local primates and monks who come from Julfa or other areas, will not be permitted to live among you, as was the custom before. Whomever we have or will appoint primate or monk in the new monastery, you should accept him in obedience. You should give him all your spiritual taxes most willingly.[7]

This encyclical was issued at a time, when Steṗanos Jułayeċi, the vicar of Dawiť was stationed in Ṗeria, where he was occupied with the construction of the monastery of Hazarǰarib.[8] The Kaťołikos could have tried to secure the cooperation of Steṗanos. Probably that is why, in his encyclical he avoided naming a primate for the new diocese.

With a second encyclical issued in the same year, Kaťołikos Yakob likewise declared the quarters of Erewan, Gask, Tawriz, Dašt and Gawrapat of New Julfa and the districts of Linǰan, Alinǰan, Geandiman and J̌łaxor as a separate diocese.[9] Thus the diocese of New Julfa was reduced to its original jurisdiction, covering only the two thousand families of the old quarters of the town.

The reaction of the New Julfa Armenians to this division must have been strong enough to force the kaťołikos reverse his decision one year later. In a new encyclical dated September 4, 1660, and addressed to the people of Erewan, Gask, Tawriz, Dašt, Gawrapat, Linǰan, Alinǰan, Geandiman and J̌łaxor, he wrote:

Our intention was the common benefit in spiritual salvation, the dissemination of monasteries and monks in certain places, so that instruction and spiritual consolation would always be available to people living far away. That is why we separated you from the monastery of Julfa.

But now we see that the separation was not as beneficial as we thought it would be. Moreover, divisions and enmity crept into the atmosphere of love and unity. Therefore, we reinstate you in the diocese of the All Saviour's monastery.[10]

---

[7] See the complete text of the encyclical in Appendix I, doc. #11.

[8] Minasean L.G., *Patmu ŭwn Ṗeriayi Hayeri*, pp. 45-48.

[9] I have not seen the text of this second encyclical, which is utilized by Y. Tēr Yovhaneanċ, (vol. II, pp. 96-7). According to Tēr Yovhaneanċ, Kaťołikos Yakob appointed a certain Yovhan *Vardapet*, as primate of the communities listed in the encyclical. Obviously Tēr Yovhaneanċ has confused the chronology. Yovhan *Vardapet*, known also as *Tntesi tłay* (son of custodian) will be a player in the conflict between Ējmiacin and New Julfa only after 1675, as will be seen later. Furthermore, two manuscript colophons written in Marnan and Govdēh Zayenderud (in the vicinity of Isfahan) in 1659 and 1660, mention the name of a certain Bishop Sahak as their primate. See Hakobyan V., *ŽĒ Dari Hišatakaranner*, vol. III, pp. 902, 959-960.

[10] See the complete text of the encyclical in Appendix I, doc. #12.

Following his return to Ējmiacin, and less than three years after his conciliatory encyclical of 1660, Katolikos Yakob once again reversed his position and tried to divide and weaken the diocese of New Julfa. With a new encyclical dated April 30, 1663, he declared the districts of Geandiman and Jlaxor a separate diocese under Sahak *Vardapet*.[11] He may also have created similar administrative divisions in other areas of the diocese of the New Julfa as well, though no documentation for this is available. The leaders of New Julfa community reacted once again and obtained a royal decree from Shah Sulayman, according to which, all the Armenians of Isfahan and the neighbouring districts were to remain under the jurisdiction of the All Saviour's monastery and no administrative changes were to be allowed.[12]

Between 1664 and 1671, Katolikos Yakob faced a serious challenge from Eliazar Ayntapci, the patriarchal vicar of Jerusalem, who presented himself as anti-katolikos and sought to be recognized officially by the Ottoman government, as the spiritual head of all the Armenians of the Ottoman Empire.[13] Katolikos Yakob was therefore compelled to travel to Jerusalem and Constantinople and remain in Ottoman territories for seven years[14] in order to neutralize Eliazar Ayntapci and safeguard his own spiritual authority. As a result of this, he had no direct means of pursuing his plans for the division of the diocese of New Julfa during those years.

In 1671, the relations between Katolikos Yakob and the diocese of New Julfa deteriorated further, due to an incident which became the source of great troubles for the diocese. According to Zakaria Aguleci[15] and a manuscript colophon[16] dated 1671, a certain priest from Peria named Yovhan, ignored the authority of Bishop Stepanos Julayeci, the vicar of Peria and his teacher, travelled to Constantinople and was consecrated bishop by Katolikos Yakob who was still in residence in the Ottoman capital. Upon his return to Isfahan, Yovhan was punished by Dawit, the bishop of New Julfa, and Stepanos Julayeci. He escaped, took refuge with the *Shaykh al-Islam*, apostatized and brought charges against

---

[11] AASM (Cab. 5, dr. 3, doc. 8).
[12] Y. Tēr Yovhaneanč, vol. II, pg. 97.
[13] Ormanean M., vol. II, pp. 2550-2577.
[14] Ališan Ł., *Kamenic*, Venice, 1896, pg. 267.
[15] Zakaria Aguleci, pg. 103.
[16] Tēr Awetisean S., vol. I, pp. 301-302.
Xačatur Julayeci and Stepanos Erec, both of them late eighteenth century sources, narrate the same incident quite differently. Obviously their information is not accurate as those of the above cited sources. However, a number of scholars have simply repeated the information provided by Xačatur and Stepanos.

the Armenian Church and clergy. As a result, both Dawit and Stepanos were arrested and imprisoned for more than six months, the newly built monastery of Hazarjarib was destroyed, and church treasures were confiscated. An annual tax of 424 *tomans* was imposed on the churches of New Julfa, Peria and Burwari by Shah Sulayman.[17] Those taxes were to burden the churches for fifty years, until the fall of the Safavid Kingdom.[18]

On his return from Constantinople to Ējmiacin in 1671, Katolikos Yakob was very heavily burdened with debts. He had borrowed large sums from Armenian as well as non-Armenian creditors for his campaigns against Eliazar Ayntapci, in order to pay the customary bribes to Ottoman officials and to secure their cooperation against Eliazar.[19] Therefore, he now faced a new dilemma, and was under heavy pressure from his creditors, who had turned to Safi-quli *Khan*, the Safavid governor of Erevan and secured his assistance to recover their loans,[20] creating a golden opportunity for the *Khan*, who was entitled to keep a portion of the recovered money.

Pressured by Safi-quli *Khan*, Katolikos Yakob fled from Erevan in 1673 and reached Isfahan,[21] where, he sought the financial and moral assistance of the Armenian community of New Julfa. But faced with the traditional opposition, which was revived due to the hardship caused by the conversion of Yovhan to Islam, Katolikos Yakob once again adopted his old policy of "divide and rule."

In a letter written from Tabriz in 1674 or 1675,[22] Yakob instructed a certain Mesrop *Vardapet*, possibly his legate,[23] to arrange for the payment of his debts and for the return of his books, deposited at the house of *Khwaja* Haykaz, as collateral for his loan. In the same letter he also made the following statement about his relations with the Armenian community of New Julfa:

---

[17] Y. Tēr Yovhaneanc, vol. II, pp. 239-242.

[18] Ibid., pg. 251.

[19] Hovhannisyan A., *Drvagner Hay Azatagrakan Mtki Patmutyan*, vol. II, pp. 155-156.

[20] Zakaria Sarkawag, vol. II, pg. 78.

[21] Ibid., pp. 78-79.

[22] AASM, cab.2, file 99. The letter is dated only December 27. It could not have been written before 1672, since Katolikos Yakob makes reference to Setpanos *Vardapet* and the church taxes. On the other hand, Katolikos Yakob was in New Julfa from early 1673 to late 1674. He could have written the letter on his way back to Ējmiacin, possibly, in December 1674.

[23] In a letter dated 1683, Katolikos Eliazar Ayntapci suggests cooperation between Mesrob, the legate of Ējmiacin and Stepanos *Vardapet*, the new bishop of New Julfa. AASM, cab. 5, dr. 3, file 17/d, doc. #10.

> I know what will be the reaction of the people of Julfa, towards the appointment of a new pimate. Close your ears and do not respond to their arguments, ... whatever they say is fine. I am insulted by them and they are insulted by me. Let it be whatever pleases God.

In another encyclical dated February 20, 1676,[24] Kaťoťikos Yakob argued that the diocese of New Julfa originally included only the refugees from Old Julfa, while the Armenians of Isfahan and the neighbouring districts were under the direct jurisdiction of the kaťoťikoi of Ějmiacin. Kaťoťikos Movsēs had expanded the administrative jurisdiction of the diocese of New Julfa over all the Armenians of Isfahan, Linjan, Alinjan, Geandiman, Peria and Burwari. He continued his complaints for the lack of financial support from the community of New Julfa, by saying:

> At that time [under Xačatur Kesaraći] the churches were flourishing, people were united, they were not selfish, and they were all working for the benefit of the church. But since people have become extremely selfish, disputes and quarrels have increased. While one is starving to death, the other is satiated with wealth. Let the care and mercy of the generous God always be upon the people of Julfa and their possessions. With the mercy of God, they can support as many as four monasteries, instead of one.

Lengthy arguments supported by historical facts and principles of Christian morality, were then presented by the kaťoťikos, in justification of his primary intention. Finally, he concluded his encyclical by declaring:

> For this reason, I ordained bishop my beloved son, Yovhan *Vardapet*.[25] I appointed him vicar of Holy Ějmiacin and sent him to you as primate, dean and pastor ... [He] will be your primate for three years. If I am satisfied with his performance, and if he is able to console you with love and God's words, ... I will send another encyclical to reappoint him for another three years. But if he does not act according to these written instructions, I will send you another primate and Yovhan *Vardapet* will return to the Holy See.

The upper portion of the encyclical, which would indicate to whom it was addressed, has not survived. However, judging from its content and taking into consideration future developments, as described in the following few pages, it is easy to conclude that Yovhan *Vardapet*, was

---

[24] See Appendix I, doc. #13.
[25] Also known as *Tntesi Tłay* (Son of custodian). He should not be confused with the other Yovhan, who converted to Islam in 1671.

appointed primate of a large diocese, which included the quarters of Erewan, Gask, Tawriz, Dašt, Gawrapat and the districts of Linĵan, Alinĵan, Geandiman, Ĵŧaxor and possibly Ṗeria and Burwari. Therefore, at least in theory, the jurisdiction of the diocese of New Julfa, once again, was reduced to the old quarters of the town.

The death of Kaŧolikos Yakob Ĵuŧayeči in 1680, and the elevation of Kaŧolikos Eŧiazar Aynŧapči to the pontifical seat of Ējmiacin in 1681, brought about a temporary peace between the kaŧolikate and the diocese of New Julfa, primarily because Kaŧolikos Eŧiazar had been invited to assume the pontificate of Ējmiacin by general consensus[26] and the Armenians of New Julfa were very supportive in this initiative, since Eŧiazar had sought their support, before accepting the office of the kaŧolikate.[27] Yovhan *Vardapet* however, still remained in New Julfa, though isolated in the church of St. Sargis, also known as *Ohanay Vanḱ* (the monastery of Yovhan), in the quarter of Erewan.

In 1683, Archbishop Dawiŧ of New Julfa died and was succeeded by his vicar of many years, Steṗanos Ĵuŧayeči. In the same year Yovhan *Vardapet* supported with a petition signed by his followers, travelled to Ējmiacin and succeeded in obtaining reconfirmation of his episcopal office from Kaŧolikos Eŧiazar.[28] This action generated an internal conflict in New Julfa, which was settled only in 1689, through two encyclicals issued by Kaŧolikos Eŧiazar. In the first encyclical to the Armenians of Julfa, Erewan, Tawriz, Gask, Gawrapat, Šexsapan, Ŧaragel, Ṗeria, Burwari, Geandiman, Linĵan and Alinĵan, dated April 7, 1689, the Kaŧolikos declared:

> We, the humble servant of the Lord, Kaŧolikos Eŧiazar, according to the authority given to us from above and by the high order of the Holy See of Ējmiacin, reestablished your blessed towns and districts in the diocese of All Saviour's monastery of Julfa. This was not an impulsive decision; it was the result of consultations with many theologian *vardapets* and notables. ... I did this, so that the soul of the late Kaŧolikos Yakob might be saved because many people are offended and curse him. Much as in the days of Kaŧolikoi Movsēs and Ṗilibbos of blessed memory and the time of Xačatur and Dawiŧ *vardapets* the people were united under one diocese, love, peace, and success prevailed, benevolence and peace reigned in the world and the kings were favourable towards our suffering nation, we wish to create unity and pray to God to have mercy upon us and grant us the same order and success.[29]

---

[26] Zaḱaria Sarkawag, vol. II. pg. 106.
[27] See Appendix I, doc. # 16.
[28] Y. Tēr Yovhaneanč, vol. II, pg. 98.
[29] See Appendix I, doc.#14.

The second encyclical, dated August 5, 1689, was issued in condemnation of the rebellious behaviour of Yovhan *Vardapet* and his followers, in the strongest possible way. The Kaťolikos warned *Tntesi Tłay* Yovhan *vardapet* to obey Stepanos *vardapet*, the bishop of New Julfa or return to Ējmiacin. Ignoring these orders would bring severe punishments on the rebels.[30]

Unfortunately, the death of Kaťolikos Ełiazar two years later, on August 8, 1691[31] reversed the situation in New Julfa once again. The day following the Kaťolikos' death, one of Ełiazar's pupils, Bishop Nahapet Edesaċi, supported by Bishop Minas Astapatċi and few other monks,[32] declared himself kaťolikos and was immediately consecrated, avoiding the formal process of election. According to Ałekˈsandr Jułayeċi:

> Nahapet was consecrated without the knowledge of the people and the agreement of the church leaders... On the day of Kat'ołikos Ełiazar's burial and during the very Divine liturgy, while the body of the deceased in his casket was still placed on the altar, the new Kaťolikos was first ordained and then the deceased was anointed and buried. This was a kind of ordination, not suitable even to a village priest, let alone a kat'ołikos, who is the head of the nation.[33]

Despite the general opposition to his self promotion, in 1692, Kaťolikos Nahapet succeeded in securing the support of *Khwaja* Awet, the *kalantar* of New Julfa, and in obtaining confirmation of his office from the Safavid court.[34] This provoked a great tension in New Julfa. Removed from office by the community leadership of New Julfa, *Kalantar* Awet converted to Islam and retaliated against Bishop Stepanos Jułayeċi, by accusing him of alleged anti-Muslim writings. The Muslim high court of Isfahan sentenced Stepanos to be burned. But upon the intervention of the Queen mother, the patron of New Julfa, a second trial acquitted Stepanos.[35] However, two hundred *tomans* had to be spent to secure the acquittal.[36]

Taking advantage of the confused situation in New Julfa and in order to weaken his opponents, Kaťolikos Nahapet reclaimed direct jurisdiction over the *teruni*[37] people, or the communities under dispute

---

[30] AASM, cab. 5, dr. 3, file 27/d, doc. #13.
[31] Ormanean M., vol. II, pp. 2659-2660.
[32] See Appendix I, doc. #16.
[33] *Kondak Ktakaranaċ Tearn Ałek'sandri Jułayeċwoy* , pg. 94.
[34] See Appendix I, doc. #16.
[35] *A Chronicle of the Carmelites in Persia*, vol. I, pg. 468.
[36] Stepanos Jułayeċi, *Ktak*, (AASM, Cab. 1, file 27/13).
[37] Pontifical domain.

between the Katołikate of Ējmiacin and the diocese of New Julfa, since the days of Katołikos Yakob. He reappointed *Tntesi Tłay* Yovhan *vardapet* as bishop of Erewan, Gask, Tawriz, Linjan and Alinjan, and considered Ałeksandr Julayeci as a possible candidate, to oversee the remaining *teruni* communities,[38] namely P̀eria, Burwari, Geandiman, and Jłaxor. In an undated encyclical, Katołikos Nahapet presented a specious justification for his action, by claiming to have fulfilled the will of late Katołikos Ełiazar:

> At the time of his death, when he [Ełiazar] entrusted everything into our hands, he also gave the following order, saying: 'I bestowed upon Yovhan *vardapet* the episcopal title for St. Sargis monastery and the people in the domain of our Great See. But later I deprived him of that office. And that greatly bothers my conscience. You should appoint him to his seat and entrust to him the people of the above mentioned patriarchal domain, leaving the rest of the people [in other patriarchal domains] under the care of Ałeksandr *vardapet*.[39]

The coalition of Katołikos Nahapet, *Kalantar* Awet and Yovhan *vardapet*, provoked a very strong reaction from the bishop of New Julfa, the diocesan leadership and the people at large. On May 1, 1693, in a printed open letter from the members of the Religious community of All Saviour's monastery to the members of the Religious community of Ējmiacin, Katołikos Nahapet and his chief supporter Bishop Minas Astapatci were strongly condemned for having illegally seized the Holy See. The Katołikos was also accused of every type of corruption, including bribery, intolerance, ostentatious living, illegal ordinations and arbitrary administrative arrangements for the dioceses. Twelve preconditions were listed for any possible compromise with him, and in conclusion, the letter declared bluntly:

> We demand the listed twelve conditions to be met by the Katołikos, whoever he might be, and we forward the present appeal to you in brotherly love, since we belong to the same body and must console each other. Show [our demands] to him. If he agrees and accepts [our demands], let him seal his written response, have it certified by the blessed bishops and forward it to us, so that we may keep it as an indelible memorial and be willing to obey him as our [spiritual] head

---

[38] Katołikos Nahapet was obviously trying to divide the ranks of the opposition, since Ałeksandr was the closest assistant of Step̀anos, the primate of New Julfa.

[39] Appendix I, doc. #15. L.G. Minasean has classified this encyclical under the year 1695. (See *Diwan S. Amenap̀rkič Vanki*, pg. 58) But I think it was written in 1692 or early 1693. My assumption is based on the developments between 1693 and 1695 and related documents presented below.

and so that he may rule our Church the way the sun [shines above the universe]. But if he does not accept our arguments and considers our letter worthless, then we would like you to return our letter and be assured that we will take all the necessary measures to deal [with him] as harshly as possible.[40]

Simultaneously with the open letter, a second document, entitled "The order of ordination [election] of the Katolikos, written by Movsēs *vardapet* Bǰneći and approved by the Holy *vardapets* and bishops, who have signed this document" was printed in New Julfa.[41] According to this document, in 1665, a meeting had been held with the participation of numerous bishops, *vardapets* and lay nobility from Eastern Armenia and other regions of the Safavid Kingdom, to condemn the practice of katolikoi naming their successors, and the intolerable behaviour of other high ranking clerics who attempted to occupy the patriarchal throne of Ējmiacin with the support of Muslim officials, through bribes, or by other illegal means. According to this document, only two procedures for the selection of a legitimate new katolikos were acceptable. There were either a formal election or the general consensus of all the sees of the Armenian Church. Anyone who occupied the Holy See without being officially elected or agreed upon by the Church leadership, would be rejected and dethroned. The document had been signed by nineteen high ranking clerics and eight lay noblemen.

This document had originally been aimed against Katolikos Yakob Julayeći, who had succeeded Katolikos Pilippos, without being officially elected and had irritated many bishops by his authoritarian rule, and arbitrary administrative interventions in their sees. But now, twenty eight years after its composition, it was printed in New Julfa, to discredit Katolikos Nahapet and demonstrate that his spiritual authority was not legitimate.

Popular opposition to Katolikos Nahapet and his ill-intentioned policy towards the diocese of New Julfa, also expressed itself through public protests in the communities separated from the diocese by the katolikos. In August 1693, a public petition, expressing full loyalty to the bishop of New Julfa, and rejecting any other spiritual authority, circulated in the districts of Peria and Burwari. The signatures and seals of the *kalantars* Melik (Peria), and Zakarē (Burwari), the parish priests and headmen of at least forty Armenian villages appear on the

---

[40] See the complete text of the letter in Appendix I, doc. #16.

[41] *Yałags Kargi Katutikos Jernadrutean Greal I Movsisē Vardapetē Bǰnečwoy Srbazan Vardapetać ew Episkoposać Veragreloć I Kartisis*, New Julfa, 1693. This document was printed together with the open letter, on May 1, 1693.

surviving fragment of the petition.[42] A similar petition, also dated August 1693, and signed by more than thirty priests and village chiefs from the district of Geandiman, can also be found in the archives of All Saviour's Monastery.[43]

Bowing to the pressure of the prevailing opposition, Kaťolikos Nahapet was forced to restore the jurisdiction of the bishop of New Julfa over all the communities in dispute. In a letter dated January 3, 1695, and addressed to Yovhan *vardapet*, the Kaťolikos expressed his concerns for the unity of the people and the prosperity of the Holy See. Admitting that the dispute had lasted for a long period of time and the only solution was the unification of all the communities under the diocese of New Julfa, he relieved Yovhan *vardapet* from his pastoral duties and ordered him to obey Stepanos, Bishop of new Julfa. He also gave the following advice to Yovhan:

> Stay with Stepanos *vardapet* in peace and humbly accept all his words...
> live with each other in love and unity like father and son. If he
> [Stepanos] decides to let you live as a beloved son in his monastery or
> in your current residence, and if you agree to that, you must live
> together in love, peace and unity. Do not follow the ill-willing people
> and keep them away from you.[44]

In a second letter, dated March 20, 1695, Kaťolikos Nahapet strongly reprimanded *Tntesi Tłay* Yovhan *vardapet* for his rebellious behaviour. Once again, he ordered him to be reconciled with Stepanos and all the members of the Religious community of All Saviour's monastery, to accept the authority of Stepanos, transmit to him all the encyclicals and the chrism in his possession, and to live peacefully in the All Saviour's Monastery. The kaťolikos also proposed that Yovhan return to Ejmiacin and be assigned to another diocese. The letter concluded with the following warning:

> If you disregard our order to live in the monastery with Stepanos
> *Vardapet* or return here, you will suffer greatly and be severely
> punished by us. You are not permitted to live in that blessed district. I
> will destroy your house on your head and you will not be called
> *vardapet* anymore. Wake up from your stupidity, use your brain and

---

[42] See Appendix I, doc. #17.

[43] AASM, file 30B, doc. #3.

[44] AASM, cab. 5, dr. 3, #27d, doc. #15. «Խաղաղութեամբ կացցես ընդ Ստեփանոս վարդապետին եւ հեզութեամբ ունկնդիր լինիցիս յամենայն բանից նորին ... այլ կացջիք ընդ միմեանս սիրով եւ միաբանութեամբ որպէս հայր եւ որդի. եւ եթէ մեծ առ իւր ի միջի վանաց իւրոց որդիական սիրով պահել կամիցի եւ եթէ ի Գահանագոյ օթեւանի քում հաճցից, եւ դու յօժարիցիս ի կեալն. բայց սիրով եւ խաղաղութեամբ եւ միաբանութեամբ. եւ մի լինիցիք ունկնդիր չարաբարոյից դմանց, այլ ի բաց հերքիցէք զայնպիսիսն»:

choose the way beneficial for you. A late repentance will not help. Your blood be upon your own head. With this, I am warning you in advance. You are responsible for the future.[45]

Yovhan *Vardapet* was apparently forced to leave New Julfa and return to Armenia.[46] But Kaťolikos Nahapeťs conciliatory gesture did not satisfy the leaders of the See of New Julfa, or help ease their anger. For several years, they had lived in constant turmoil as a result of their opposition to the kaťolikos, the apostasy of their former *kalantar* Awet, the provocations of Yovhan *Vardapet*, the aggressive behaviour of Catholic missionaries and the Muslim fanaticism dominating the Safavid court. For them, Kaťolikos Nahapet's gesture was too little, too late. He had not yet satisfied the twelve conditions required in their open letter of 1693. His withdrawal of Yovhan *Vardapet* was seen only as a strategy to neutralise his opponents in New Julfa, because of the growing opposition he faced at the Holy See and in the dioceses of Naxčawan and Goľťn in Armenia.

Indeed, according to Zaḱaria *Sarkawag*, Kaťolikos Nahapet had established an authoritarian rule at the Holy See and was very brutal towards the clergy. Priests were subjected to severe physical punishments for minor mistakes.[47] As a western Armenian, he had adopted a mode of life and introduced new rules, not compatible with the taste and traditions of Eastern Armenian clergy.[48] Therefore, a great number of monks and bishops from the Holy See, the dioceses of Naxčawan and Goľťn and other monasteries of Eastern Armenia united against the Kaťolikos. They wrote a joint letter to Steṗanos Ĵulayeči, to express their despair and invited Steṗanos to the Holy See, to replace Kaťolikos Nahapet. Matťēos Karbeči was delegated to go to Isfahan and convince Steṗanos Ĵulayeči to accept their proposal.[49]

Encouraged by the anti-Nahapet movement in Armenia, the leaders of the New Julfa community intensified their protests against the kaťolikos. They sought the intervention of the Safavid court for his

45 AASM, cab. 5, dr. 3, #27d, doc. #16. «Եւ եթէ անուես արարիր զհրամանս մեր եւ ոչ ñնազանդեցար, ոչ վանքն զ.նացիր առ Ստեփան վարդապետն եւ կամ ոչ եկիր ի տեղոյ, մեծ ñեղութիւն եւ պատիժ անñնարհին կրեցելոյ ես ի մէջ բարկութեամբ մեծաւ, եւ ոչ miñիս իշխանութիւն եւ ñրաման յորñնեալ զաատող կեալոյ եւ զբնակարանդ բո զլխոյդ կու բակեմ եւ ոչ կոչ ի վերայ բո անմն վարդապետունական: Զթափեաց յանñխլութենէ, եւ միտրդ ժողովէ եւ զոգտունն բո ընտրեալ որ վերջին աաշաñին նշñ օգնէ: Արñին բո ի գլուխ բո եղիցի, աñա յառաջագոյն գրեցի, զապագայն դու գիտես»:
46 In a letter dated November 25, 1698, Yovhan *Vardapet* stated: "...When I received a written order to return that region to their control, I did not resist. I went to live in my place..." AASM, cab. 2, file #99.
47 Zaḱaria Sarkawag, vol. II, pg. 136.
48 Ibid. pg. 107.
49 Ibid. pg. 136.

ouster. In May 1696, Shah Sultan Husayn issued a decree,[50] ordering Muhammad-quli *Khan*, the *Beglarbegi* of Erevan, to remove immediately "the former Kaťolikos" from Ějmiacin and send him to the monastery (of Taťew) in Qapan (Łaṗan). Based on "a petition signed by the *Kalantar*, the clergy, the *Kadkhudas* and the people of New Julfa and other areas in general," the Shah issued a new decree in June 1696,[51] in which he proclaimed the ouster of Kaťolikos Nahapet and his replacement by Bishop Steṗanos of Julfa. He also ordered the *Beglarbegi* of Erevan, to support the new Kaťolikos.

On September 8, 1696, Kaťolikos Nahapet was expelled from the Holy See. Ten days later, Ałekśandr *Vardapet* J̌ułayeći arrived in Ějmiacin,[52] to organise the reception and the consecration of the new kaťolikos. Steṗanos left New Julfa on October 3, 1696,[53] and accompanied by the newly appointed Farz-Ali *Khan* of Erevan, arrived Ějmiacin on November 1, 1696. The next day he was consecrated Kaťolikos by Patriarch Minas Amteći of Jerusalem, in the presence of fourteen diocesan bishops and heads of religious orders.[54]

The pontificate of Kaťolikos Steṗanos J̌ułayeći was not to be of long duration. Nahapet Edesaći, the ousted kaťolikos, who had been ordered to retire to the monastery of Taťew, managed to flee to Tabriz and to take refuge in a special asylum, where those convicted enjoyed temporary immunity, pending a final review of their case.[55] From there he secured the support of Awet, the former *Kalantar* of New Julfa and of the Jesuit missionaries of Iran, who had found a serious opponent in the person of Steṗanos J̌ułayeći.[56] Their efforts soon obtained a new decree from Shah Sultan Husayn, reinstating the pontifical rights of Kaťolikos Nahapet and ordering Farz-Ali *Khan*, to arrest Kaťolikos Steṗanos and impose on him a fine of one thousand *tomans*.[57]

In January or early February 1697,[58] Kaťolikos Steṗanos J̌ułayeći

---

[50] See Appendix I, doc. #7. The decree is dated *Shawwal* 1107 (May 5-June 2, 1696).

[51] See Appendix I, doc. #8. The decree is dated *Dhu Al-Qa'da* 1107 (June 3-July 2, 1696).

[52] Hakobyan V., *Manr Žamanakagrut'yunner*, vol. II, pg. 423.

M. Ormanean is mistaken in concluding that Steṗ'anos J̌ułayeći held the pontifical office between April 1695 and February 1696. See *Azgapatum*, vol. II, pg. 2677.

[53] *A Chronicle of the Carmelites*, vol. I, pg. 481.

[54] Hakobyan V., *Manr Žamanakagrut'yunner*, vol. II, pp. 310, 419, 423.

[55] Zaḱaria Sarkawag, vol. II, pg. 137.

[56] Leo, *Hayoć Patmut'yn*, vol. III, book I, pg. 343.

[57] Zaḱaria Sarkawag, vol. II, pg. 137.

[58] One of the letters written by Kaḱolikos Steṗanos from prison is dated February 28, 1697. AASM, cab. 5, dr. 3, file 27/d, doc. #18. Printed in my article, "*Step'anos Kat'ołikos J̌ułayeći*," *Hask Hayagitakan Handes*, N.S., vol. II-III, pg. 338.

was arrested, together with Petros of Vayoć Jor, Grigor of Mułnu Vank and Yovhannēs of Całkunoć Jor, by the governor of Erevan, tortured and imprisoned under the harshest conditions, pending the payment of the fines.[59] In a letter written from the prison and dated April 15, 1697, Stepanos provided the following information to the monks of All Saviour's monastery of New Julfa:

> Ałeksandr *vardapet*, who was here, knows how many times Nahapet forced us to appear before the *Khan*, the *begs*, the *shaykhs* and the *Qazi*.[60] ... Also, consequent to a payment of forty *tomans* by Nahapet, on the Tuesday of Holy Week, they moved me to a dungeon, proudly declaring that it is the King's order to finish me by the Easter Sunday. On the first Sunday following the Easter, they took me alive out of the dungeon and brought me back to the first prison, where currently we stay with the *vardapets*. We have written to you many times, but they do not let our letters reach you. We have received your letters of February 2 and March 11. Pursue the plans described in your letters for the sake of a successful result... I am prepared to die for the glory of Christ and as a scapegoat for them. But they know, they have sacrificed their honour to selfishness.[61]

Katołikos Stepanos was unable to raise enough funds to pay the enormous fines and other related expenses. For almost a year, he remained in prison, where he died on January 4, 1698, and was buried in the monastery of Xor Virap, according to his wish.[62]

---

[59] Zakaria Sarkawag, vol. II, pp. 137-138.

[60] Arabic Qadi, Judge.

[61] AASM, cab. 5, dr. 3, file 27/d, doc. #20. Also printed in my article, *"Stepanos Katołikos Jułayeci,"* pp. 338-341. «Աղեքսանդր վարդապետն տեղս իբեւան թէ քանի քանի զմեզ խաշի բեկի, շիխի, ղազու դիւան տանիլ ետուր Նահապետն: ... Մէկ այլ այս, որ Նահապետն խ թուման է տվլեր, որ աւագ շաբաթէ Գ. շաբթի օրն տարան զիս, երիդն ի զնդան, եւ իրեանք սկսան պարծիլ, թէ թագաւորի հրամանն է որ մինչ ի Զատիկ կիրակին զիս բթթարափ կանեն: Այլու Զոր կիրակէին զիս սաղ հանեցին, բերին առաջին բանտս, որ այժմս վարդապետոբն կամք ի մհասին: Մեք ձեզ գիր շատ եմք գրել, չեն թողում հասանիլ ձեզ: Իսկ ձեր Բ. գիրն, մէկն փետրվարի երկութն էիբ գրեալ, մէկն մարտի ԺԱ, մեզ հասաւ: Զոր ինչ գրեալ էիբ տեղ հասուցանէք, կատար հանէք: ... Եւ իմ մեռնելույս յօժար եմ, ի վրաս Քրիստոսի եւ իրեանց մատաղ, բայց իրեանք գիտեն իրեանցն Ճամոս դայրաբն է»:

In his letter, Katołikos Stepanos refers to the publication and distribution of a book, for which he had been blamed by his rivals. He does not mention the title of the book or the name of the author. He refers to the publisher simply as *Baspac Erec* (Priest the Printer), who had produced the book by his own initiative. Katołikos Nahapet and his followers had traced twenty five copies of the book throughout Armenia and had turned them over to the *Khan* of Erevan, for shipment to Isfahan. In the present state of our knowledge, nothing more can be said about the book in question.

[62] Zakaria Sarkawag, vol. II, pg. 138.

Following his victorious return to Ějmiacin, immediately after the imprisonment of Stepanos, Katołikos Nahapet sought to solidify his position there by eliminating or neutralizing his opponents. On March 1, 1697, he issued a sharply worded encyclical,[63] claiming ownership over all the parishes of Iran, which "from the very beginning were established as pontifical domains [*Teruni vičak*]," including the capital city Isfahan, the quarters of Erewan, Tawriz, Dašt, Bałatay, Gask, Gawrapat, the two Laragēls, and the districts of Peria, Burwari, Linjan, Alinjan, Geandiman and Jłaxor, and once again, appointing his "beloved son, and right hand man, Yovhan *Vardapet*, as pastor, bishop and personal representative" over all the said communities. Thus the katołikos was trying to establish direct control over the entire diocese of New Julfa, excluding only the All Saviour's monastery and the few older quarters of the town, which were mainly inhabited by the leaders of the New Julfa community.

Katołikos Nahapet's encyclical had not even reached New Julfa, however, when massive protests against his legitimacy and administrative policies erupted again throughout the diocese. The surviving fragment of a petition,[64] dated March 10-26, 1697, and signed by the priests and the lay leaders of more than twenty villages of Burwari, expressing their loyalty to the All Saviour's Monastery of New Julfa demonstrates the opposition of people towards Katołikos Nahapet and to his attempt to fragment the see. Still a more eloquent testimony to that effect, is another open letter from the clergy and lay leaders of New Julfa, to the Armenian clergy and laity at large. This undated letter, written immediately after the death of Katołikos Stepanos, denounces Katołikos Nahapet in the following words:

> But the second Cain and Juda [Nahapet], succeeded in having him [Stepanos] tortured and eventually killed. Last year, in Tabriz, without even being tortured or facing hardship, he [Nahapet] was ready to apostatize. That son of Satan is the type of man who cannot bear even the slightest pressure. Because of that and because of his vicious nature and ambitions, he renounced his faith before kings and princes and caused the death of such a true servant of Christ and hard working laborer after making him suffer various kinds of tortures...

> Beloved brothers, we were greatly amazed when you accepted him again, because in your joint letter of agreement, signed and sealed by all *vardapets*, bishops and prelates—which is in our hands—you had called him devil and falcon. He was a falcon then, a corpse full of

---

[63] AASM, cab. 5, dr. 3, file 27/d, doc. #19.
[64] AASM, file 30B, doc. #4.

devils, although he had not yet denounced Christ and not killed the Kat'oŧikos. Now, when he has committed those sins and has followed his father, Satan, he has become hospitable and acceptable to you. Alas! to the blindness of our minds.[65]

In their letter, the leaders of New Julfa claim to have obtained a new order from the Shah, for the ouster of Kaŧoŧikos Nahapet. They announce "the good news" to the faithful of the Armenian Church, proposing to have their "elderly father Isahak *Vardapet*"[66] serve as *locum tenens* at the Holy See, until the election of a new kaŧoŧikos. They reject in advance the possibility of electing a kaŧoŧikos from among the western Armenian clergy, because of their strange customs, already introduced at the Holy See by Kaŧoŧikoi Eŧiazar and Nahapet, and they require from the future kaŧoŧikos the elimination of those customs.

Contrary to the claims and hopes of New Julfa Armenians, Kaŧoŧikos Nahapet was able to maintain his pontificate at Ějmiacin until 1705, albeit in very difficult circumstances. For the rest of his life, he faced enmity, and was deprived of the important financial support of the see of New Julfa. In a letter dated as early as March 12, 1698, and addressed to a certain *Kalantar* Zaḱum,[67] Kaŧoŧikos Nahapet complained bitterly against the clergy of New Julfa and begged the *Kalantar* to support and protect his legate, Yovhan *Vardapet*.[68] In another letter, dated August 1, 1698, the Kaŧoŧikos appealed to a certain *Paron* Petros, to use his personal friendship with *Naqqash-Bashi*, the lord of the pontifical (*teruni*) quarters of New Julfa, and secure his assistance for the cause of the Holy See.[69] In a joint letter, dated June 28 of the same year, the clergy and the lay leaders of Ějmiacin and Erevan, appealed on their side to the leaders of the diocese of New Julfa for peace and compromise. They praised the late Kaŧoŧikos Steṗanos for his strong faith and martyrdom and cited the adverse consequences of the conflict between the kaŧoŧikos and the community of New Julfa, during which,

---

[65] See Appendix I, doc. #18.
[66] Isahak *Vardapet* born in New Julfa in 1626 was a student of Xačatur Kesaraċi. For many years he had served in Ějmiacin under Kaŧoŧikos Ṗilippos. (See his manuscript colophon in Tēr Awetisean S., vol. I, pg. 386.) Later he was the bishop of St. Thaddeus Monastery. (See *A Chronicle of the Carmelites*, vol. I, pg. 48.)
[67] The *Kalantar* of a certain pontifical (*teruni*) community, possibly of Linjan or Alinjan. The *kalantar* of New Julfa at the time was Łukas. (see Appendix IV)
[68] AASM, cab. 5, dr. 3, file 27/d, doc.#22.
[69] AASM, cab. 5, dr. 3, file 27/d, doc. #9. L.G. Minasean is obviously mistaken in classifying this letter under the year 1678, when Nahapet was not even kaŧoŧikos. He must have read the Armenian date ՌՃԽԷ (1147) as ՌՃԻԷ (1127). See his *Diwan S. Amenaṗrkič Vanḱi*, pg. 57.

thousands of *tomans* had already been spent by both sides for bribes and fines.[70]

The (cited) letters of Nahapet, as well as the aggressive campaigns of Yovhan *Vardapet* and his few assistants throughout the diocese[71] did not weaken the determination of New Julfa Armenians. They rejected the pontificate of Nahapet altogether, as clearly evidenced by manuscript colophons dated 1699-1703, in which, only the name of late Kaťołikos Step'anos is mentioned.[72] The faithful at large maintained their loyalty towards All Saviour's Monastery of New Julfa, ignoring Yovhan *Vardapet* and the pontifical legates, who visited the dioceses once every three years, to collect various kinds of dues and donations, on behalf of the Holy See.

Completely deprived of the financial support of New Julfa, Kaťołikos Nahapet took the unusual step, in 1704, of granting full authority to a layman, a certain Sahak *Agha*, to collect the unpaid dues and possible donations to the Holy See, throughout the diocese of New Julfa.[73] In February 1705, only four months before his death, once again disappointed in his expectations, the kaťołikos attempted to travel to New Julfa in order to defend the rights of the Holy See. But due to his advanced age and poor health, he was unable to travel beyond Naxčawan, and was reduced to delegate Yovsep̄, the Archbishop of Smyrna, "to establish peace and love" with the New Julfa community and collect the past dues on behalf of the Holy See. A letter from Nahapet himself addressed to *Paron* Seťała and *Paron* Safraz,[74] the two best known supporters of All Saviour's Monastery, "the failing Kaťołikos," begged their support "humbly, with broken heart, tearful face and lamentations".[75]

At the death of Kaťołikos Nahapet on June 13, 1705,[76] Kaťołikos Aleksandr Julayeči was unanimously elected. According to Aleksandr's

---

[70] AASM, cab. 2, file #99.

[71] In a letter dated November 25, 1698, Yovhan *Vardapet* describes some of his activities and mentions the names of two monks and two priests, assisting him in his mission. AASM, cab. 2, file #99.

[72] Tēr Awetisean S., vol. I, pp. 309, 471-472, 527, 528 and 583.

[73] AASM, cab 2, file # 99.

[74] Seťała and Safraz were the sons of *Khwaja* Minas Ťarxanean. Together with their two other brothers: Ēliaz and Ēmniaz they played a leading role in the community affairs of New Julfa. They were very close to Ałek'sandr Julayeči, the Bishop of New Julfa (1697-1706) and Kaťołikos of Ějmiacin (1706-1714). More than ten encyclicals and letters from Kaťołikos Aleksandr to the four brothers have survived in the archives of All Saviour's Monastery. (cab. 5, dr. 3, file 27/d, #30, 33-36, 39-42, 45, 53). AASM, cab. 5, dr. 3, file 27/d, #24.

[76] Ormanean, M., vol. II pg. 2732.

own account, the *Beglarbegi* of Erevan wrote to the Shah, reporting that all the Armenians of the Safavid Kingdom and the Ottoman Empire had expressed their wish in favour of Ałekśandr. Together with his letter to the shah, the *Beglarbegi* had sent many petitions signed and sealed by Eastern and Western Armenian communities, to demonstrate the unanimity of the people. Consequently, after the approval of the Shah, he was called to the presence of the Grand Vazir (*I'timad al-daula*) and was amazed to hear the news of his election. He was immediately given the royal decree (*raqam*) and the robe of honour (*khelat*) and was ordered to immediately leave for Ējmiacin.[77]

The pontificate of Kaťolikos Ałekśandr finally brought the bitter conflict of fifty years, between the Kaťolikosate of Ējmiacin and the diocese of New Julfa to a peaceful end.[78] Kaťolikos Ałekśsandr died on November 22, 1714,[79] and was peacefully succeeded by Astuacatur Hamatanči, another member of the religious community of the All Saviour's Monastery of New Julfa. Under Kaťolikoi Ałekśandr and Astuacatur, Movsēs Julayeči, the bishop of New Julfa (1706-1725), established permanent rights over his entire diocese and even expanded his jurisdiction as far as India and Java, where new Armenian communities were being established by merchants from New Julfa.[80]

---

[77] AASM, cab. 5, dr. 3, file 27/d, #27. In a statement dated Sept. 18, 1706, Kaťolikos Ałek'sandr confirms the end of his tenure in the diocese of New Julfa and his planned departure for Ējmiacin. Y. Tēr Yovhaneanč, vol. II, pg. 48.

[78] In an agreement between Kaťolikos Ałekśandr, and Movsēs *Vardapet*, the new Bishop of New Julfa, *Tntesi Tłay* Yovhan *Vardapet*, was placed under the authority of Movsēs. Letter of Kaťolikos Ałekśandr to Movsēs *Vardapet*, in AASM, cab. 5, dr. 3, file 27/d, #26.

[79] Ormanean, M., vol. II, pg. 2800.

[80] AASM, cab. 5, dr. 6, file 27/Ž, doc. #8.

Fig. 15 Entrance of Surb Sargis (Ohanavanḱ) church.

Fig. 16 Epitaph of Kaťolikos Ałeǩsandr J̌ułayeći at the entrance of Ējmiacin Cathedral.

CHAPTER SEVEN

THE OPPOSITION OF
THE DIOCESE OF NEW JULFA
TO CATHOLIC MISSIONARY EXPANSION

The mass deportation of Armenians by Shah 'Abbas I and their settlement in Iran occurred at a time when special diplomatic and trade relations were being established between Iran and European countries.

In 1589, shortly after his ascension to the Safavid throne, the eighteen-year-old Shah 'Abbas had ceded large territories to the Ottomans and had secured a temporary peace.[1] He then devoted ten years to the restoration of internal security in his realm, to the reorganization of his army and to the strengthening of the Iranian economy.[2] Before moving to liberate the Iranian territories occupied by the Ottomans, the Shah also attempted to form a military and economic alliance with the European powers who were hostile to the Ottomans and had economic interests in the East. On the one hand, military operations in Europe would force the Ottomans to commit large forces for the defence of their western borders. On the other hand, trade agreements with European countries would open new international roads for the Iranian trade, which until then had been largely dependent on the land road passing through Ottoman territories.[3]

In 1598, Shah 'Abbas admitted into his service two Englishmen: Sir Anthony Sherley and his brother Robert. The following year he dispatched Sir Anthony Sherley to Europe, to deliver his letters of

---

[1] Savory R., pg. 77.
[2] Ibid., pp. 77-85.
[3] Bayburtyan V.A., *Nor Ĵuɬayi Vačarakanutiwnə*, pg. 215.

friendship addressed to the Pope of Rome, the Holy Roman Emperor Rudolf II, King of Bohemia, King Henry of France, King Philip III of Spain, the King of Scotland, the King of Poland, the Queen of England, the Doge of Venice and the Grand Duke of Tuscany.[4]

Sir Anthony Sherley who was accompanied by an Iranian delegation headed by Husayn 'Ali Beg Bayat, failed to accomplish his entire mission. In Russia, on the first leg of their journey, strong quarrels broke out between Anthony Sherley and Husayn 'Ali Beg Bayat. After six months of a fruitless stay in Moscow, the delegation headed for Prague and was received by Emperor Rudolf II in October 1600. Amid continued quarrels, the delegation arrived in Rome in April 1601, where Husayn 'Ali Beg Bayat with his Iranian assistants abandoned Sherley, went to Spain and was received by King Philip III. But soon all his Iranian assistants were converted to Christianity and he was forced to return to Iran empty handed.[5] In Rome, Anthony Sherley was able to deliver the Shah's letter to the Pope and continue his journey to Venice, whence he maintained correspondence with the King of Spain. But his letters were intercepted by English agents and he was considered to be a traitor. In 1603, he was imprisoned in Venice for unknown reasons. After his release, he settled in Madrid where he lived in extreme poverty.[6]

The only beneficiary from Sherley's mission was the Catholic Church. During his meeting with Pope Clement VIII, Anthony Sherley, among other things, proposed the following on behalf of Shah 'Abbas I:

> a) to cause to submit to the obedience of your Holiness and the Holy Apostolic See all schismatic Christians in his realm, whether Georgians, Armenians or of whatever other kind they may be; b) to bring into his realm preachers and 'founders' of the Christian religion, and the free practice of the Christian religion with very genuine privileges for all.[7]

Taking advantage of the offer, in his immediate response dated May 2, 1601, and addressed to Shah 'Abbas I, Pope Clement VIII answered:

> As to that which you signify that you desire, and which those whom you sent to us have also related in our presence, that the Christian kings and princes should enter into league against the Turk with you,

[4] Savory R., pg. 109.
[5] Ibid, pp. 109-110.
[6] Ibid., pp. 109-110.
[7] A Chronicle of the Carmelites , vol. I, pg. 78.

we desire the same and we shall pledge to this our functions and character of papal authority. Meanwhile there are not lacking those of our princes such as are keeping him [the Turks] engaged with military operations and attacking him, especially our most dear son, Rudolf the Emperor elect, who constantly wages war with him and even now, this very summer, is about to wage it: and we also are helping him and are sending our auxiliary forces against the Turks, and by every sort of pressure we are working on the Catholic princes our sons to bring help to the same Emperor-elect...

We derived incredible pleasure from that portion of your letter and from the conversation of those same two distinguished men whom you sent to us (where it was said) that it is your great wish that entry to your realm and countries shall be open to Christians and especially to those who shall be sent by us, trade be free to Christians and Persians, and that the Christians themselves shall enjoy and possess not only immunity and many favours and privileges abundantly granted by you, but also that they may build churches and temples to God most high for the Christian rite within your realm and jurisdiction, that they may have priests and presbyters to perform the Divine office, administer the sacraments, preach the word of God and everywhere spread it... so in a short time we shall dispatch to you priests, doctors of the truth and teachers of salvation.[8]

Since the early fourteenth century, Catholic missionary activities had produced tangible results in northern Iran, where Persians, Turks, Mongols, Kurds, Assyrians and Armenians lived side by side. As already mentioned,[9] the Dominican archbishopric of Sultaniyya was established in 1318. Subsequently, the Dominicans had managed to expand their activities across river Arax, into Naxčawan in Armenia, where Bartholomew of Podio, a Dominican bishop had succeeded in converting to Catholicism eleven Armenian monks living at the monastery of Ќrna, thus laying the foundations of the future Catholic Archbishopric of Naxčawan.[10] By the end of the sixteenth century, this archbishopric had grown to ten active churches in Ќrna, Aparaner, Saltał, Aprakunis, Xoškašen, Jahuk and some other Armenian villages of Naxčawan, with a total of 19,000 faithful.[11]

For the Church of Rome, Iran could serve as a unique base in the East, for the task of "saving the souls" of local peoples, especially "schismatic" Christians. Therefore, Pope Clement VIII wasted no time in

---

[8] Ibid., vol. I, pp. 83-84.
[9] See pg. 30.
[10] Frazee C.A., *The Catholic Missions to Azerbaijan and Nakhichevan*, pp. 253-256.
[11] Ibid., pg. 259.
Bayburtyan A.V., "*XVII Darum Arevelyan Hayastanum Katolik Misionerneri Gorcuneutyan patmutyunić*," *Patma-Banasirakan Handes*, 1989, #2 (125), pp. 148-149.

accepting the offer of Shah 'Abbas I. In 1603, only two years after Sherley's meeting with the Pope, three Portuguese missionaries from the Order of St. Augustine established the first Catholic mission in Isfahan.[12] Four years later, in 1607 three missionaries from the Carmelite Order arrived from Rome and established the second Catholic mission in the Safavid capital.[13]

In the sixteenth and early seventeenth centuries, the Catholic missionary activity partly depended on European monarchs, who underwrote the expenses of the missionaries. Besides their religious task, missionaries were expected to serve the interests of their patron countries. As a result, missionaries from one nation or order would sometimes look upon those from another nation or order as rivals, not partners in a common cause.[14] The Augustinians in Isfahan were supported by the King of Spain and the Viceroy of the Portuguese Indies.[15] Therefore, in Iran, they played the role of ambassadors for the King of Spain, who promised Shah 'Abbas to send "Artillery gunners, engineers, artillery, if he ['Abbas] allowed the Holy Gospel to be preached in his realm."[16] The Carmelite missionaries, who were mostly of Italian and Spanish origin, were considered in Isfahan as guests sent by the Pope.[17]

In Iran or in any other Muslim country, the missionaries faced the all but impossible task of converting Muslims, because, according to Islamic law, any Muslim renouncing his faith would automatically face execution. Therefore, the Catholic missionaries in Iran focused their attention mainly on non-Muslim minorities, namely Zoroastrians, Jews, Assyrians, Georgians and Armenians. Furthermore, in his efforts to please the Church of Rome and the European monarchs for the sake of a military alliance against the Ottomans and greater trade opportunities, Shah 'Abbas I had clearly offered the allegiance of his non-Catholic Christian subjects to the Pope. Therefore, the almost simultaneous settlement of tens of thousands of Armenian refugees in Iran in 1605, seemed to have created a golden opportunity for missionary work for the Augustinians and the Carmelites, especially since the Dominicans had managed to save their faithful from forced deportation[18] and

---

[12] *A Chronicle of the Carmelites* , vol. I, pg. 92.
[13] Ibid., vol. I, pg. 105.
[14] Frazee C.A., *Catholics and Sultans*, Cambridge, 1983, pg. 88.
[15] 1580-1640 Portugal and Spain were united under the King of Spain.
[16] *A Chronicle of the Carmelites* , vol. I, pp. 92-93, 284.
[17] Ibid., vol. I, pg. 284.
[18] Gouvea, Anthonio De. pg. 146.
Gulbenkian R., *Hay-Portugalakan Haraberutyunner*, pp. 212-213.

continued to maintain their archbishopric in Naxčawan, Armenia. Only a few Armenian Catholics headed by the Šahrimanean and Łaramean families were among the refugees who were settled in New Julfa.

The Augustinian prior in Isfahan, Father Diego de Santa Ana was very ambitious in his plans to achieve a union between the Armenian and Catholic Churches, under the supreme authority of the Pope of Rome. Immediately after the arrival of Kaťołikos Dawiť Vałaršapatči, in 1605 as a refugee in Isfahan with thousands of his faithful, Father Diego de Santa Ana made every effort to overcome the resistance of the kaťołikos, who did not accept the supremacy of the pope and considered him simply "a spiritual brother like other patriarchs, who were the successors of the holy apostles."[19] Finally, in May 1607,[20] "partly by exhortations, partly by more than 1000 scudi, which he had brought from India, given by the archbishop (of Goa, Alejo de Menezej) for the purpose, he drew up a document for union" and secured the signatures of Kaťołikos Dawiť, as well as of many Armenian monks and priests.[21] Other members of the Augustinian Order in Isfahan did not take this event seriously and even blamed Father Diego de Santa Ana for wasting his time and not devoting himself to the service of the people at large.[22]

In June 1607, armed with the document of Union signed by the Kat'ołikos, Father de Santa Ana travelled to Šamaxi-Shirvan, on the western shores of Caspian Sea, where Shah 'Abbas I was occupied with military campaigns. During an audience with the Shah, he requested royal confirmation for the submission of the Armenians to the papal authority.[23] The Shah's initial reaction was favorable, but later he angrily rejected the request. According to a report sent from Isfahan to Rome by the Carmelite father John Thaddeus:

> Some Armenians told him ['Abbas] that the Father wanted to make them Portuguese and deprive them of the faith they had kept for so many centuries. The King was greatly displeased at this, because of the deep hatred he has for the Portuguese on account of the onerous impositions they daily in Hormuz place on his [the Shah's] subjects.[24]

According to the Augustinian version of the same episode, the Shah was very upset when he learned from merchants coming from Aleppo

---

[19] Gulbenkian R., Ibid., pg. 177.
[20] Ibid., pg. 180.
[21] *A chronicle of the Carmelites*, vol. I, pg. 101.
[22] Gulbenkian R., *Hay-Portugalakan Haraberutyunner*, pg. 180.
[23] Ibid., pp. 113, 183.
[24] *A Chronicle of the Carmelites*, vol. I, pg. 101.

that Emperor Rudolf II had concluded a peace agreement with the Ottomans. Therefore, he bitterly complained saying:

> While the Christian princes fail to fulfil their promises, you expect to have churches in my realm... So far I have not received more than words and letters from you and the princes who have send you.[25]

Father de Santa Ana's attempt at unity with Kaťoŀikos Dawiť apparently did not have a lasting effect, because only one year after that event, Father John Taddeus, the Carmelite missionary, reported the following from Isfahan:

> Till now there has been small success, for the Muslims are as already described, and the Armenians (so the Augustinian Fathers say) take no account of the Pope unless it be to get some alms or temporal benefit... it appears to us that great results could be gained in this country if there were a college for Armenian, Georgian, Circassian and Persian boys, who might be purchased out of money offered for sale and if we were to bring them up among us and teach them our habits and standard of conduct, in order to send them to Italy when bigger and they would serve as interpreters: and the King of Persia would not interfere with such work. We do not doubt that, because it is the habit here that the slave must take the religion of his master, many souls would be released from the bonds of Satan, since many of them would become our brethren and others would follow them.[26]

Three years after Father de Santa Ana's failure in his ambitious undertaking, another Augustinian stationed in Isfahan, Father Gileerme de Santo Augustino became involved in a serious act of provocation against the Armenian Church. Accompanied by Agostino d'Abreo, a catholic from Syria, Father Gileerme travelled to Naxčawan and Ējmiacin, openly preaching the Catholic faith.[27] In Ējmiacin, he succeeded in gaining the confidence of Kaťoŀikos Melkiset Garneci and was allowed to enter the Armenian churches of the area. At the church of St. Hripsimē, he secretly dug the tomb of the most venerated female saint of the Armenian Church, Hripsimē, and intended to smuggle her relics out of Armenia. He was caught by two Armenian bishops but was able to flee with some pieces of the Saint's relics, part of which he left in Aparaner, with the Dominicans of Naxčawan, and he took the other portions to the Augustinian monastery of Isfahan.[28]

---

[25] Gulbenkian R., *Hay-Portugalakan Haraberutyunner*, pp. 113-114, 190-191.
[26] *A Chronology of the Carmelites*, vol. I, pg. 165.
[27] Gulbenkian R., *Hay-Portugalakan Haraberutyunner*, pp. 103-104.
[28] Aťaḱel Dawriževi, pp. 178-185. The names of Father Gileerme and his companion are registered by Dawriževi as Patri Glēlun and Patri Arḱanjeli (pg. 187).

The news of the theft created an uproar among the Armenians of Isfahan. Headed by Kaťolikos Dawiť, the *kalantar* of New Julfa *khwaja* Safar and his brother *khwaja* Nazar, the head of the Erewanči community of Isfahan *Agha* Terter and others, the Armenians protested to Shah 'Abbas I.[29] The Shah issued written orders to investigate the matter and identify all the accomplices of Father Gileerme in the theft and the smuggling of the relics.[30] In Naxčawan, several catholic clerics were tortured. In Isfahan the Augustinian monastery was searched. The stolen relics were fully recovered both in Naxčawan and Isfahan,[31] but Father Gileerme was able to avoid punishment. In 1615, during a second visit to Naxčawan, he was trapped and killed by Qizilbash officers.[32]

Earlier in 1608, having in mind a large upcoming campaign against the Ottomans aimed at the occupation of Baghdad,[33] Shah 'Abbas I had sent a second mission with Robert Sherley to Europe bearing specific proposals. During his audience with Pope Paul V on October 4, 1609, Robert Sherley begged him, on behalf of the Shah, to persuade the King of Spain to undertake an expedition to Cyprus, move on to Syria and join the advancing Persian army. Furthermore, he asked the Pope to persuade every sovereign in Europe to attack the Ottomans from their frontiers. To please the Pontiff, Robert Sherley added:

> The King of Persia invites your Holiness to post an archbishop and establish him at the Three Churches[34] in Greater Armenia, the place of residence of the patriarch of that race, through whom your Holiness would easily be able to convince the latter and make him submit to the obedience of the Holy Roman Church.[35]

Pope Paul V was delighted with the prospects of bringing the Armenians into his fold. On October 9, 1609, only five days after his meeting with Robert Sherley and possibly even before bothering to urge the European sovereigns to military action against the Ottomans, he wrote to the Shah, saying:

---

[29] Ibid., pp. 186-187.

[30] Paṗazyan H.D., *Matenadarani Parskeren Hrovartaknerǝ*, vol. I, Book II, pp. 90-91, 482-483.

[31] Aṛaḱel Dawrižeči, pp. 186-189.

[32] Ibid., pp. 191-193.

Gulbenkian R., *Hay Portugalakan Haraberutyunner*, pp. 106-107.

[33] *A Chronicle of the Carmelites*, vol. I, pg. 165.

[34] Ějmiacin. Official Persian documents of this period commonly refer to Ějmiacin as *Učkilisa* (three churches), due to the presence of three churches (the cathedral of Ějmiacin and the churches of St. Hṙipsimē and St. Gayanē) in the same place.(See Chardin Jean, vol. I, pg. 214.)

[35] Ibid., vol. I, pg. 148.

> Regarding moreover those things which your same ambassador promised us in your name... and regarding the setting up of a Catholic archbishop in Greater Armenia, we give your Highness very great thanks and we shall deliberate about both topics and shall decide only on one worthy of so great an office and one who can satisfy you and his post, even as we shall also take pains that of such kind too shall be the rest of the Religious whom we shall send into Persia.[36]

The Pope's dream was never to be fulfilled partly due to his failure to mobilise the European sovereigns against the Ottomans and partly due to his selection of Father Antonio de Gouvea, a Portuguese Augustinian missionary, for the task of supervising the submission of the Armenians to the Catholic Church.

For several years father de Gouvea had already served in Isfahan, when late in 1608, Shah 'Abbas decided to dispatch a new delegation to Spain, to conclude a trade agreement with King Philip III. Along with his ambassador Dengiz Beg Rumlu, and a merchant named *Khwaja* Rajabo, the Shah included father de Gouvea in the delegation. In addition to the gifts for King Philip, the Shah sent with the delegation 76 bales of silk, the proceeds of which were to be brought back. The Shah's main proposal was to channel all the export of Iranian silk through the strait of Hurmuz to deprive the Ottomans of their custom duties earned from the Iranian trade through their territories. The delegation was also instructed to persuade King Philip to wage war on the Ottomans.

The mission proved a total failure. The members of the delegation had presented the entire stock of the silk as a gift to the King of Spain. In 1613, when they returned to Iran with only some gifts for the Shah, Dengiz Beg was immediately executed and Father de Gouvea was compelled to write to the King of Spain and request payment for the "donated" silk. The Shah was further angered with the fact that Father de Gouvea had returned from Europe with the title of "Apostolic Visitor to the Armenians" and was claiming the Armenian subjects of the Shah as his flock. This attitude was seen by the Shah as a serious provocation. Feeling threatened, in October 1613 de Gouvea fled from Isfahan under the pretext of receiving the new Spanish Ambassador to Iran, Don Garcia de Silva y Figueroa, in Hurmuz. Shah 'Abbas sent orders to the Governor General of Fars, Imam Quli *Khan*, to detain him, but it was too late. Father de Gouvea had left the Iranian territory through Hurmuz, without waiting for the Spanish Ambassador, who would arrive in Iran only four years later.[37]

---

[36] Ibid., vol. I, pg. 150.
[37] Gulbenkian R., *Hay-Portugalakan Haraberutyunner*, pp. 115-119.
Savory R., pp. 115-116.

After the escape of Father de Gouvea, the remaining two Augustinian missionaries temporarily left Isfahan in November 1613, fearing reprisals from the Shah who had threatened to force all of his Christian subjects to convert to Islam.[38] But, surprisingly, the Shah's attitude towards the Christians changed very soon.

With a special decree issued in 1614, the Shah announced his intention to build for his Armenian subjects "a large, magnificent, high and elegantly adorned church in the capital, which will serve for them as a place of worship and where they may pray according to their traditions and rules." In the same Decree, the Shah nevertheless emphasized his "friendly relationship" with the Pope of Rome and the King of Spain and his intention to "send a messenger to the Holy Pope of Rome and ask him to send a Christian priest or cleric," this time "to the Capital of Isfahan to pray in the said church, so that the people may learn." He ordered the dismantling of the cathedral of Ējmiacin in Armenia, and the transportation of its sacred stones to Isfahan for use in the construction of the new church.[39]

The Shah sought to please his Armenian subjects with this project, particularly the merchants of New Julfa, and to secure their attachment and permanent settlement in Isfahan. His declared intention was to make the Armenians "living in the Royal capital of Isfahan hold their heads high, due to the special attention paid to them by our great kingdom."[40] He was also trying in a sense to reconfirm the offer he had made to the Pope five years earlier for the appointment of an archbishop in Ējmiacin. This time, however, Ējmiacin was being relocated in Isfahan and the offer was limited to the assignment of a pastor or chief priest at the planned church. As noted earlier,[41] the Armenian merchants were able to persuade the Shah to abandon the project.

The mission to Iran of Ambassador Don Garcia de Silva y Figueroa, coming after the failure of Father de Gouvea, proved another blunder for the Spanish and Portuguese interests in the Persian Gulf. During his meeting with Shah 'Abbas in 1617, the ambassador demanded the return of the Island of Bahrain and the port of Gambrun captured by the Shah from the Portuguese in 1602 and 1614 respectively. In addition, he demanded the expulsion from Iran of the English East India Company factors. He was immediately dismissed by the Shah and was forced to leave Iran empty handed.[42]

---

[38] Gulbenkian R., Ibid., pg. 119.
[39] See Appendix I, Doc. #2.
[40] Ibid.
[41] See pg. 85.
[42] Savory R., pg. 116.

Between 1620 and 1622, with the help of the naval forces of the English East India Company, Shah 'Abbas was able to capture the island of Hurmuz and expel the Portuguese from the Persian Gulf.[43] Consequently, the Augustinian mission in Isfahan was marginalized, never to recover and serve its intended purpose adequately. But soon, another Catholic missionary order succeeded in establishing a presence in Isfahan.

In 1627, the French Cardinal de Richelieu sent a mission to Iran to obtain permission from Shah 'Abbas for the establishment of a Capuchin mission in Isfahan.[44] With the assistance of *khwaja* Nazar, the *kalantar* of New Julfa,[45] Cardinal de Richelieu's envoy, père Pacifique, was able to obtain permission and establish the mission which would serve the interests of the Catholic church and the kingdom of France.[46] In August 1629, a letter of appreciation was sent to *khwaja* Nazar from Rome by the Sacred Congregation for the Propagation of the Faith.[47] Three months later, on November 23, 1629, a letter signed by King Louis XIII and Cardinal de Richelieu, granted special trade privileges to the Armenian merchants of New Julfa, traveling between Iran and Marseille.[48]

During the first three decades of the seventeenth century, relations between the Armenians of Isfahan and the Catholic missionaries were generally calm, despite the aggressive behavior of the Augustinians. Under Shah 'Abbas I, who admitted the missionaries in Iran due to his own political and economic agenda, the Armenians tried to avoid open confrontations with the missionaries so as not to provoke the Shah. The Armenian merchants of New Julfa even cooperated with them at times, particularly with the Carmelites and the Capuchins, for their own economic interests in the European market. The poor benefited from their alms, their free medical services[49] and the bail they occasionally furnished on behalf of poor Armenians, to save them from their Muslim debtors and forced conversion to Islam.[50] The Provincial of the Carmelites, Father Dimas of the Cross, reported the following in June 1631:

---

[43] Ibid., pp. 116-117.
[44] Ibid., pg. 120.
[45] P. Pacifique, *Relation du Voyage en Perse*, Lille 1632, pg. 423.
[46] Savory R., Iran Under the Safavids, pg. 120.
[47] Akinean N., *"Movsēs G. Taťewaċi Kaťołikos"*, *Handēs Amsoreay*, Vienna, 1934, pg. 513.
[48] Ališan Ł., *Sisuan*, pg. 456.
[49] *A Chronicle of the Carmelites*, vol. I, pp. 120, 207, 265-271, etc.
[50] Ibid., vol. I, pp. 206-207.
Aťaḱel Dawriżeċi, pg. 154.

If on some occasions in the year food was eaten outside the house, it was in the convent of certain monks in Julfa, who live more than 3 miles away from our convent: and this is done to keep up and foster fellowship with those religious. For both they and their patriarchs and bishops are very well disposed towards us, making us substantial alms from time to time: and it is not a month ago since they sent us a mule-load of flour: and on every occasion, when serious affairs occur, they assist us greatly, always giving us credit with the Armenians also. We too have always maintained good relations with them and shown them kindness when they come to visit us: and the whole serves as a means to their conversion, and to dispose them to it.[51]

After 1630, the relations between the Armenians of New Julfa and the Catholic missionaries of Isfahan slowly and gradually deteriorated due to external and internal factors and turned into a bitter struggle, which lasted for almost a century and at certain stages, caused great turmoils in the internal life of the Armenian community of New Julfa.

The main external factor which sparked the tension was the submission of the Armenian diocese of Poland to the Catholic Church. In 1626, Katołikos Melkiset Garneci, who was wandering around Ottoman territories and Eastern Europe after his escape from Ējmiacin, as we have seen, ordained Bishop Nikol Torosovič, the twenty three years old son of a wealthy Armenian merchant of Lwow. He appointed him bishop of the Armenian diocese of Poland despite strong opposition from the majority of the local Armenian population.[52] Two years later, Grigor Kesaraci, a highly respected Armenian theologian and famous teacher visited Poland as legate from Ējmiacin. Witnessing liturgical practices which were against the traditions of the Armenian church, Grigor Kesaraci reprimanded the young bishop. In retaliation, Nikol Torosovič complained to Polish authorities, accused the legate as an Ottoman spy and succeeded in obtaining his expulsion from Poland, an act which intensified the internal opposition against the bishop.[53]

In 1630, Xačatur Kesaraci, the bishop of New Julfa arrived in Lwow as legate of Katołikos Movsēs Siwneci.[54] He attempted to mediate the conflict between Torosovič and the community, but neither was ready for compromise. Moreover, Nikol Torosovič once again approached the Polish authorities and accused Xačatur of being an Ottoman spy. But sensing that the people's anger had reached its climax and fearing for his own physical safety, he now took refuge with the Carmelite mission

---

[51] *A Chronicle of the Carmelites in Persia*, vol. I, pg. 320.
[52] Aṙakel Dawrizeci, pp. 363-366.
[53] Ibid., pp. 366-369.
[54] See pg. 91.

in Lwow and converted to Catholicism. With the support of the Carmelites and of the Jesuits, he secured the protection of the Polish authorities, and was soon able to occupy all of the Armenian churches, depriving his opponents of their own churches. The diocese of Poland was lost in this manner to the Armenian Church.[55]

In 1631, Xačatur Kesarači was forced to leave Poland and return to Ējmiacin to report to the kaťolikos. Later the same year, he moved back to New Julfa and resumed his responsibilities as bishop.[56] But this time he returned after a bitter experience in Poland, in which the Catholic Church had played a negative role, through its missionaries.

The relations between the Armenians and the Catholic missionaries of Isfahan after 1630 were also affected by the following two factors:

a) In 1622 the Sacred Congregation for the Propagation of the Faith (usually known as the Propaganda Fide) was formed in Rome to strengthen and control the missionary activity of the Roman Catholic Church.[57] Five years later, in 1627, a school and a multi-lingual publishing house were established in Rome by the Propaganda Fide. The school was primarily to provide for the education and training of students selected from abroad. The publishing house would produce religious books in various languages, including Armenian, for distribution by missionaries abroad.[58] During the following two decades, new missionaries armed with Catholic publications arrived Iran and generated a new and very aggressive wave of missionary activity among the Armenians of Iran and Eastern Armenia.

b) After the death of Shah 'Abbas I in early 1629, his successors did not follow his policy towards Western Europe. In 1639 Shah Safi concluded the Treaty of Zuhab with the Ottomans and secured a long lasting peace.[59] Also under Shah Safi, royal control in trade gradually diminished,[60] when English and Dutch companies and Armenian merchants dominated the Iranian trade with Europe. Therefore, the Safavid Court had no reason to favor the missionaries with a privileged status.

In June 1632, upon the recommendation of the Propaganda Fide, Pope Urban VIII appointed Father John Thaddeus, a Carmelite, as

[55] Ibid., pp. 371-378.
Ormanean M., vol. II, pp. 2410-2415.
Akinean N., *Movses G. Tatewači Kaťolikos*, pp. 5-17.
[56] See pg. 92.
[57] Frazee C.A., *Catholics and Sultans*, pg. 88.
[58] Leo, *Hayoč Patmut'yun*, vol. III, book I, pg. 318.
[59] Cook M.A. (ed.) *A History of the Ottoman Empire to 1730*, pg. 147.
[60] Ferrier R.W., *The Armenians and the East India Company*, pg. 41.

bishop of Isfahan. Father Thaddeus had already served in Isfahan for more than twenty years and was in Rome on a visit when he was appointed to his new position. He was given "as coadjutor, with future right of succession, Fr. Timothy Perez, calced Carmelite, with the title of Baghdad or Babylon," in order to avoid a vacancy in the Diocese after his death.[61] According to a decree prepared by the Propaganda Fide for the occasion:

> The Bishop of Isfahan can use the faculties to be granted him in the whole empire of Persia except that part of Assyria now subject to the same King, which is assigned to the Bishop of Baghdad: also (he can use them) in Greater and Lesser Armenia, except in the Province of Nakhciwan, which has its own Dominican bishop.[62]

Bishop Thaddeus died in 1633, on his way back to Isfahan. For unknown reasons, Father Timothy Perez, his coadjutor, did not replace him and the new diocese of Isfahan remained vacant for at least the following sixty years.

In 1640, Bishop Barnard of Baghdad arrived in Isfahan with a letter from the Pope, requesting the fulfilment of the promise made by Shah 'Abbas I, to build a church in Isfahan for the bishop whom the Pope would dispatch. Shah Safi denied that any such promise had ever been made by his grandfather and simply granted a permit to the bishop to purchase a house in the city of Isfahan at his own expense.[63]

For the greater part of the seventeenth century, Armenian sources, including the archives of All Saviour's monastery provide only marginal information on the conflict with the Catholic missionaries and the measures taken by the leadership of the Armenian Church in their struggle against the Catholics. We must therefore turn primarily to the missionary reports which are full of details and alarming news from Isfahan. In April 1644, Father Joseph de Rosario, an Augustinian wrote the following to the Propaganda Fide:

> We constantly suffer persecution from the Armenians, on account of which the removal of all missionaries from these parts is to be foreseen if against those who dwell without hindrance[64] in the lands of Catholic sovereigns it were threatened, and by some demonstration made clear to them, that the Catholic sovereigns would take ill any molestation caused us, perhaps we should be freed [from it.][65]

---

[61] *A Chronicle of the Carmelites*, vol. I, pg. 299.

[62] Ibid., vol. I, pg. 300.

[63] Ibid., vol. I, pg. 346.

[64] Referring to the Armenian merchants.

[65] Ibid., vol. I, pg. 375.

Xačatur Kesarači, the bishop of New Julfa presumably adopted various measures to fight off Catholic influence throughout his diocese. But the only tangible examples of his activities known to us are the establishment of the All Saviour's school for higher education and the printing press he created purely by local means in 1636. By the late 1630's, the graduates of the school became the main defenders of the Armenian faith against Catholic encroachment. Between 1638 and 1642, four volumes were printed, all for daily use by the community at large, partly to counter balance the influence of the Catholic publications in Armenian.[66]

Shortly before Xačatur Kesarači's death in 1646, Father Paul Piromalli, a Dominican missionary arrived in Isfahan and started an aggressive preaching campaign. Father Piromalli had been sent to Naxčawan by Pope Urban VIII as early as 1613, to establish a Catholic seminary and train new recruits for the Dominican order.[67] But because of his aggressive character, he soon turned against his own superior, Augustin Baječi, the Armenian Dominican archbishop of Naxčawan and sent false reports to the pope about the archbishop. Baječi, in turn, sent written complaints to the pope against Piromalli and had him jailed by local Safavid authorities for almost two years. After his release from prison, Piromalli spent more than ten years in Eastern Armenia, during which time he learned the Armenian language and studied Armenian religious literature.[68]

After his arrival in Persia, Father Piromalli preached openly and aggressively in Isfahan and New Julfa about the "errors of the Armenians" and was convinced that "outspoken methods should be employed to overcome the schism." His aggressive style of missionary work was greatly resented by the Armenians and considered "unsuitable" and "violent" by his fellow missionaries in Isfahan, as described in the reports of the Capuchin and Carmelite missionaries to the Propaganda Fide.[69]

In an undated letter addressed to Yakobjan, the Armenian *Naqqash-Baši* of the Safavid court, Katołikos Pilippos accused Piromalli of a damaging involvement in the continued crisis of the Armenian Church of Poland and of his ultimate goal to subject the Armenians to the

---

[66] For a detailed presentation of the school and the printing press of All.Saviour's Monastery, see Chapter IX of this study.
[67] Kevorkian R.H., *"Livre Missionaire et Enseignement Catholique Chez les Armeniens 1583-1700," Revue des Etudes Armeniennes*, N.S., Tome XVI, Paris 1982, p. 594.
[68] Ormanean M., vol. II, pp. 2408-2409, 2437-2439.
Akinean N., *Movses G. Tat'ewači Kat'ołikos*, pp. 507-511.
[69] *A Chronicle of the Carmelites*, vol. I, pg. 360.

Church of Rome. He also reported that Piromalli came to Isfahan with the aim of obtaining a royal decree to fulfil his dreams. He requested the assistance of Yakobjan for the extradition of Piromalli to Ējmiacin, where he would be held accountable for his role in the affairs of the Armenian Church of Poland.[70]

Following the death of Xačatur Kesaraci, in 1646 the see of New Julfa officially remained vacant for six years, as we have seen, until 1652, when Dawit Julayeci was installed as bishop by Katołikos Pilippos.[71] In the same year New Julfa was practically overrun by a large number of Catholic missionaries, belonging to five different orders.

The first three missionary orders: the Augustinians, the Carmelites and the Capuchins were stationed in the city of Isfahan. In 1651 the Capuchins had managed to open a school in New Julfa, followed by the Carmelites, who established a residence there on June 15, 1652. According to the report of a Carmelite Father Balthazar of St. Mary:

> Our fathers began the Residence of Julfa on Sunday in the octave of Corpus Christi (June 15, 1652). At the first they were well received and welcomed by the principal men, who showed them many kindnesses. Fifteen days after the new Residence (was opened) there arrived in Isfahan the Reverend Fathers of the Society of Jesus... Two or three days after their arrival, they all went into Julfa to pay a visit, and as already for a year past the Capuchin Fathers had been there, our (Carmelite) Fathers following, when the populace saw so many European Religious they were struck with amazement and stupefaction, and in a short time a small storm arose so that 'commota est universa civitas'—the whole town was in uproar—commencing with the clergy, and the bishop did not fail to stop the Julfa people from sending their sons to our Fathers to be taught (for the Capuchin Fathers already had a considerable number of boys).[72]

The Jesuits, the most militant and aggressive Catholic missionary order, penetrated Iran with the support of the King of France. In 1652, Father Aymé Chezaud arrived in Isfahan[73] and obtained a permit from the Shah to establish a church in New Julfa. The Armenians reacted promptly and very energetically. They presented a petition to Shah 'Abbas II and in January 1654 obtained a royal decree, saying:

---

[70] AASM, cab. 5, dr. 3, file 27d, #2.
[71] See pg. 100.
[72] *A Chronicle of the Carmelites*, vol. I, pg. 378.
[73] Machault, Jacques de. *"History of Mission of the Fathers of the Society of Jesus, Established in Persia by the Reverend Father Alexander of Rhodes,"Bulletin of the School of Oriental Studies*, #4 (1925) pp. 686-687.

> Previously we had responded favourably to the request of the representative of His Royal Majesty the King of France, to allow the Francs build the church they intend to build in the town of Julfa, near the capital city of Isfahan. But now, the Armenian *ra'yats* who reside in the capital have presented petitions, arguing that the construction of such a church may cause divisions among the *ra'yats* and result in their affiliation with the French infidels. At this time we order that the construction of the said church be stopped. This order should be followed even after the return of the French envoy from the land of infidels.[74]

Following this order, the Jesuits, the Capuchins and the Carmelites were forced to abandon their houses in New Julfa and move back to Isfahan.[75] Meanwhile, according to his own report to Rome, Father Paul Piromalli, the Dominican missionary, was persecuted and heavily tortured at the hands of the Armenians of New Julfa.[76] In 1657, after a new written request from the King of France, the Jesuits were granted "full permission to establish a fixed and permanent abode near his [the Shah's] palace and to build a church there (in Isfahan)."[77] But the Jesuits continued to pursue their dream of having a base in New Julfa. In the words of Father Jacques de Machault, a Jesuit missionary:

> If this takes place a wide field will be opened for the preaching of the Gospel, especially if the project entertained and assiduously aimed at by the founders of the Mission--namely the general reunion of the Armenians in this kingdom with the Church of Rome— is realized.[78]

After 1658, when they had secured the support of the Safavid Prime Minister,[79] the Jesuits were finally permitted to obtain a house in the newly established Erewan quarter of New Julfa, where many European residents of Iran were settled.[80] Father Alexander of Rhodes—also known as Rhodes of Vietnam for his thirty years of service in the Far East—had already arrived in Isfahan in 1655, to head the Jesuit mission.[81] A few years earlier, on his way back from the Far East to Rome, he had passed through Isfahan and had found there at least ten

---

[74] See Appendix I, doc. #19.
[75] *A Chronicle of the Carmelites,* vol. I, pg. 381.
[76] Terzean M., *Yakob D. Ĵulayecĭ,* Beirut, 1956, pg. 11.
[77] Machault, Jacques de, pg. 697.
[78] Ibid., pg. 701.
[79] Ibid., pg. 705.
Rabbath P.A., *Documents Inédits pour servir à l'histoire du Christianisme en Orient,* vol. I, Paris, 1907, p. 84.
[80] Chardin, Jean. vol. II, pg. 107.
[81] Machault, Jacques de, pp. 681-685.

Carmelite and five Capuchin missionaries. He had also made the following observations:

> In this great conclave of all nations of the world I found so few Catholics, there were practically as many religious as lay Christians. I had the great consolation of seeing three fine convents of religious there who enjoy the free exercise of their faith, each wearing his habit without anyone offering him the slightest affront. The King guarantees them this freedom, as great as they could enjoy in France.[82]

At his establishment in Isfahan at the head of a group of five Jesuit missionaries and having secured a foothold in New Julfa, Father Alexander started his new mission, being convinced that "the poor Armenians, who are schismatics and Eutychian heretics... can be persuaded to relinquish their errors without any fear."[83] But soon, like most other missionaries, he found success with only dying children. In the words of his biographer:

> The first and most important fruits won in early days by our missionaries in this promising field was the Baptism of a number of small children on the point of death. This could be done easily, as the parents themselves often brought them, in the hope of procuring some bodily remedy for them; when, however, the case was so serious that the Fathers judged that there was no hope of recovery, they secured Eternal Life for these children by means of Baptism.[84]

Besides the few Catholic families, namely the Šahrimaneans and the Larameans who had migrated from Old Julfa in 1605, the missionaries had practically no followers or converts among the Armenians. According to Bishop Joseph of Hierapolis, a Carmelite, there were only six Armenian Catholic families in New Julfa in 1658.[85] According to the famous traveler Jean Baptiste Tavernier, who was a protestant and understandably had little respect for the Catholic missionaries, in the mid-seventeenth century, the number of the Catholic teachers was far greater than the number of hearers and the Armenians were "so obstinately fixed to their own religion, that they would hear of no other; and nothing but money had sometimes caused them to feign the

---

[82] Rhodes of Viet Nam, *The Travels and Missions of Father Alexander de Rhodes in China and other Kingdoms of the Orient*, Maryland, 1966, pp. 222-223.

[83] Ibid., pp. 224-225.

[84] Machault, Jacques de, pp. 687, 705. Also see, Rabbath P.A., vol. II, pp. 310-311.

[85] *A Chronicle of the Carmelites*, vol. I, pp. 381-382.

embracing of another."[86] Yet the reports sent to Rome by the missionaries were full of false or exaggerated accounts. Even so, Father Felix of St. Anthony admitted in a report to the Propaganda Fide, dated 1673, that:

> I suppose your Eminences there wish to hear the truth, and do not desire to be deceived with the false and exagerated accounts, which greatly transcend the limits of the truth... as to the conversion of Muhammadans, save for one now and then and a marvel, there are no conversions at all, not from any failure on the part of the missionaries, who do their best, but by the suitable design of God, who has not yet raised the veil from the eyes of these poor people. For the space of 26 years approximately that I have been in the East I have neither heard of any conversion of a Muhammadan, except of one or two and that very rarely, nor among the Armenians, more than very few, for they are obstinate and deceitful... But, as there are some here who have had some reports printed of the great progress made, the harvest and conversions which certain religious have effected—which are all fables and fictions—I beg to inform your Most Illustrious Lordship that such false accounts have caused much scandal and distinct harm to the Faith, and to the authority of ecclesiastical reports.[87]

Following the conversion of an Armenian monk named Yovhan *Vardapet* to Islam in 1671, and the charges he brought against the Armenian Church, the bishop of New Julfa and his vicar were jailed for six months by the Safavid authorities.[88] The Catholic missionaries were shaken by these events as well. For a certain time, they avoided public activities or any appearance at the court.[89] Even a few years later, in 1675, they were mainly occupied with secret negotiations with Kaťołikos Yakob Ĵułayeći, trying to convince him that in his undertakings for the liberation of Armenia, he should seek the assistance of the Christian princes, particularly the King of France. And, in order to secure that assistance, first "he should acknowlege the Pope's Sovereign Authority and submit himself thereto."[90]

By the end of the 1670's, the struggle between the Armenian Church and the Catholic missionaries intensified again. In 1679, the Armenian merchants of New Julfa were ordered by their primate, bishop Dawiť, not to maintain any relationship with the Franks.[91] Marriages between

---

[86] Tavernier, J.B., pg. 160.
[87] *A Chronicle of the Carmelites*, vol. I, pg. 449.
[88] See pp. 108-109.
[89] *A chronicle of the Carmelites*, vol. I, pg. 407.
Chardin, Jean. vol. I, pg. 310.
[90] Chardin, Jean. vol. I, pg. 350-351.
[91] Terzean M., pp. 11-12.

Armenians and Catholics were forbidden.[92] Consequently, the few Armenian Catholics of New Julfa, particularly members of the famous Šahrimanean family were faced with great difficulties. Five brothers of the Šahrimanean family, whose wealth was estimated to be 70,000 *tomans*,[93] were the main financial supporters of the Catholic missionaries in Iran during the last quarter of the seventeenth century. They annually paid 30 *tomans* to the Carmelites alone.[94] They also sustained the cost of the construction and maintenance of churches and houses for the missionaries and provided them with income generating properties.[95] For their daily spiritual needs and the education of their children and followers, they even established a private Catholic institution, headed by Father Basil, an Armenian Catholic priest who graduated from the Urban college of Rome.[96] As a result, they were disliked by the community and were socially isolated. In marriages, they were "unable to find anyone of a condition in life equal to themselves," therefore, the missionaries were compelled to request on their behalf special permission from Rome, to "form unions in the second degree of consanguinity."[97]

In 1682, a new figure emerged on the scene of the conflict between the Armenians and the Catholics. Father Elias of S. Albert, the prior of the Carmelite convent of Isfahan joined Father Basil at the Catholic institution of the Šahrimaneans.[98] For the following two decades, he became the most active and dominant missionary and helped create the sharpest encounter between the Armenians and the Catholics. Thanks to his enormous correspondence with Rome, we have very detailed (although often exaggerated and biased) information on the affairs of New Julfa between 1682 and 1705.[99]

As we already noted, Bishop Dawit̀ of New Julfa died in 1683 and was succeeded by Bishop Step̀anos J̌ułayeći,[100] who was to lead the opposition to the Catholics. The following fifteen years, until his tragic death in early 1698, Step̀anos faced a chain of vicissitudes, due to his uncompromising opposition both to the Catholics and Kat̀ołikos Nahapet Edesaći of Ējmiacin.[101]

92 *A Chronicle of the Carmelites*, vol. I, pg. 456.
93 Ibid., vol. I, pg. 458.
94 Ibid., vol. I, pg. 501.
95 Ibid., vol. I, pp. 436, 500-501.
96 Ibid., vol. I, pg. 457.
97 Ibid., vol. I, pg. 458.
98 Ibid., vol. I, pg. 456.
99 Ibid., vol. I, pg. 456-512.
100 See pg. 95.
101 See tpp. 96-102.

Shortly after being installed as primate, Steṗanos focused his attention on the printing press of All Saviour's monastery, which had been closed for almost thirty years. This press could serve as a very effective tool to counterbalance the Catholic propaganda. Consequently, he published, with the assistance of his fellow monks, the following three volumes between 1687 and 1688:

— *Girḳ Atenakan or Asi Vičabanakan* (Book of Discourse or Polemics) by Ałek'sandr Ĵułayeči .

— *Girḳ Žołova čoy Ẓnddem Erkabnakač* (A collection against the Dyophysites), which included treatises from the following Armenian and other anti-Chalcedonian church fathers: Mat̓usała Siwneči, Steṗanos Siwneči, Połos Taronači, Steṗanos Siwneči son of Prince Tarsayič, Grigor Tat̓ewači and the Syrian Jacobite Patriarch Michael.

— *Girḳ Hamarot Vasn Iskapes Čšmarit Hawatoy-Dawanu t̓iwn Hayoč ew Neracu t̓iwn Anułič* by Yovhannēs *Vardapet* Ĵułayeči-Mrkuz. Also entitled in Latin *Symbolum Armeniorum et Introductio de Di Directam.*

All these works were purely anti-Catholic in nature and were written or compiled by wellknown monks at the All Saviour's Monastery. The books were printed in a relatively large quantity, five hundred copies,[102] at a total cost of two hundred *tomans*.[103] According to the introduction of the third book, more publications were planned.[104] But due to unknown reasons, no further publications appeared.

In response to a letter of recommendation from the Holy Roman Emperor, Shah Sulayman granted the Carmelites in 1683 full permission "to establish themselves anywhere in the Shah's realm, without any hindrance."[105] Consequently, New Julfa was once again invaded by Catholic missionaries. With the financial assistance of Šahrimanean brothers, a new Carmelite convent was established in New Julfa. In 1694, a total of more than 25 missionaries were on duty in New Julfa alone.[106] Father Elias, who had resigned his office as prior of the Carmelite convent at Isfahan and was permanently settled in New Julfa, had adopted a very effective method to secure followers among poor Armenians. In an anonymous report describing the duties carried out by the Carmelites in Iran, the following agenda was presented:

> In Julfa the principal mission work consists of singing mass to Gregorian Chant and preaching every Sunday and feast-day. When the

---

[102] Minasean L.G., *Nor Ĵułayi Tparann u ir Tpagrač Grk'erə*, pg. 58.

[103] Steṗanos Ĵułayeči, *Ktak,*.

[104] Minasean L.G., *Nor Ĵułayi Tparann u ir Tpagrač Grk'erə*, pg. 58.

[105] *A Chronicle of the Carmelites* vol. I, pg. 458.

[106] Ibid., vol. I, pp. 459-461.

sermon is over, the Catholics, on leaving the Church, are in the habit of giving some small alms for distribution to the poor, who gather in large numbers. They remain round the church till the end of the office. When all is over, one or two of our scholars get them together and make them sit in a circle: the hour-glass is turned, and they begin to teach them the catechism for one hour: after that the alms are distributed among them. On the other days of the week there is school—usually 60-80 Catholics and heretics: some have to be taught to read and write Armenian, others rhetoric and others philosophy and the older ones too the moral theology of Blessed Albert, geometry, etc.[107]

Naturally, the leaders of the Armenian community, headed by Bishop Step̄anos J̌ulayeći and the *kalantar* of New Julfa, also used every possible means, including bribes, to gain the support of Safavid officials and protect their people against the Catholic encroachment. But gaining the sympathy of Shah Sulayman was not easy. In 1692, a petition signed by six hundred Armenians was presented to the Shah, protesting against Father Elias. But the Shah "tore in pieces the memorial, saying that for the sake of 'four dogs of Armenians' he was not going to invite the hostility of the Christian princes, who had recommended to him the Carmelites."[108]

Encouraged by the negative attitude of the Shah towards the Armenians, Father Elias attempted to expand his premises in New Julfa. According to his long report dated July 1694, he negotiated the purchase of a house adjacent to his own house, planning to build a new church. An Armenian crowd, headed by the bishop and the *kalantar*, went to the house in question and pressured the landowner into canceling the agreement. The crowd was dispersed by armed men sent by the Polish ambassador, Father Ignatius Zapolski, himself a Jesuit. To avoid any further disturbances, the *kalantar* of New Julfa tried to convince Father Elias to be satisfied with the house and the church he already possessed and abandon his plans for the construction of a new church. The *kalantar* was rebuffed and the foundations of the new church were laid in the presence of the Catholic archbishop of Naxčawan, the Polish ambassador and all the missionaries and catholics of New Julfa.[109]

In 1694, a new petition signed by nine hundred Armenians was presented to the Queen Mother, patron of New Julfa, bitterly complaining against Father Elias and the Šahrimanean brothers. Having learned about the petition, all the Catholic missionaries presented the

107 Ibid., vol. I, pp. 517-518.
108 Ibid., vol. I, pg. 460.
109 Ibid., vol. I, pp. 461-463.

following joint proposals to the *kalantar* of New Julfa, as a precondition for any possible compromise:

> a) That they (the Armenians should allow them (the missionaries) to reside in peace at Julfa, without molesting them, both because the Persian King had so given orders, and because a like liberty (of residence) is allowed in Europe to all Armenians, both ecclesiastics and lay-people;
> b) That they should not speak ill of the Pope and of our countries;
> c) That they should molest no one going to communion with us, or having dealings with us.[110]

Reasonable as they seemed, the proposed terms were not acceptable from the Armenian point of view, because they indicated that the missionaries were trying to solidify their presence in New Julfa and to secure a peaceful environment for future activities. Therefore, they ignored the proposals. The missionaries, having not received an answer from the *kalantar*, were prepared to approach the Shah and present their own complaints against the Armenians, when they were taken by surprise and deeply shaken.

In response to a request made by the Queen Mother, Shah Sulayman ordered his *Divan-begi*[111] to raze the new church to its foundations, expel the Carmelites from New Julfa and collect a fine of 550 *tomans* from the Šahrimanean brothers. The order was carried out promptly.[112] Father Elias who has described all these events in great details, concludes his report by making the following suggestion to the Propaganda Fide:

> In any event, in order to insure the mission and the Bishop of Isfahan (whom I hear you have chosen me, all unworthy, to be) against similar insults from the schismatics, all here are of opinion that it would be very expedient to show some resentment of such violences against the principal leaders of this persecution, who are the *Kalantar Khwajeh* Lucas (whose brother *Khwajeh* Kalandarandeh and Stepanos, father of Aviet who too helped much to fan this fire, perhaps are still in Venice, or in Leghorn), Hovannes and his son Gregory,... their correspondents and agents, some of whom are always in those parts of Italy. If here they were to hear but once that the smallest reprisal would be made against them for the harm caused to Catholics, financial interest being the mainspring of all actions with these people, all here would come to our feet, and be the first to beg the court to have satisfaction given us, in order to obtain by our mediation their effects there.[113]

---

[110] Ibid., vol. I, pg. 464.
[111] The Lord High Justice.
[112] Ibid., vol. I, pp. 464-466.
[113] Ibid., vol. I, pg. 467.

Early in 1695, Father Elias was successful in obtaining a favorable decree from the newly installed Shah Sultan Husayn for his return to New Julfa. But once again, with the help of the Queen Mother, Stepanos Julayeci obtained another order from the Shah, which not only restricted Father Elias to Isfahan, but also threatened to expel all the other missionaries from New Julfa. Under these circumstances, Father Elias reported the following to Rome:

> So now, humanly speaking, there remains no other hope of preserving the Catholic community here except that suggested in my previous letters, either some embassy to the new king with congratulations on his accession to the throne, accompanied by complaints about the terms thus infringed, or else some resentment to be manifested against the schismatic Armenians trafficking in all parts of Christendom, in order that they themselves be obliged to arrange for the fire they have lit here to be extinguished.[114]

Bishop Stepanos Julayeci, who for several years had also led a strong opposition to Katolikos Nahapet Edesaci, as we have seen, now won the approval of Shah Sultan Husayn for his move to Ejmiacin and his elevation to the pontifical seat. When he left New Julfa,[115] in October 1696, the Catholic missionaries were in a very weak position. Before his departure, he left a written testimony, in which, he listed among other achievements, his victory over the Catholics with a total expenditure of 200 *tomans*.[116]

Stepanos was consecrated Katolikos on November 2, 1696, but his success received a set back almost at once. Three months later, Katolikos Nahapet Edesaci and a renegade former *kalantar* of New Julfa, supported by the Jesuits, succeeded in obtaining a new decree from the Shah, in favour of Nahapet. As a result, Stepanos Julayeci was deposed and thrown in prison, where he died in January 1698.[117]

In December 1696, Father Elias was consecrated Bishop of Isfahan. At the same time the Portuguese Ambassador Don Gregorio Fereira Fidalgo personally delivered a letter from the Pope to Shah Sultan Husayn and obtained a new decree in favour of the missionaries. On February 27, 1697, Bishop Elias, "with the Shah's *raqam* [decree] placed on his hat" and surrounded by all the missionaries, made a triumphant re-entry into New Julfa and "made the round of the Armenian

---

114 Ibid., vol. I, pg. 475.
115 See pg. 117.
116 Stepanos Julayeci, *Ktak,*.
117 See pp. 117-118.

township" on horseback.[118] Four months later he wrote to Pope Innocent XII:

> With the expression of gratitude due I lay at the feet of Your Holiness the reply from the King of the Persians to the Briefs, which You had deigned to write in our favour with regard to the matter of our expulsion from Julfa, and along with this I offer you the congratulations of a joyful heart for the success so desired, which the recommendation of so great weight and authority has obtained. For from it there ensued the restoration of our apostolic mission in this chief colony of the Armenians: and thus the bishopric of Isfahan becomes established in the midst of exulting Catholics and of schismatics gnashing their teeth.[119]

Indeed, Bishop Elias had reason to be delighted and hope for a new and prosperous era of missionary work, since Stepanos, "the declared enemy of the Franks" was eliminated and Ałeksandr Julayeči, the new bishop, and the people of New Julfa—who continued their opposition to Katolikos Nahapet—, were "separated not only from the Roman Church, but also from their own Patriarch."[120] His enthusiasm was not to be long lived. In 1699 he witnessed the fall of his prime supporters: the Šahrimanean brothers.[121]

Bishop Elias returned at once to Rome with the following three primary objectives:

---

[118] *A Chronicle of the Carmelites*, vol. I, pp. 478-480.

[119] Ibid., vol. I, pg. 478.

[120] Ibid., vol. I, pg. 482.

[121] The famous French merchant-traveller Jean Baptiste Tavernier had established cooperation with the Šahrimanean brothers and had invested with them a large amount of money. When he died in 1689, the money was still deposited with the Šahrimaneans. Few years later, a certain adventurer known as Count Philip de Zaghly or Imam-quli Beg arrived Isfahan and claimed the inheritance of Tavernier. According to the missionary sources, Philip de Zaghly was the son of an Armenian goldsmith from New Julfa. As a young man he had travelled to Europe, where he had spent more than twenty years. He had specially befriended with the brother of King Louis XIV, had converted to Catholicism, had been rebaptised, taking the name Philip de Zaghly, and had married Tavernier's sister in law. On his return to Iran, he had converted to Shi'ism, taking the name Imam-quli Beg.
In Isfahan, taking advantage of his muslim status and supported by a former Prior of the Augustinian mission, named Antonio, Philip de Zaghly claimed 28,000 *tomans* from the Šahrimanean brothers for Tavernier's original investment and accumulated interests. Broken by severe pressure and harsh persecution, two of the four Šahrimanean brothers converted to Islam, hoping to save their wealth. Their apostasy was a terrible blow for the Catholic missionaries in Iran, whom it deprived of their main financial source. See Gulbenkian R., "Philip de Zagly...", *Revue des Études Arméniennes*, N.S. VII (1970), pp. 361-426. Also *A Chronicle of the Carmelites* vol. I, pp. 484-486.

a) To secure financial assistance for the missionaries in Iran,

b) to develop broader political support for their cause in Iran,

c) to create obstacles for the Armenian merchants of New Julfa trading in Europe and force them to compromise with the missionaries. He spent eight years in Europe, meeting with the Pope, the cardinals of the Propaganda Fide, and lobbying at various European courts. He secured new funds and obtained letters of commendation from Pope Clement XI and several Christian princes, addressed to Shah Sultan Husayn. But he died in Lisbon, on his way back to Iran.[122]

The tension between the Armenians and the missionaries was briefly eased between 1699 and 1705. Bishop Aleksandr Julayeći, the new primate of New Julfa was mainly occupied with leading the opposition to Kaťolikos Nahapet Edesaći,[123] while the troubles of Šahrimanean brothers and the absence of Bishop Elias checked the initiatives of the Catholics. Nevertheless, the bishop, the *kalantar* and the Armenian clergy of New Julfa complained once more in a petition presented to the Safavid Court in 1705, against a certain "Frank missionary-ambassador," who had presented to them "unacceptable offers" and had tried to impose certain obligations on them.[124]

With the death of Kaťolikos Nahapet in 1705 and the election of Bishop Aleksandr Julayeći as Kaťolikos of Ējmiacin, the decade long conflict between Ējmiacin and the diocese of New Julfa was finally resolved in favor of the latter. In his new position, Kaťolikos Aleksandr, an ardent anti-Catholic, would now be free to devote all his energies to the elimination of the Catholic missionaries in Eastern Armenia and Iran. In 1706 Kaťolikos Aleksandr left New Julfa for Ējmiacin. On his way he visited Tabriz and found the Catholic missionaries operating freely and aggressively within the local Armenian community. In a letter dated August 7, 1706 and addressed to Movsēs Julayeći, his successor in the diocese of New Julfa, he reported:

> We arrived safely in Tabriz on August 2 and found the city in turmoil and confusion, because the accursed and wicked Catholics had persecuted the Orthodox faithful even more severely than Diocletian and Maximian. They have imposed a collatoral on the priests to prevent them from preaching against the Francs in the churches, ... they have imposed a bond of fifty *tomans* on laymen, who slander the Francs and prevent their fellow Armenians from visiting the houses of

---

[122] Ibid., vol. I, pp. 485-513.

[123] See pp. 119-121.

[124] Hakobyan T. H., "*Hayeri Paykarə Kaťolikakan Misionerneri Asimilyatorakan Jgtumneri Dem Iranum (XVII-XVIII D.D.)," Arewelagitakan Žołovacu*, vol I, Erevan, 1960, pg. 276.

the Francs... We sent Bejanbeg to *Jahnšin*[125] [sic] to ask him why was he ignoring our one thousand and two hundred years old tradition? He replied as follows: 'I do not exchange the dog of an Armenian with one thousand Francs. I also know that they have paid some gold to obtain that *eltezam*.[126] I can not do anything against the order. Bring me a new order and I will hang them along with dogs' ... You must obtain such an order—signed and sealed by the shah—that whenever an Armenian is proved to be Catholic, the local judge should give him a warning, declare his conversion invalid, make him pay fines and punish him... We must obtain an order to prevent them [the missionaries] from living in Tabriz.[127]

In 1707, Katotikos Alekśandr also presented the following petition to Shah-quli Khan, the governor of Tabriz:

This is to inform and petition your lordship and sovereignty that our first and last request from you will be the following: Let the Armenians be Armenian and the Francs be Franc. But, the Francs want to preserve their identity and convert the Armenians. We do not accept that. We do not want to see the King's subjects become Francs, like the twenty six persons from Tabriz, priests and laymen who went to the country of the Francs and did not return. It is thirty years now since they became Francs.

Now we ask your Highness for an order and decree, indicating that the Armenians should remain Armenian and the Francs should remain Franc. The Armenians should not go to the Church of the Francs and they should not be allowed to send their children to their schools. If they do, they should be considered guilty and the local judge should punish them...

We will be grateful if you show us mercy; otherwise, respond to our pleas once and for all, saying: Let the subjects of the King of Kings become Franc. Our lives and rights are in your hands.[128]

Katotikos Alekśandr's initiatives against the Catholics of Tabriz appear to have alarmed the missionaries. At least two missionary reports dated 1707[129] describe the "fear" of the people, of having any contact with them. According to one of these reports, Katotikos Alekśandr asked the governor of Tabriz "not to permit the Armenians to come to our church, but to punish them (for it) and, if they want to abandon their faith, to compel them to adopt Muhammadanism rather

---

[125] Possibly *Janeshin* - vice governor.
[126] Collatoral.
[127] See Appendix I, doc. #20.
[128] See Appendix I, Doc. # 21.
[129] *A Chronicle of the Carmelites,* vol. I, pg. 521. One of the reports is dated 1704. It must be a typographical error.

than Catholicism." In this report, the content of Ałekّsandr's letter to the governor is clearly falsified and exagerated, indicating the panic of the missionaries. In the letter of Ałekّsandr, which is quoted above and fully presented in the Apendix I (doc. #21) of this study, there is no suggestion to compel anybody "to adopt Muhammadanism rather than Catholicism."

The pontificate of Katّolikos Ałekّsandr Ĵułayeči (1706-1714) strengthened the Armenian Church internally and restored the authority of Ējmiacin, shaken under the katّolikoi Yakob Ĵułayeči (1655-1680) and Nahapet Edesači (1692-1705). But, perhaps even more importantly, it marked almost the final defeat of the Catholic missionaries in Eastern Armenia and Iran.

According to Father Jacques Villotte, a Jesuit missionary who spent twelve years (1696-1708) in Isfahan and other parts of the Safavid Kingdom,[130] Katّolikos Ałekّsandr persecuted the Catholics not only in Tabriz, but also in Ganja, Šamaxi and Tbilisi. Father Villotte also blames his arch-enemy the Katّolikos for the "death of many Armenian Catholics" in Constantinople.[131] This accusation stems from the petition sent to Katّolikos Ałekّsandr from the Armenians of Constantinople, signed by 448 individuals and dated December 20, 1706, protesting against the abduction of their Patriarch Awetikّ by the Catholics and requesting the assistance of the Katّolikos for his liberation. The names of 175 Armenian supporters of the Catholics were listed in the petition. Katّolikos Ałekّsandr wrotc to the Ottoman Grand Vezir, complaining against the aggressive behaviour of the Catholics. Consequently, eleven Armenians suspected of having opposed Patriarch Awetikّ and collaborated with Charles Feriol, the French ambassador in Constantinople and the Jesuit missionaries, who had arranged the abduction and the transportation of the Armenian Patriarch to France, were tried and sentenced to death or to conversion to Islam. Ten of them apostatised and only one Armenian priest, Gomitas Kĕomiwrčean opted for a martyr's death.[132]

The Catholic missionaries of Isfahan were greatly weakened and reduced in number,[133] when, Pierre Victor Michel, a secretary at the French Embassy of Constantinople, arrived in Isfahan in 1708, as an envoy of King Louis XIV and successfully negotiated the first official

---

[130] Sefeanč M. Y., "*Haykaban Vardapet mi Yisusean,*" *Bazmavep,* 1922, pp. 326-327.
[131] Cited from a manuscript of Jacques Villotte by Tĕr Yovhaneanč , vol. II, pp. 47-48.
[132] Ormanean M., vol. II, pp. 2751-2759.
[133] *A Chronicle of the Carmelites* vol. I, pp. 516-517.

trade agreement between France and Iran.[134] As part of the treaty, Michel negotiated an article for the protection of Catholic missions in Iran, according to which, the Shah undertook the following:

> The French bishops and (other) religious residing in the whole of our empire shall be able to say their prayers and carry out their religious duties in the places and houses where they shall be lodged, without anyone being able to prevent them or trouble them... as to the Europeans living at Naxčawan and other places in our empire, nobody shall contravene the decrees which have been granted to them in the past or shall trouble them. We promise, besides that, to confirm and ratify the decrees which our predecessors have granted them, and if those of the Armenian nation or the religious of the other nations of Europe have attacked them and maltreated them... against right and reason, they shall, after proof and conviction be made to pay into the royal treasury the sum of 50 Tabrizi tomans.[135]

The Catholic missionaries undoubtedly benefitted from the French envoy's visit to Iran, but their success proved only temporary. Soon after Michel's departure from Iran, Katołikos Ałeksandr and Movsēs, the bishop of New Julfa obtained in June 1710, a decree from Shah Sultan Husayn, which not only cancelled all the privileges and rights granted to the missionaries, but also ordered regional and local Iranian officials not to allow the Catholics to interfere in the religious affairs of the Armenians in order to convert them or to bring their children to Catholic churches and schools. The Catholics were also forbidden to marry Armenian women, to purchase lands or to build churches in Iran.[136]

In his effort to curtail the activities of the Catholic missionaries, Katołikos Ałeksandr even maintained correspondence with Pope Clement XI. In a letter dated February 25, 1709, the Katołikos addressed the Pope with expressions of Christian love and high respect. After elaborate compliments for the pope and his spiritual leadership, the katołikos presented the confession of the Armenian Church in trying to convince the Pontif of the Roman Catholic Church that the Armenians were genuine Christians, not schismatics or heretics, as presented by the Catholic missionaries. Then he bitterly complained against the missionaries, in the following words:

---

[134] Savory R., pg. 122.

[135] Lockhart L., pg. 450. While in Iran, the French envoy also succeeded in exposing the manipulations of Philip de Zaghly and have him beheaded by the governor of Tabriz, thus eliminating a very dangerous enemy of the Catholics. Ibid., pp. 144-145.

[136] A copy of Shah Sultan Husayn's decree in the archives of Caro Owen Minasean at UCLA Library.

We can state in the clearest possible way that we live among such people who do not accept Christ as God and do not follow him. However they do not bother us, or make us to suffer. They live with us in peace and love, even when we debate with them the Divinity of Christ and his teachings, or when we praise the Christian faith... Also our King... who is a non-Christian... care for us and protect us...

But the fathers [Catholic missinaries] who have come to our country behave differently by opposing us and by creating obstacles for us. And when we complain against their behaviour, they present to your greatness false and groundless reports. Being unaware [of the reality] you believe them. In the presence of non-Christians, they call the Armenians schismatic and heretic.

Now, based on the above presented confession, if you condemn the Armenians as schismatic, blessed be the will of your Holiness. Otherwise, we beg you, the father of all, to warn them [the missionaries] in writing, so that they may correct their mistakes, because this situation is not befitting to the name of Your Holiness. If for the hope and love of Christ and as a caring father you grace us with the requested favor and send the letter through us, we will accept it as the godgiven commendments to Moses and will show it to the fathers [missionaries], so that they may be restrained in their hatred towards the Christians... Also we would like to ask you to grant [or return] the Armenian Church in Venice, because the poor Armenians who live there, are deprived from communion and all other sacraments.[137]

---

137 Ałekʻsandr's letter was first published by Y. Tēr Yovhaneančʻ in *Aršaloys Araratean*, Smirna, 1857, ## 557-555. Later it was reproduced in his work, vol. II, pp. 38-46. Եւ զի յստակագոյն ասացմոր, մեք որ բնակեալ եմք ի մէջ այսպիսի ազգաց, որ ոչ ընդունին զքրիստոս Աստուած եւ ոչ են պաշտոնեայք քրիստոսի, ոչինչ իրիք զգուշցուցանեն զմեզ կամ տառապեցուցանեն, այլ մանաւանդ կան ընդ մեզ խաղաղութեամբ եւ սիրով, յաւէտ եւս զի յոլով անգամ ընդդիմաբանեմք ընդ նոսա, եւ վիճեմք յաղագս Աստուածութեան քրիստոսի եւ օրինաց նորա, եւ լինիմք քատագով քրիստոնէութեան կրօնից, ... Այլ եւ թագաւորն մեր... եւ սա այլազգ է... այսպիսի գթով գթայ եւ նախախնամեալ պահպանէ զմեզ...

Իսկ առ մեզ եկեալ պատրիքն ոչ այսպէս, այլ ներհակական վարին ընդ մեզ, խոչընդակն առնելով, եւ յորժամ ներհակեմք անկարգ արարմանց նոցին՝ զուր եւ ունայն բանիք ամբաստան լինին առ մեծութիւն ձեր, եւ անիրործ գոլով նոցին բանից հաւատայք, բանցի ի մէջ այլասեհիցն, զհայք հերձումող եւ հերետիկոս անուանեն: Այլ ըստ վերոյ գրեալ դաւանութեանցն եթէ մեծապատումութիւն բոյ զհայս հերետիկոս դատապարտես, եղիցի կամք վեհափառութեանդ օրհնեալ իսկ եթէ ոչ, խնդրեմք ի հաւարակագ հորէդ որ այնանխեցագ սատ սպանանեցագ գրես որ դադարին յայնպիսի սխալութենէ, զի եւ Սրբազան անոնն Տեառնդ ոչ է վայելոչ այնպիսի իրակութիւն: Եթէ վասն յուսոյն եւ սիրոյն քրիստոսի այդ շնորհ մեզ առնիցես ըստ հայրախնամ գթոյդ, Նոցա թողութ առաքես ի ձեռ մեր, եւ ընկալեալ մեր իբր զԱստուածատուր պատգամն Մովսիսի, ցուցցմոք պատրոնացն թերեւս սակաւ մի կասեցին յաւէլութենէ քրիստոնէից: ... Նաեւ շնորհել մաղթեմք եկեղեցին հայոց ի Վենետիկ, բանցի ողորմելի ազգն հայոց որք անդր են առանց հաղորդութեան եւ ամենայն խորհրդոց:

In Rome, however, this letter was translated into Latin by the Jesuit missionary Father Jacques Villotte, who interpreted the document as a letter of submission to the Catholic Church.[138] His translation presumably misled the Pope, who, responded to the Katolikos on March 15, 1710, and sent him with a document containing the Catholic confession and urging the Katolikos to accept and sign this document for the final admission of the Armenian Church into the Catholic fold.[139]

In April 16, 1711, even before receiving the Pope's answer, Katolikos Aleksandr repeated his appeal to the pope and wrote a second letter, whose content was almost identical with that of the first.[140] This second letter, was taken to Rome by Archbishop Tovma Vanandeci, who was unable to meet the pope, so that, the letter remained undelivered.[141]

Presumably angered by the pope's attitude, Katolikos Aleksandr never responded to his letter. Instead, in October 1711, he travelled back to New Julfa,[142] creating a great panic among the Catholic missionaries. A few days after Aleksandr's arrival in New Julfa, Father Paul Augustine, a Carmelite stationed in Isfahan, reported the following to the Cardinal prefect of the Propaganda Fide:

> So your Eminence should know that about 20 years ago this patriarch wrote and gave to be printed a booklet[143] (which I have read) in which he spoke with very great contempt of the Holy See, S. Leo and the Council of Chalcedon,and this booklet, about one finger thick, was read by those who have so ill informed Your Eminence: to say that since then the Patriarch has changed signifies nothing; because besides that book still remaining in circulation, on receiving the reply from His Holiness he (Aleksandr) cast ridicule on that letter... and now he has come here to molest us. What will be God knows.[144]

During Katolikos Aleksandr's visit to New Julfa, Monseigneur Gratien de Galiczean, titular Bishop of Agathopolis and Bishop

---

[138] J. Villotte, *Meknutiwn Dawanutean Utlapari Hawatoy* (Explanation Professionis Fidei Orthodoxae), Rome 1711, pp. 79-82.
Based on the interpretation of J. Villotte, Father Michel Camcean and some other 19th century Armenian Catholic scholars, who have not seen the text of Alek'sandr's letter, have accepted the theory of submission. (See Camcean M., *Patmut'iwn Hayoc*, vol. III, pg. 749).
[139] See an Armenian translation of the Pope's letter in Galemkearean G., "*Yovakim V. Julayeci Arkepiskopos Ejmiacni,*" Handes Amsoreay, 1914, pp. 553-555.
[140] See the texts of Aleksandr's two letters Ibid., pp. 540-552. The second letter of Aleksandr is also published in *Maseac Alawni*, 1856, #5, pp. 110-123, and *Puros*, 1873, #2, pp. 6-28.
[141] Galemkearean G., Ibid., pg. 552.
[142] *A Chronicle of the Carmelites* , vol. I, pg. 523.
[143] Referring to *Girk Atenakan or Asi Vicabanakan*, New Julfa, 1687.
[144] Ibid., vol. I, pg. 524.

coadjutor of Babylon arrived at Isfahan to lodge an official protest on behalf of the King of France and the Pope, against the ill treatment of the Catholic missionaries, and obtained in April 1712, a decree in favour of the missionaries.[145] But, once again, Kaťolikos Aleksandr reacted and gave a final blow to Catholic aspirations throughout the Safavid Kingdom. In a decree dated November 1712, the Shah declared:

> At this time, the chief of the Christians, Aleksandr... petitioned us based on a royal decree issued in the month of *Rabi' Al-Thani*, 1122,[146] according to which the *Amirs*, the *Hakims* and the *Vazirs* of Iran must not allow anyone from among the Francs and Catholic missionaries to interfere in the religious affairs of the Armenians... We hereby issue a decree ordering that the Honorable Governors... implement all the terms of the previously issued decree, and in all circumstances act accordingly... Catholic missionaries and Francs living in Iran, particularly in the Royal capital of Isfahan, Tabriz, Gurjistan, Ganja, Qarabagh, Shirvan, Chukhur-i Sa'd and Hamadan... should not be allowed to interfere in the religious affairs of the Armenians or to mislead their children and youth and convert them to the religion of Franks and they should let them in every aspect act according to their religion and tradition. Nobody should prevent them from being governed by their own laws. In that respect, everybody should extend assistance to the Armenians and not permit some Armenians—who have converted to Catholicism—to go to Catholic churches and associate with the Catholics. All transgressors should be punished.[147]

The Catholic missionaries had unquestionably suffered a major defeat at the hands of Kaťolikos Aleksandr Julayeci. In two separate appeals, dated November 1713 and August 1714, Pope Clement XI desperately "begged" the Shah to protect the missionaries from "slanders, molestation and ill-treatment" and permit them "to dwell everywhere freely, and without any impediment and attend to the duties of their office."[148] However, the pope had nothing to offer in return, and Shah Sultan Husayn had no reason to please the pope or the Western powers anymore. He left the pope's letters unanswered.

When Kaťolikos Aleksandr, the "great persecutor" of the Catholics, died on March 12, 1714,[149] very few missionaries were left in the entire Safavid Kingdom.[150] Their very presence is largely ignored by the Armenian sources after 1715. An anti-Catholic document entitled *Dašanc̆*

---

[145] Lockhart L., pg. 454.
[146] May 31-June 28, 1710.
[147] See Appendix I, doc. # 22.
[148] *A Chronicle of the Carmelites* , vol. I, pp. 527-528.
[149] Ibid., vol. I, pg. 528.
[150] Ibid., vol. I, pp. 516-517.

Gir,[151] (Letter of Agreement) issued in 1721 by the Armenian clergy of New Julfa, simply refers to past missionary activities, when a few Armenians, "ignorant men and women" were misled by the missionaries and converted to Catholicism, in order to justify the words of St. Paul: "For there must be also heresies among you, that they which are approved may be made manifest among you."[152]

---

[151] AASM,
[152] I Cor. 11: 19.

CHAPTER EIGHT

THE DECLINE OF THE ARMENIAN COMMUNITY OF NEW JULFA

The prosperous years of the Armenian community of New Julfa were limited to five or six decades, 1615-1670, and were largely conditioned by the economic and ethnic policies of the Safavid rulers. Shah 'Abbas I and his two successors: Shah Safi and Shah 'Abbas II were well disposed towards the Armenian community of New Julfa, mainly because of the benefit of the Safavid economy, from the international trade endeavours of the Armenian merchants. However, during the reigns of Shah Sulayman (1666-1694) and Shah Sultan Husayn (1694-1722), the situation changed drastically, when the Armenian merchants experienced religious and economic pressures and most of them moved their trade headquarters, their families and their wealth out of Iran, causing the gradual decline of the community of New Julfa.

Before ascending to the Safavid throne, both Shah Sulayman and his son Shah Sultan Husayn were confined to the harem and had never received the necessary training for future kingship under the supervision of a tutor (*lala*). They both were under the great influence of eunuchs or Shi'ite clergy. Their administrations were marked by inefficiency and corruption at all levels of government, and there were no powerful ministers or military leaders to control the situation.[1] They had little tolerance for non-Shi'ite minorities, including the Armenians, and would not treat the community of New Julfa as an important

---

[1] *The Cambridge History of Iran*, vol. VI, pp. 304-331.
Lockhart L., pp. 25-34.

element for the economic prosperity of the country. The Armenians of New Julfa, who had enjoyed freedom in religious, cultural, economic and internal administrative matters for sixty years, felt the anti-Christian bias from the very beginning of Shah Sulayman's rule. In late 1660's, in a number of *Fatwas*[2] issued by the *Divan al-Sadarat*,[3] Kaťolikos Yakob Julayeči was quoted arguing that according to the existing laws, the Armenian subjects of the King have to pay *Jizya* once a year and only in the place of their permanent residence and not in other places where they travel for trade purposes. But the merchants were often forced to pay *Jizya* in various places during their travels and some of them pretended to have converted to Islam to avoid paying the same tax many times.[4]

In 1671, *Khwaja* Ałapiri, the *Kalantar* of New Julfa who was "a sort of half scholar"[5] and an ardent reader of philosophy[6] was persuaded by Shah Sulayman to convert to Islam. He apostatized in the presence of the Shah, the Grand Vazir and *Shaykh al-Islam* and was honored by the Shah with a "Royal Garment, of that sort which is given to Governors of provinces, with a horse, and the trappings set with precious stones."[7] Following the *Kalantar*'s conversion, the Grand Vazir sent for the Armenian clergy of New Julfa and told them:

> The king had a great zeal for their conversion, and that for his part, he should esteem it the greatest happiness of his life, if during the time of his Ministry, they would embrace the true Religion. They trembling made answer, that his Majesty having a world of Mahometan slaves, his Goodness might permit to live in the Religion of the Prophet Jesus Christ the humblest of his slaves, and let them have their churches, where they did nothing oftener, and with more fervour, than pray to God for his Majesty's life, and that their factors who were gone to Europe, would not return, which would be the loss of immense riches to the state; moreover that the Christian princes would not suffer them to traffick in their dominions any longer. This said, no further urgences were made to them on that account.[8]

On May 22, 1671, An Armenian monk named Yovhan, being punished for his rebellious acts against the authority of Bishop Dawiť,

[2] Judgment, verdict.

[3] The office of the supreme religious leader.

[4] Papazyan, H., "*Sefyan Irani Asimilyatorakan Kałakakanutyan Harci Šurja*", pp. 93-94.

[5] Chardin, Jean. vol. I, pg. 349.

[6] *Stepanos Dašteci*, pg. 48.

[7] Chardin, Jean. vol. I, pg. 350. "Habit Royal, de la sorte qu'on donne aux Gouverneurs de province, avec un cheval et le harnois de pierreries."

[8] Ibid., vol. I, pg. 350. English translation of the passage taken from Chardin's travels in Persia, Dover publications, New York, 1988, pg. 68.

the bishop of New Julfa and his Vicar, Step̌anos *Vardapet*, took refuge with the *Shaykh al-Islam*, converted to Islam and brought charges against the Armenian Church and clergy.[9] As a result, both Bishop Dawit̔ and Step̌anos *Vardapet* were jailed for more than six months, paid heavy fines,[10] the newly built monastery of Hazarǰarib (P̌eria) was destroyed, church treasuries were confiscated and with a royal edict, an annual tax of 424 *tomans* was imposed on the churches of New Julfa, P̌eria and Burwari.[11] For many years, the Armenians of New Julfa tried unsuccessfully to have the church taxes cancelled. Large amounts of money were spent for petition fees and bribes. In 1695 a royal edict was obtained from Shah Sultan Husayn, exempting the Armenian churches from the taxes imposed on them by Shah Sulayman in 1671.[12] Shah Sultan Husayn's edict of 1695 did not have much effect, nor did his three other edicts issued in 1703, 1709, and 1712 for the matter. The Armenian churches were forced to continue paying the annual taxes and other extra charges imposed by various state officials at least until the fall of the Safavid Kingdom.[13]

As already mentioned, in 1691, Awet, the *Kalantar* of New Julfa apostatized and caused a new uproar in the community. The Armenian clergy and the lay leadership of the community reacted fiercely and succeeded in ousting Awet and replacing him with *Kalantar* Łukas.[14]

Shah Sultan Husayn, a devoted Muslim, who was deeply concerned with religious affairs and was very closely associated with the Shi'ite clergy, adopted a number of measures against the non-Muslim minorities of Iran. Soon after his ascension to the throne in 1694, the Shah started building the palace of Farahabad on the south western edge of New Julfa, adjacent to the Armenian cemetery and Gawrabad, a quarter inhabited by 200 Zoroastrian families[15] along with few Armenians. That move brought the Shah into closer contact with his

---

[9] Zak̔aria Aguleci, pg. 103.
Minasean L.G., *Patmuti'wn P'eriayi Hayeri*, pp. 48-49.
[10] Tēr Awetisean S., vol. I, pp. 301-302.
[11] See the Armenian translation of the edict and the list of churches burdened with the 424 tomans annual tax in Tēr Yovhaneanc̔ Y., vol. II, pp. 239-242. A partial and slightly different list of churches and their respective taxes, dated 1675, has survived in AASM. (Cabine 1, file 35A).
[12] Step̌anos J̌ułayeci, *Ktak*. See the printed text in my article: *Step'anos kat'ołikos J̌ułayeci*, pg. 336. According to the will, which is dated November 13, 1695,175 *tomans* were spent for official petition fees, and an additional 40 *tomans* for bribes, to obtain the edict for the cancellation of the tax.
[13] Tēr Yovhaneanc̔ Y., vol. II, pp. 243-251.
[14] Step̌anos J̌ułayeci, *Ktak*. Also Appendix I., doc. #16.
[15] Tēr Yovhaneanc̔ Y., vol. I, pg. 202.

non-Muslim subjects. Manipulated by the Muslim clerics, the Shah issued a decree for the forcible conversion of the Zoroastrians to Islam. The name Gawrabad was changed to Husaynabad, the local Zoroastrian temple was destroyed and replaced with a mosque and a *Madrasa*.[16] A large number of Zoroastrians were compelled to turn Muslim and only a few were able to escape and reach Kerman, where the persecution was less severe.[17] The Armenians of New Julfa were subjugated to constant humiliations. The Shah personally visited the All Saviour's Monastery and entered into theological discussions with the Armenian monks, particularly with Yovhannēs *Vardapet* Mrk'uz.[18] Occasionally Muslim heralds were sent to New Julfa to announce special benefits and privileges for those Christians who would convert to Islam.[19] In order to be easily identified in public, the Armenians were forced to wear their shirts with the collar opened below the nape[20] and a tattered piece of cloth hanging on their back. They were not allowed to go into the city on horseback or enter the bazaar on a rainy day to avoid spoiling goods belonging to Muslim merchants with their wet clothes, or to have physical contact with the Muslims.[21] They were charged with the humiliating duty of carrying the bodies of executed criminals and were forced to pay an extra tax to cover the cost of cereals fed to the poultry of the royal household.[22] Thousands of tombstones in the Armenian cemetery were cut on one of the upper four angles by Muslims to symbolise the circumcision of the dead Christians and their conversion to Islam.[23]

Tadeusz Juda Krusinski, a Polish Catholic missionary, who for twenty years in early eighteenth century was the procurator of the Jesuits at Isfahan, provides the following example of anti-Christian bias under Shah Sultan Husayn:

> "Under the former kings justice was done them according to lex Talionis; but since Schah Hussein came to crown, the Moulahs

---

[16] Religious school.

[17] Lockhart L., pp. 72-73.

[18] See the text of the theological discussions between the Shah and Yovhannēs Mrḳuz in: Yovhannēs *Vardapet* J̣uɫayeči, *Vičapanut'iwn Aṙ Šah Slemann Parsič*, Calcutta, 1797.. Also see: Tēr Yovhaneanč Y., vol. I, pg. 202-203.

[19] Tēr Yovhaneanč Y., Ibid., vol. I, pg. 203.

[20] Ibid, vol. I, pg. 203. Also many references in AASM.

[21] Ibid., vol. I, pg. 203.

[22] See the Armenian translation of a decree issued by Shah Sultan Husayn in 1716, freeing the Armenians from the burden of carrying the bodies of executed criminals and the cereal tax for poultry, Ibid., vol. I, pg. 208.

[23] Ibid., vol. I, pg. 206.

pretended it was a shameful thing that a Mussulman's Head should pay for an infidel's, that is, in their phrase, a Christian. And on this principle they got it to be established, not by law but custom, in all the provinces, that every Mussulman who killed an Armenian should only be condemned to pay the defunct's family, for their nourishment as much corn as an ass can carry.[24]

The law of *Imam* Ja'far, according to which any convert to Islam was entitled to inherit the property of his non-Muslim relatives, was enforced more systematically by Muslim officials in the reigns of Shah Sulayman and more specially Shah Sultan Husayn, who was under the great influence of *Mullabashi* Muhammad Baqir Majlisi.[25] The impact of *Imam* Ja'far's law was best demonstrated in the case of Šahrimaneank, one of the most wealthy Armenian families of New Julfa, as presented in the previous chapter.[26]

For the protection of their faithful against the unjust law of apostasy, the Armenian Kat'olikoi Yakob Julayec'i (1655-1680), Aleksandr Julayec'i (1706-1714), Astuacatur Hamatanc'i (1715-1725) and the bishops of New Julfa presented many petitions to the Safavid rulers and state officials, mainly arguing that the Armenians who regularly pay their poll taxes and all other dues to the state are still pressured to become Muslim. New apostates are encouraged and supported by Islamic courts in claiming the inherited property of their distant relatives, even if the inheritance has been acquired many years before the apostasy of the claimant.[27]

In a letter dated 1714 and addressed to Movsēs *Vardapet*, the Archbishop of New Julfa, Kat'olikos Aleksandr stated: "... As you know, this country is devastated because many people go and betray the Christ for the sake of silver."[28] In another letter dated 1720 and addressed to the same Movsēs *Vardapet*, Kat'olikos Astuacatur Hamatanc'i reported on the receipt of a letter from the Ottoman territories, written, signed and sealed by five to six hundred Armenian merchants from eastern Armenia[29] and addressed to him and the governor of Erevan. The merchants had threatened not to return to their country, unless a royal

---

[24] Krusinski, Tadeusz Juda, S.J. *The History of the Late Revolutions of Persia...*, London, 1729, pg. 219.

[25] Savory, R., pg. 251.

[26] Pg. 148.

[27] Papazyan, H., "Sefyan Irani Asimilyatorakan K'alakakanutyan Harc̄ Šurja," pg. 92.

[28] AASM.

[29] The merchants in question were mostly from Erevan and the district of Goltn. This shows how well spread was the problem of apostasy throughout the Safavid kingdom.

decree was obtained against the unjust claims of *Jadid al-Islam*. Having the support of the governor, the Katołikos expressed hope of obtaining the requested edict.[30]

The Armenian merchants of New Julfa were experiencing the religious and economic pressures in Iran at a time when both Russia and the English East India Company in India were trying to co-opt them into their own service. Two agreements concluded with the Russian government in 1667 and 1673 respectively, gave the Armenian merchants of New Julfa the privilege of transit over the Russian territories.[31] Another agreement concluded with the English East India Company on June 22, 1688, stated:

> First, that the Armenian Nation shall now and at all times hereafter have equal share and benefit of all indulgences this Company have or shall at any time hereafter grant to any of their own Adventurers or other English Merchants whatsoever. Secondly, that they shall have free liberty at all times hereafter to pass and repass to and from India on any of the Company's ships on as adventagious terms as any Freeman whatsoever. Thirdly, that they shall have liberty to live in any of the company's cities, Garrisons, or Towns in India, and to buy, sell, and purchase Land or Houses, and be capable of all Civil Offices and preferments in the same manner as if they were Englishmen born, and shall always have a free and undisturbed liberty of the exercise of their own Religion... Fourthly, that they... may have liberty to trade in China, the Manillas, or any other parts or places within the limits of the company's charter, upon equal terms, duties, and freights with any free Englishman whatsoever.[32]

The trade agreements with Russia and the East India Company did not trigger an immediate mass exodus of Armenian merchants from Iran. However, they served as a point of departure for the gradual relocation of several prominent families to India, Russia and Europe, during the last quarter of the seventeenth century.[33] The exodus of the Armenian merchants from Iran became more common during the first two decades of the eighteenth century, when, under Shah Sultan Husayn, the anti-Christian bias in Iran had reached its peak. The departing merchants were taking their treasures out of Iran, thus precipitating the silver haemorrhage in Persia and causing the

---

[30] Ibid.

[31] Xačikyan Š.L., *Nor Jułayi Hay Vačarakanutyunə...*, pp. 21-22.

[32] Ferrier R.W., *The Agreement of the East India Company*, pp. 438-9.

[33] From the most prominent twenty families of New Julfa, Velijaneank, Gērakeank and Ałanureank settled in India. Nazareteank (later known as Lazareank), Xaldareank and Tarxaneank settled in Russia. A part of Šahrimaneank settled in Italy. See Tēr Yovhaneanč Y., vol. I, pp. 94-157.

debasement of the coinage.[34] The transfer of treasures abroad was also affecting the Armenian Church in Iran. In a letter dated 1718 and addressed to Movsēs *Vardapet*, Kaťołikos Astuacatur Hamatanći complains:

> You have written from your place [New Julfa] that, Julfa is in a very bad situation and when you ask for money, there is nobody to give. Under the sun, there is only one Julfa, not two. If Julfa has reached to that point, then compare and conclude what the situation would be in Erevan?[35]

The Armenian community of New Julfa received a most devastating blow in 1722, during the Afghan occupation of Isfahan. The Afghans, a tribal society who were Sunni Muslims, were oppressed under the Safavid rule. In 1709, the Ghazali tribe of Afghanistan revolted and during the following few years defeated all the Safavid forces, who were sent to the region to restore order.[36] In 1721, Mahmud of Qandahar, a tribal chief commanding a small army of Ghazali fighters, departed from Qandahar for an expedition against Persia. He easily captured the city of Kerman, advanced towards Yazd and before capturing the city of Yazd, made a bold move and marched on Isfahan. On March 8, 1722, in the battle of Gulnabad, only ten miles from Isfahan, he defeated a huge Safavid army, encircled the Safavid capital, plundered and devastated the suburbs of the city and nearby villages, until the abdication of Shah Sultan Husayn, on October 23, 1722.[37]

On the eve of the battle of Gulnabad, the entire Safavid army was mobilised to stop the advancing Afghans. The defense of Isfahan was entrusted to a small number of Persian troops and new recruits from the local population. The Armenian community of New Julfa, at the request of the Safavid Court, had sent 300 fully armed young men, to guard the Shah's palaces in Isfahan. But they were immediately disarmed by the Persian troops and dismissed.[38] Deserted by the Persians, the Armenian community was able to defend itself for only a few days, when the Afghans arrived in Isfahan. On March 22, 1722, New Julfa was occupied by the Afghans.[39]

---

[34] Ferrier R.W., *The Agreement of the East India Company*, pg. 432.
[35] AASM. «Դու տեղէն գրեալ ես թէ Ջուղա այն օրուան է որ յումմէ փող ես ուզում տուող չկայ, ի ներքոյ արեգականն մէկ Ջուղա եւ ոչ երկու: Ջուղա որ այդ տեղդ հասած լինի համեմատեալ եւ կշռեայ թէ Երեւան ինչ տեղ կամ որ հասած կու լինի»:
[36] Lockhart L., pp.80-92.
[37] Ibid., pp. 130-170.
[38] *Chronicle of Petros Di Sarkis Gilanentz*, pg. 9.
Krusinski, Tadeusz Juda, S.J., pg. 220.
[39] *Chronicle of Petros Di Sarkis Gilanentz*, pg. 10.
Krusinski, Tadeusz Juda, pg. 221.

Unlike Persian villages in the vicinity of Isfahan, New Julfa was spared total destruction and massive killings by the Afghans.[40] However, it was subjugated to exorbitant fines and all houses and churches were broken into, ransacked and looted. Mahmud, the Afghan leader levied an indemnity of 70,000 *tomans* on New Julfa. First he received from the leadership of the Armenian community 17,000 *tomans* in cash and a promise for the payment of the balance within a short period of time. But because the Armenians were unable to pay the remainder of the indemnity within the specified time, four prominent members of the community, including Xačik, the *Kalantar* of New Julfa were beheaded by Mahmud to force the community raise the total amount demanded.[41] In addition to the levied indemnity, 5000 Satin coats (*kapa*), cotton material (*ghutni*), sufficient material (*chokha*) to make up 8000 long coats for the Afghan soldiers and a large quantity of quilts, mattresses and pillows, made of textiles (*qumash*) and gold (*zar*) thread were collected from New Julfa.[42] Furthermore, sixty two Armenian girls were taken away by the Afghans, giving the most grievous blow to the community of New Julfa.[43]

The Afghan occupation of Isfahan, which lasted for seven years, until 1729, brought about the final downfall of the Armenian community of New Julfa. During this period, the economy was in total shambles and the physical security of the people was at stake. Many Armenians, being robbed of their wealth and persecuted, were abandoning their homes in a panic and fleeing to Iraq, India and Russia. According to a written statement made in 1725 by Bishop Dawit of New Julfa, 156 Armenian families from the parishes of *Surb Hogi* (Holy Spirit) and *Surb* Yovhannēs (St. John) churches alone had already fled, leaving behind vacant houses.[44] A letter written by three Armenian brothers from Basra (Iraq) in 1753 and addressed to their mother living in New Julfa, expresseed the plight of expatriates in the following words:

> We can not expect any good from that country [Iran] anymore, and that is obvious to all of you. What happened to the three Xaldarean families or the houses of Šahrimanenk, Salənjenk, Šaxatunenk, Bedłenk, Jamalenk, Gerakenk, Kaṙasmankenk, Kamalenk, *Khwaja* Połosenk, *Khwaja* Šarfrazenk, Frangsisenk, *Agha* Dawutenk, *Khwaja* Nikołosenk, *Cik* Mukelenk, *Agha* Babenk, Parsadanenk, *Mec* Šahenk and all other families? Honorable mother, you well know that none of

---

[40] *Chronicle of Petros Di Sarkis Gilanentz*, pg. 10.
[41] Ibid., pg. 35-36.
[42] Ibid., pp. 38-39.
[43] Ibid., pp.12-14. Krusinski Tadeusz Juda, pg. 222.
[44] Tēr Yovhaneanč Y., vol. I, pg. 293.

them has remained. We are not going to be their [Persians] servants. During the time of Kings, under stable conditions and amid a large population they [the said families] perished. Therefore, beloved mother, how are we, four or five families, going to live in that country at a time of confusion and instability.[45]

Indeed, by the second quarter of the eighteenth century, the Armenian community of New Julfa was greatly reduced in size and economic power. The prominent and wealthy families had either fled the country or were terriby weakened. The economic survival of the remnants of the community or the churches was now largely conditioned on the assistance of the expatriates, who were mostly settled in India and had formed new communities under the spiritual jurisdiction of the diocese of New Julfa.[46]

According to a census conducted in 1770's by Bishop Mkrtič, the number of Armenian "clergy and laymen" of New Julfa was reduced to 1517.[47] Even if the women and children were excluded from this census, as appears to be the case, the total inhabitants could barely be more than 6000 or equal to less than one third of the 17th century Armenian population of New Julfa.

[45] Ibid., vol. I, pg. 297. «Ոյշիտ գայիր այ որ էլ էտ երկիրն մեզ համար խէր չի առում, ինչ եւալ Խալդարէնց երեք օջադն, Ճարիմանէնց՝ Սայրնջէնց՝ Ջախաթունէնց՝ Բղղղէնց՝ Ջամայէնց՝ Գերապէնց՝ Քառասմանկանց՝ Քամայէնց՝ Խոջայ Պողոսէնց, Խոջայ Ճարֆրագէնց, Ֆրանգզիխէնց՝ ադայ Դաութոնց՝ Խոջայ Նիկողոսէնց, ձիք Մրքէլէնց՝ ադայ Բարէնց փարատանաէնց՝ Մեծ Ճաֆէնց, եւ այլ մհս օջադան՝ որ ձեր հրամանքն եւս առաէլ պատութէլի մայս լէվաս խքար, մինն մնացէլ չի, մենք խո Նանգան Նորարն չէնք դառման, էնպէս ավատ եւ մարթաոյ եւ համատատ թագատորութեան ժամանակումն որ Նանքան փշացան՝ մէնք մին չորս հինգ տունն էս խարաս եւ անհատատ ժամանակումն ինչպէս պիտոի ապրէնք Նանիջան:»
[46] For the establishment of the Armenian communities in India See: Seth M., *Armenians in India*, Calcutta, 1937. Irazek Y., *Patmu ñwn Hndkahay Tpagruſean*, Antelias, 1986.
[47] Tēr Yovhaneanč Y., vol. I, pg. 315.

Fig. 17 General view of the Armenian cemetery of New Julfa.

Fig. 18 Tombstone of Tĕr Sukias (left), dated 1690, in the cemetery of Vastikan, Geandiman. An extremely large piece of rock, measuring 126x34x37 inches.

CHAPTER NINE

THE CULTURAL LEGACY
OF THE DIOCESE OF NEW JULFA

The end of the Safavid-Ottoman wars in the early seventeenth century and the re-creation of secure conditions in the region, permitted a cultural as well as religious revival. Kaťołikos Movsēs Siwneći, Xačatur Kesaraći and a few other religious leaders in the monasteries of Ējmiacin, New Julfa, Taťew,[1] Lim, Ktuč[2] and Amərtolu[3] assumed leading roles in the religious, intellectual and artistic rebirth of the Armenian people. Among these, All Saviour's Monastery of New Julfa was to become the most important center of higher education and a scriptorium devoted to literary activity, as well as printing and painting.

Xačatur Kesaraći had established a school in the All Saviour Monastery during the first period of his pontificate at New Julfa (1623-1629). After his return to New Julfa in late 1631, he was to concentrate particularly on the development of this school. Kesaraći gathered many students, reorganised the teaching system, introduced a new curriculum which included all the areas of knowledge known at the time, namely grammar, rhetoric, philosophy, natural sciences, geometry, music, theology and biblical studies and turned the school into a center of higher education, a "university, where he taught and trained his students in the Old and New Testaments and all the areas of liberal arts and metaphysics."[4]

---

[1] Known also as *Siwneač* or *Mec Anapat.*
[2] Lim and Ktuč were two small islands in Lake Van.
[3] In Bitlis, Western Armenia.
[4] Xačtur Ĵułayeći, *Patmuťiwn Parsić,* pg. 117.

Kesaraći took great care of all his students, provided them with reasonable living means and encouraged them to concentrate exclusively on their studies.[5] He showed particular care for Simeon Julayeći,[6] his senior disciple, a brilliant and hard working young priest, who had accompanied him during his travels to Poland and had studied with him under Melkiset Vžaneći at Ejmiacin.

After their return to New Julfa, for three years (1632-5), Simeon Julayeći continued his extensive studies and became "superb and gracious in preaching, dialectics, biblical commentaries, analytical and philosophical arts and was preeminent among all the contemporary *vardapets*, who humbly came and learned from him...".[7] Simeon became the backbone of the school as a teacher and close assistant to Xaćatur Kesaraći. Until 1641, he taught philosophy and grammar to three classes of his fellow students[8] and wrote a grammar, *Girk or Koči Kerakanuťiwn* (A book called grammar),[9] which was widely circulated until late eighteenth century and commonly used as a textbook in Armenian schools.[10] In 1641 he was given the title of *vardapet* by Xaćatur Kesaraći,[11] and invited by Kaťolikos Pilippos Ałbakeći to serve as a teacher in Eastern Armenia. Soon he took charge of the school of Ejmiacin, where fifty students attended his courses.[12] During the years of his studies and teaching career both in New Julfa and Ejmiacin, Simeon Julayeći acquired a wide range of knowledge reflected in his grammar and his two other works: *Girk Tramabanuťean* (logic),[13] completed in 1649 and *Meknuťiwn Prokli* (Commentary on the works of Proclus),[14] completed in 1651. For these he utilised multiple works by Armenian and non-Armenian thinkers, including Grigor Taťewaći, Dawiť Anyałt (the invincible), Plato, Aristotle, Philo of Alexandria, Porphyry, Nemesis of Emessa, Gregory of Nyssa, Proclus Diadochus, Pseudo-Dionysius the Areopagite, Albertus Magnus, Thomas Aquinas, Peter of Aragon and others.[15]

---

[5] Aŕakel Dawrižeći, pp. 402-403.

[6] Ibid. pp. 402-403.

[7] Ibid. pg. 403.

[8] Ibid. pp. 404-405.

[9] Written in 1637. Printed in Constantinople in 1725.

[10] Only in the collection of Mesrob Maštoć Manuscript library (*Matenadaran*) of Erevan, more than 40 copies of this grammar book are preserved.

[11] *Haranč Vark'*, New Julfa, 1641, Colophon on pg. 704.

[12] Hakobyan V., *ŽĒ Dari Hišatakaranner*, vol. III, pg. 5.

[13] Printed in Constantinople in 1728 and 1794 and until early nineteenth century used as a textbook of Logic in Armenian schools. More than 100 manuscript copies preserved in the collection of Mesrob Maštoć *Matenadaran* alone.

[14] Commentary on the *Syntagma Theologica* of Proclus Diadochus, unpublished, survived in many manuscripts, mostly in the collection of Mesrob Maštoć *Matenadaran* .

[15] Mirzoyan H., *Simeon Julayeći*, pp. 35-36. For Armenian translations of listed authors, see Ter Petrosian L., *Ancient Armenian Translations*, pp. 3-25.

In the colophons of books printed by him, Xačatur Kesarači lists the names of at least twenty students who have assisted him in the printing.[16] Among them are Simeon Julayeči, Yakob Julayeči, the future Katołikos of Ējmiacin, Dawit Julayeči, the successor of Kesarači as bishop of New Julfa and Yovhannēs Julayeči, who was later known for his achievements in printing. Oskan Erewanči, the printer of the first Armenian Bible and a number of other major works, was also a student of Kesarači for several years.[17] Among the textbooks used at the school of All Saviour Monastery was Euclid's geometry, a translation of which, possibly by Grigor Kesarači, was made specially for the school.[18]

For Xačatur Kesarači, the maintenance of a school was not just a matter of principle or moral duty. For him the school had a special cultural and religious mission. On the one hand, it had to serve for the religious and cultural revival of Armenians, after a long period of serious stagnation and chaos. On the other hand, it was essential for the higher education of the Armenian clergy, who had to face the growing and aggressive missionary activities of Catholic religious orders in Armenia and Iran.

Following the death of Xačatur Kesarači, Dawit Julayeči took over the school of All Saviour's monastery. He gathered a new generation of students and maintained its rich curriculum of higher education. In a manuscript colophon dated 1686, Ałeksandr Julayeči lists the names of Dawits thirty students. He also presents the school's curriculum, which included psalm reading, hymn singing, music, poetry, arithmetic, grammar, philosophy, natural sciences, theology and Biblical studies.[19] In the same colophon, Ałeksandr mentions his own father, Kostand *vardapet*, better known as *varžapet*,[20] who maintained a school for 250 children.[21] Following the death of his wife, Zebetia, in 1654, Kostand had apparently become a monk at the All Saviour's monastery. His name among the members of the religious order of All Saviour's monastery also appears in other contemporary manuscript colophons.[22]

A textbook written by Kostand and entitled *Ašxarha žołov*[23] (general collection) presents the basic rules of trade, trade roads of New Julfa

[16] Oskanyan N.A., Korkotyan Ḱ.A., Savalyan A.M., *Hay girk' ə 1512-1800 Tvakannerin*, pp. 21-27.

[17] *Patmut'iwn Kenač Oskanay Vardapeti Erewanečwoy*, pp. 228-230.

[18] Mirzoyan H., *Simeon Julayeči*, pg. 36.

[19] Tēr Awetisean S., vol. I, pg. 751.

[20] Teacher.

[21] Ibid. pg. 752.

[22] Minasean L.G., *Čučak Jeragrač*, vol. II, pp. 73-74, 152.

[23] Ms. #5994 in Mesrob Maštoč *Matenadaran* .

merchants and currencies, weights and measures used in different Asian and European countries. Consequently, in the second half of the seventeenth century, a program of business education conducted by Kostand *var žapet*, for the children of New Julfa merchants was evidently maintained at the All Saviour's monastery, side by side with its theological and literary school.[24]

With the foundation of All Saviour's monastery and other churches throughout Iran, the diocese of New Julfa also became one of the most important Armenian scriptorium. Many scribes and miniaturists who settled in New Julfa, Isfahan and surrounding villages, were fully occupied with copying and illuminating manuscripts for the use of the churches, the clergy and other persons. They were financially supported and encouraged by wealthy individuals, for whom, as is often specified in the colophons, the manuscripts were imperishable treasures and the warrants of their salvation.[25] Master scribes and illuminators residing at the All Saviour's Monastery and other parish churches had many apprentices, who in due course would be trained enough, to become masters in their own rights. Mesrop Xizanči, one of the best known master scribe-illuminators, who lived and worked in Isfahan and New Julfa between 1608 and 1652, copied and illustrated some thirty manuscripts and trained numerous pupils.[26]

More than 350 manuscripts written in New Julfa and the surrounding areas have survived[27] and are currently part of various collections, primarily at the All Saviour's monastery, the Mesrob Maštoč Manuscript Library (Matenadaran) in Erevan and the University of California at Los Angeles. In addition, almost one thousand other manuscripts brought to Iran by Armenian immigrants or acquired by traveling merchants of New Julfa can also be identified in existing collections throughout the world.[28]

These manuscripts, which are an eloquent testimony of the rich cultural heritage of the diocese of New Julfa, were much greater in number in the seventeenth century. Unfortunately, All Saviour's monastery which had a large collection of manuscripts in the

---

[24] According to his tombstone inscription, Kostand died in 1702, probably at a quite advanced age. The tombstone of his wife Zebetia, the mother of Katolikos Aleksandr, is dated 1654. Minasean L.G., *Nor Julayi Gerezmanatuna*, pp. 29, 40.

[25] Hakobyan V., *ŽE Dari Hišatakaranner*, vols. I-III.

[26] Der Nersessian S, *Armenian Miniatures from Isfahan*, pg. 156.

[27] Minasean L.G., *Čučak Jeragrac*, vol. II, pg. IX.

[28] The present collection of All Saviour's monastery alone includes 750 manuscripts. In addition, 54 manuscripts in private hands are listed in the second volume of the manuscript catalog of the All Saviour's monastery.

seventeenth century, suffered great losses during the Afghan invasion of Isfahan in 1722 and more particularly between 1748-1755, when manuscripts were sold to grocers, spice sellers and gun powder makers of Isfahan,[29] in order to raise funds, for the payment of the 6000 *tomans*, imposed on the Armenians of New Julfa by Azadkhan,[30] the Afghan chieftain from Khorasan, who occupied Isfahan, and terrorised its population.

In addition to his establishment of schools and his encouragement and support the work of scriptorium, Xačatur Kesaraci was fully aware of the potential of a printing press for his efforts at a religious and cultural revival. Printed books could best serve to reach out to all segments of his community, to educate and protect it against Muslim pressures and Catholic influences. For several years he actively pursued the idea of establishing a printing press at the All Saviour's monastery. The first Armenian book, *Urbatagirk'*[31] had been printed in 1512 by Yakob Mełapard in Venice, who printed four additional volumes during the next two years. In 1565, two volumes had been printed, still in Venice, by Abgar Toxateci, who then moved his printing press to Constantinople and between 1567 and 1569 printed six additional volumes.[32] During the following sixty five years, until 1634, thirteen volumes, all of them Catholic publications in Armenian, were printed in Rome, Venice, Milan and Paris,[33] mainly for the use of Catholic missionaries in the Middle East. Finally, according to the *Chronicle of the Carmelites in Persia*, the Carmelites introduced a printing type, with Arabic and Persian script, to Iran in December 1628—January 1629,[34] but no further information is available on the use of that printing type in any publication.

The establishment of an Armenian printing press in New Julfa was a very difficult task, since the technology of printing was not familiar throughout the Middle East and there was an acute shortage of type, paper and printers. Even so, Kesaraci was fortunate enough to find in his community a very talented artisan named Yakobjan, who was later to be *Naqqash-Bashi*, "head of royal painters." According to Tavernier,

---

[29] See the quotation from a letter by bishop Mkrtič on pg. 8. According to the oldest available inventory of the Library of All Saviour's monastery, in 1833, the monastery possessed only 111 manuscripts and 45 printed volumes. Minasean L.G., *Cucak Jeragrac*, vol. II, pg. IX.

[30] Tĕr Yovhaneanc, vol. I, pp. 286-292.

[31] Literally means book of passion. A prayer book for the healing of the sick.

[32] Abgar *Dpir* Toxateci was the first person who established a printing press in the Middle East.

[33] Oskanyan N., *Hay girkə*, pp. 1-21.

[34] *A Chronicle of the Carmelites*, vol. I, pg. 306.

Yakobjan was a genius in mechanical arts and the author of many inventions, who introduced the art of printing into Iran and personally made the fonts.[35]

In 1636, the first printing press was established in the All Saviour's monastery, and after seventeen months of hard labour, the first volume: *Sałmos Dawtí*[36] (The Psalms of David) was printed in 1638. In the colophon of the book, Xačatur Kesaraci acknowledges the active participation of Yakobjan in the publication of the book.[37] In 1641, Kesaraci printed two more volumes: *Haranc̣ Varḳ* (Lives of the church fathers) and a *Xorhrdatetr* (Missal). In the following year he printed a fourth volume, the *Jamagirḳ Ateni* (Breviary).[38] In the colophons of his publications, Kesaraci emphasised that the whole printing process was created locally. No one in New Julfa had any previous experience or knowledge of printing. Even the paper and the ink had to be produced at the monastery. Therefore, he asked the readers not to be critical of technical defects in his publications. He also revealed that he had sent Yovhannes *Vardapet*, one of his students to Europe, to learn the art of printing and secure new printing equipment for the All Saviour's monastery.[39] Xačatur Kesaraci's printing work ended with the publication of the *Breviary* in 1642. The class of scribes who earned their living by writing, led a strong opposition[40] and forced Kesaraci to end his printing activities. According to an unsubstantiated statement by L.G. Minasean, even the printing press was burnt down.[41]

The legacy of Xačatur Kesaraci in the field of printing was to be continued by his disciple, Yovhannes Julayeci, also known under the name Ḱ̇ršenc̣, who was sent to Europe in 1639 to learn the art of printing. After an entire year of travel, he arrived in Venice and a little later moved to Rome, where he established a printing press and started printing the book of Psalms. But before completing the work, for unexplained reasons, he moved again and settled in Livorno, where the printing of the book was completed in 1644.[42] In the preface of the book, Yovhannes reported to his teacher, Xačatur Kesaraci:

---

[35] *Tavernier, J.B. Les Six voyages...*, Paris 1930, pg. 225.
[36] Only two copies of this publication are known. One has survived in the collection of the Bodleian Library at Oxford University, the second at St. James Armenian Monastery of Jerusalem.
[37] *Sałmos Dawtí*, New Julfa, 1638, pp. 341, 572.
[38] Oskanyan N.,*Hay girk'ə*, pp. 21-27.
Minasean L.G., *Nor Jułayi Tparann U Ir Tpagrac̣ Grk'erə*, pp. 17-34.
[39] Oskanyan N., Ibid. pp. 26-27.
[40] Tavernier, J.B., pg. 229.
[41] Minasean L.G., *Nor Jułayi Tparann U Ir Tpagrac̣ Grk'erə*, pp. 34-45.
[42] See the preface and the colophon of the book in Oskanyan N., *Hay girḳə*, pg. 29.

> We were able to complete a perfect publication with various styles and sizes of type, including material [notes] for songs and hymns and many other ornamentations, with which it will be possible to print everything... This book was printed in a great haste, only as a sample... 1050 copies were printed.[43]

Late in 1646, few months after the death of Xačatur Kesaraći, Yovhannēs Julayeći returned to New Julfa with his new printing press, the fonts and many engraved illustrations depicting biblical scenes and the martyrdom of St. Gregory the Illuminator.[44] Amidst confusion resulting from the absence of a clear successor to Kesaraći and the opposition of the scribes, Yovhannēs reestablished the printing house and in 1647 printed a calendar, impressive for its layout and the style of its scripts, the *Girk Tumarač or ev Parzatumar Koči* (Book of calendars, which is also called simple calendar).[45]

Soon after, Yovhannēs Julayeći attempted the first publication of the Armenian Bible. According to Jean Baptiste Tavernier, he

> Printed the Epistles of St. Paul, the seven penitential Psalms, and was going about to print the whole Bible, but not having the way of making good ink, and to avoid the ill consequences of the invention, he was forced to break his press. For ... many persons were undone by it, that got their living by writing.[46]

The following information concerning Yovhannēs' attempt for the publication of the Bible is given by the eighteenth century historian Xačatur Julayeći:

> They printed many books and started the printing of the Bible. But due to our sins, the work remained incomplete. [The printed parts] are still available. The quality of the paper and the scripts are improved in comparison with older publications.[47]

Not a single sample of the printed parts of the Bible has survived, nor is anything known about the "Epistles of St. Paul" and "the seven penitential Psalms" mentioned by Tavernier. Probably they were some of the printed parts of the Bible which never materialised. Yovhannēs Julayeći closed the printing house because of the prevailing opposition

---

[43] Ibid. pg. 29.

[44] Minasean L.G., *Nor Julayi Tparann U Ir Tpagrač Grkera*, pp. 45-49.

[45] Ibid. pp. 39-44.

[46] *Les six voyages...* pg. 225. This part is omitted in the English edition of 1684 of Tavernier's book.

[47] Xačatur Julayeći, pg. 121.

to his work. He left New Julfa and moved to Armenia in 1650/1.[48]

The printing house of All Saviour's monastery remained closed thereafter for more than 35 years. In 1687, when the tensions between the Armenian clergy of New Julfa and the Catholic missionaries had reached to its climax, Bishop Steṕanos of New Julfa (1683-1696) reactivated the press and between 1687 and 1688, printed three books, as already presented.[49] Addressing the readers in the introduction to the third book, Steṕanos Ĵułayeċi stated:

> We searched and found many useful and luminous books, written by the blessed fathers of our church, which are kept here and there and are, not commonly known or utilised. Therefore, strengthened by the Holy Spirit, we reopened the printing house in order to publish the old holy books, which we will soon print and send to you.[50]

Even so, Steṕanos was not able to fulfil his promise for more publications. In 1693, two documents, the previously mentioned open letter[51] and a one page "rules for the election of Kaṫołikos" were printed, openly declaring opposition to Kaṫołikos Nahapet Edesaċi. The printing house was closed once again, not to be reopened for nearly two centuries, until 1863.

According to Xaċatur Ĵułayeċi, the historian, Shah Sultan Husayn ordered the closing of the printing house following allegations made by Catholics, and fined Steṕanos heavily.[52] Y. Tēr Yovhaneanċ, who probably had not seen the work of Xaċatur Ĵułayeċi,[53] also blames the Catholics for the closing of the printing house. According to him, the Catholics presented Steṕanos' publications as being opposed to the teaching of the Koran, and succeeded in convincing the Muslim officials. As a result, the printing house was closed and four hundred *tomans* had to be spent for fines and bribes, in order to settle the matter.[54]

The information of both Xaċatur Ĵułayeċi and Tēr Yovhaneanċ seems open to question on the following grounds:

a) In 1693, five years after the publication of the three books for

---

[48] Yovhannēs was consecrated Bishop by Kaṫołikos Ṗilippos and appointed primate of Old Julfa, where a small community had survived or resettled after the mass deportations of 1604. Soon after his arrival in Julfa, Yovhannēs was killed by Muslims, trying to help an Armenian save his daughter from the hands of a Muslim. See Ibid. pg. 120.

[49] See pg. 144.

[50] Minasean L.G., *Nor Ĵułayi Tparann U Ir Tpagraċ Grk'erə*, pg. 57.

[51] Appendix I, doc. #16.

[52] Xaċatur Ĵułayeċi, pg. 120.

[53] Tēr Yovhaneanċ, vol. I, pg. 15.

[54] Ibid. vol. II, pp. 31-32.

which the printing house was allegedly closed, Stepanos was still able to print the two documents mentioned above.

b) In his will, Stepanos Julayeci listed his main achievements and the most troubling episodes of his pontificate. With regards to his publications, he has merely mentioned the expenditure of 200 *tomans*, without any reference to fines or any hardship. The "anti-Koran" charges made against him for which he has spent 200 *tomans*, are mentioned as a separate incident.[55]

c) According to a report by Elias, the very active Carmelite missionary stationed in Isfahan during the last quarter of the seventeenth century, the "anti-Koran" charges were made by Awet, the *kalantar* of New Julfa, who was forced out of office by the Armenian community in 1692, as already noted,[56] converted to Islam, and retaliated against Stepanos, who had instigated his removal from office.[57] The Catholic missionaries may have been the ones who sought to prevent Stepanos' publications, but a final conclusion cannot be reached at the present stage of our knowledge.

The decorative arts occupied an important place in the seventeenth century cultural life of New Julfa. They were expressed primarily through easel paintings on wood or canvas, wall paintings, ceramic tiles and stucco decorations. Monumental painting was not prevalent in the Armenian church until the seventeenth century, in part because, the stone construction of churches lent itself better to carved than to painted decoration.[58] More importantly, Armenian tradition was deeply antagonistic to the iconophile position of the Byzantine church. Painted decoration of churches was consequently limited.[59]

The seventeenth century was marked by an enormous upsurge of Armenian painting in New Julfa, thanks to the following favourable conditions:

a) Several European painters, employed by the Safavid court, were settled in New Julfa. Therefore, they were in direct contact with the

---

[55] Stepanos Julayeci, *Ktak*.

[56] See pg. 112.

[57] *A Chronicle of the Carmelites*, vol. I, pg. 468.

[58] Der Nersessian S., *Armenia and Byzantine Empire*, Cambridge, 1947, pg. 110.

[59] Traces of wall paintings can be found mainly in the following VII-XIII century Armenian churches: Mren, Tekor, Talin, Aruč, Aḷtamar, Gndevank, Tatew and St. Gregory of Ani built by Tigran Honenc. (See Thierry J.M., Donabedian P.,*Armenian Art*, France 1989). However, a treatise against the iconoclasts (*Ǝnddem Patkeramartic*), written by Vrtanes Kertoł in early seventh century, enumerates an extensive cycle of paintings presented in the Armenian churches and concludes: "All that the Holy Scriptures relate is painted in the churches." (See Durean E., *Usumnasirutiwnk ev Knnadatutiwnk*, Jerusalem, 1935, pp. 304-305).

Armenian churh and community.[60]

b) Armenian merchants developed a taste for painting during their travels in Europe. They consequently imported European paintings to Iran or employed local painters to decorate their homes and churches.[61]

c) Finally, the Armenian churches of New Julfa were architecturally a combination of Armenian and Persian styles. The Armenian style pertained primarily to the ground plans and the main divisions of the churches, based on liturgical requirements. The Persian style, which may have been dictated by the Safavid authorities so as not to provoke Muslim fanaticism, applied mainly to the onion-shaped or shallow and lid shaped domes.[62] In order to realise this architectural feature, Persian brick-building techniques with a plaster coating were constantly used. Taking advantage of these plaster surfaces and in order to strengthen the Christian character of the church buildings, the Armenians turned to wall paintings for didactic as well as decorative purposes.

Wall paintings or easel paintings on canvas can still be found in almost all the thirteen churches of present day New Julfa. The most complete series of wall paintings that have survived are to be found in the church of the Holy Mother of God, the Bethlehem church and All Saviour's cathedral. Large series of paintings, mostly plastered over, subsequently can also be traced in the following churches: St. Stephen, St. Catherine, St. Gregory the Illuminator, St. Sargis and St. Minas, all of them built between 1610 and 1659.

The study of the New Julfa school of painting has been primarily based so far on the wall paintings of All Saviour's cathedral, which presents a complete cycle of Old and New Testament illustrations.[63] But for a more complete study and a better understanding of the evolution of painting in New Julfa, the wall paintings of at least the Bethlehem church also require careful investigation. The Bethlehem church was built in 1628 and it was probably decorated immediately after the

---

[60] Carswell J., *New Julfa*, pg. 21.

[61] Many pieces of seventeenth century European paintings acquired by Armenian merchants are presently part of the collection of the Museum of All Saviour's Monastery. As for the wall paintings of private houses, see Carswell J., *New Julfa* and Karapetian K., *Isfahan, New Julfa*.

[62] Carswell J., *New Julfa*, pg. 20.

[63] Boase T.S.R., "*A Seventeenth-century Typological Cycle of Paintings in the Armenian Cathedral of Julfa*," *Journal of Warburg and Courtland Institutes*, vol. XIII, #3-4, 1950, pp. 323-327.
Carswell J., *New Julfa*, pp. 21-29.
Łazaryan M., *Hay Kerparvestə XVII-XVIII Darerum*, pp. 13-96.

completion of the construction.[64] The interior walls of the church, including the drum of the dome, are entirely covered with paintings of evangelical scenes, standing figures of saints, scenes from the life of St. Gregory the Illuminator and other martyrs of the Christian church, floral designs, stucco decorations and ceramic tiles. The decoration displays a variety of styles. Those paintings depicting evangelical scenes and the martyrdom of St. Gregory the Illuminator and other saints are presented in European style. The standing figures of saints, twelve in number,[65] are clearly a reflection of the traditional Armenian manuscript illumination art. The floral designs and the ceramic tiles are inspired by Persian decorative art.

Whereas the wall paintings of the Bethlehem church indicate a transitional stage from the traditional Armenian painting style to European style, those of All Saviour's cathedral are fully in European style. They are modelled mostly on the *Biblica Sacra*[66] by the engraver Christoffel van Sichem (1581-1658)[67] and are of high artistic quality.

The wall paintings of the cathedral are arranged horizontally. Those in the drum of the dome and in the upper row of the walls depict themes from the Old Testament, while the themes from the New Testament are presented in the second row. In the third row, Biblical parables, the seven sacraments and episodes from the life of Christ are presented in oval shaped pictures. A series of smaller pictures form the fourth row and depict the torments of St. Gregory the Illuminator and the victory of Christianity in Armenia as they are traditionally narrated in the *History* attributed to Agatangełos. A huge painting of the last judgment adorns the western part of the North wall of the nave of the cathedral. Below the paintings, a row of magnificent ceramic tiles encircles the interior of the cathedral.[68]

---

[64] Chronologically, the last inscription left in the church by the benefactor, *Khwaja* Petros Vēlijanean, is dated 1635. According to the inscription on his tombstone, *Khwaja* Petros died in 1649. See Tēr Yovhaneanč, vol. II, pp. 175-179.

[65] A total of 76 complete paintings can be found on the interior walls of the church. Tēr Yovhaneanč, vol. II, pp. 176-177.

[66] Printed in Anvers, 1646.

[67] Van Sichem's engravings were also used in a number of Armenian publications, specially in the first printed Bible (Amsterdam, 1966). Copies of these engravings or the *Biblica Sacra* could have been brought to New Julfa by Yovhannēs Vardapet Julayeči, for possible use in his project of printing the Holy Bible. At least twenty other engravings, depicting the torments of St. Gregory the Illuminator, which were brought to New Julfa by Yovhannēs, have survived. They have also served as models for Yovhannēs *Vardapet* Mrkuz, the artist of a series of wall paintings in the All Saviour's cathedral. See Minasean L.G. *Nor Julayi Tparann U Ir Tpagrač Grkera*, pp. 45-49.

[68] Paintings, later covered by a coat of plaster, are also discovered on the walls of the parvis of the cathedral.

Iconographically, the paintings of the cathedral "are worked out with remarkable thoroughness and with some unusual typological features," as was first observed by T.S.R. Boase.[69] Indeed, in the upper two rows of the wall paintings, scenes from both the Old and New Testaments are harmonised to a great extent with theological understanding and are presented as twenty six typological pairs. In the parallel rows, among other typological pairs, depicted are the following:

- Joseph reading the moon and the stars. The angel appearing to the shepherds of Bethlehem.

- Melchisedek worshipping Abraham. The worship of the Magi.

- The persecution of the Israelites by the Egyptians. The massacre of the innocents of Bethlehem.

- The Ark being brought into Jerusalem. The entry of Christ into Jerusalem.

- The passover. The last supper.

- The judgement of Solomon. Christ before Caiaphas.[70]

Bishop Dawit, who supervised the construction and the decoration of the cathedral, undoubtedly played a decisive role in the selection and the typological classification of the paintings. According to Stepanos Julayeci, Bishop Dawit built the cathedral

> With a fine dome of heavenly design at great expense, three storeys high reminiscent of Noah's Ark and the temple of Solomon. He had it painted with paints of various colours, had it gilt and designed beautiful flowers like the paradise of Sion.[71]

The decoration of the cathedral must have been carried out immediately after the construction of the cathedral. An inscription on the ceiling above the altar, dated April 27, 1661, identifies *Khwaja Awetik* as the sponsor of the decorations.[72] An undated inscription below the window on the northern wall of the cathedral indicates that, Khwaja Awetik, the benefactor who sponsored the decoration of the church, died on February 5, 1669, and seems to indicate that the decoration was mostly completed.[73]

Unlike the manuscript illuminators, whose names are known through the colophons of the manuscripts they decorated, the painters

---

[69] Boase T.S.R., pg. 324.

[70] See the complete list of typlogical cycle, Ibid. pp. 324-325 and *Album, All Saviour's Cathedral New Julfa, Isfahan*, Teheran, 1975, pp. 19-20. The total number of individual paintings are well over 100.

[71] Tēr Awetisean S., vol. I, pg. 5.

[72] Tēr Yovhaneanc, vol. II, pp. 4-5.

[73] Ibid., pg. 4, The ceramic tiles around the altar were added in 1716, Ibid. pg. 5.

of the churches have mostly remained anonymous. Consequently, for the past sixty years, scholars have either avoided the difficult task of identifying the artists of the wall paintings, or presented speculative conclusions.[74] In the absence of tangible information and mainly guided by stylistic considerations, western scholars have attributed most of the wall paintings of All Saviour's cathedral to European artists. In the opinion of T.S.R. Boase:

> Stylistically these paintings, which with the exception of the side walls of the High Altar and some of the small panels in the fourth and fifth bands seem to be by the same artist or group of artists, suggest the Italo-Flemish schools of the late seventeenth century.[75]

John Carswell admits that the identification of the artist or the artists remains a matter of speculation, but he concludes:

> The use of van Sichem's engravings from a recent Dutch edition, the known presence of Dutch artists in Isfahan in the seventeenth century, and the close link the Armenians had with Amsterdam, where their merchants were established, all indicate that it was probably a Dutchman.[76]

Going still further, Otto Meinardus even makes the controversial statement that

> "There is no doubt that these paintings, specially those of the Last Judgment, are the work of European rather than Persian or Armenian artists. The dependence of the Armenians upon non-Armenian artists in the XVIIth century is an interesting phenomenon, especially in view of the traditional iconoclastic tendencies and the anti-Byzantine attitudes of the Armenians."[77]

Traditionally the names of a few Armenian painters, including Minas, Yakobjan, Simeon, Stepanos, Kirakos, Barseł, Awet, Karapet, Dawit, Apov, Astuacatur and Yovhannēs *Vardapet* Mrk̕uz have survived. All of them are somehow considered to be affiliated with the wall paintings of the New Julfa churches in general.[78] Armenian

---

[74] T.S.R. Boase, John Carswell, Otto Meinardus, Aram Eremean, Manya Łazaryan and others.
[75] Boase T.S.R., pg. 326.
[76] Carswell J., *New Julfa*, pg. 24.
[77] Meinardus O., "*The Last Judgment in the Armenian Churches of New Julfa,*" pp. 182-183.
[78] *Album*, All Saviour's Cathedral, pg. 18.

scholars, among them Aram Eremean and Manya Łazarian have depended primarily on tradition and fragmentary, often imprecise and confusing information concerning the paintings or the painters, in their attribution of most of the paintings to Armenian artists.[79]

Ařak̇el Dawriževi mentions the two most famous painters; Minas and Yakobǰan, both laymen and natives of New Julfa, "who are a source of pride and benefit for our nation."[80] The detailed information on Minas, provided by him can be summarised as follows: As a child, Minas was taken to Aleppo, where he was trained under a European master painter and became an accomplished artist. After his return to New Julfa, he was employed by the Armenian nobility, anxious to have their houses decorated richly. Having visited the house of *Khwaja Sarfraz* and being very impressed by the decorations, Shah Safi (1629-1642) summoned Minas to his presence and ordered him to paint the portrait of *Čřal Khan*, one of his ministers. After he had painted the portrait successfully on the spot, Minas became the favourite artist of the royal court and was commissioned to paint for the king and the ministers. A falcon sent to Shah Safi from Russia was painted by Minas, who was rewarded with a *khelat* (robe of honor), as well as a gift of twelve *tomans* and was offered permanent employment with an annual salary from the royal treasury. But being a Christian, he declined the offer and preferred to practice his art independently. Minas was a great artist, who could paint with equal success on canvas, wood, metal or plastered walls. He created a variety of subjects: plants, animals, birds or human beings, as well as accurate representations of Persians, Armenians, Jews, Indians, Europeans, Russians or Georgians. His knowledge of medical, biological, psychological and chemical sciences was a key element for his successful portrayal of human beings of different ages, backgrounds, outfits or moods.[81]

Dawriževi provides no information on Yakobǰan. J.B. Tavernier identifies him as the *naqqash-bashi*, head of the royal painters and a very talented artist.[82] He is also mentioned in manuscript colophons and

---

[79] Eremean A., "Nkarič Minasi Keank'i ev Stełcagorcutean Himnakan Gcerə," *Anahit*, 1938, May-August, pg. 45.

―――――, "Noragiwt Ějer nor J̌ułayi Ormnankarčut'iwniǰ," *Anahit*, 1939, Jan-March, pp. 24-32.

Łazaryan M., *Hay Kerparvestə XVII-XVIII Darerum*, pp. 13-96.

[80] Ařak̇el Dawriževi, pg. 409.

[81] Ibid. pp. 409-413.

[82] *Les Six voyages*, pg. 225.

other seventeenth century Armenian documents.[83] His position at the royal court is the most eloquent testimony for his prominence in the artistic life of the seventeenth century Isfahan.

The third famous Armenian painter from New Julfa is Yovhannēs *Vardapet* Mrkʿuz, also known as *Tiezeraloys* (universal illuminator), for his activities as a great teacher, a theologian and an artist. Xačatur Ĵułayeći, the historian, devoted more than fifty pages to the description of the educational, theological and artistic merits of Yovhannēs Mrkʿuz. He also credited him with the decoration of All Saviour's cathedral.

Finally, a document dated 1666 and submitted by *Khwaja* Zakʿar to the Russian court indicates that artistic workshops where several painters were employed, existed in New Julfa.[84] A painting of the Last Supper, produced in one of these workshops and presented to Tsar Aleksei Mikhailovich by *Khwaja* Zakʿar in 1660 was so appreciated that Zakʿar was asked to arrange for the transfer of the painter from New Julfa to Moscow. In 1667, a young painter from New Julfa, named Astuacatur, was employed by the Tsar and was soon acclaimed as a great artist. For more than thirty five years he lived and painted in Moscow under the names Bogdan Sulťanov or Ivan Iewliewic Sulťanov.[85]

Until recently, only a few Armenian painters could be directly linked to a particular painting or the decoration of a particular church. Two inscriptions dated 1666, identified Dawiť and Ēreċpox Apov as the artists of some of the paintings in the church of Holy Mother of God.[86] One inscription, dated 1662 mentioned the name of Karapet as the painter of the altar of Saint Yakob church of Bałaťay.[87] Another inscription, gave the name Stepanos the picture maker, on the lower part of painting of the Virgin Mary on the north wall of the chancel of the cathedral.[88] In 1972 however, during the restoration of the Bethlehem church, the following inscription was discovered on the ceiling above the altar: "The paintings were drawn by Minas and Martiros. The floral decorations were drawn by Astuacatur." This was a major key for the identification of the artists of one of the two most richly decorated churches of New Julfa. Indeed, in the light of the artistic quality of the

---

[83] *Sałmos Dawťi*, New Julfa, 1638, pp. 341, 572.
Hakobyan V., *Žē Dari Hišatakaranner*, vol. III.
Also a number of documents in AASM.
[84] Xačatur Ĵułayeći, pg. 210.
[85] Łazaryan M., *Hay Kerparvestə XVII-XVIII Darerum*, pp. 51.
[86] Tēr Yovhaneanċ, vol. II, pg. 192.
[87] Ibid. pg. 168.
[88] Carswell J., *New Julfa*, pg. 25.

paintings of Bethlehem church, Dawriǯeći's evaluation of Minas is fully justified.

Dawriǯeći who completed the writing of his *History* in 1662, clearly indicated that both Minas and Yakobǰan were still living in New Julfa. This corresponds to the time when All Saviour's cathedral was being built. Therefore, it is reasonable to assume that Minas, whose European style paintings can now be seen and evaluated at the Bethlehem church, could have contributed his share to the decoration of the cathedral, along with other Armenian and possibly non-Armenian painters.

The information provided by Xačatur J̌ułayeći on the participation of Yovhannēs *Vardapet* Mrk̇uz in the decoration of the cathedral can be verified only through a close examination of the paintings and their style. As already observed by T.S.R. Boase,[89] John Carswell[90] and others, a group of twenty one small paintings, mostly depicting the torments of St. Gregory the Illuminator on the fourth row of the cathedral paintings, and above them, thirteen oval shaped paintings of the Holy Sacraments, parables and scenes from the gospels, form a separate series and must be considered the work of a single artist. The last painting of that series presents a white bearded monk, over fifty years of age, hooded and in Armenian style monastic outfits, praying before the Holy Virgin and the child. On the upper right corner of the painting is the image of the Mandylion.[91] The monk depicted is evidently the painter. In the oral tradition of New Julfa, the monk is identified with Yovhannēs *Tiezeraloys Vardapet*[92] (Mrk̇uz).

Yovhannēs *Vardapet* Mrk̇uz died in 1715.[93] Assuming that he lived for more than eighty years, in the early 1660's, when the construction of the cathedral was completed, he would have been 25-35 years old, not the age of the white bearded monk depicted in the said painting. However, considering the fact that the decoration work started only after the construction of the cathedral and possibly lasted for many years, we can assume that Yovhannēs Mrk̇uz painted the last phase or row of the paintings in the late 1670's or early 1680's, when he was already a middle aged man, like the depicted white bearded monk.

---

[89] Boase T.S.R., pg. 325.

[90] Carswell J., *New Julfa*, pg. 25.

[91] According to the tradition of the Syrian and Armenian Churches, King Abgar of Edessa sent messengers to Christ and invited him to his kingdom. Christ could not accept the invitation. However, He put a handkerchief on His face and His image was printed on the handkerchief, which later was sent to King Abgar. This tradition is narrated in a number of sources, including Labubna of Edessa, Josephus and Movsēs Xorenaći.

[92] Tēr Yovhaneanć, vol. II, pg. 1

[93] See his epitaph in Minasean L.G., *Nor J̌ułayi Gerezmanatunə*, pg. 30.

The influence of cultural works from New Julfa were not limited to the geographical boundaries of Isfahan or of its diocese at large. They spread far enough to enrich culturally both the people of Armenia and the Armenian communities of the Diaspora. Graduates of the school of All Saviour's monastery, including Simeon, Dawit́ and Yovhannēs J̌ułayeċi, Oskan Erewanċi, Yovhannēs Mrk̇uz, Kat́ołikoi Yakob, Steṕanos and Ałek̇sandr J̌ułayeċi and Astuacatur Hamatanċi[94] played important roles in the religious and cultural life of the Armenian people. The Armenian merchants of New Julfa were the main financial supporters of all kinds of religious and cultural endeavours in New Julfa, Armenia and various cities of Europe. In the field of publication alone, more than half of the 160 known titles of the seventeenth century Armenian printed books, including the first printed Armenian Bible, were produced by printers of New Julfa origin or were financially supported by merchants from New Julfa.[95] In the eighteenth and nineteenth centuries, Armenians from New Julfa, settled in India, Russia and Europe, continued to play crucial roles in publication of Armenian books and journals,[96] the establishment of large and permanent educational institutions[97] and the promotion of the growing ideology for the liberation of Armenia.[98]

The cultural legacy of New Julfa is best evaluated in the following words of the nineteenth century Armenia writer Mesrop T́ałiat́eanċ:

> Alas Julfa! with all the savants of the world
> Greece was barely able to build an Athens during her entire history.
> But your sons, all of whom wandered during their entire lives,
> Wherever they reached, there they built an intellectual Athens."[99]

---

[94] The interior decoration of the cathedral of Ējmiacin was commissioned by Kat́ołikoi Ałek̇sandr J̌ułayeċi and Astuacatur Hamatanċi.

[95] Oskanyan N.,*Hay girk̇a*, pp. 16-132.

[96] Irazek Y., *Patmutiwn Hndkahay Tpagrut́ean*. The Armenian printing houses of Ējmiacin (1771), Madras-India (1772) and St. Petersburg (1783) were established by merchants of New Julfa origin. The publication of *Azadarar*, (the first Armenian magazine, published in Madras in 1794) and Mik̇aēl Čamčean's monumental *History of Armenia* (Venice 1784-6), were also financed by New Julfa merchants.

[97] Mardasirakan Ċemaran of Calcuta (1811), Lazarean Ċemaran of Moscow (1816) and Murat-Raṕaelean schools of Venice (1835) and Paris were established by benefactors of New Julfa origin.

[98] Kat́ołikos Yakob J̌ułayeċi, Yovseṕ Ēmin, Šahamir Šahamirean and his son Yakob (all of them of New Julfa origin), were the champions of the liberation ideology.

[99] Set́eanċ M., "I Širakay Ċhndiks kam Cagumn J̌ułayeċwoċ́ew Hndkahayoċ́," *Parskahay Tareċbyċ́*, vol. I, Tehran, 1927, pg. 172.

Ալիաս Ջուղա, զի ՅովՆաստան գիտնովք ՆաՆոր աշխարՆիՆ,
ՆազիՆ կարաց իւր ըզկԵաց կացուցանԵլ զԱթԵՆ մի,
իսկ որդիք քո՛ աստանԳնակաԳ լիրԵանԳ տխս,
որ որ ՆասիՆ՛ աՆԳ կացուցիՆ մԵծ մի ԱթԵՆ իմասաքis:

Fig. 19 Interior view of Surb Beťłehēm church.

Fig. 20 Baptism, Surb Beťlehēm church.

Fig. 21 Transfiguration, Surb Betłehēm church.

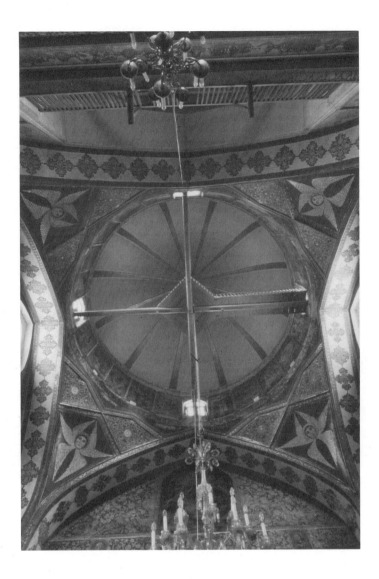

Fig. 22 Surb Astuacacin church, interior view of the dome.

Fig. 23 Interior view of All Saviour's Cathedral.

Fig. 24 Interior view of the dome of All Saviour's Cathedral.

Fig. 25 Last Judgment, All Saviour's Cathedral.

Fig. 26 Resurrection and ascension, All Saviour's Cathedral.

Fig. 27 Yovhannēs Vardapet Mrkuz, All Saviour's Cathedral.

Fig. 28 Detail of interior decoration, All Saviour's Cathedral.

CONCLUSION

As noted in the introduction, this has been the first attempt since the publication of Yarufiwn Tēr Yovhaneanč's *History of New Julfa* in 1880-1, to treat the seventeenth century Armenian communities of Iran as a large diocesan unity, of which New Julfa, the focal point of most scholars, was only the central component. There has been little attempt at a quantitative analysis of the Armenian deportees of 1604 and the geographical distribution of the surviving refugees in Iran. The present discovery of thirty-two new names of seventeenth century Armenian villages in the vicinity of Isfahan, has shown the urgent need for further exploration of the geographic aspect of the diocese of New Julfa, which I have undertaken in order to achieve a balanced evaluation of the entire community.

A study of the social composition of the seventeenth century Armenians of Iran clearly indicates that far from being an economic elite, the absolute majority of the settlers were poor and barely able to maintain a physical existence. Only a small minority, settled in New Julfa and engaged in local and international trade, was socially and economically privileged.

For the greater part of the seventeenth century the official Safavid policy towards the Armenians of Iran was largely conditioned by economic considerations. New Julfa was the domain of the Queen Mother and an important source of her income. The profits made by Armenian merchants in the international trade markets were largely brought to Iran and benefited the state treasury and the local economy. Consequently, the merchant community of New Julfa was fairly well treated by the Safavids and enjoyed relative freedom of worship and limited internal autonomy. The civil administration of the town was headed by an Armenian *kalantar* (mayor), who was in charge of administrative and judicial matters and the collection of royal taxes. He was assisted by a council of Armenian wardens (*tanuterk*). A Persian official called *Darugha* was however in charge of security and criminal matters. Unlike New Julfa, the other communities of Iran, which were largely composed of common artisans and agricultural laborers, were subject to religious and economic hardship and were largely left to the mercy of local state officials. The merchants of New Julfa would do little, and only when urged by the church, to support these poor communities and help ease their sufferings.

With the establishment of the town of New Julfa in 1605, a small diocesan see was created at the All Saviour's monastery for the spiritual administration of the local community. But less than three decades later, the diocese of New Julfa emerged as one of the most important sees of the seventeenth century Armenian church. The principal factors contributing to the fast growth of the diocese were: the election of Katołikos Movsēs Siwneći in 1629, who was enthusiastically supported by the Armenian community of New Julfa, the appointment of Xačatur Kesaraći, a close associate of Movsēs Siwneći, to the See of New Julfa in 1623 and his personal merits as a religious leader and a great teacher, the unlimited financial support of the Armenian merchants of New Julfa, their influence among the Armenians of Iran and Eastern Armenia and their good relations with the Safavid court, the geographical location of the diocesan headquarters near the Safavid capital, which would serve as a bridge of communications between the Armenian Church and the Safavid court, the religious freedom and the internal autonomy granted to the community of New Julfa by Shah Abbas I and his two immediate successors.

The All Saviour's monastery was a religious as well as an administrative center for internal community affairs, which included maintenance of parish churches, collection of church taxes, management of church properties and operation of community courts. In addition, during the long tenure of Xačatur Kesaraći, the monastery turned into a center of higher education, scriptorium, printing and painting, and assumed a leading role in the seventeenth century Armenian cultural life. Some of the best educated and most prominent clerics of the seventeenth century Armenian church were graduates of the School of New Julfa. Hundreds of surviving Armenian manuscripts were copied and illuminated at the monastery and parish churches of the diocese of New Julfa. The first printing press in the Safavid Kingdom and the greater part of the entire Middle East was established at the monastery in 1636. Wall paintings by Armenian artists decorated many churches and private houses.

The death of Xačatur Kesaraċi in 1646 created a serious division within the monastic community of All Saviour's monastery and a temporary vacuum of leadership. For six years, three contenders for the office dominated the religious scene of New Julfa. Finally, in 1652, one of them, Dawit́ Julayeċi, was officially installed as bishop of New Julfa. Yakob Julayeċi, another contender for the diocesan office and an important protagonist in the conflict, left for Armenia and a few years later, in 1655, occupied the pontifical seat of Ējmiacin.

Even after his election to the pontifical seat, Kat́olikos Yakob Julayeċi did not find any support from the diocese of New Julfa. In retaliation, he attempted to reduce the diocese to its original size and jurisdiction by declaring all the Armenian communities of Iran, except New Julfa, as pontifical domains. Thus, a major administrative conflict was created between the Holy See and the diocese of New Julfa, which lasted for half a century, until 1706 and was finally settled in favor of the diocese.

Parallel to its tense relationship with the Kat́olikate of Ējmiacin, during the second half of the seventeenth century, the diocese of New Julfa had to wage a bitter struggle against catholic missionaries, who practically invaded New Julfa with at least two dozen missionaries, belonging to five different orders. Financially and politically the missionaries were supported by Rome and European states and were tolerated in Iran by Safavid authorities, for economic and political considerations. By Islamic law, Muslims were not permitted to convert to any other religion, therefore, the Armenians were the primary target for the Catholic missionaries in Iran. The decades long missionary work of the Catholics in Iran resulted in not more than a handful of Armenian converts, thanks to the strong reaction of the diocese of New Julfa to the Catholic encroachment. By 1715, the missionaries were almost completely eliminated from new Julfa and other Armenian communities of Iran.

Under Shah Sulayman and more particularly Shah Sultan Husayn, between 1667 and 1722, the Armenian community of New Julfa experienced religious and economic pressures. As a result, Armenian merchants gradually relocated their trade centers from Isfahan to India, Russia and Europe. However, New Julfa remained a fairly active and influential community until the Afghan occupation of Isfahan in 1722, which devastated the town and caused a mass exodus of people.

Despite its ultimate decline, New Julfa created a cultural legacy, which was not limited by time and geography. Until the mid-nineteenth century, textbooks originally produced at the All Saviour's monastery were commonly used in the schools of Armenia and various communities of Armenian diaspora. Armenian merchants of New Julfa origin, who, in the eighteenth century were established in India, Russia or Europe were the principle financial supporters for most of the Armenian publications. They were also the benefactors of several Armenian printing presses and schools in Armenia, India, Russia and Europe.

APPENDICES

Document #1

The Decree of Shah 'Abbas I, concerning the settlement of Armenians in the suburbs of Isfahan.[1]

[The Royal Seal]

A high order is issued.[2]

To His Highness, Mirza[3] Muhammad, supreme and most brilliant Vazir[4] of the capital city of Isfahan. Be informed that we have received the petition that you wrote concerning the fight between the Armenians of Julfa and the inhabitants of Marbanan.[5] Well done! Shame on them. Is that the way to treat guests? For a few melons, a few *mans* of grapes and cotton, is it worth to fight with these people, who, for our sake have migrated from their fatherland of some thousand years and have come to your homes, leaving behind loads of gold and silk?

In [Old] Julfa there used to be certain houses on which up to two thousand *tomans* were spent. They destroyed these houses and came here with their families. Is it fair to treat them in that manner? They [the people of Marbanan] have behaved very badly. It is surprising that the people of Marbanan are not killed. Didn't they learn from the inhabitants of Murchakhurd,[6] who were punished for having offended the guests? At any rate make sure that the people of Julfa are happy with you in a perfect way, so that they may be comforted and satisfied. During this winter, lodging should be provided for them in the Royal estates of Arsa'abad, Falashan and Marbanan. For some of them you should rent the houses of peasants, who must evacuate their homes, until next year, when by God's will, they [the Armenians] will build their own houses. We order that the people of Marnanan, who have fought against them be punished severely. Issued in *Rabi' Al-Thani*, 1014.[7]

---

111 Persian text in AASM (cabine 6, file 41, document 6). Other versions in *Matenadaran* of Erevan. Armenian tr. by Tēr Yovhaneanč, vol. I, pg. 46.

1 *Hukm-i Jahan Muta' shud*, an opening formula of administrative orders. Literally "an order to which the world should obey is issued." See *Tadhkirat Al-Muluk*, pp. 202-203.

2 King's steward administering territories under the Royal Household.

3 King's steward administering territories under the Royal Household.

4 Marnan, an area on the western edge of New Julfa, originally inhabited by Persians and in 1656 granted to the Armenians by Shah 'Abbas II. See Tēr Yovhaneanč, vol. I, pg. 83. Mentioned as Marnun in Armenian sources.

5 A village, 35 miles to the North-West of Isfahan.

6 August 16-Sept. 13, 1605.

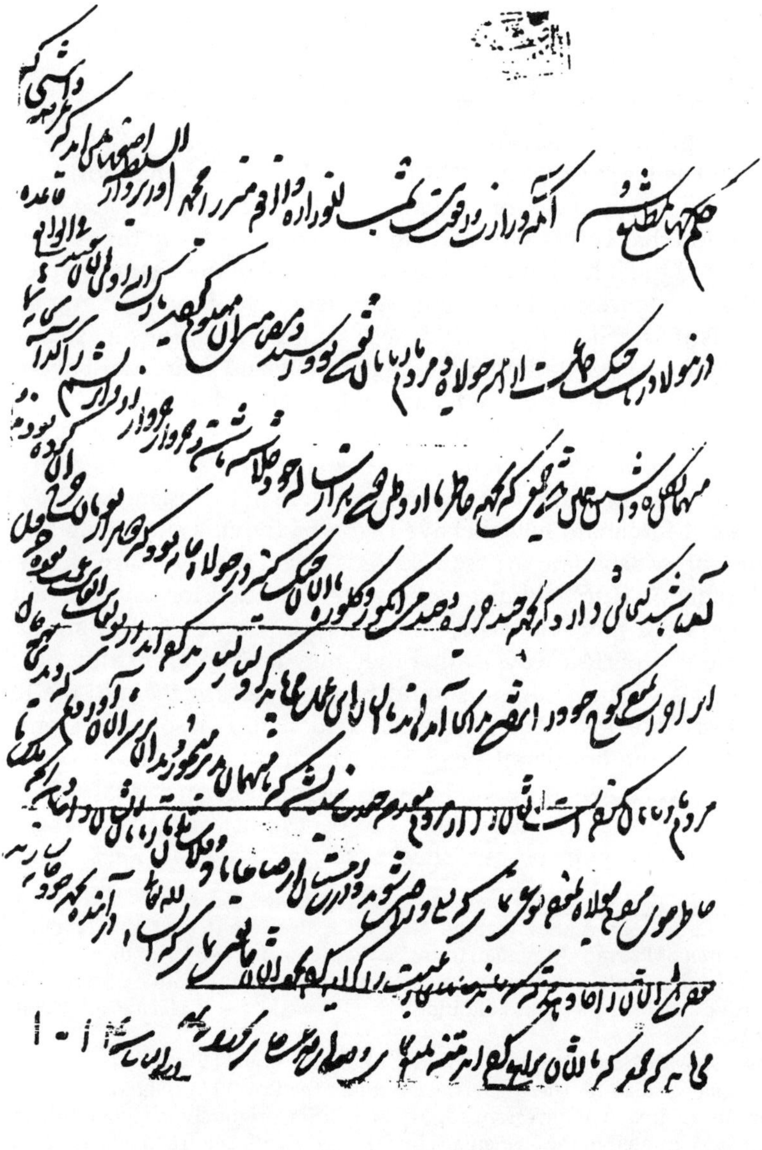

فرمان شاه عباس اول صفوی
سال ۱۶۰۵ م.

حکم جهانمطاع شد آنکه وزارت و رفعت پناه شمس الوزاره والرفعه میرزا محمدا وزیر دارالسلطنه اصفهان بداند که عرضه داشتی که دربنولا در باب جنگ جماعت ارامنهٔ جولاه و مردم ماربانان نوشته بود رسید و مضامین آن معلوم گردید. بارک الله روی ایشان سفید فی الواقع قاعده میهمان نگاه داشتن همین باشد؟ جمعی که بجهت خاطر ما از وطن دو سه هزار ساله خود جلا شده باشند وخروار خروار زر و ابریشم را گذاشته بخانهٔ شما آمده باشند گنجایش دارد که بجهت چند خربزه و چند من انگور وکلوره با ایشان جنگ کنید؟ در جولاه خانه بود که دو هزار تومان خرج آن کرده بودند و آنرا خراب نموده کوچ خود را برداشته بدانجا آمده اند با ایشان این عمل می باید کرد؟ بسیار بسیار بد کرده اند از تو بغایت الغایت عجیب بوده که قتل مردم ماربانان نکرده است ایشانرا از مردم مورچه خورت بند نشده که با میهمان بد برمیخوردند آن برسر ایشان آوردیم که دیدی.

بهر حال خاطر جوئی مردم جولاه نموده نوعی نماید که تسلّی و راضی شوند و درین زمستان از صاغاباد و فلاشان تا ماربانان ایشان را جا دهند آنچه ملک ما بوده باشد ایشان را جا دهند تتمه که بماند خانهای رعیت را کرایه کرده بجهت ایشان جا تعیین نمایند انشاالله تعالی در آینده بجهت خود خانه سازند می باید که جمعی که با ایشان نزاع کرده اند تنبیه بلیغ نماید و درین باب قدغن دانند.

تحریرا فی شهر ربیع الثانی سنه ۱۰۱۴

Document #2

The Decree of Shah 'Abbas I, to build a Cathedral in New Julfa, with the Sacred Stones of Ējmiacin.[1]

The present high order is issued, so that Armenian priests, clerics, elders, leaders and people living in the Royal Capital of Isfahan, will be able to hold their heads high, due to the special attention paid to them by our great kingdom.

Let them know that there exists a friendly relationship between our great kingdom and the Christian states, particularly with the Lord Pope of Rome and His Majesty the King of Spain and that we are inseparably united in love with the Armenian nation. We have friendly communications with the Pope of Rome, because people travel between all the Christian states and our kingdom; Isfahan is the Capital of our famous kingdom, where there are people of different origins and nationalities; therefore, we wish to build for the Armenians a large, magnificent, high, and elegantly adorned church in the Capital, to serve as a place of worship for them, where they may pray according to their tradition and rites. We will send a messenger to the Holy Pope of Rome and ask him to send a Christian priest or cleric to the Capital Isfahan to pray in the said church, so that the people may learn and we may also benefit from the prayers.

There are sacred stones in *Učkilisa*[2] of Erevan, which is mostly in ruins and whose reconstruction is not possible. The bones of saints buried there were dug out and sold to foreigners by the local priests;[3] thus, the place has lost its glory and its ability for miracles. Therefore, We ordered that the stones be removed and sent to Isfahan, so that We may use them for the construction of the famous Church.

When the said stones are brought, the Armenian community must gather and with great honours receive them, and together with 'Ali-Vazir of Isfahan and Mohebb 'Ali Beg,[4] the tutor of the princes, they should place the stones in a safe place. The Armenians, the Vazir and Mohebb 'Ali Beg in concord, should take with them skilful architects to

---

[1] Persian text in AASM (cab. 6, file 41, doc. 7). Armenian tr. in Tēr Yovhaneanč, vol. I, pp. 52-53. Another English translation based on the Italian and Spanish versions of this decree is presented in the *Chronicle of Carmelites in Persia*, vol. I, pg. 196.
[2] Ējmiacin.
[3] Referring to the theft of St. Hripsimē's relics by Catholic missionaries. See Aṙakel Dawrižeči, pp. 178-197.
[4] Mohebb 'Ali Beg is mentioned also by E. Monshi, vol. II, pg. 1170.

the rear of *Baghzeresk*,[5] the place that We have designated for the Church, where they should lay the foundations of the famous church according to the wishes of the priests and the fathers.[6] They should send the designs to Our Majesty, which we will study and order the builders to begin the work and bring the construction to completion. They must exercise great care in this matter, for which they will be assured of favours by Our Kingdom. Written in the year 1023.[7]

---

[5] A garden on the eastern edge of New Julfa.
[6] Catholic missionaries.
[7] Feb. 11, 1614-Jan. 30, 1615.

فرمان همایون شد...

مذهبه پادشاه ...

اسلامبر العبود...

وجوانب کیتنید...

مذکور کلیسیا...

ارکشیشان و ربانیان...

بوده مند بدنیم...

وکشیش آنجا...

سکنیها...

بهی طوایف مسیحیه...

محبت مشبک...

ترکشیشان و پادریان...

۱۰۲۳

فرمان شاه عباس اول صفوی
سال ۱۶۱۴ م.

فرمان همیون شد آنکه کشیشان و رهبانان و ملکان و ریش سفیدان و کدخدایان و رعایا ارامنه ساکنین دارالسلطنه اصفهان بعنایات بیغایت شاهانه و شفقت و مرحمت بینهایت پادشاهانه مفتخر و سرافراز و مستظهر و امیدوار بوده بدانند که چون میانه نوّاب کامیاب همیون ما و حضرات سلاطین رفیع الشّأن مسیحیه خصوصاً سلطنت و شوکت کرامت پناهی قُدوة السلاطین العیسویه کمال محبت و دوستی است و در میانه ما طوایف مسیحیه یگانگی است و اصلاً جدایی نیست و توجّه خاطر اشرف بدان متعلّق است که همیشه طوایف مسیحیه از اطراف و جوانب این دیار آمد و شد نمایند چون دارالسلطنه اصفهان پایتخت همایون است و او از همه طبقه و هر طایفه و مردم هر مَلّت در آنجا هستند میخواهم که جهت مردم مسیحیه در دارالسلطنه مذکور کلیسیای عالی در کمال رفعت و زیب و زینت ترتیب دهیم که معبد ایشان بوده جمیع مردم مسیحیه در آنجا بکیش و آئین خود عبادت نماید و کس نزد حضرت با با خواهیم فرستاد که یکی از کشیشان و رهبانان مَلّت مسیحی را بدارالسلطنه اصفهان فرستد که در آن کلیسیا بآداب عبادت قیام نموده طوایف مسیحیه را بطاعت و عبادت ترغیب نماید و ما نیز از ابواب آن عبادات بهره مند باشیم و چون چند عدد سنگ متّبرک در اوج کلیسیای ایروان بود و عمارت آن کلیسیا منهدم گشته خرابی تمام بآن راه یافته بود که دیگر شایستگی تعمیر نداشت و کشیش آنجا نیز استخوانهای پیغمبران را که در آن مکان مدفون بود از آنجا بیرون آورده بجماعت نصارا و ترسایان فروخته آنمقام را از عزّت و سراقت انداخته بود بنابر آن سنگهای مذکور را از آنجا بیرون آورده روانه دارالسلطنه اصفهان فرمودیم که در کلیسیای عالیی که بدانجا آورند در آنجا ترتیب میدهیم نصب فرمائیم می باید که چون سنگهای مذکور را بدانجا آورند همگی طوایف مسیحیه را جمع نموده از روی تعظیم و احترام تمام استقبال کرده سنگها را آورده باتّفاق سیادت و وزارت پناه شمسالّلوزاره عُلیا وزیر دارلسلطنه مذکور و رفعت پناه کمالاً للرفیعه مُحّب علی بیک لله در جایی که مناسب داند بگذارند و باتّفاق و یکدیگر معماران خاصه شریفه را همراه برده در پشت باغ زرشک در زمینی که بجهت کلیسیا قرار داده بودیم طرح کلیسیای عالی که کشیشان و پادریان عظام قرار دهند انداخته طرح آنرا در تخته و کاغذ کشیده بخدمت اشرف فرستند که ملاحظه نمائیم و بعد از ملاحظه امر فرمائیم که استادان شروع در کار کرده باتمام رسانند درین باب اهتمام لازم دانسته بهمه جهتی بشفقت بیدریغ خسروانه واثق و امیدوار باشند

تحریراً فی شهر شعبان المُعظّم سنه ۱۰۲۳

Document #3

The Decree of Shah 'Abbas I, granting Royal Lands to the Armenian Community of New Julfa.[1]

A high order is issued.

At this time, due to our endless Royal benevolence and mercy towards the Armenians of Julfa, and for the betterment of their life, We decided to grant them, free of charge, the land at the bank of river Zayandarud, in the Capital City of Isfahan, which is part of our royal property and where they have already built houses.

Honorable and great treasurer of the Chancery, delete the above mentioned land from the list of royal properties and register it in the books as a gift to the Armenians. *Vazir, Kalantar* and public officers of Isfahan, obey the present order and consider the said land as accorded property to the Armenians. Issued in the month of *Shawwal*, 1028.[2]

---

[1] Persian text in AASM (cab. 6, file 41, doc. 8). Printed by Isma'il Ra'in, pg. 114. Armenian translation in Tĕr Yovhaneanč, vol. I, pg. 36.

[2] Sept. 11 - Oct. 9, 1619.

ز علی

کمیجه مطلع گشته آنکه در سوابق بر عادت بعضی امه و شفقت پادشاهی

در باره ارامنه علیاه و ترقیم صلاحیت ایشان از اهمی نوریان واقع در کار رفته

دار السلطنه اصفهان که ایشان را زانجا خانه برنهاده اند و ملک کذا خوان

بعضی دیگر از آنها در ستم مسندنشینان عظام کرام دیوان را بین بد کرده

بطرف مساجد بانعام از امنه مذکور در دفعات عمل نرسیده و زرد و کلام

اصفهان حبیب الطور موذر در مسجد از قرار مسق در مکذ زید و راین مذکور

معین ده اسید محرر الامه شوال ۱۰۲۸

فرمان شاه عباس اول صفوی
سال ۱۶۱۹ م.

حکم مطلع شد آنکه در اینوقت بنابر عنایت بی غایت شاهانه و شفقت بلانهایت پادشاهانه درباره ارامنه جولاه وترقیه حال ایشان راضی و زمین واقعه در کنار رودخانه زاینده رود ، دارالسلطنه اصفهان که ایشان در آنجا خانه ترتیب داده اند و ملک نواب همایون است، به انعام به ایشان شفقت فرموده ، ارزانی داشتیم.

مستوفیان عظام کرام دیوان، زمین مذکور را از ملکیت دیوان برطرف ساخته، به انعام ارامنه مذکور ، در دفاتر عمل نمایند. وزیر کلانتر و عمال اصفهان ، حسب المسطور مقرر دانسته، از فرموده در نگذرند، و زمین مذکور را به انعام ایشان مقرر دانند.

تحریراً فی شهر شوال سنه ۱۰۲۸

Document #4

The *Fatwa*[1] of *Shaykh Al-Islam*,[2] concerning the hereditary rights
of Muslim heirs of *Zimmi*[3] subjects.[4]

He knows the Truth

How would the wise clergy and theologians of the *Shi'a*
dogma—Let their wise utterings be perpetuated in the world–
resolve the following question?

A person called Mehdiqoli, who had newly converted to Islam
died, leaving behind a Muslim son called Shahnazar and two grand
daughters: Mariam and Fatimē, offsprings of another Muslim son
called Zakaria. In this case, based on the principal of "the closer
relatives take precedence over the distant ones," does the
inheritance of the above mentioned Mehdiqoli—after all necessary
deductions—belong to the above mentioned Shahnazar or not?
Clarify.

He has the knowledge. Glory to His light.

Yes, it belongs to Shahnazar.

God is the wisest.

Written by '*Abd*[5]

Seal "Servant of the Lord, Yousef, 1030"[6]

Let the wise men, whose word be preserved forever among
nobles, also give their verdict concerning the following question:

A certain *Zimmi* called Baba, who has two Muslim nephews, an
infidel brother and nephews, died. In this case, should the infidels
be deprived of the inheritance of the *Zimmi* or not? Clarify.

He has the knowledge. Glory to His Light.

Yes, when there are Muslim heirs, the infidel is
deprived of the inheritance.

God is the wisest.

Written by '*Abd*

[The same seal]

---

[1] Verdict.

[2] Chief religious official of the larger cities.

[3] Non-Muslim, Christian.

[4] Persian text with Armenian trans. in Y. Papazyan, *Matenadarani Parskeren Hrovartakner∂*, vol. I, Book II, pp. 101-103, 496-7.

[5] Slave, servant.

[6] Nov. 26,1620-Nov. 15-1621.

Let them also give their verdict concerning the following question:

If the infidel brother converts to Islam before the inheritance of the said *Zimmi* is distributed among the two Muslim nephews, would the nephews, in this case, be deprived of the inheritance and would the newly converted brother who is a closer heir than the nephews inherit the entire property? Clarify.

He is

Yes, that is the way it happens and

the inheritance belongs to the closest heir.

God the wisest

Written by *'Abd*

[The same seal]

Let them also reveal their decision concerning the following question:

The said brother, who was the only heir of his *Zimmi* brother died, leaving behind a son, the said Shahnazar and the said grand children. If , at this stage, when Shahnazar is the only heir and is entitled to inherit everything, the other above mentioned *Zimmi* son converts to Islam to claim the inheritance, would he be able to deprive an earlier convert (Shahnazar) of his inheritance, given the fact that he is the older of the two? Clarify.

He is

No

And God is the wisest

Written by *'Abd*

[The same seal]

فتوی شیخ‌الاسلام ایروان
سال ۱۶۲۱ م.
هوالعالم بالحق

چه فرمایند علماء امامیه وفقهاء اثنی عشریه ابدت ایام افادائهم بین البریه در بیان اینمسئله که هرگاه مهدیقلی‌جدیدالاسلام فوت شود از سربسری شاه نظر اسلامی و از نوادگان پسری اسلامیه هَن مریم و فاطمه بنتان ذکریاء ابن مهدیقلی مذکور والحالة هذه بمدای کل اقرب بمنع البعد بعد از اخراج مایحب اخراجه عن‌المتروکات متروکات مهدیقلی مذکور ایا مخصوص شاهنظر مذکور است یا نه بینوا توجروا.

هوالعالم عز نوره
بلی مخصوص شاهنظر مذکور
است الله اعلم. حرر العبد
— نقش مهر —
بندهٔ شاه ولایت یوسف. سنهٔ ۱۰۳۰

ایضاً بیان فرمایند علماء انام ابدت ایام افاداتهم بین الکرام در بیان اینمسئله که هرگاه بابأ ذمی فوت شود از سر دو برادر زادهٔ مسلمان و برادر کافر وپسران کافرین والحالة هذه کفار ممنوع از ارث ذمی اند یا نه بینوا توجروا.

هوالعالم عز نوره
بلی با وجود وارث مسلمان
کافر از ارث ممنوع است. الله اعلم. حرر العبد (همان مهر)

ایضاً بیان فرمایند در بیان اینمسئله که هرگاه برادر زادگان اسلامی قبل از آنکه ارث ذمی مذکور را میانهٔ یکدیگر قسمت نمایند برادر ذمی مذکور که ذمی باشد مسلمان شود چون اولی از برادرزادگان است بمیراث آبا برادرزادگان مذکوره ممنوع از ارث میشوند وارث مخصوص برادر واحد میشود یانه بینواتوجروا.
هو
بلی میشود وارث مخصوص وارث اقرب میگردد...والله اعلم.
حرر العبد(همان مهر)

ایضاً بیان فرمایند در بیان اینمسئله که هرگاه برادر مذکور که واحد است در ارث بردن از برادر ذمی فوت شود از سربسری که شاه نظر مذکور است وپسرزادگان مذکورین و شاه نظر که وارث واحد شده مستحق ارث شده باشد و متروکات مخصوص او شده پسر ذمی مذکور مسلمان شود بعد از اسلام وارث واحد مذکور والحاله هذه پسر متأخر فی‌الاسلام با وجود اقربیت آنوارث واحد را که قبل ازین مسلمان بوده منع از ارث میتواند کرد یا نه بینوا توجروا.
هو
نه والله اعلم . حرر العبد

Document #5

The Decree of Shah 'Abbas II, confirming the election of Kaťolikos
Yakob Julayeci.[1]

The position of His Majesty's sacred seal

May God rest the soul of my father the King in peace.
A high order is issued.

According to the Royal Decree issued in the month of *Safar*, 1055,[2] the spiritual leadership of Armenians–priests, clergy[3] and others–in *Uckilisa* and *Chukhuri Sa'd* was entrusted to *Khalife*[4] Pilippos. At this time, *Khalife* Yakob informed us that *Khalife* Pilippos has died and asked that the duties be entrusted to him. Therefore, with Our Royal mercy, we entrust the spiritual leadership of *Uckilisa* and the Armenians of *Cokur-e Sa'd*, etc.—which was previously given to *Khalife* Pilippos—to the above mentioned *Khalife*. All the Armenians of *Cokur-e Sa'd*—clergy and others—should follow this order, accept him as their *Khalife* and follow his orders. This should be considered as an obligation.

Issued in *Jumada Al-Aula*, 1069.[5]

---

[1] Persian text in AASM (cab. 6, file 41, doc. 53).

[2] March 30-April 27, 1645.

[3] *Mehrasayan* or *Mehrasyaban*.

[4] Caliph. A general term used for all high ranking Christian clergymen. In this text it refers to the Kaťolikos.

[5] Jan. 26-Feb. 24, 1659.

شاه بالم انار الله سرئم

حكم جهو طاع شس

سرطی ترسم بدارخانال صراكماب صادر ساد كشه حلاف اىكم والامه جهودمعود

ومهراساها وعن نخليفه ملكبس مرحع شم بموف ودرميون علم بسوف

سعالم يوس سا مدكم طهوملكمس فوس شوا سدعا صه ميسلم

شاه درمان شه رله حلا ىكم والامه جهودمعود اعما راى سد

لمومرى انمجهودذ تر نمعطار لصروا شمع امراسجهدمعود

ممت رله راجلهو جهونىسدار منخ رسلاح سا بردان سر

۱۰۶۹

علل لهر حهامد الا د سه

فرمان شاه عباس ثانی صفوی
سال ۱۶۵۹ م.

حکم جهانمطاع شد آنکه چون بموجب رقم اشرف که بتاریخ شهر صفر ۱۰۵۵ برطبق رقم نواب خاقان رضوانمکانی صادر گشته خلافت اوچ کلیسیا و ارامنه چخور سعد و کشیشان و مهراساها و غیره بخلیفه پیلیپوس مرجوع شده بود و در اینوقت عمدةالمسیحیه یعقوب خلیفه بدرگاه معلی آمده بعرض رسانیدکه خلیفه پیلیپوس فوت شده و استدعای خدمت مزبور باسم خود نمود بنا بر شفقت شاهانه دربارهٔ مشارالیه خلافت اوچ کلیسیا و ارامنه چخورسعد و غیره را بدستوری که در وجه خلیفه پیلیپوس مقرر بود بمومی الیه شفقت و مرحمت فرموده ارزانی داشتیم جماعت ارامنه چخور سعد و کشیشان و مهراساها و غیره حسب المسطور مقرر دانسته مشارالیه را خلیفهٔ خود دانند و از سخن و صلاح حسابی او برون نروند و در عهده شناسند

تحریراً ۲۴ شهر جمادی الاخر سنه ۱۰۶۹

Document #6

The Decree of Shah Sulayman, forbidding Persian officials to intervene in the religious affairs of the Armenian community.[1]

The position of His Majesty's Sacred Seal

A high order is issued.

At this time, the honorable Stepanos *Vardapet* came to the court and informed us that the spiritual leadership of the Armenian communities in Julfa, Faridan,[2] Burwari, Geandiman and Linjan belongs to him. He complained that the local *hakems*,[3] *tiuldars*,[4] *hamesaledars*[5] and others were intervening in his Jurisdictional affairs, and were forcing him to perform illegal weddings, preventing him from collecting ecclesiastical taxes and act according to the Christian laws. Some Armenians also were intervening in his affairs, refusing to obey him and failing to follow the customary rites.

Therefore, We are sending this Royal Decree to *Yuzbaši*[6] Safi-quli *Beg*, having decided that he—if the accusations are true—not let the *hakems, tiuldars, hamesaledars* and others intervene in his [Stepanos'] affairs and in the proper order of Armenian weddings or prevent him [Stepanos] from collecting ecclesiastical taxes. The above mentioned Armenian communities must be governed the way they used to be governed in the past and he [Stepanos] should be treated accordingly. Whatever religious taxes they [the people] use to pay, they should not stop paying him. In that respect *Yuzbaši* Safi-quli *Beg* should be responsible, so that new decrees will not be required to be issued every year.

Shawwal, 1079.[7]

---

[1] Persian text in AASM (cab. 6, file 41, doc. 63).
[2] Peria.
[3] Regional governor or judge.
[4] Military officer.
[5] Military or administrative officers, who were paid by local taxes.
[6] A Turkish military title, meaning commander of hundred soldiers.
[7] March 4-April 1, 1669.

حکم جهان مطاع شد انکه چون در زمان تازه و ... استفانی و رعایت پرکار و چهینی ... آمده موضوع رسیده محررست

ارمنه جلد بزرگان و بروباری و کنیسه مال و لبجان ... را پیش حکم و جولداران ... جمله جولداران و غیره نقل درجات ...

عفو و نفع ... از امنیت رو در آخذ گرفت و لقد قان از آن ارمنه نوروز مانع شده ... از ... و ...

نور حل در ام نوزمیع ... عن ... و در آدار رسم مرجع مول ... ... قل فنیار در باب ... عارفم امرف نهود ...

لبای ... المف ... می نفرم اردیم که ... و تولید شد ... احراز حکم و جولداران و جمله داران و غیره نگاه حکم حسن نقل والیهم ...

مانع احراز گرفت و لقد قان آز ارمنه نوروز نگرو مع و و در عقد و کنا هار مه نوزو رکمه چها عت آدر و مه نوزیرانی این خود کردانیده ...

ام راه ... در رسمی چهل آزبی میواد و ... ... رالور رتمه موقوف آز از نهود و الوسی ... فات نفساتی گلاتی ...

در سال ... غنی انته بسال ... تم ... نظیفه محررآ می ... نورانیس ۱۰۲۹

فرمان شاه سلیمان صفوی
سال ۱۶۶۹ م.

حکم جهانمطاع شد آنکه چون در اینوقت زبده الاشباه استفان و رطابیت بدرگاه جهان پناه آمده بعرض رسانید که محراسیائی ارامنه جولاه و فریدن و برواری و کندمان ولنجان بمشارالیه متعلق است حکام و تیولداران و همه‌ساله داران و غیره مدخل در مهمات متعلقه باو نموده عقد نکاح ملّت مزبور را جبراً مینمایند و در اخذ زکوات و تصدقات از ارامنه مزبوره مانع شده نمیگذارند که بدین و آئین آل مسیح عمل نمایند و بعضی از ارامنهٔ آنجا نیز مدخل در امر مزبور نموده اطاعت نمی‌نمایند و در ادای رسومی که معمول است تعلل مینمایند در این باب استدعای رقم اشرف بعهده رفعت و معالی پناه صفی قلی بیک یوز باشی ابداللوعود بنابرین مقررفرمودیم که هرگاه نموده واقعی بوده باشد احدی از حکام و تیولداران وهمه‌ساله داران و غیره بخلاف حکم وحساب مدخل در مهمات متعلقه با و ننموده مانع اخذ زکوات و تصدقات ارامنه مزبور نگردند و دخل در عقد و نکاح ارامنه مزبور نکنند و جماعت ارامنه مزبور موافق آئین خود که با مهراسیاهانی سابق عمل مینموده اند با مشارالیه نیز عمل نمایند و رسومی که قبل از این میداده اند بدستور واصل مشارالیه ساخته موقوف ندارند بعهده رفعت و معالی پناه صفی قلی و بیک یوزباشی که امداد حسابی تقدیم بتقدیم رساند و درین باب قدغن دانسته هر ساله رقم مجدّد نطلبد.

تحریراً فی شهر شوال سنه ۱۰۷۹

Document #7

The Decree of Shah Sultan Husayn sending Kat́olikos Nahapet into exile.[1]

The position of His Majesty's Sacred Seal

A high order is issued.

His Excellency the *Amir*[2] of *Amirs*, who has been raised in the royal house, the sun of the state and the kingdom, Muhammad-quli *Khan*, the *Beglarbegi*[3] of *Chukhuri Sa'd*, who has been honored by royal mercy, should know that, as soon as he receives the present royal order, he should send Nahapet, the former *Khalife* of *Učkilisa* to the monastery located in Qapan,[4] and keep him there under royal protective custody.

Issued in *Shawwal*, 1107.[5]

---

[1] Persian text in AASM (cab. 6, file 41, doc. 78).
[2] Prince in Arabic.
[3] Governor General of a bordering province.
[4] Refering to the Monastery of Tat́ew.
[5] May 4-June 1, 1696.

فرمان شاه سلطان حسین صفوی
سال ۱۶۹۶م.

حکم جـهانمطاع شد آنکه ایالت و شـوکت پناه حـشمت و جـلالت دسـتگاه عـالیـجاه امیرالامراوالعظام پرورده خاندان شاهی شمس الایاله والشوکه والجلاله والقبال محمد قلی خان بیگلر بیگی چخورسعد بشفقت شاهانه سرافرازگشته چون بر مضمون رقم ا شـرف مطلع گـردد نهابید خلیـفهٔ سابق اوچ کلیـسیا را بکلیـسیای واقعـه در قپان فرستد و بتوجّهات پادشاهانه مستمال باشـد.

تحریراً فی شهر شوال ۱۱۰۷

Document #8

The Decree of Shah Sultan Husayn replacing Katołikos Nahapet by
Steṗanos, bishop of New Julfa.[1]

A high order is issued.

At this time, the *Kalantar*, the priests, the *Kadkudas* and other
Armenian *ra'iyyat*[2] of Julfa, Isfahan, Our Capital City, complained
against the immoral deeds and negligence of *Khalife* Nahapet of *Učkilisa*
and presented us with a petition signed by all the *ra'iyyat* of Old and
New Julfa and others, and asked us to dethrone him and entrust the
spiritual authority of the Christians to Steṗanos, the *Khalife* of Julfa.

Therefore, effective from the first day of the year of the *rat*,[3] and in
accordance with Our decree concerning the former *Khalife* Nahapet, the
spiritual leadership of *Učkilisa* and the Armenians—priests, clergy and
others— of *Čokur-e Sa'd* is granted to the Honorable *Khalife* [Steṗanos] of
Julfa.

The Armenians—priests, clergy and others—of *Čokur-e Sa'd* should
behave according to this order. They should accept him as their *Khalife*
and should not disobey his orders for the benefit of Christians.

The Honorable *Beglarbegi* of *Čokur-e Sa'd* should not let anyone
interfere in the affairs of the above mentioned *Khalife*. This should be
considered as an obligation. Issued in the month of *Dhu al-Qa'da*, 1107.[4]

---

[1] Persian text in AASM (cab. 6, file 41, doc. 79).
[2] Subjects, peasants.
[3] August 12, 1695.
[4] June 2-July 1, 1696.

فرمان شاه سلطان حسین صفوی
سال ۱۶۹۶ م.

حکم جهانمطاع شد آنکه چون دراینوقت کلانتر وکشیشان وکدخدایان و سایر رعایای ارامنه جولاه دارالسلطنه اصفهان شکوه از سوء سلوک و نامقیدی نهابید خلیفه اوچ کلیسیا و محضری بمهر همگی رعایای جولاه قدیم و جدید وغیر هم ابراز واستدعاء تغییر مشارالیه وتفویض امر مزبور بعهده المسیحیه استیفانوس خلیفه جولاهی نمودند بنابراین از ابتداء ده ماهه سیچقان ئیل خلافت اوچ کلیسیا و ارامنه چخور سعد و مهراساها و غیرهم را بدستوری که در وجه (نهابید) خلیفه سابق مقرر بود بموی الیه شفقت و مرحمت فرموده ارزانی داشتیم جماعت ارامنه چخور سعد وکشیشان و مهراساها و غیر هم حسب المسطور مقرر ومشارالیه را خلیفه خود دانسته از سخن و صلاح حسابی او که هر آینه موافق ملت مسیحی بوده باشد بیرون نروند و رعایت و مراغبت اورا لازم دانند بعهده عالیجاه بیگلر بیگی چخور سعد که نگذارد که احدی در امر خلافت مذکور که نسبت بخلیفه مشارالیه دارد مدخل نماید ودر عهده شناسند

تحریراً فی ذیقعده الحرام سنه ۱۱۰۷

Document #9

The Decree of Shah Sultan Husayn, confirming the election of
Movsēs, Bishop of New Julfa.[1]

The position of His Majesty's Sacred Seal

A high order is issued.

Since the *Kalantar* and the *Kadkudas* of Armenians living in Julfa, the
Capital City of Isfahan, petitioned us that according to the most ancient
and effective decree, the spiritual leadership of Armenians living in Julfa
and other areas surrounding the capital, namely Faridan, Burwari,
Geandiman and Linjan has been entrusted to the *Khalifes* [bishops of
Julfa], and that *Khalife* Aleksandr was the [last] bishop. But now it has
been one and a half years since His Eminence [Aleksandr] was
appointed *khalife* of *Učkilisa*; therefore, they [the Armenians of New
Julfa] petitioned for *Khalife* Movsēs to be entrusted with the office [of the
bishop of New Julfa], since all of them are satisfied with his conduct.

In response to the petition presented by the Christian *Khwaja*
Yarutiwn, the representative of *Khalife* Aleksandr, the primate of the
Armenians of Old and New Julfa in the Capital City and other places,
the following decree was issued in the month of *Rajab* 1111.[2]

"Yarutiwn petitioned us that certain Armenians from Julfa, Faridan,
Burwari, Geandiman and Linjan under the spiritual jurisdiction of the
above mentioned bishop [Aleksandr] and the *hakems, tiuldars,
hamesaledars* and others should not intervene in his [Aleksandr's] affairs,
force him to conduct illegal weddings, and that the above mentioned
Armenians should not withold the payment of their church taxes, they
should obey his orders and be governed according to their religious law.
Therefore, should this be the case, we order that no one from among the
hakems, tiuldars, hamesaledars and others intervene illegally in the affairs
of the above mentioned bishop and force him to conduct illegal
weddings. The said Armenians should be governed as they were
governed during the time of former bishops and the church taxes should
be paid on a regular basis."

With our Royal kindness towards the Armenians and following the

---

[1] Persian text in AASM (cab 6, file 41, doc. 87).
[2] Dec. 24, 1699-Jan. 22, 1700.

petition of the *Kalantar* and *Kadkudas* of Armenians, effective end of month *Rabi' Al-Awal*, the year of the *rat*, 1120,[3] we entrust to *Khalife* Movsēs the primacy of the Old and the New Julfa in the Capital City of Isfahan, Faridan, Burwari, Geandiman, Linjan and other areas, which previously belonged to *Khalife* Aleksandr, because all are satisfied with the conduct of Movsēs. Let everybody be guided according to previously issued decrees. Nobody from among the *hakems, tiuldars, hamesaledars* and others is allowed to intervene in his affairs, whether they are Franks, Assyrians, Georgians or other Christians, and force him to conduct illegal weddings or prevent the collection of church taxes. He should be allowed to act according to the Christian religion and faith. Any internal dispute between the *Khalife*, the priests and the representatives of the Christian community should be handled by the said *Khalife*, in collaboration with the *Kalantar* of New Julfa. The said Armenian community should be governed by its own traditional religious laws. As they [the Armenains] used to be [governed] under previous clerics, the same should be now and whatever religious taxes they used to pay, they should pay the same exclusively to him [Movsēs].

It is the duty of everyone, the *hakems* and officials in each region, to cooperate and assist in this matter.

Issued in the blessed month of *Ramadan*, 1120.[4]

---

[3] June 20, 1708.
[4] Nov. 15-Dec. 14, 1708.

فرمان شاه سلطان حسین صفوی
سال ۱۷۰۸ م.

حکم جهان‌مطاع شد آنکه چون کلانتر و کدخدایان ارامنه جولاه دارالسلطنه اصفهان بعرض رسانیدند که بموجب رقم قدرشیم از قدیم‌الایام خلیفه‌گی ارامنه جولاه و بلده و بلوکات و نواحی دارالسلطنه مزبوره و فریدن و برورود و کندمان ولنجان بخلیفه‌گان مرجوع و قبل از این خلیفه‌گی مذکور با خلیفه الکسندر بوده و حال مدت یکسال و نیم است که مومی‌الیه بخلیفگی اوچ کلیسیا مأمور گردیده استدعا نموندندکه خلیفه‌گی مزبور بخلیفه موسس که همگی از حسن سلوک او راضی‌اند مرجوع گردد و از سرکار خاصه نوشته‌اند که بموجب رقم اشرف که بتاریخ شهر رجب المرجب ۱۱۱۱ بر طبق عرض خواجه هاروتون مسیحی وکیل الکسندر خلیفه جولاه قدیم و جدید و بلده و بلوکات دارالسلطنه مزبوره باین مضمون شرف صدور یافته آنکه چون هاروتون بعرض رسانیده که مهراسائی ارامنه جولاه و فریدن و برورود و کندمان ولنجان بخلیفهٔ مشارالیه متعلق است که حکام و تیولداران و همه‌ساله داران و غیر هم مدخل در مهمات متعلقه بخلیفه مزبور ننموده عقد و نکاح ملت مزبور را بجبر ننمایند و در اخذ زکواة و تصدقات ارامنه مزبوره ننموده اطاعت او نمی نمایند و در ادا و رسوم معمولی تعلل میکنند بنابراین مقرر فرمودیم که هرگاه نموده واقعی باشد احدی از حکام و تیولداران و همه‌ساله داران و غیر هم بخلاف حکم و حساب مدخل در مهمات متعلقه بالکسندر خلیفه مزبور ننمود. مانع اخذ زکواة و تصدقات مزبوره نگردیده و مدخل در عقد و نکاح ارامنه مزبوره نکنند و جماعت ارامنه مزبوره موافق آئین خود که مهر آسایان سابق عمل مینموده‌اند با مشارالیه عمل نموده رسومی که قبل از این باو میداده‌اند بدستور واصل او ساخته موقوف ندارند بنا بر شفقت شاهانه درباره ارامنه مزبوره از تاریخ شهر ربیع‌الاول ۱۱۲۰ سیحقان ئیل خلیفگی و مهراسانی ارامنه جولاه قدیم و جدید و فریدن و برورود و کندمان و لنجان و بلده و بلوکات دارالسلطنه (اصفهان) مزبور که سابقاً با خلیفه الکسندر بوده حسب استدعا کلانتر و کدخدایان جماعت ارامنه مزبوره بدستور خلیفه موسس که همگی از حسن سلوک او راضی‌اند شفقت و مرحمت فرموده ارزانی داشتیم که بشرح رقمی که قبل از این صادر شده عمل نموده احدی از حکام و تیولداران و همه‌ساله داران و غیر هم خواه فرنگی و صوریان و خواه گرجی و ملل دیگر از مسیحیان مدخل در مهمات متعلقه از عقد و نکاح و اخذ زکاة و تصدقات ننموده گذارند که او بدین و آئین آل مسیح عمل

نماید و نـزاع و گـفتگـوئی که فیما بین خلیفه و کشیش و سایر جماعت مسیحی رود خلیفهٔ
مزبوره باتفاق کلانتر جولاه رسیده فیصل دهد . جماعت ارامنه مزبوره موافق آئین
خود که مهر آسایان سابق عمل مینموده اند با مشارالیه عمل نموده و رسومی که قبل از
این میداده اند بدستور مخصوص او دانسته واصل سازند بعهده حکام و عمال هر محل
که در این باب امداد و اعانت بتـقدیم رسانیده و در عهده شناسند

تحریراً فی
شهر رمضان المـبارک ۱۱۲۰

Document #10

Encyclical of Kaťolikos Ṕilippos, appointing Bishop Dawiť Primate of
New Julfa.[1]

The Servant of Jesus Christ, Ṕilippos, Kaťolikos of all Armenians
and Patriarch of the majestic, angelic, paradisiacal and heavenly Holy
See of Ēĵmiacin in Vałaršapat, whose letter of blessing and protection,
apostolic grace and Divine blessing will reach the city of Isfahan and our
people in Julfa, Erewan,[2] Ṕeria, Burwari, Geandiman and Linĵan, and the
God worshipping and Christ loving *dowla ťawork*, priests and people at
large, old and young, men and women, elderly and children, youths and
maidens, and people of all ages, Amen.

Grace and peace be with you from Almighty God, the Father, our
Saviour Jesus Christ and life giving and generous benefactor Holy Spirit.
Amen.

Let the blessing of Father, the protection of Son and the providence
of Holy Spirit be always with you and everyday make you blossom in
glory, honours and abundant riches, like leafy and fruitful vine and
branches planted in paradise, grant you a peaceful and long life and
make you reach advanced age, Amen.

Let also our Lord, God bless you and enrich you spiritually and
physically, with a home and place, a family and children, sons and
daughters, beloved ones and friends, possessions and goods, cultivation
and products, and fill you with all kinds of spiritual and physical
goodness, and at your departure from this world, let Him make you and
your deceased ones worthy to the heavenly kingdom and unfading
crown, in the company of his saints, Amen.

With blessings, be informed my beloved people in the Lord,
according to the words of the apostle I have to care for all the churches;
therefore, I have to provide for all their needs as much as I can, so that I
may face Christ with an open countenance. Moreover, I should carry on
the message of God, who says to the primates through the Prophet
Ezekiel: "Son of man, I have made thee a watchman unto the house of

---

[1] Armenian text AASM (cab. 5, drawer 3, doc. 1).
[2] A quarter in the south western edge of New Julfa.

Israel,"[3] and He concludes by saying: "... thou givest him [the wicked] not warning... his blood will require at thine hand."[4]

We see the needs of your churches, because it has been quite a long time since Xačatur *Vardapet*[5] died and you have been without a bishop; therefore, We ordained Our spiritual son Dawit *Vardapet* and sent him to be your pastor and bishop. We elevated him to the rank of primate so that he may guide you. Blessed be who he blesses and cursed be who he curses. Let whatever he binds be bound and whatever he looses be loosed. Those who obey him obey God and those who oppose him oppose God.

Therefore, my beloved people, do not go and meet him in the manner you have been used to meeting him until now, but obey him as beloved children and do whatever he orders you to do, because he does that which is to your benefit with joy and not with discontent. Assist and support him in all his affairs so that with your help he may advance his works and be able to say: "Behold I and the children which God hath given me."[6]

Provide the needs of the monastery and pay all the church taxes to strengthen him in his duties. And for whatever you pay or you do, you will be awarded during the second coming of Christ, who is blessed for ever and ever, Amen. Our Father which art.

Written on April 23, 1101[7] at St. James Monastery in the Holy City of Jerusalem.

---

[3] Ezekiel II, 17.
[4] Ibid. II,8.
[5] Xačatur Kesaraći, died in 1646.
[6] Hebrews, II,13.
[7] 1652.

ԿՈՆԴԱԿ ՖԻԼԻՊՊՈՍ ԿԱԹՈՂԻԿՈՍԻ, 1652
(կնիք)

Յիսուսի Քրիստոսի ծառայ Փիլիպպոս կաթողիկոս ամենայն հայոց եւ
պատրիարք Վաղարշապատու վեհափառ եւ հրեշտակապար աղիւնասարաս եւ
երկնահանգէտ սրբոյ աթոռոյ Էջմիածնի: Յորմէ ժամանեալ հասցէ գիր օրհնութեան եւ նամակ պանիպանութեան, շնորհք առաքելական եւ աստուածային օրհնութիւն ի վերայ տիրախնամ եւ աստուածապաշ քաղաքիդ Սպանանու եւ աստ-
ւածաբնեալ ժողովրդեան մերում որ ի Ջուղայ, ի ՚երեւան, ի Փերիա, ի Բուրվարի,
ի Գանտիման եւ ի Լինճան, աստուածապաշշու եւ քրիստոսասէր ղօլվաթաւորաց,
նաեւ առ հասարակ քանանայից եւ ժողովրդոց ամենեցուն, մեծի եւ փոքու, ա-
րանց եւ կանանց, ծերոց եւ տղայոց, երիտասարդաց եւ կուսից, եւ ամենայն չափու հասակի ամէն:

Շնորհք ընդ ձեզ եւ խաղաղութին յԱստուծոյ հօրէ մերմէ, եւ ի տեառնէ
ամենակալէ Յիսուսէ Քրիստոսէ, եւ ի Սուրբ Հոգոյն կենարարէ, առասածաւալ
պարգեւատուէ, եւ շնորհատու բարերարէ եւ մարդասիրէ, ամէն:

Օրհնութիւն Հօր, պանպանութիւն Որդւոյ, եւ նախախնամութիւն ամենասուրբ Հոգւոյն, միշտ եւ հանապազ ի վերայ ձեր լիցի, եւ որ ըստ օրէ լցուացէ
զձեզ փառօք պատուօք եւ արգասաւիր ճոխութեամբ, իբրեւ գործս եւ գոստ
սաղարթախիսի եւ պտղալից դրախտ տնկեալ ի գնացս ճոգոյն վտակաց կալ
մնալ ձեզ խաղաղական կենօք եւ պարագայծ ամօք մինչեւ ի խորին ծերու-
թիւնն, ամէն:

Այլ եւ օրհնեսցէ զձեզ Տէր Աստուած մեր, եւ զարդարեսցէ ճոգով եւ
մարմնով, տամբ եւ տեղօք, զարմօք եւ զաւակօք, որդօք եւ դստերօք, սիրելեօք
եւ բարեկամօք, ընչիւք եւ ապրանօք, վարօք եւ վաստակօք եւ ամենայն բարու-
թեամբ ճոգոյ եւ մարմնոյ լցուացէ զձեզ, եւ յետ աստենայս ելանելոյ, զձեզ եւ
զննչեցեալսն ձեր երկնից արքայութեան եւ անթառամ պսակացն արժանաորս
արասցէ զձեզ ընդ սուրբս իր, ամէն:

Եւ ընդ օրհնութեանս ծանիք սիրելիք մեր ի Տէր, զի ըստ առաքելոյ բանին
ճոգք ամենայն եկեղեցեաց ի մեզ ունիմք, վասն որոյ պարտիմք զամենայն պակասութիւն ձռցս ճոգալ որ քան կար մեր է, զի ճամարձակութեամբ կացցուք
պարզերեսս առաջի Քրիստոսի: Մանաւանդ թէ ազատ լիցուք ի սպառնալեաց
պատգամացն Աստուծոյ որ մարգարէիւ Եզեկիէլիւ ասէ առ առաջնորդս թէ որդի
մարդոյ դէտ կացուցի զքեզ ի վերայ տանն իսրայէլի եւ յաւարու հասուցեալ ասէ
թէ բարութ ոչ զգուշացուցես զարինն ձռցս ի ձեռաց քոց խնդրեցից:

Վասն որոյ եւ մեր տեսեալ զզակասութիւն եկեղեցւոյ ձերոց որ այսքան
ժամանակ որ լուսաոր ճոգի Խաչատուր վարդապետն առ Աստուած է փոխեր
դուք առանց առաջնորդի էք: Ջեռնաւրեցաք գնողեռւո որդի մեր զԴաւիթ վարդապետն եւ առաքեցաք ձեզ ճովիւ եւ առաջնորդ եւ տուաք նմա իշխանութիւն
առաջնորդական որ ճովմւեցէ զձեզ: Օրհնեալն նորա օրհնեալ է եւ անիծեալն
անիծեալ: Կապեալն կապեալ է եւ արձակեալն արձակեալ: Հնազանդեալքն դ-
րա Աստուծոյ են ճնազանդ եւ ընդդիմացօղքն նորա Աստուծոյ են ընդդիմակք:
Վասն որոյ եւ դուք սիրելիք, մի ըստ ձեր սովորութեանն որպէս միշչեւ ցայժմ
զնայցէք առ դա, այլ իբրեւ սիրելի որդիք ճնազանդք լերուք դմա, եւ գոր ինչ
հրամայեսցէ արասջիք զի խնութեամբ արասցէ զայն եւ մի յոգոց ճանելով. զի
այն ոչ յոգուտ ձեր է: Այլ եւ յամենայն գործս օգնական եւ թիկունք լինիջիք զի
զգործս իր ձեռօք յառաջեցուցցէ, եւ ճամարձակ լիցի ասել, թէ աha ես եւ ման-

կունք իմ: Այլ եւ զամենայն պակասութիւն վանացն լիով ՟նգաւշիք եւ զամենայն կանոնական ՟աս եւ զիրաւունս անպակաս առնիցէք, զի ինքն իր գործոյն
՟աստատ կացցէ: Եւ դուք ըստ տրոց եւ ըստ իրաքանչիւր վաստակոց վարձս ի
Քրիստոսէ առնուցուք ի միսանգամ գալստեանն նորա, որ է օրՀնեալ յաւիտեանս ամէն: Հայր մեր որ:

Գրեցաւ թուին ՌՃՆ յապրիլի ամսոյ ԻԳ: Ի սուրբ քաղաքն Երուսաղէմ, ի
դրան սրբոյն Յակոբայ:

Document #11

Encyclical of Kaťolikos Yakob separating the districts of Burwari and
Ṗeria from the diocese of New Julfa.[1]

The Servant of Jesus Christ, Yakob, Kaťolikos of all Armenians and
the Patriarch of the heavenly, paradisiacal and luminous great See of
Ējmiacin in Vałaršapat, whose letter of blessing and protection, apostolic
grace and abundant Divine blessing will reach the districts of Burwari
and Ṗeria which are under the protection of God and Christ.

To the churches, priests, headmen, *dowlaťawork̇* and the people at
large, to the old and young, men and women, the elderly and the
children, youths and maidens and to the faithful in all ages. Grace and
peace be with you from God the Father, our Saviour Jesus Christ and
our life giving benefactor the Holy Spirit, Amen.

God bless you all and enrich your souls and bodies, your homes
and places, your families and children, your sons and daughters, your
beloved ones and friends, your possessions and goods, your labour and
earnings, your fields and gardens and all the things you possess.

With blessings, dear people, I would like to announce that after
your deportation from the old country to this country—as you all
know—you were under the direct jurisdiction of Kaťolikoi Dawiť and
Melḱiseť until the time of Kaťolikos Movsēs. But due to the shortage of
primates, Kaťolikos Movsēs temporarily placed you under the
jurisdiction of Xačatur *Vardapet,* until the time, when by Divine grace
the number of clerics would increase.

Now, by the grace of Christ, monasteries have been established
everywhere and primates have been appointed. With the grace of the
Holy Spirit, a monastery is established among you.

From now on, non-local primates and monks who come from Julfa
or other areas, will not be permitted to live among you, as was the
custom before. Whomever We have or will appoint primate or monk in
the new monastery, you should accept him in obedience. You should
give him all your spiritual taxes most willingly, namely *hogebažin, ptli*
and *srbadram.* Do not pay taxes to anybody other than your primates.

---

[1] Armenian text in AASM (cab. 5, dr. 3, doc. 5).

Since We appoint them as your pastors and primates, you ought to care for their physical needs, so that day and night they may care for your spiritual needs and make you live your spiritual and physical life in peace. Worships and Divine liturgies celebrated there [in the monastery] will benefit you and your departed loved ones, in this world and in the eternal life, Amen. Our Father which art in heaven.

Written in the Armenian year 1108,[2] August 26, in the village Xaǩuar.[3]

---

[2] 1659.

[3] A village most probably in the vicinity of Isfahan. Kaťołikos Yakob obtained the royal confirmation for his election in early 1659 (Jan. 26-Feb. 24). Probably he spent months in the vicinity of Isfahan before returning to Ějmiacin.

ԿՈՆԴԱԿ ՅԱԿՈԲ ԿԱԹՈՂԻԿՈՍԻ, 1659

Յիսուսի Քրիստոսի ծառայ Յակոբ կաթողիկոս ամենայն հայոց եւ պատրիարք Վաղարշապատու երկնասարաս եւ աղինատարաց, աղինադիտակ եւ
արեգակնագայծառ մեծի աթոռոյ Սրբոյն Էջմիածնի, յորմէ ժամանեալ հասցէ
գիր օրհնութեան եւ նամակ պահպանութեան, շնորհք առաբելական եւ աստ-
ւածածառայ բազմապատիկ օրհնութին ի վերայ աստուածապաշ եւ քրիստո-
սախնամ երկրացդ Բուրվարու եւ Փէրիու եկեղեցեաց, քահանայից, տանուտերաց,
դոյվաթատուրաց եւ առհասարակ ամենայն ժողովրդոց, մեծամեծաց եւ փոքունց,
արանց եւ կանանց, ծերոց եւ տղայոց, երիտասարդաց եւ կուսից, եւ ամենայն
չափու հասակի հաւատացելոց իւր:

Շնորհք ընդ ձեզ եւ խաղաղութին յԱստուծոյ հօրէ եւ ի փրկչին մերմէ
Յիսուսէ Քրիստոսէ եւ ի Սուրբ Հոգւոյն կենսարարէ եւ առատածառալ պարգեւա-
տրութ եւ բարերարէ, ամէն:

Օրհնեսցէ զձեզ տէր Աստուած մեր եւ զարդարեսցէ հոգւով եւ մարմնով,
տամբք եւ տեղօք, զարմօք եւ զաւակօք, որդւովք եւ դստերօք, սիրելեօք եւ բարեկամօք, ընչիւք եւ ապրանօք, վարօք եւ վաստակօք, անդաստանօք եւ բուրաստանօք եւ ամենայն գոյականօք:

Եւ ընդ օրհնութիւն ծանուցումն եղից ձեզ սիրելիք, զի ձեր այն երկրէն
բշելն այս երկիրս յայտ է ձեզ ամենեցունց որ Դաւիթ եւ Մելքիսէթ կաթողի-
կոսքն հովլին զձեզ, մինչ ի Մովսէս կաթողիկոսն, եւ Մովսէս կաթողիկոսն վասն
սակաւութեան առաջնորդաց յանձնեաց զձեզ ի խաչատուր վարդապետին մինչեւ
այժ առասցէ տէր եւ գրող աշակերտ բազմասցին: Այժմ, շնորհիւքն Քրիստոսի,
ամենայն տեղիս վանդրեայք հաստատեցան եւ առաջնորդք եղան նոսա, որպէս
եւ այժմ ի ձերում միջի շնորհիք սուրբ հոգւոյն վանք հաստատեցան որպէս այլ
վանդրեայքն: Այսուհետեւ օտար առաջնորդ եւ սեւագլուխ մի իշխեսցէ ի ձերում
միջի շրջել ըստ առաջին սովորութեան, թէ Չուղոյ եւ կամ այլ տեղեաց: Այլ գով
որ որ նոր վանիցն մերոյ սեւագլուխ եւ առաջնորդ կարգեալ եմ եւ կարգեմք,
զնոսա ընդունէք եւ հնազանդ նոսա կայջիք. զոր ինչ հոգեւոր հաս եւ իրաւունք
լինի, թէ հոգեբաժին, պտող եւ սրբադրամ, զամենայն ի ձեռս նոսա հասուցանէք
ամենայոծար սրտիւ եւ կամօք:

Զատ ի յառաջնորդաց ձերոց այլոց բնաւին մի տայք: Չերա գդրաս կարգեցաք ձեզ հովիւ եւ առաջնորդ, դուք պարտիք դոսա զմարմնաւոր կարիքն հո-
գալ, որ զի եւ դոքա գիշեր եւ ցերեկ զձեր հոգեւոր հոգան քաշեսցեն որ խաղաղութեամբ եւ անդորրութեամբ զձեր հոգեւոր եւ մարմնաւոր կեանս անցուցանէք:
Եւ որք անն պաշտոնէ եւ պատարագ մատչի ձեզ եւ ընչեցելոց մասն եւ բաժին
լիցի աստ եւ ի հանդերձեալն, ամէն: Հայր մեր որ յերկինս:

Գրեցաւ ի թուին հայոց ՌՃԸ եւ յոգոստոսի ամսոյ ԻՉ եւ ի գիւղ
Խաթրար:

Document #12

Encyclical of Kaťolikos Yakob, restoring the administrative jurisdiction of the diocese of New Julfa over all the Armenian communities around Isfahan.[1]

The Servant of Jesus Christ, Yakob, Kaťolikos of all Armenians and the Patriarch of the heavenly, paradisiacal, luminous and Christlike Holy See of Ējmiacin, whose letter of blessing and protection, apostolic grace and abundant Divine blessing with provident mercy will reach your districts, cities—which are under the protection of God and Christ—and you, the faithful people of Erewan, Gask, Tawriz, Dašt, Gawrabad, Linjan, Alinjan, Geandiman and Jłaxor. To the holy priests at large, Christ loving and pious *dowlataworḱ*, headmen, church trustees, merchants, craftsmen and people at large, to men and women, the elderly and children, youths and maidens and to the faithful of Christ-God in all ages, Amen.[2]

With my blessings, be informed my spiritual and beloved children. The Saint apostle says: "Providing for honest things, not only in the sight of the Lord, but also in the sight of men."[3] Our intention was the common benefit in spiritual salvation, the dissemination of monasteries and monks in certain places, so that instruction and spiritual consolation would always be available to people living far away. That is why we separated you from the Monastery of Julfa.

But now We see that the separation was not as beneficial as We thought it would be. Moreover, divisions and enmity crept into the atmosphere of love and unity. Therefore, We reinstate you in the diocese of All Saviour's monastery, and as your bishop we install our brother Dawiť *Vardapet*, so that you may be "one fold and one shepherd."[4]

From now on, obey all his orders and express your obedience with love and faithfulness which befits the faithful of Christ. We have also suggested to Dawiť *Vardapet* to always provide you with preachers and

---

[1] Armenian text in AASM (cab. 5, dr. 3, doc. 6).
[2] The translation of a large part of customary and supplicant expressions is omitted.
[3] Second Corinthians, VIII, 21.
[4] John X, 16.

instructors, which you should host with love and fruitful works, so that you may be worthy of graces and blessings, glories and crowns from Jesus Christ, our Lord, who is blessed for ever and ever, Amen.

Written in the Armenian year 1109,[5] September 4.

---

[5] 1660.

ԿՈՆԴԱԿ ՅԱԿՈԲ ԿԱԹՈՂԻԿՈՍԻ, 1660

Յիսուսի Քրիստոսի ծառայ Յակոբ կաթուղիկոս ամենայն հայոց եւ պատ‐
րիարք Վաղարշապատու երկնահանգէտ եւ աղինասարաս, լուսական եւ քրիս‐
տոսանկար սուրբ աթոռոյս Էջմիածնի: Յորմէ ժամանեալ հասցէ գիր օրհնութեան
եւ նամակ պահպանութեան, շնորհիք առաքելական եւ աստուածային բազմազեղ
օրհնութիւն հանդերձ նախախնամական գթութեան ի վերայ աստուածապահ եւ
քրիստոսասիրեան գաւառացդ, եւ վեհախնամ քաղաքացդ, եւ բարեպաշտ ժողո‐
վրդոցդ: Նախ երեւանցոցդ, կաղկցոցդ, թաւրիզեցոցդ, դաշտեցոյց, գաւրապա‐
տեցոցդ: Նաեւ Լինջանու, Ալինջանու, Գանդիմանու եւ Ջղախոռու հանօրէն եւ
միագումար սրբազան քահանայիցդ, քրիստոսասէր եւ բարեպաշտոն տօլվաթա‐
ւորացդ, տանուտերացդ, երեսփոխանացդ, վանականակնացդ, արուեստաւորացդ,
եւ միանգամայն ամենայն ժողովրդոցդ, արանց եւ կանանց, ծերոց եւ տղայոց,
երիտասարդաց եւ կուսից եւ ամենայն չափու հասակի եւ տիոց, ի Քրիստոս
Աստուած հաւատացելոց, ԱՄԷՆ:

Շնորհ ընդ ձեզ եւ խաղաղութիւն յԱստուծոյ հօրէ ամենակալէ, եւ որդւոյն
միածնէ Յիսուսէ Քրիստոսէ, եւ ի սուրբ հոգւոյն կենարարէ եւ մարդասէր բարե‐
րարէ եւ շնորհիածաւալ պարգեւատուէ, եւ ամենեցունցդ նախախնամողէ, ԱՄԷՆ:

Զոր եւ բազկատարած մախրանօր եւ բարեխօսութեամբ սուրբ Աստուա‐
ծածնին, եւ ամենայն երկնագումար ընտրելոցդ սրբոցն հայցեմք եւ խնդրեմք
յամենասուրբ երրորդութենէն ի ի մի աստուածութենէն, զի պատճառն բոլորից
անեղդ Աստուած, հայցմ երկնաւոր, հաշտութեան ընդ ձեզ միշչ ի կատարած, օրհ‐
նելով զձեզ ամենայն հոգեւոր օրհնութեամբ երկնաւորս ի Քրիստոս առաւել քան
զլերանց մշտունշենաւորաց, եւ բլրոց յաւիտենականաց: Ծագումն ի հօրէ անանա
ծննդեամբ միածինն որդին բանն Աստուած որ յոշրանշէ գոյացոյց զամենայն
արարածս, եւ պատրաստեաց զարքայութիւն արդարոց ի սկզբանէ աշխարհի,
արժանի եւ պատրաստո արասցէ զձեզ մոից առագաստին եւ անվախճան
ուրախութեանցն: Ամենասուրբ հոգին որ զարդարեաց զտիեզերս ամենայն,
զարդարեսցէ զձեզ ի զարդն անկողոպտելի, եւ ի պսակն անթառամելի:

Այլ եւ օրհնեսցէ զձեզ Տէր Աստուած մեր, եւ տացէ կրկին բարութիւն,
առատութիւն եւ լիութիւն, խաղաղութիւն եւ խնդութիւն, առողջութիւն եւ կարո‐
ղութիւն, զօրութիւն եւ արիութիւն, անշարժութիւն եւ անխոովութիւն, ուրախու‐
թիւն եւ բերկրութիւն, եւ ամենայն բարի իրաց յաջողութիւն եւ կատարելութիւն,
աստուածապաշտութիւն եւ սիրոյ առանկապակցութիւն, յուսոյ պնդութիւն եւ հա‐
ւատոյ անեղկրայութիւն, եւ միանգամայն ամենայն հոգեկան եւ մարմնական
գործող բարեգործութիւն եւ պայծառութիւն, ԱՄԷՆ:

Այլեւ օրհնեսցէ զձեզ Տէր Աստուած մեր, եւ զարդարեսցէ հոգով եւ
մարմնով, տամբ եւ տեղօք, զարմօք եւ զաւակօք, որդւք եւ դստերօք, սիրելեօք
եւ բարեկամօք, ընչիւք եւ ապրանօք, վարօք եւ վաստակօք, այգեստանօք եւ
բուրաստանօք փառօք եւ մեծութեամբ եւ ամենայն գոյականօք, լցուցէ զձեզ
Տէր Աստուած մեր որ ոչ անցանէ աստ:

Այլ եւ փրկեսցէ եւ ազատեսցէ զձեզ Տէր Աստուած մեր յամենայն փոր‐
ձանաց, յերեւելեաց եւ անյերեւունից, յանօրինաց, յանիրաւաց, ի ծննգաւորաց, ի
չարաց, ի պատրանաց, ի հերձուածողաց, ի կեղծաւորաց, ի մարդադէմ գազա‐
նաց, ի քարասիրտ բռնաւորաց, ի յանիրաւ պահանչողաց, ի սուտ եղբարց, ի
սուտ ընկերաց եւ ամենայն յորոգայթից, ամէն:

Եւ ընդ օրհնութիւնս ծանէրուք հոգեւոր եւ սիրելի որդիք մեր, զի աստ
սրբազան առաքեալն թէ խորհիմք զբարիս առաջի Աստուծոյ եւ առաջի մարդ‐

կաճ: Արդ, մեր կամս եւ խորհուրդն ըստ այսմ բանի այն էր թէ օգուտ եւ շահ հասարակաց հոգելոր փրկութեան լինէր, ի տեղիս, տեղիս վանք եւ միաբանք բազմանայր եւ խրատն եւ մխիթարութիւն հոգելոր ի հեռաւոր ժողովրդեանն անպակաս լինէր: Սակս որոյ եւ որոշեցաք գձեզ ի վանիցն Չուղայու: Այլ այժմ զի տեսաք թէ օգուտ այնչափի ոչ երեւեցաւ ի բաժանմանէն, որպէս եւ կարծէաք, մանաւանդ թէ երկպառակութիւն եւ թշնամութիւն սերմանեցաւ ի մէջ սիրոյ եւ միաբանութեան: Յաղագս այսորիկ եւ մեք ըստ առաջին կարգին սահմանեցաք գձեզ սեփական թեւ եւ վիճակ սուրբ Ամենափրկչի վանիցն, եւ առաջնորդ ձեր եղբայր մեր Դաւիթ վարդապետն հաստատեցաք, զի լինիցիք մի հօտ եւ մի հովիւ: Այսուհետեւ յամենայնի հլու եւ հպատակ կացջիք հրամանաց նորա եւ սիրով եւ մտերմութեամբ զհնազանդութիւն ցուցանիցիք որպէս եւ վայել է հաւատացելոց Քրիստոսի: Նաեւ Դաւիթ վարդապետին պատուիրեցաք զի քարոզիցէ եւ խրատիցէ ի ձէնջ անպակաս արասցէ, զորս եւ դուք ընկալցիք սիրով եւ ընդունելութեամբ եւ արդիւնացուցիք գործովք բարութեան, որպէսզի շնորհաց եւ օրհնութեան, փառաց եւ պսակաց արժանաւոր լինիցիք ի Քրիստոսէ Յիսուսէ, Տեառնէ մերմէ, որ է օրհնեալ անզրաւ յաւիտենից յաւիտեանս, Ամէն:

Գրեցաւ ի թուին Հայոց ՌՃՀԹ, սեպտեմբեր ամսոյ Դ:

Document #13

Encyclical of Katołikos Yakob, dividing the diocese of New Julfa and appointing Yovhan, primate of the newly created diocese.[1]

The blessing of Father, the protection of Son and the providence of most Holy Spirit be always with you and everyday make you blossom in glory, honour and abundant riches, like leafy and fruitful vine and branches planted in paradise and make you live a peaceful life, Amen.[2]

And with God-given blessing be informed luminous sons of mother light Holy Ějmiacin, my spiritual and beloved children, as long as the Armenians used to live in their motherland, all the provinces were divided into certain dioceses under the jurisdiction of monasteries. But when God became angry with our suffering nation, our people scattered from their native motherland, the land and the homes of our forefathers and monasteries were destroyed. Wherever our people went and settled, some were forced to leave again. Many who were not used to their new environment died soon after and were exterminated like the Christians of Farahabad.[3] We have heard from our forefathers that eleven thousand Armenian families were taken to Farahabad and now there are less than two hundred families in the entire Farahabad region.

Those who lived in Isfahan, with the grace of the Holy Spirit, did not suffer the same fate as the others. But with Divine guidance they built churches and were adorned with all Christian rites. Julfa was under the jurisdiction of the monastery, which we have witnessed personally. But the other Christians in the city and in the villages of Linjan, Geandiman, Peria and Burwari were equally divided between Katołikoi Meliksef and Dawit, until the time of Katołikos Movsēs, who sent Xačatur *Vardapet* as legate to Poland[4] and Połos *Vardapet* Tiwrikeči became supervisor of all [Armenians of New Julfa and surrounding districts], who was later succeeded by Zakaria *Vardapet*, until Xačatur

---

[1] Fragment of the Armenian text in *Matenadaran* of Erevan (Patriarchal Archives, file 244, doc. 359). The top portion of the text is missing.

[2] The translation of two passages of customary and supplicant expressions are omitted.

[3] The capital city of Shah 'Abbas in the province of Mazandaran.

[4] 1629.

Vardapet returned from his mission and was again sent [to New Julfa] as primate for all.[5]

Again, my spiritual children, at that time the churches were flourishing, people were united, they were not selfish, and they were all working for the benefit of the Church. But since people have become extremely selfish, disputes and quarrels have increased. While one is starving to death, the other is satiated with wealth. Let the care and mercy of the generous God always be upon the people of Julfa and their possessions. With the mercy of God they can support as many as four monasteries, instead of one.

For this reason, I have ordained bishop my beloved son, Yovhan *Vardapet*. I have appointed him vicar of Holy Ējmiacin and have sent him to you as primate, dean and pastor, preacher and instructor, a disciplinarian for the guilty. Whatever he binds be it bound and whatever he looses be it loosed. Blessed be who he blesses, and cursed be who he curses.

My spiritual and beloved children, my dear son Yovhan *Vardapet* will be your primate for three years. If I am satisfied with his performance and if he is able to console you with love and God's words and is thankful to you, I will send another encyclical to reappoint him for another three years. But if he does not act according to these written instructions, I will send you another primate and Yovhan *Vardapet* will return to the Holy See. Again, my spiritual children, all the funds raised by the bishop for the Holy See, including payments for incense, candles, spices and white linen, will be used for the benefit of the poor monasteries. All the worships and the Divine liturgies celebrated there will benefit you and your departed ones. Let God grant you and your children long life free of temptations, and let Him be blessed for ever and ever, Amen.

Written in the year 1125,[6] February 20.

---

[5] 1631.
[6] 1676.

ԿՈՆԴԱԿ ՅԱԿՈԲ ԿԱԹՈՂԻԿՈՍԻ, 1676[1]
(կնիք)

Օրհնութիւն հօր պահպանութիւն Որդոյ եւ նախախնամութիւն ամենասուրբ հոգւոյն եւ միշտ եւ հանապազ եկեսցէ եւ հանգիցէ ի վերայ ձեր եւ օր ըստ օրէ լցուցէ փառօք պատուով եւ արգասալիր ճոխութեամբ իբրեւ զորթս եւ որպէս զսաղարթախիտ եւ պտղալից դրախտ տնկեալ ի գնաս հոգւոյն վտակաց կալ մնալ ձեզ խաղաղական կեանք ամէն: ...

Եւ ընդ աստուածապարգեւ օրհնութիւնս ծանիք լուսածնունդ գաւակ մօրն լուսոյ Սրբոյ Էջմիածնայ, հոգեւոր եւ սիրելի որդեակք իմ, որքան աշխարհի եւ երկիրս հայոց, իւրեանց բնիկ տեղիս կային, ամէն երկիր թեմ եւ վիճակ բաժանեալ յատուկ եւ որոյն կային վանորէիցն: Իսկ յորժամ բարկացաւ Աստուած տառապեալ ազգիս, գիր եւ ցան եղեւ ազգս մեր ի հայրենի ի բնիկ եւ ի նախնեացն երկրէն, տանց եւ բնակութեանց, քակտեցաւ եւ աւերեցաւ վանորայք եւ անապատք: Ընդ որ երկիր որ գնացին եւ անդ կալատեալ եւ բնակեցան ումանք աշխարհավարաց տեղեն: Եւ բազումք ոչ ընդ եւ զոլոյն աշխարհին եւ երկրին, կառնակեաց եւ տարածամբ եղեն, եւ բնաջինջ եղեն որպէս Փահրապատոայ քրիստոնեայքն: Ի նախնեաց լուեալ եմք թէ ժա˜ Ո տուն հայոց ազգեւ տարեալ են երկիրդ Փահրապատոայ, եւ այժմու ԲԳ տուն չկայ բովանդակ երկիրն այն: Իսկ որք Իսպահանա բնակեցաւ շնորհիօք սուրբ հոգւոյն ոչ եղեն այլ երկրի ուման: Այլ լաչողութեամբ Աստուծոյ շինեցին լեկեղեցիս եւ ամենայն քրիստոնէական կարգք զարդարեցաք, յատուկ Չուղայ իւրեանց վանից էր գոր մեք աշոր տեսեալ եմք: Իսկ այլ քրիստոնեայքն թէ ի քաղաքն Լնձանու գեօղորեայքն, թէ Դանդիման, Փարեայ եւ Բուրվարի, կէսն Մելիքսէթ կաթողիկոսն կու տիրէր եւ կէսն Դաւիթ կաթողիկոսն կու տիրէր, մինչ Մուլսու կաթողիկոսն եւ զԽաչատուր վարդապետն առապեւաց Ճութիրակ Հոմմաց տումննն, եւ լեհաց երկիրն: Տիրիկեցի Պօղոս վարդապետն էր վերակացոյ ամենեցոյն: Չկնի Ճորա Չաքարեայ վարդապետն, մինչ որ եկն ի Ճութիրակութեանէ Խաչատուր վարդապետն վերստին ուղարկեաց առաջնորդ ամենեցոյն: Դարձեալ հոգեւոր որդիք, այն ժամանակն եկեղեցեաց հնորգումն էր միմեանց ձեռնտուր էին, իմն քոլ խիստ չկայր ամէնքն ի բարեձեւութիւն կու ձկտիչն, իսկ այժմու իմն քոնն է չատացեր եւ կորին բազմացեալ, մէկն քաղ ցած է մեռանում, եւ մէկն փարթամութեամբ յոփոացեալ է կովում: Խնամք եւ ողորմութիւն բարերարին Աստուծոյ միշտ եւ հանապազ ի վերայ Չուղայու լինի եւ իւրեանց ապրանացն վերա: Ողորմութեամբ Աստուծոյ կարող են չորա վանք պահել, որ մնայ թէ մէկ վանք պահելէ:

Վասն այս պատճառի գիմ սիրելի որդի Ցոհան վարդապետն եպիսկոպոս ձեռնադրեցի եւ սուրբ Էջմիածնայ աթոռակալ հաստատեցի եւ առաքեցի ձեզ ա- ռաջնորդ, տեսու եւ հովիւ, քարոզ եւ խրատիչ, սասող եւ յանդիմանիչ յանցաւորաց: Կապեալն դորա կապեալ եղիցի եւ արձակեալն արձակեալ: Նոյնպէս օրհնեալն ի դմանէ օրհնեալ եղիցի եւ անիծեալն դորա անիծեալ եղիցի: Դարձեալ հոգեւոր եւ սիրելի որդիք մինչ երեք տարին, սիրելի որդիս Ցոհան վարդա- պետն ձեզ առաջնորդէ: Եթէ ըստ հանդիցն առնիցէ որ մեք հանին եւ ձեզ սի- րով եւ աստուածայիբ բանիւ միխիթարք, Աօլնակեա եւ ի Աս ի ձեԱչ Շնորհակալ լինի, կրկին օրհնութեան կոնդակ կուղարկեմբ, որ Գ տարի եւս մնայ: Իսկ եթէ զգրելով աս չասնէ միս առաջնորդ կու ողարկեմբ, որ Ցոհան վարդապետն գա ի սուրբ աթոռ: Դարձեալ հոգեւոր որդիք, զինչ հաս եւ իրաւունք որ լինի եպիս-

[1] Մաշտոցի անուան մատենադարան, կաթողիկոսական դիւանի ֆոնդ, թղթապանակ թիւ 244, վաւերագիր թիւ 359: Կոնդակի սկիզբը պակասատոր է:

կոպոսի գէլուրիցն, խնկի, մոմի, տաքդեղորէից, սպիտակճոթի գին լինի վասն սրբոյ աթոռոյն, աղքատ վանորէից եւ անապատից լինի: Եւ զինչ պաշտօն եւ պատարագ որ անդ մատչի ձեզ եւ ձեր ննջեցելոցն մասն եւ բաժին հասցէ: Այլ ձեզ եւ ձեր զաւակացն արեւշատութիւն եւ անփորձ կենցաղավարութիւն պարգեւեսցէ, որ է օրհնեալ անզրաւ յաւիտենիւ, ամէն:

Գրեցաւ գիրս ի ՌՃԻԵ թվին, եւ փետրվարի ամսոյ ի քսան:

Document #14

Encyclical of Kaťołikos Ełiazar,

restoring the unity and the integrity

of the diocese of New Julfa.[1]

Servant of Jesus Christ Ełiazar, Kaťołikos of All Armenians and Patriarch of the Holy and Great See of Ějmiacin in Vałaršapat, which is built with light, is God given, high, brilliant, sunlike, heavenlike and paradisiacal, surrounded by cherubs and where seraphim dwell. His letter of blessing and protection, the apostolic grace, together with multiple Divine blessings and provident mercy will reach the city, which is protected by Lord and cared by Christ, the blessed Capital Julfa and other cities and churches, namely the people of Erewan, Tawriz, Gask, Gawrapat, Šəxsapan, the two Łaragēls, as well as the districts of P̌eria, Burwari, Geandiman, Linǰan and Alinǰan. To the Divinely built churches, His Eminence the Glorious Primate, ever preaching and theologian *vardapets*, the class of priests devoted to the sacred service and the heavenly call, honorable and most glorious princes, *dowlaťaworǩ* with abundant of possessions, truth loving and just headmen, loyal and pious trustees, wise and ingenious merchants, blossomed in gray hair and dignified elderly, right-minded and decent youth, pure and virtuous virgins, modest and venerable house wives, milk-sucking and innocent-hearted children and to the entire people of all ages and ranks, the Armenian nation of St. Illuminator's confession and the people who believe in Jesus Christ, the Lord God and Saviour of all, Amen.[2]

And with God given and graceful blessings be informed our spiritual children in the Lord and the luminous sons of mother of light Holy Ějmiacin. Saint Paul the Apostle commands: "The end of the commandment is charity out of pure heart, and of a good conscience, and of faith unfeigned."[3] "For where envying and strife is, there is confusion and every evil work."[4] And the Lord says: "Every kingdom

---

[1] Armenian text in AASM (cab 5, dr. 3, doc. 12).
[2] The translation of a large passage of supplicant expressions is omitted.
[3] First Timothy, I,5.
[4] James, III,16.

divided against itself is brought to desolation; and a house divided against a house falleth."[5]

As we witnessed personally, Ganjasar,[6] as well as other monasteries, particularly the Divinely built, the light and consolation of our nation, the Monastery of Saint James of Jerusalem, were not destroyed by outsiders, but by Armenians who were against each other. They paid bribes and put the monastery under unbearable debts and insurmountable troubles, to the point that there was no cure for its sufferings. The same happened in your blessed country. When there was division, many abandoned their faith, laws and rules were dissolved, evil was established and troubles were fomented as you yourselves saw. And if We let this inflammation to grow and abandon the path established by our ancestors, there will be no solution forever.

But now, that We have thought about this matter, have examined and considered all the options and discussed this issue extensively with bishops, *vardapets*, princes and visiting pious merchants, We cannot find any other solution than the unification of the diocese.

We, the humble servant of the Lord, Katołikos Ełiazar, according to the authority given to us from above and by the high order of the Holy See of Ējmiacin, reestablished your blessed towns and districts in the diocese of All Saviour's monastery of Julfa. This was not an impulsive decision; it was the result of consultations with many theologian *vardapets* and *dowlatawork*. Neither a monk nor anybody else is permitted to enter the diocese and undertake anything without the permission of the bishop of All Saviour's Monastery and he has to obey the bishop of the said monastery. Anybody who does not agree with this order, shall come and settle at the Holy See or live at the Monastery of Naxavkay.[7] The monks are not permitted to live anywhere else, neither in any other monastery nor in their native towns and villages. As there will be one primate, his subjects will also be united and in agreement. According to the word of the Lord, "there shall be one fold and one shepherd."[8] And as long as our beloved and intimate son, Stepannos *Vardapet* is in office, all will obey him, and after him, whoever is unanimously selected by the people to be [their] primate and approved and appointed by the Katołikos occupying the Holy See at the time. Everybody will obey him and they will live together in love, as Ałeksandr, Yovhannēs and Mikayel *vardapets* and others are united as brothers in the Holy order,

---

5 Luke, XI, 17.
6 The Katołikate of Ganjasar in the province of Arčax.
7 The Monastery of St. Stepannos Naxavkay in Naxčawan.
8 John, X,16.

according to the prophet who says" "how good and how pleasant it is for brethren to dwell together in unity."[9]

As all favours to monasteries and religious orders are extended from the Holy See, in the same manner monasteries and religious orders extend favours to the monks and to the faithful. According to David, "it is like the precious ointment upon the head of Aaron, that went down to the skirts of his garments."[10] According to God given canons and commandments, the order is that children shall obey their parents and that the mercy and the care of the parents will always overflow upon their children.

Beloved people, we did not do this out of envy or avarice, God the reader of hearts, knows that. We did this to eliminate internal divisions and barriers, so that the love of Christ and peace will prevail. As saint Paul says: "Charity edifieth,"[11] and we may win the Christ and live happily in peace.

I did this, so that the soul of the late Katołikos Yakob might be saved because many people are offended and curse him. Much as in the days of Katołikoi Movsēs and Pilippos of blessed memory and the time of Xačatur and Dawit *Vardapets* the people were united under one diocese, love, peace, and success prevailed, benevolence and peace reigned in the world and the kings were favourable towards our suffering nation, we wish to create unity and pray to God to have mercy upon us and grant us the same order and success.

God loving people, upon receiving this order, all of you will obey whoever is appointed bishop of All Saviour's by Divine selection. Priests will reside in those churches which are considered to be monasteries. These churches will serve as places of worship for the people. All churches will obey All Saviour's monastery, as the latter obeys the Holy See and carries its orders. The churches will obey All Saviour's monastery and its bishop, because whoever obeys him obeys us and the Holy See, and whoever opposes him opposes us and the Holy See.

We also address you, the so called bishops and *vardapets* living in that areas. According to Gregory the Theologian,[12] ignorant and impious people, who have not studied under philosophers, claim honors for themselves. Having lived a marginal life, they do not know

---

9 Psalms, CXXXIII, 1.

10 Ibid, CXXXIII, 2.

11 First Corinthians, VIII, 1.

12 Gregory of Nazianzus, *"Apologeticus de Fuga,"* A Select Library of Nicene and Post-Nicene Fathers of the Christian Church, tr. & ed. by Schaff P., Wace H., Second Series, vol. VII, Michigan, pg. 215.

their limits. Suddenly they creep into the society, and walk in the street trying to pass themselves off as rabbis, for which the Lord reprimands them saying: "be not yet called Rabbi: for one is your master, even Christ."[13]

In the same manner we entrust you in the hands of the primate of the monastery. Whatsoever he calls you, that will be your name, according to the Divine order given to Adam, and "whatsoever Adam called every living creature, that was the name thereof."[14] All monks at the monastery, bishops or *vardapets* should obediently carry out the orders of the primate for the service of the people, as it is ordered in the Canons and the By-Laws.[15] Whoever dares [to disobey] will be condemned.

People loyal to [the unity of] the diocese should not build [new] monasteries just for the sake of opposing the existing order. There are many churches in the dioceses of the Agulis Monastery[16] and Surb Karapet,[17] as well as in the other dioceses which are built to serve as places of worship and not as new diocesan centers.

Therefore, we did this [the reunification of the diocese] for your own sake, so that there will not be troubles among you and confusion among the clergy, but instead there will be prosperity and reform. The blessed Kaťolikos Yakob did not enjoy peace ever since he divided the diocese causing the troubles to increase. We did this so that his soul might find peace and to clear our conscience. We all acted in unity, guided by the Holy Spirit. Let us all say Amen. Let it be. Those of you, who follow our orders, will be blessed by God and by all saints, Amen.

Written in April 7, 1138,[18] at Holy Ějmiacin.

---

[13] Matthew, XXIII, 8.

[14] Genesis, II, 19.

[15] *Sahmanadru ťiwn*, literally meaning constitution. Probably it is a reference to the traditional order, rather than a written By-Laws.

[16] St. Tovma Monastery of Agulis.

[17] St. Karapet Monastery of Muš.

[18] 1689.

ԿՈՆԴԱԿ ԵՂԻԱԶԱՐ ԿԱԹՈՂԻԿՈՍԻ, 1689
(կնիք)

Յիսուսի Քրիստոսի ծառայ Եղիազար կաթողիկոս Ամենայն Հայոց եւ
Պատրիարք Վաղարշապատու լուսակառոյց եւ Տեառնամատոյց, Արփիադիտակ եւ
արեգակնաբառնակ, երկնահանգէտ եւ աղինասարաս, սրովբէական, եւ քրով-
բէապար, սրբոյ եւ մեծի Աթոռոյս Էջմիածնի։ Յորմէ ժամանեալ հասցէ գիր օրհնութեան եւ ճամակ պահպանութեան, շնորհք առաքելական հանդերձ աստ-
ւածային բազմապատիկ օրհնութեամբն եւ նախախնամական գթութեամբն ի
վերայ Տիրապաh եւ քրիստոսասիրաւմ օրհնեալ մայրաքաղաքիդ Զուղայու, եւ այլոց քաղաքաց եւ եկեղեցեաց, Երեւանցոց, Թարվիզցոց, Գաղկեցոց, Գարա-
պատցոց, Շրիսսապանցոց եւ երկու Ղարագէլին։ Նաեւ աստուածային աջոյն
օրհնեալ եւ նախախնամեալ գաւառաց Փէրիու, Բուրվարու, Գանտիմանու, Լըն-
ճանու եւ Ալինճանու։ Աստուածաշէն եկեղեցեաց, Արհի եւ պանծալի Առաքնոր-
դիդ, մշտաբարող եւ աստուածաբան վարդապետաց, սրբանւէր եւ երկնաքրաւէր
քահանական դասոց, պերճապատիկ եւ փառագարդ իշխանաց, գոյիք գեղուն եւ
ընշիք յոգնաբեղուն դովվաթաւորաց, իրաւաէր եւ արդարադատ տանուտեարց,
հաւատարիմ եւ հեզամիտ երեսփոխաս, իմաստնախոհ եւ հանճարեղ վաճառականաց, ալեոք ծաղկեալ եւ գանիք պատուեալ ծերոց, ողջամիտ եւ պարկեշտա-
բարոյ երիտասարդաց, սրբասունգն եւ մաքրակենցաղ կուսից, համեստ եւ հարկե-
ւոր տանտիկնաց, կաթնասունգ եւ անմեղասիրտ տղայոց եւ միահամուռ ամենայն
չափու եւ հասակի, տիոյ եւ կարգի, ազգանց հայկականաց, լուսատոր\sհաբանեան
ժողովրդող, հաւատացելոց ի Քրիստոս Յիսուս ի Տէր Աստուածն եւ փրկիչն
ամենայնի, ամէն։

Շնորհք ըն ձեզ եւ խաղաղութիւն յՍատուծոյ հօրէ ամենակալէ եւ ի
վիրկչէ մերմէ Յիսուսէ Քրիստոսէ եւ ի Սրբոյ Հոգւոյն կենարարէ, եւ յաrա-
տւածաւալ պարգեւատու քարերբարէ, Ամէն։ Զոր օրհնութիւն աստուածային եւ
աղօթք Սուրբ Աստուածածնին եւ Յովhան«ու Կարապետին, եւ Սրբոյն Ստեփան-
նոսի նախավկային, եւ Սրբոյն Գրիգորի մերոյ Լուսատուրշին, եւ ամենայն սրբոց
երկնաւորաց եւ երկրաւորաց, միշտ եւ հանապազ եկեսցէ եւ հանգիցէ ի վերայ
ձեր, ի տուէ եւ ի գիշերի, ի ննդլ ի տան, ի գնալ ի ճանապարհ, ի ննչել եւ ի
յառնել, ի գնել եւ ի վաճառել, ի սկսանիլ եւ ի գործել, ի նւնլ եւ ի կատարել, ի
սկիզբն տարուոյ եւ ի կատարած տարուոյ, կրկին կեանոր եւ երկու աշխարhօր։ Եւ
եղիցի աստուածային օրհնութիւն եւ օգնութիւն ի վերայ hոգւոց եւ մարմնոց ձերոց, տանց եւ ընտանեաց ձերոց, Ամէն։

Եւ ընդ աստուածապարգեւ եւ շնորhագեղում օրհնութիւնն ծաներnուք
հոգեւոր որդիք մեր ի Տէր, եւ լուսածնունդ գաւակք մոսս լուսդ Սուրբ Էջմիածնի։
Զի hրամայէ Սրբագան Առաքեալն Քրիստոսի Պօղոս, եթէ գլուխ պատուիրանին
սէր է, ի սուրբ սրտէ եւ յանկեղծաւոր հաւատոյ։ Եւ թէ որ ոնն եւ Ննախանէ գոյ,
անդ է անկարգութիւն եւ ամենայն իրբ շարք։ Եւ Տէրն ասէ, ռաժանեալ տունն
յանձն իւր աւերի, եւ քաղաք յիւրաբանՁիր անձն ռաժանեալ կործանի։ Որպէս
տեսաւք այժմու աշոք մերոյք, թէ Գանձասար եւ թէ այլ վաճռալք, մանաանդ
աստուածաշէն եւ ազգիս լոյս եւ միախատութիւն Սուրբ Յակոբ որ յերոասաՁէմ։
Ոչ եթէ այլազգիք աւերեցին, այլ մերայիմ աղիքբ, միմեանց ներհակ եւ հարակ
լինելով եւ դրամ տալով, անտաանելի պարտող եւ անգերծանելի Ֆեղութեանg
մէջ արկին, որ ոչ իմիք ննարիք բուժումն լինի ցաւոյն այնորիկ։ Ըստ այսցo
սարասի եղել ի ձերում կոմանg եւ օրհնեալ երկրիդ, յորժամ բաժանումն երկուg
եղել, թէ քանի՞ս hաւատող եղան, ո՞րքան օրհնագ եւ սահմանag քակտումն եղել

Եւ ո՞րպիսի չարիք կալկացաւ, եւ զի՞նչ խոռովութիւն արմատացաւ, որպէս տեսիք բարի աշօր ձեռոմք։ Եւ թէ թողումք այս բորբոքումն եւ զնախինեաց կարգեալ շաւիղն, ոչ գոյ ճնար բժշկութեան միձտեւ աոյապայն։

Այլ արդ՝ քննեցաք եւ յոլովից ճնարից բուռն ճարաք, եւ խստագոյն խուզումն արարաք ճանդերձ միաբան եւ միախոհ որդւոյք Սրբոյ աթոռոյ՝ եպիսկոպոսք, վարդապետոք, եւ իշխանոր եւ երթեւեկող աստուածասէր վանառա-կանոր, ի խորքուրդս բազումն մտաք իբրեւ Ժ ամօք սակս այսմ բանի, եւ ոչինչ յելս իրաց գտաք, բայց միայն ի մի աձել եւ միապետութիւն առնել։

Աճա եւ ճուսատ ծառայ Ստեանձ, Եղիազար Կաթողիկոսս, ըստ ի վերուստ տուեալ իշխանութեամբդ, եւ բարձր ճրամանաւ Սրբոյ աթոռոյս Էջմիածնի, վերստին կարգեցաք եւ ճաստատեցաք այդ օրճնեալ քաղաքքդ եւ գաւառդ թէմ եւ վիճակ Ձուղայու Սուրբ Ամենափրկչի վանիցն։ Եւ ոչ երեէ մտացածին բանիւ կամ այլ ինչ պատճառի արարաք, այլ այսքան աստուածաբան վարդապետոր եւ դոլվաթաւորոք կարգեցաք եւ սաճմանեցաք, որ այլ ոչ ոք ճրամանն չունի յերկիրն մտանելոյ, առանց ճրամանի ամենափրկչի վանից առաջնորդին, եւ ձեռնամուխ լինիլ, ոչ սեւագլուխ եւ կամ այլ ոք։ Եւ գող ինչ սեւագլուխք կան յայդմ կողմանքդ, գնաս միաբանք լինին Սուրբ Ամենափրկչին, եւ ճորին առաջնորդին ճլու եւ ճնազանդ։ Եւ երէ ոք ծածրութիւն ճամարի գայս, կամ գայ ի սուրբ աթոռս գետերիդ եւ կամ ի սուրբ Նախավկայեալ բանիք, եւ այլ որտեք բնակելոյ ոչ գող ճրաման սեւագլխի, ոչ ի վանք եւ ոչ յիր ճայրենիքն կամ ի գիւղ, եւ որպէս առաջնորդն մի լինի, եւ իր ճնազանդեալքն պարտին միաբան եւ միախորճուրդ լինի։ Ըստ Ստեանձ բանի՝ եղիցի մի ճօտ եւ մի ճովի։ Եւ որքան սիրելի եւ ճարազատ որդիս մեր Ստեփանձու վարդապետն կայ՝ նմա ճնազանդ լինին, եւ յետ նորա ո՞վ ոք ժողովուրդն միաբանութեամբ խնդրեն իրեանց առաջնորդ եւ ճովիւ յետ Ստեփանձու վարդապետին, եւ ճաւանութեամբ եւ կամօք սուրբ աթոռիս ճնսոր կարգութիւն ճրամանաւն կարգեալ առաջնորդին ճնազանդ լինին եւ սիրով կացցեն առ միմեանս, որպէս Աղէբրասնրդ, Ցովճաննէս եւ Միքայէլ վարդապետոք եւ այլ մի եղէն երբարք սուրբ ուխտին։ Ըստ մարգա-րէին՝ զի՞ բարի կամ զի՞ վայելիչ զի բնակին երբարք ի միասին։ Եւ որպէս ամենայն շնորճարաշխութիւնք ի սուրբ աթոռս տարածի յամենայն վանորայք եւ ի սուրբ ուխտոսն, նոյնգունակ եւ ի ցացանէն տարածի ի ներբոյ եղեալ ժողո-վուրդն եւ ի միաբանան Վանից, ըստ Դաւիթ, որպէս իւղ զի իջանէ ի գլուխն Աճարոնի, եւ միձտեւ ի գրապան զգեստու նորա։ Ըստ աստուածաճիր կանոնաց եւ ճրամանաց այս է կարգն եւ սաճմանադրութիւն, որ որդիք ճնազանդ լինին ծնողացն ամենայնի, եւ ծնողաց գութն եւ խնամարկութիւն զեղցի միշտ առ որ-դիացեալոյն իւր։ Սիրելիք, զայս բանս ոչ թէ ճակառակն կամ սակս թամանի ինչ արարաք, քաւ լիցի։ Զոր սրտագէտն Աստուած գիտէ, այլ վասն միջի կրճիման եւ միջնորմն խոռովութեան բարձից, եւ կայսաց սէրն Քրիստոսի եւ խաղաղութիւն, ըստ աստեղէն Պօղոսի, ամենայն ինչ ձեր սիրով լինի։ Որով գ Քրիստոս շաճիմք եւ մեր անխռով լինիմք, եւ ճոգիով գուպ։ Այլ եւ զայս վասն այն արարի, զի որդրած ճոգի Ցակոբ Կաթողիկոսի ճոգւոյն վիրկութիւն լինի, որ բազումք գայ-թակղեալ են եւ աննձս ասէն նմա։ Ձի որպէս լուսաճոգիք Մովսէս եւ Փիլիպպոս կաթողիկոսաց աւուրքն, Խաչատուր եւ Դաւիթ վարդապետաց ժամանակն միջ-թիւն էր ի ժողովուրդն եւ առաջնորդն մի, որպէս սէր գոյր առ միմեանս եւ խա-դաղութիւն, ամենայն իրաց յաջողութիւն եւ բարեաց լիութիւն, եւ աշխարճի ան-դորրութիւն եւ թագաւորաց սիրող քաղցր ան մերայից տատանապեալ աղգս, նոյգ գունակ եւ այժմ մեր կամք այս է, որ ճաստատեցի միապետութիւն։ Որ եւ խնդր-րեմ յԱստուծոյ նոյգ կարգ եւ ողորմութիւն տացէ եւ յաջողեսցէ։ Եւ դուք աստ-ւածասէր ժողովուրդք, զայս ճրաման առ ձեզ գալով, ամենեքեան ճնազանդ լինիք ճլու եւ ճպատակ Սուրբ Ամենափրկչի առաջնորդին, ո՞վ ոք աստուածային ընտրութեամբ ճովիւ կարգեալ լինի։ Եւ այն եկեղեցիք որ վանք աննմ էին եղ-եալ, քաճանայ բնակեցէ եւ աղօթից տեղի լինի ժողովրդեան, եւ այլ եկեղեցիք ճնազանդ լինին ամենափրկչի սուրբ ուխտին, որպէս եւ իրենք սուրբ աթոռս ճանգագանդ է եւ հրամանակատար, նոյնպէս եւ նորա ճանգագանդ լինին Զուդայու վանգիսն եւ առաջնորդի նորին, զի ճանգագանդք նորին մեզ եւ սուրբ աթոռոյս են ճակառակք, իսկ ճակառակքն մեզ եւ սուրբ առողոյս են ճակառակք:

Գրեմ եւ առ ձեզ որք եպիսկոպոսք եւ վարդապետք անուամբ յորջորջեալ կայք ի կողմանդ այդոսիկ, քստ Գրիգորի աստուածաբանին, որպէս ասէ, արք երեկեան եւ յերանդեան, որք ոչ վարժեալ առ ուոս ձերոց եւ ոչ դեզերեալ ի դրուեն իմաստասիրաց, այլ անձամբ յանձին առեալ պատիւ ի քունջս եւ յան- կիւնս կենցաղավարեալ եւ գշաիի իր ոչ գիտացեալ, եւ յանկարծօրէն սպրտեալ ի մէջ ժողովրդեան ճեմեալ եւ ճօճեալ, ուսբրի՞ ուսբրի՞ կոչելով շրջեալ, որոց ասասն ի Տեառնէ ընկալեալ, թէ մի կոչէք զձեզ վարդապետս եւ ուսուցիշս, այլ ուսուցիչ ձեր Քրիստոս է: Նոյն գունակ կոչեմ զձեզ առ Վանից Հայրն եւ զոր ինչ կոչեցէ զձեր անուն, այն եդիցի ձեր անուն, քստ աստուածային հրամանին որ առ Աղամ ասաց, զոր ինչ կոչեցէ անուն, այն եդիցի անուն: Եւ որքան ի մէջ վանից իցէն, ի քահանայի կարգի իցէն, եւ զոր ինչ հրամայէ առաջնորդն եթէ եպիսկոպոսական եւ եթէ վարդապետական գործ ինչ կատարել ի մէջ ժողովրդ- եանն, զայն ունի հրաման կատարելոյ, որ կանոնք եւ սահմանադրութիՆ այսպէս հրամայէն: Եւ ո՞վ ոք յանդգնի, ի ներքոյ կապանաց է: Եւ թէ ամենայն վանից ներքոյ շինեալ վանորայք թէմի եւ վիճակի տեարք լինէին, ոչ լինէր շինութիՆ վանից եւ վիճակացն առ միճեանց ճակառակ լինէին: Որպէս բազում գործ գոն եկե- ղեցիք յԱգուլեաց վանից վիճակումՆ եւ սուրբ Կարապետի եւ ամէնայն վիճակի մէջ կան, որ ողորմի տալոյ տեղիս շինէին եւ ոչ թէմի տէր: Վասն որոյ խնայեցի ձեզ զայս առնելով, որ ոչ խռովութիՆ եւ գայթակղութիՆ ի միջի ձերում լինիցի եւ սեաագլխոց շփոթման տեղի եւ աշխարհի խոռվութիՆ, այլ շինութիՆ եւ բարեկարգութիՆ:

Որ լուսաճոգի Յակոբ կաթողիկոսն քանի զազդ արար, ոչ ինչն ճանգեաւ, եւ օր զաւուր խռվութիՆ բարձրացաւ: Եւ զայս վասն այնորիկ արարի, որ ոչ ի ներքոյ խղճմտանաց Յակոբ ճոգեւորին մնայցէք եւ ոչ ի մեր: Նոյն գունակ ևս եւ մեք աղխիՆ մնացուք: Եւ զոր ինչ ճոգիՆ սուրբ Աստուած տնօրինեաց, եւ միաբանութեամբ կարգեցաք, ամէնեքեան ի մի բերան ասասցուք ԱՄէն, եդիցի եւ եդիցի: Կատարող հրամանաց մերոց օրհնին յԱստուծոյ եւ յամէնայն սրբոց եւ դասաց հրեշտակաց, ԱՄէն:

Գրեցաւ ի թուին ՌՃԼԸ եւ յամսեանն Ապրիլի Է, ի Դրանն Սուրբ Էջմիածնի:

Document #15

Encyclical of Kaťołikos Nahapet, dividing the Diocese of New Julfa and appointing Yovhan *Vardapet* primate of St. Sargis Monastery.[1]

The Servant of Jesus Christ, Nahapet, Kaťołikos of all Armenians and the Patriarch of the luminous and the heavenly Holy See of Ējmiacin at Vałaršapat, whose letter of blessing and protection, the apostolic grace, together with multiple divine blessings and provident mercy will reach the blessed capital Isfahan, the three churches of Erewan, Gask, Linǰan, Alinǰan and the two Łaragēls and their Divinely built churches. Reverend clergy, distinguished and honorable princes, faithful *tanuťerk̄*, opulent noblemen, wealthy *dowlaťawork̄*, pious trustees, wise merchants, skilled artisans, honest labourers and people at large, old and young, men and women, the elderly and children, youths and maidens and people of all ages, Amen.[2]

With God given and gracious blessings be informed, the spiritual and genuine children of mother of light Holy Ējmiacin. Saint Paul the apostle of Christ commands: "Let every soul be subject unto the higher powers. For there is no power but of God: the powers that be ordained of God."[3] In that respect he also advises: "Obey them that have the rule over you, and submit yourselves: for they watch for your souls."[4]

Now, our spiritual children, our Lord Jesus Christ made all the apostles leaders—equal in rank—as an example for us. That is the rule of nature. As the flock needs a shepherd, and the family needs a householder, so the subjects need a prince and the whole country needs a monarch. In the same manner, our Lord Jesus Christ adorned his Holy Church. He fortified it by apostles, strengthened it by prophets, crowned it by martyrs and made it rejoice by doctrinal teachings. Saint Paul the apostle lists them as follows: "And God hath set some in the Church, first apostles, second prophets, third teachers."[5]

---

[1] Text in AASM (cab 5, dr. 3, doc. 14).
[2] A large paragraph full of suppliant expressions is omitted.
[3] Romans, XIII, 1.
[4] Hebrews, XIII, 157.
[5] First Corinthians, XII, 28.

Following this order and [to fulfil] the will of our spiritual father, the late Kaťołikos Ełiazar, we did not let our faithful to remain without pastors. During his [Ełiazar's] pontificate, the Holy See, our whole nation, monasteries and churches flourished. He appointed suitable primates and trustees everywhere. At the monastery-church of St. Sargis, he appointed our spiritual son Yovhan *Vardapet* to serve as primate and trustee for our people in the pontifical domain. But later his heart burnt for the deprivation of St. Sargis monastery and Yovhan *Vardapet*. At the time of his death, when he entrusted everything into our hands, he also gave the following order by saying: 'I bestowed upon Yovhan *Vardapet* the episcopal title for St. Sargis monastery and the people in the domain of our Great See. But later I deprived him of that office. And that greatly bothers my conscience. You should appoint him to his seat and entrust to him the people of the above mentioned patriarchal domain, leaving the rest of the people [in other patriarchal domains] under the care of Ałeǩsandr *Vardapet*." Therefore, following the will of our spiritual father, with the high authority of our Great See and our patriarchal order, and in accordance with everybody's wish, we reinstalled our spiritual and beloved son Yovhan *Vardapet* as primate of St. Sargis monastery and entrusted the people of the above mentioned patriarchal domain to his trusteeship, so that he may lead the people with his episcopal authority and annually forward all your spiritual taxes to the Holy See.

Following the will of our spiritual father, we left the other half of the people in patriarchal domains under the trusteeship of Ałeǩsandr *Vardapet*.

Therefore, we strongly urge you, our spiritual and genuine sons, that from now on you recognise Yovhan *Vardapet* as your spiritual leader and trustee, assigned by us and the Holy See over our people of patriarchal domain. Honour and respect him and obey all his words and orders. From now on nobody is authorised, neither primate nor clergy, to live among you and to rule over you, except our spiritual son Yovhan *Vardapet* and members of the Religious Order of St. Sargis monastery. Let nobody oppose him, because such a person will be opposing us and the Holy See. In the same respect, those who obey him [will be obeying us and the Holy See]. Let whatever he binds be bound and whatever he looses be loosed, according to the order of Christ.

Your dues to the Holy See—which are confirmed by the canons— namely *Ptłi, Srbadram, Žamuč, k'arasnič, harsanič, hogebajin, kołoput, tnakan*,[6] as well as the taxes of priests, warden, trustees, those who suffer

---

[6] A tax paid by each household.

sudden death, adulterers, personal incomes, beadles and heads of villages should be delivered in full to our spiritual and beloved son Yovhan *Vardapet* who will annually transfer them to the Holy See.

You should also help St. Sargis monastery by offering butter, cheese, chicken and other similar gifts. And again you will be worthy of blessings and graces. All the psalm singings, worships and Divine liturgies celebrated at the Holy See will be beneficial to you and to your departed ones. For all taxes and presents you give, you and your departed ones will receive thousands and ten thousands times more from our Lord Jesus Christ in this world and in the eternal life, Amen. Our Father.

Again and again I give the following order to my spiritual and beloved son Yovhan *Vardapet*: be strong, courageous and firm in the spiritual work to which you are called by the grace of the Holy Spirit. Always maintain your genuine love towards the Holy See, gird thyself and take good care and be loyal to the patriarchal rights. From now on, every year you ought to send more presents to the Holy See and you, together with your collaborators will be compensated for your services by the graces of the Holy See.[7]

---

[7] L.G. Minasean has classified this encyclical under the year 1695. (See *Diwan S. Amenap'rki č Vank'i*, pg. 58). But more likely, it was was written in 1692 or 1693. This assumption is based on documents #16 and #17, both written in 1693, probably as reactions to the present encyclical.

ԿՈՆԴԱԿ ՆԱՀԱՊԵՏ ԿԱԹՈՂԻԿՈՍԻ, 1692/3
(կնիք)

Յիսուս Քրիստոսի ծառայ Տէր Նահապետ կաթուղիկոս ամենայն հայոց եւ
պատրիարք Վաղարշապատու լուսանկար եւ երկնահանգէտ Սրբոյ Աթոռոյս Էջմիածնի: Յորմէ ժամանեալ հասցէ գիր օրհնութեան եւ ճամակ պահպանութեան,
Շնորհք առաքելական, հանդերձ Աստուածային բազմապատիկ օրհնութեամբն եւ
նախախնամական գթութեամբն, ի վերայ Աստուածապան մայրաքաղաքի Աս-
պահանու, Երեւանայ երից եկեղեցեաց եւ Գաղկեցոց, Լրնջանայ եւ Ալրնջանայ,
եւ երկու Դարագէլցոց, եւ Դոցին Աստուածաշէն եկեղեցեաց, սրբանուէր քահանայից, պերճապատիւ իշխանաց, հաւատարիմ տանուտերաց, փարթամայոց մե-
ծատանաց, գոյիք գեղում դուլվաբատրաց, բարեպաշտոն երեսփոխաց, իմաստնախոհ վաճառականաց, վայելչագործ արուեստատւորաց, արդարավաստակ երկրագործաց, եւ ատ հասարակ ժողովրդոց, մեծամեծաց եւ փոքրունց, արանց եւ կանանց, ծերոց եւ տղայոց, երիտասարդաց եւ կուսից եւ ամենայն չափու, ամէն:

Շնորհք ընդ ձեզ եւ ողորմութիւն, եւ երկնաւոր խաղաղութիւն յԱստուծոյ
հօրէ ամենակալէ, գթութիւն եւ քաղցրութիւն ի Տեառնէ մերմէ Յիսուսէ Քրիստոսէ, պարգեւ ձիր եւ զեղմունք առատաբաշխ յամենասուրբ հոգւոյն կենարարէ
իջցէ եւ հանգիցէ, եկեսցէ եւ բնակեսցէ առ ձեզ, իբրեւ գյորձանան գետոզ եւ որպէս զվտակս աղբերաց, անսպառ խաղացմամբ եւ առատապէս ծաւալմամբ,
ընդ որոյ հովանաւորութեամբն զօրասջիր եւ պահպանեսջիր յամենայն ժամու,
ամէն:

Այլ եւ օրհնութիւն հոր, պահպանութիւն որդւոյ եւ նախախնամութիւն ամենասուրբ հոգւոյն միշտ եւ հանապազ եկեսցէ եւ հանգիցէ ի վերայ ձեր, եւ որ
ըստ որէ լցուսցէ զձեզ փառօք պատուոց եւ արգասալիր ճոխութեամբ, իբրեւ
գորդս եւ գուստ սաղարթախիտ եւ պտղալից դրախտ տնկեալ ի գնագս հոգւոյն
վտակաց, կալ մնալ ձեզ խաղաղական կենօք, եւ պարագայից ամօք, եւ յա-
մերամ ժամանակոք, Ամէն:

Եւ ընդ Աստուածապարգեւ եւ շնորհագեղուն օրհնութիւն ծանուցումն լից-
գի հոգեւոր եւ հարագատ որդւոցդ մորս լուսդ Սուրբ Էջմիածնի: Զի հրամայէ
սրբագայ առաքեալն Քրիստոսի Պօղոս, եթէ նենգին անձն որ ընդ իշխանութեամբ է, ի հնագանդութեան կացցէ: Քանզի ոչ ուստերէ է իշխանութիւն, եթէ
ոչ յԱստուծոյ, եւ որ եննն, յԱստուծոյ են կարգեալ: Նաեւ ի սոյն յորդորէ ասելով,
եթէ ունկնդիր լերուք առաջնորդաց ձերոց եւ հպատակ կացէք բանից նոցա, զի
նոքա տրջինն վասն ոգւոցն ձերոց փրկութեան: Արդ՝ հոգեւոր որդիք մեր, զի ինքն
Տէրն մեր Յիսու Քրիստու հաճադապտ առաքելովքն յորինական մեզ ամենեցուն
գլխատրաբար կարգատրեաց զամն: Քանզի ամենայն կարգ բնութեան ի սոյն
կարօտանայ, որպէս հօտք հովլի, եւ ընտանիք տանունտեանն եւ իշխեցեալք իշ-
խանի, եւ աշխարհի ամենայն ինքնակալ թագաւորի: Այսպէս եւ Տէրն մեր Յիսու
Քրիստու զարդարեաց զեկեղեցի իր սուրբ, պարսպեալ առաքելովք, ամրացոյց
մարգարէիք, պասակագզեաց արար մարտիրոսաօք, եւ զուարճացոյց վարդապետական բանիւ: Որպէս եւ սուրբ առաքեալն Պօղոս թուէ ասելով, եթէ գորս եդ
Աստուած յեկեղեցւոջ այս են, նախ զառաքեալս, երկրորդ զմարգարէս եւ երրորդ զվարդապետս: Ըստ այսմ հրամանի եւ մեզ ոչ թողաք զհոգեւոր որդիդ
մեր առանց հովուաց անխնամ մնալ, ըստ կտակի հոգեւոր հօրն մերոյ Տեառն
Եղիազարու կաթողիկոսի:

Քանզի յորժամ եկն նա ի սուրբ աթոռս, ամենայնիւ զարդարեաց զաս եւ
զազգս ամենայն, զվանրայս եւ զեկեղեցիս, կարգելով ամենայն ուրեք ըստ

արժանիոյն առաջնորդս եւ ռոգաբարառու։ Որպէս եւ ի վերայ վանից եւ եկեղեցւոյն սրբոյն Սարգսի եւ ի վերայ օրհնեալ տէրունի ժողովրդականացդ մերոյ
կարգեաց առաջնորդ եւ ռոգաբարառւ գռոգետոր որդին մեր գՅոռան վարդա-
պետունն։ Բայց յետոյ տոչորեէր սիրտ ննդին սակս գրկանաց վանիցն սրբոյն Սարգսի
եւ Յոռան վարդապետինն, իսկ ի ժամ վախճանինն իւրոյ յորժամ ամենայն ինչ
վերջին կտակաւ ի մեզ յանձնէր, զայս եւս պատուիրէր ասելով, եթէ պասկեցաք
գՅոռան վարդապետունն եայիսկոպոսական իշխանութեամբ ի վերայ վանից սրբոյն
Սարգսի եւ ի վերայ օրհնեալ տէրունին ժողովրդականաց մեծի աթոռոյս, բայց
յետոյ գրկեցաք, այդ խիղն է ինձ ոչ սակաւ։ Պարտոս վերստինն ռասատատել գնա
յաթոռ իւր, եւ գտէրունին ժողովուրդադ՝ գոր ի վերայ գրեցաք ի նա յանձնել, եւ
զայլ մնացեալւն թողուլ ի ռոգաբարառութիւն Աղեքսանդր վարդապետինն։

Ցաղագս որոյ, ըստ կտակի ռոգեւոր ռօրն մերոյ, շնորհիօք սուրբ ռոգւույն,
բարձր իշխանութեամբ մեծի աթոռոյս, եւ ռայրապետականական ռրամանաւ մերով, եւ
ռանունութեամբ ամենեցողծ, իրաունս վարկաք, եւ կրկնակի եւ վերստին կարգեալ
ռասատատեցաք Առաջնորդ վանիցն սրբոյն Սարգսի, գռոգետոր եւ գսիրելի որդիդ
մեր գՅոռան վարդապետդ, եւ զվերոյ գրեալ տէրունին ժողովուրդադ ի ռոգաբարառութիւն դորին յանձնեցաք, որ ռովւեացէ գտէրունին ժողովուրդադ մեր եպիսկոպոսական իշխանութեամբ, եւ գռոգետորական արդիւնան ձեր ամ յամէ լիակա-
տար եւ անթերի ի սուրբ աթոռս ռասուսցէ։ Եւ զմնացեալ տէրունին ժողովուրդան
այղպէս կիսաբաժին առնելով, թողաք ի ռոգաբարառութիւն Աղեքսանդր վարդապետինն, ըստ կտակի ռօրն մերոյ ռոգետորի։

Վասն որոյ պատուիրելով պատուիրեմ ռոգետոր եւ ռարագատ որդեացդ մերոց, զի այսուռետեւ գՅոռան վարդապետդ ծանէրուք ռոգետոր առաջնող ձեր եւ
ռոգաբարառու ի մէնջ եւ ի սրբոյ աթոռոյս ի վերայ տէրունին ժողովրդոցդ մերոց,
պատուիցէք եւ մեծարեցէք գդա, ռլու եւ ռնազանն կացցիք յամենայն բանից եւ
ռրամանաց դորին, զի այսուռետեւ ոչ օք ունին իշխանութիւն ոչ այլ առաջնորդ եւ
ոչ կարգաւոր շրջել ի միջի ձերում եւ իշխել ի վերայ ձեր, բայց միայն ռոգետոր
որդիդ մեր Յոռան վարդապետունն, եւ միարաբար վանիցդ Սրբոյն Սարգսի։ Մի օք
իրէ որ ռակառակ եւ դիմադարձ երեւեսցի դմա, զի այնպիսին մեզ եւ սուրբ
աթոռոյս է ռակառակ, ոյնպէս եւ ռնազանդքն։ Այլ եւ կապեալն ի դմանէ կապեալ է եւ արձակեալն արձակեալ, ըստ ռրամանին Քրիստոսի։ Նաեւ զամենայն
գտէրունին ռասս եւ գիրաունս ձեր որպէս կանոնիք ռասատատեալ է, այսինքն՝
զպտղին, զզոբռաղրամն, զզմանցն, զզքաոասանիցն, գռարասանիցն, գռոգերածին,
զկողոպուտն, զտնականան։ Այլ եւ տուք քառանացից, տանունտերաց, երեսափոխաց,
յանկարծամարիից, պռոնկաց, եկամտից, ժամկոչաց, գզրաց տէրունին է։ Դոցա
արդիւնքն եւ այլ զամենայն ռասս եւ գիրաունս ձեր լիով եւ անթերի ռասուսցա-
նիցէք ի ձէնն ռոգետոր եւ սիրելի որդւոյ մերոյ Յոռան վարդապետինն, որ գիտութեամբ ձերով ամ յամէ ռասուսցէ ի սուրբ աթոռս։ Նաեւ թէ ինչ, թէ պանիր, թէ
ռաւ, եւ թէ այլ ինչ դոյնպիսին նուիրոգ յօգնութին ռասանիցէք վանիցն սրբոյն
Սարգսի։ Որով եւ դուք կրկին օրհնութեանց եւ շնորռաց արժանի լինիչիք։ Եւ որքան ի Սուրբ աթոռս սաղմոսերգութինք, պաշտոնք եւ պատարագ եւ ամենայն
շնորռաբաշխութինք կատարի, ձեզ եւ ձեր անչեղելոյց մասն եւ բաժին եղիցի։
Եւ ըստ տրոգ նուիրաց եւ արդեանց ձերոց ռազարապատիկ եւ բիւրապատիկ ընկալցիք ի քրիստոսէ Աստուծոյ մերմէ ռանդերձ անչեղելովք ձերովք աստ եւ ի
ռանդերձեալումն, Ամէն։ Հայր մեր։

Դարձեալ պատուիրելով պատուիրեմ ռոգետոր եւ սիրելի որդւոյդ մերոյ
Յոռան վարդապետիդ, զի եւ դու արի եւ քաջ եւ ռասատատուն կացցես ի վերայ
ռոգետոր գործօդ, լոր շնորհիօք սուրբ ռոգւոյն կոչեցար եւ գռարագատական սերն
քո մի պակաս առնիցես ի սրբոյ աթոռոյս, եւ գտուն ի վրայ գտուոյ աճեալ լաւ
ռոգաբարառութին եւ ռասատարմութին արասցես արդեանցն տէրունականացն եւ
քան զառաջինն այլ աւելորդոք պարտիս գնութրան եւ գարդինան ամ յամէ ռա-
սուցանել ի սուրբ աթոռս, որով եւ դու ըստ վաստակոց քոց ամենայնի զվարձս
ընկալցիս ի շնորռաց սրբոյ աթոռոյս ռանդերձ քոյովք ամենեքեամբք։

Document #16

An Open Letter from members of the Religious Order of the All
Saviour's Monastery to the members of the Religious Order of
Ējmiacin, against Kaťoŀikos Nahapet.[1]

To our Holy and beloved, intimate and faithful colleagues, to our
blessed, truthful and honest brethren and overseer bishops, the
residents of our very celebrated mother, the Holy an sanctifying See of
Ējmiacin. Also to those in the provinces of Ayrarat and Atrpatakan,
bishops, priests and all pupils and clerics of our Holy Church, who
consider Holy Ējmiacin their common mother.

We greet you in Christ. Let our most sacred love and heavenly
peace be with you. We the Christians of Šoš,[2] clergy and laymen, would
like to inform your excellencies about certain events which occurred in
our unfortunate time, due to our carelessness and unpreparedness, and
because of which everybody's will was shaken like a wind-tossed ship.
We understand that there will be peace where there is order. Eliminate
order and confusion is what you will be left with. Ever since Kaťoŀikos
Eŀiazar of blessed memory died, the misdeeds of imprudent and ill-
advised men corrupted by their passion for glory and led by Minas
Astapatči,[3] have spread confusion among us. As a child, he [Minas] was
never educated in the morals of the truth. He has learned neither the
theory[4] not its practical application. He has adopted vulgar and earthly
values and has spent his life wallowing in material pleasures. He has
made a written agreement with Nahapet on the condition that he will be
the Vicar. We also know more about them, but it is not worth to mention
everything in this letter.

Now, who is Minas Astapatči who dares to do that? Is our nation
his father's slave which he thinks he can sell to anybody of his choice,
just to fulfil his own ends? If that is the way of consecrating kaťoŀikos,

---

[1] Armenian text printed in new Julfa, 1693. Copies in AASM, *Matenadaran* of Erevan
and UCLA. Printed in Tēr Yovhaneanč, vol. II, pp. 114-122.
[2] Isfahan.
[3] Astapat was a famous village in Naxčawan.
[4] The curriculum of higher education which included the *trivium* and the *quadrivium*
divisions of seven liberal arts.

then everybody will seek to consecrate someone who will always be at their back and call. There are many monasteries and bishops in your as well as in our country. If it is right to consecrate someone kat'ołikos, without holding elections or without obtaining written authorisation, who will be there to refrain from that of what Minas Astapatči has done? Who is less worthy than the person consecrated by him? If the person consecrated by him is acceptable, then people consecrated by others must be acceptable as well. If they are not acceptable, then the person consecrated by him [Minas] should not be acceptable either, because Minas Astapatči has acted against the social order. He is the most illiterate and therefore the most wicked and worthless person. Ignorance is considered the source of all vices. He must be made accountable for the evils he has caused to our nation. They [Minas and his cohorts] provided us with two reasons for their deeds only after they had already consecrated Nahapet as Kaťołikos.

First they claim to have acted according to the will of the Spiritual Lord.[5] Secondly, they say, "we acted according to the letter sent by you." To their first argument we respond: As you already knew and as we later came to know, the Spiritual Lord Ełiazar is not the author of that will. If you wish, we can tell you what the true will of the Spiritual Lord was. If he had really made that will, why didn't he sign it personally? It was his custom to sign at the bottom of his writings, saying: "In confirmation, I put my signature on this." There are many letters in our possession, which are written and duly signed by him. He was under more obligation to follow the same custom in this case, because this document was addressed to the general public and its implementation concerned everybody. Therefore it is obvious that the said will is not authentic.

Let us suppose that the will is authentic and then look into the orders and canons of the church fathers and our blessed forefathers and see if there is such a law, authorizing the Kaťołikos alone—without the council of bishops, *vardapets*, monks, hermits and *A šxarha žo łov*[6] —to promote someone of his own choice to the pontifical office. If that kind of practice has been allowed before or is allowed at present, it has only been allowed against the order of our forefathers, and is therefore not acceptable. If they are not willing to follow that ancient canons set by our early church fathers, at least they have to obey the church fathers of our own times.

---

[5] Kaťołikos Ełiazar.
[6] General Assembly participated by clergy and lay leadership of Armenia.

In the year 1115[7] of the Armenian era, famous *vardapets*, notables and prominent people gathered at the Holy See of Ējmiacin and guided by the holy fathers, they adopted new rules consisting of several articles, concerning the ordination [election] of Katołikos. If those rules are not respected, then [the new Katołikos] will be unacceptable. The rules copied by Movsēs *Vardapet* and signed and sealed by other *vardapets* are available here. We have already sent you a copy of that document. If the rules are respected in the present case, we will accept [the election], if not, we will feel free to free ourselves of any obligations. This is our response to their first argument.

In response to their second argument, we can say that we have written to Katołikos Ełiazar—a fact which we can not deny—saying: "As long as you are alive, you are our Katołikos and after your death, we will abide by your will and will elect a katołikos from among your followers."

Katołikos Ełiazar had many disciples, not just one. Had we referred to any specific name in our letter, then your accusations [of us] could have been justified. But since the statement we have made is fairly vague and general, we find your accusations to be ungrounded. Nobody has ever heard that before the burial of a deceased katołikos, a new katołikos may be anointed. But that is exactly what happened. Some people [are mistaken] if they think that the Spiritual Lord Ełiazar was an ignorant person. When he left Jerusalem, he was wise enough to go to Constantinople and wait there, saying: "I will not go to the Holy See, unless I receive the *mansar*[8] from Isfahan." When we sent the *mansar* he came to the Holy See.

This is the way a wise man would act. If he [Ełiazar] himself was so scrupulous going through the proper channels, how can you expect him to allow others to bypass our *mansar*? They [Minas and his cohorts] requested a *mansar* from us, only after completing their work without a written authorisation.

We, the authors of the present letter were in the process of writing [the *mansar*], when the second Holofernes[9] and Goddos,[10] the fallen and destroyed Awet,[11] being bribed and blinded by silver and having received bribes twice and thrice, obtained and sent *Libasi hukm*[12]

---

[7] 1666.

[8] Letter of agreement.

[9] The chief general of King Nebuchadnessar's army. Judith, II, 4.

[10] Godołia? (Ged-a-li-ah, governor of Judah, appointed by the King of Babylon.)

[11] *Kalantar* of New Julfa.

[12] Royal confirmation-order for the new Katołikos.

without our knowledge and agreement, as a result of which he was destroyed and replaced by a new *Kalantar*, the blessed *Khwaja* Łukas, son of *Mahtasi*[13] *Khwaja* Petros, a pious man like his father. From now on the bribes will be eliminated and the truth will prevail and guide us. Beloved brethren, it is time to awake, time to reject darkness and to embrace light.

We are sending the present letter to your honors, so that you may explain to the person, who claims to be Kaťołikos, that if he intends to rule us by force, he will not succeed, because we are nobody's slave. Even God, whose rule is unquestionable and natural, does not rule over anybody by force, let alone man [who is not God]. But if he intends to rule justly and lawfully, we will obey him unconditionally.

But what do justice and law mean? To follow the path of our blessed forefathers, if not the early and supreme ones, at least the recent ones, who adopted the morals and the virtues of the early ones by following the true order and religion. We mean kaťołikoi Movsēs and Pilippos of blessed memories who enlightened our Church and the Armenian nation.

We briefly list our arguments in the following twelve points:

- First: The Kaťołikos must constantly read the Bible and be guided by it and administer the Church accordingly.

- Second: He must establish schools everywhere, as it is the custom of other Christian nations, but more particularly, our own [tradition]. The Persians also make great efforts in that respect as all knowledgeable people know. The development and stability of a nation depends on education. We see the uncivilized and useless Georgian people for example, who do not care for education.

- Third: He must wear woollen, not cotton or linen clothing, and must not permit others [to wear cotton or linen].

- Fourth: He should not pray or eat alone, but must be with the members of the Religious Order during prayers and share their meals at the refectory.

- Fifth: There should not be a separate stewardship and pantry. Also everything in the common house should be shared. He and his followers must not have more than what they need and others must not be left aside in desperate need. Everything must be shared, including the treasury, the storage, the pantry and the refectory.

- Sixth: He should not demonstrate pride mounting on adorned and stalking horses, but he should use mules for his travels, as we have seen the antecessors doing.

---

[13] *Mukdesi* in Arabic, a title given to men who have visited Jerusalem as pilgrims.

- Seventh: He should not keep two, three or four footmen, as we hear he does. He must employ only one messenger, as the former katolikoi used to.

- Eight: He should avoid strange and ridiculous things: when he travels, he should not surround himself with a retinue of horses the way princes do. Also, he should not wear saber and broad sword, because these are not suitable to spiritual leaders. According to the apostle, "The weapons of our warfare are not carnal, but spiritual."[14]

- Ninth: Teenage boys in beautiful clothing should not be kept in service to avoid scandals of wicked people. Instead, grown-ups, wearing beards and oversized black clothes should be employed to silence opponents and slanderers.

- Tenth: He should not elevate ignorant and uneducated people to the rank of bishop or bestow upon them the title of *vardapet*. Because, those who are eager to receive higher education might eventually quit their studies, when they see that others have been elevated to the rank of bishop and received the title of *vardapet* without much effort and work. As a result of this, our people will remain in darkness. As Aristotle says: "If you want to reform your house, separate the good from the bad and the worker from the lazy." And according to Solomon, "The wise shall inherit glory."[15]

- Eleventh: He should not impose unreasonable punishments on people of order and rank. We have often been told that he has cut somebody's beard and has tied somebody else to a pillar. Who has taught him to impose such awful punishments on people? How can he tie a bishop to a pillar during a banquet, cut his beard and have ruffians and bandits bastinade him without first giving [the bishop] a fair trial and without [seeking the approval] of the council? The pious [Emperor] Constantianus held that [trial] for Arius, who deserved death. Emperor Theodosius II did the same for Nestorius. According to the church fathers, that was the legal way to try the clerics, especially the bishops. As Saint Cyril of Alexandria referring to the abominable Nestorius, says: "With the authority of the Council, we defrocked him from his bishophood." Did you ever heared that Katolikos Pilippos, who held the office for twenty four years, cut somebody's beard or tied somebody to the pillar? Also Katolikos Yakob, who held the office for twenty five years, gave that punishment only to Onoprios,[16] and everybody know

---

[14] Second Corinthians, X, 4.

[15] Proverbs, III, 35.

[16] Onoprios Erewanci is described by Zakaria Sarkawag as a person who has initiated many conspiracies against Kat'olikos Yakob and the Holy See of Ějmiacin.

that the latter deserved death and not just a punishment. But we have heard that during the last one and a half years, many people have been humiliated for no reason. Only civil courts, not the Church, have the power to assign punishments of that sort. Therefore, we are against trying and punishing bishops or *vardapets* without a Council or contrary to the canons.

- Twelfth: He should not introduce any changes in the dioceses of bishops following the examples of Brgišo and Šmuel.[17] As Movsēs *Ḱertolahayr*[18] describes in his *History*, one of them used to annex the dioceses of deceased bishops [to his own domain], while the other used to take over the dioceses of living bishops. According to the apostolic and patriarchal canons, each bishop should rule in his diocese and each diocese should be under the See to which it is assigned from the beginning. But if a bishop errs, he should be tried according to the canons of the Church and should be punished accordingly. According to the Divine word, changes and divisions have, do and will bear only evil: "Every kingdom divided against itself is brought to desolation; and every city or house divided against itself shall not stand."[19] It is common knowledge that each see is attached to a certain diocese, and that they ought not be separated. After Kaťolikos Pilippos of blessed memory, illegal divisions were created in certain dioceses due to unjust interventions. From now on we do not want and will not tolerate such disorders to take place.

But above all, Minas Astapatči should be expelled from the Holy See and the Province of Ayrarat. He should be exiled to his native village and all his belongings should be confiscated. He, not others, deserves beard cutting and bastinado. Persecute and destroy him by written order, so that he may not again set foot in Erevan; otherwise, let it be clear that we will do that by Royal Decree. We have the ability to destroy him by subjecting him to inexpressible humiliations and persecutions because we know that he has bribed this detestable and humanlike beast[20] to accomplish his evil work. Therefore, we can not accept such an adversary and slanderer to remain in that Holy and famous place. He deserves to be discarded in a remote corner.

We demand the listed twelve conditions to be met by the Kaťolikos, whoever he might be, and we forward the present appeal to you in

---

[17] Brkišo and Šmuel (both of them Assyrians) were successively placed on the Patriarchal Seat of Armenia (329-337) by the Sasanids, while Kat'olikos Sahak was deprived from his office.

[18] A title given to Movsēs Xorenači. Literally meaning chief poet or father of poets.

[19] Matthew, XII, 25.

[20] *Kalantar* Awet.

brotherly love, since we belong to the same body and must console each other. Show [our demands] to him. If he agrees and accepts [our demands], let him seal his written response, have it certified by the blessed bishops and forward it to us, so that we may keep it as an indelible memorial and be willing to obey him as our [spiritual] head and so that he may rule our Church the way the sun [shines above the universe]. But if he does not accept our arguments and considers our letter worthless, then we would like you to return our letter and be assured that we will take all the necessary measures to deal [with him] as harshly as possible.

Two hundred copies are printed at All Saviour's monastery of New Julfa, city of Isfahan, in the year 1693 of the Christian era, and the Armenian year 1142, May 1.

ԳԻՐ ԸՆԴՀԱՆՐԱԿԱՆ, ՆՈՐ ՋՈՒՂԱ 1693

Սուրբ եւ սիրելի պաշտոնակցաց մերոց, եւ ճարագատաց ճառատարմաց երջանկացելոց եղբարց ճշմարտախոհից եւ ուղղասիրաց, վերադիտողացդ սրբազանից զետեղելոց ի գերահռչակ, ի սուրբ եւ ի սրբարար Աթոռդ էջմիածին ի մայրդ ճասարակաց, նա եւ որդ ընդ ճովանեաւ դորին որդիացելոց յաշխարհիդ արաբացւոյ եւ յատրպատականին, Քանճանայապետից, եւ Քանճանից, եւ ճամօրէն լրման ուխտի ժառանգաւորաց եւ վիճակաւորաց սուրբ եկեղեցւոյ:

Ողջոյն ի Քրիստոս մատուցանեմք սիրալրական սիրով սրբութեան երկնաւոր խաղաղութեամբն ճանդերձ, մեք ի Շօշ եղեալ քրիստոնեկախումբ դասք եկեղեցականաց եւ աշխարճականաց: Ընդ որոյ եւ որով ծանուցանեմք պատուականութեան ձերոյ գեղելոց իրաց դիպելոց, որ ի մերումս եղեալ թշուառութեան ամմանակի յանգգուշութեան եւ յանկատրասատութեան մերոյ պատճառէ, որով կամք ամենեքեան երերեալ եւ տատանեալ իբրեւ զնաւ խռովեալ յալեաց ծովու: Քանզի սկիզբն եւ աւարտ խաղաղութեան գրաբեկկարգութիւնն շիճել իմանամք, զի ուրացօր բարձրեալ է բարեկարգութիւն` արմատացեալ լինի արմտակ խռովութեան, որպէս եւ տեսանեմք մերով տեսանելիօք: Քանզի որքան վախճանա առեալ է կենցաղոյս ընդ երանելիին ճանգուցեալ երջանկիդ Հայրապետին մեր Տէր Եղիազար` վրդովումն խռովութեան ոչ պակաս ի մէջ, պատճառն անխոճեմ եւ անճանաճար մարդոց գործ եւ արարմունք, որք լիրեանց փառամօլութեանց ախտից ձգեալք եւ պարապեալք, որոց գլուխ եւ զօրավիգ զաստապատ զդ Մի-նասն, որ ոչ գրոց աշակերտեալ, ոչ զտեսական ծանուցեալ, եւ ոչ գործնական-ին մասին ճաղորդեալ, այլ զօրէն գտնկիաց գերկրատրս ետիթ ողջոնեալ եւ ի ճղն ցանկ դեցերեալ, ժամանդիր եղեալ ընդ Նախասպետին ձեռագրով եւ կնքով միմեանց թէ միշու ի քո կատրողիկոսութեանն եւ եղէց աթոռակալ, այսու պայ-մանաւ յառաջեցուցեալ զալդ գործ, որ մեզ ամենեցուն ստոյգ եւ իրաւապէս յայտնի եղեւ որ այդ այդպէս է, եւ առաւել քան զալդ գիտակ եղաք ամենայնի` գոր չէ պարտ մի ըստ միոջէ արձանացուցանել ի գիր:

Արդ ո՞վ իցէ աստապատցի Մինասն որ զայդ առնիցէ, միթէ ազգա ար-ծարթագին է Հոր դորա, որո՞ւմ եւ կամիցի վաճառիցէ յաղագս պորտոյ եւ յորո-վալին իւրոյ, եթէ այդպիսի է կարգ եւ կանոն կաթողիկոս ձեռնադրութեան` ո՞վ պակաս քան զնա որ ոչ կարիցէ գումն կատարող ախտի իւրոյ ձեռնադրել կաթողիկոս, քանզի ի ձեռում աշխարճի լուլմք գն վաճառուպք եւ Եղիսկ-պոսունեք եւ ի մերս աշխարճին. եթէ այդպիսւ իցէ որ առանց ընդոտութեան եւ վկայականի թղթոլ ձեռնադրեալ է կատողիկոս, որում պարտ է ճնազանդել` ո՞վ է որ ոչ կարիցէ իբրեւ զաստապատցին օծանել գոբ ի պատճի կատողիկո-սութեան, ո՞վ է որ պակաս է քան զնա որ օծեալ ննրա լիցի կատողիկոս, եւ այլոցն ոչ, եթէ ննրայն ընդունելի` ուրեմն այլոցն պարտ է լինիլ եւ ընդունելի, իսկ եթէ այլոցն ոչ` ուրեմն եւ ննրայն ոչ, տճնա` որ աստապատցին ոչ է ի կարգի ճասարակաց, այլ յոտի եւ անարգ քան զամենեսեան յաղագս աննուման եւ ան-վարձութեան իւրոյ, գոր տգիտութինն մայր զլ սամբանեցին ամենայն մոլու-թեանց, որով դա կաչ պարաւանդեալ որ այդպիսի ոճրագործութիւն գործեաց ի մէջ ազգիս, որ եւ լետ կատարման գործծոց գրեալ են ան մեջ կրկին պատճառ:

Նախ թէ ըստ կտակի ճոգելոր տիրին արարաբ զայս, երկրորդ թէ ի ձէնջ առաքեալ թղթոյն քանին գործծեցաբ: Առաջնոյն զայս պատասխանեմբ, թէ Եղիազար ճոգելոր Տէրն ոչ է արարեալ զայդ կտակ, որպէս եւ կանխագոյն լայտ իսկ է ձեզ, եւ լետոյ մեզ եւս եղեւ զրստուլցն յայտնին. գոր եթէ կամիք մեք ծա-նուցումք ձեզ զգշմարիտ կտակ ճոգելոր տիրին, արդ որովճետեւ արար` վասն է՞ր

ոչ դրոշմեաց ձեռամբ իրով ի քարտիսի՝ զոր կանխագոյն իսկ ունէր սովորութիւն
լաւարտ բանին դնէր ձեռս աւելով՝ թէ առ ի հաստատութիւն բանիս եդի զձե-
ռագիր ի վերայ. որ բանի թուղթ առ մեզ գոյ այսպիսի գրեալ եւ դրոշմեալ,
հարկաւորապէս եւ առաւելապէս դմին՝ իրի լաւին պարտեր զայդ սովորութիւն ի
գործ ածել, զի համաշխարհականէ բանն եւ իրագործութիւն, որով երեւի ոչ գոլ
ճմշարիտ զգասացեալն։ Անսէմբ թէ եւ ասացեալ ես լիցի, հայեցարուք ի կարգս
եւ ի կանոնս հարցն սրբոց եւ երանելի ճախճնեաց, եթէ այդպէս է սովորութիւն եւ
կարգ կաթողիկոսաց, թարգ ժողովոց Եախկոպրոսաց եւ վարդապետաց, ճանէ հարց
վանականաց լեռնականեաց կրոճաւորաց, եւ աշխարհաժողովով հանդիսի, ինքնահաւ
կամօք դստ ախորժական սրտի իրոյ, կռշեացէ զոք ի պատիւ կաթողիկոսութեան,
եթէ այնպիսին ընդունելի եղեալ է եւ այժմ լինիցի, ապա թէ թիւր եւ զարտուղի
է լրնթացից ճախճնեաց՝ ուրեմն ոչ է ընդունելի, եթէ հարցն առաջնց եւ ճոգին
կանոնաց ոչ անսաճ՝ զոճէ ի մերումս եղեալ ժամանակի հարցն անսասցեն, որ ի
թուճաշչուութեան տոճմիս հայկական հացար երրորդի հարիւրորդի եւ տասն եւ
ճինգ ամի մեծանունն վարդապետք, երեւելիք եւ ճշանաւորք ժողովեալ են ի սուրբ
Աթոռդ Էջմիածին ճետեւելով հարցն սրբազանից, եւ բանի գլխով բան կարգեալ
լաղագս կաթողիկոսա ձեռնադրութեան, թէ որ ն՛չ լինի այնպէս՝ խոտելի է, որոց
գրեալ բանքն լուսաւոր ճոգի Մովսէս վարդապետին ձեռնագրով եւ այլ սրրա-
զան վարդապետաց կնքով եւ գրով առ մեզ է, որս սասատ ես առ ձեզ առաքեցաք, եթէ այլ բանից միոյն համաձայնի արարեալն ներկալիս՝ ապա է մեզ
ընդունելի, իսկ թէ ոչ՝ մեք ումէք ոչ եմբ պարտական եթէ զպարտոն պաճանձ-
ցէ, այսքան առ առաջինն։ Երկրորդին զայս տամբ պատասխանի, թէ գրեալ եմբ
մեք առ Տէր Եղիազար կաթողիկոսն եւ ոչ կարեմբ լուրաստ լինել, թէ որբան
դու կենդանի ես՝ մեր կաթողիկոս դու ես եւ լետ քո կատարոզ եմբ կամաց քոց,
եւ թոյրցն առնելոց եմբ կաթողիկոս. աճա Եղիազար ճոգելորն տիրին ոչ մի՛ ունէր
աշակերտ՝ այլ լոլով, եթէ մեք լանունանէ մարդոյ անունՆ գրեալ եմբ, ապա թէ
մեզ վերայ հաստատուդի բանն, իսկ թէ անորրոշակի եմբ գրեալ՝ ապա զոր եւ Աա-
ճիր է մեզ վերայ ասացեալս եւ անսասոշաճ արարեալն։ Ի լաիիտենից ոչ որ
լուաս թէ ճախբան թաղումն վախճանեալ կաթողիկոսի օձանից նոր կաթողիկոս, զոր աճա եղեն, մի՛ թէ Եղիազար ճոգելորն Տէր այր տգետ երեւցաս լաչս
ումանց, քանզի իր խոճեմութեամբն եւ խորագիտութեամբն ի գալն լերոսա-
ղէմայ ճստաւ ի Կոստանդնուպոլիս, աճելով թէ ոչ եկից ի սուրբ Աթոռն միճչեւ
ոչ զայցէ մանսար իսսաճանու եւ լորժամ առաքեցաք՝ իսկլն եկն, այսպէս լինի
արարք առն խոճեմագունի, եթէ լաղագս ինքեան այսպէս խորճէր՝ ապա վասն
այլոց զի՞արդ հրամայէր լինել առանց մեր մանսարի, զոր լետ գործոնձա կա-
տարման թարգ վկայական թղթով, ապա ինձրեալ էին ի մեզշ մանսար զոր
մեզ արդեասա գրեալս լայնժաման էաբ գրելոց. բայց երկրորդ ՀողեփենՆս եւ
Գոդոս անկեալ եւ կրոճանեալ զաճետ կաշառակուր եղեալ եւ արծաթով կու-
րացեալ. կրկին եւ երեքկին անգամ ընկալեալ զկաշառ լիպսիս թուրմ ճանեան եւ
առաքեալ առանց մեր մանսարի, սպաճի եւ գիտութեան, որով վասն եւ ինքՆ
կրոճանեցաւ եւ նոր Քաղանթար հաստատեցաւ Մաճմետի Խօջա Ղուկան ամե-
նեինՆ լար եւ ճման բարեպաշտութեան ճորն իրով։ Այսուճետեւ կաշառն անգործ
եղեալ ճշմարտութիւնՆ է թագաւորելց եւ ողողութինՆ ճաստատելց։ Ժամ է
այսուճետեւ մեզ սիրելիք ի բաց զարրնելով, քանզի գիշերս մերձեցաւ եւ տին
մերձեցաւ։ Ջայս թողուր վասն այլոր առաքեցաք առ մեծութիս ձեր մի ցուցանե-
ցէք կաթողիկոս եղնողիդ եթէ կամ դա բոնութեամբ, եւ ումգնութեամբ բազկի
իրոյ տիրել մեզ՝ ոչ կարէ, քանզի մեզ ոչ ումէք եմբ արծախագինՆ, զի բարձր-
եալն որդ տերութինՆ սեփական է եւ իշխանութինՆ բնութեամբ՝ բնաւար ոչ
ումէք տիրէ, թող թէ մարդ։ Իսկ ապա թէ արդարութեամբ եւ իրաւամբբ տիրէ՝
ճնազանդիմբ եւ մեք առաւել բան զսասաւն։ Եւ թէ զի՞նչ է արդարութինՆ եւ
իրաւունբ, այսինբն է զնալ անխոտոր զշաւիղս լասաշցնցն սրբոց, եթէ ճախ-
նեացն եւ գերագունիցն ոչ՝ սակայն լետնոցն որ ի մերումս աճանակի զառաշ-
նոցՆ ստացան վարս եւ առաբինութիւնս, ճշմարտութեան կարգաց եւ կրոճից

ռետևեյով, զլուսաւոր ռոգիք Մովսէս եւ Փիլիպպոս կաթուղիկոսացն ասեմք, որ ի
վերջին ժամանակս փայլեցան իբրեւ զարեգակն ջաhատորեալք ի մէջ սուրբ եկեղեցւոյ եւ յաղագս Հայաստանեայց: Եւ զի՞նչ է խնդիր մեր եւ գորս ռամառո-
տաբար կարգեցուցք երկոտասան գլխօք: Նախ զի կաթուղիկոսն միշտ եւ անա-
րատ ընթերցցի զԱստուածային գիրս եւ ինքն ռովիմք վարեսցի եւ վարեսցէ
զեկեղեցի: Երկրորդ գի դպրատուն եւ գդասատուն ռաստատեսցէ յամենայն
տեղիս, որպէս սովրութիւն է այլազգեաց Քրիստոնէից, եւ մանաւանդ թէ մեզ
իսկ զլխովին նա եւ պարսից եւս, գոր գիտողացն է բաշալ բայթ որբ ռանան ունենն
ջանք եւ փոյթ յայդմ իրի, բանդ զ շնորհ է աստուծոյ ծ ագգի դոցա
լինի: Որպէս եւ տեսանեմք խոպտանացեալ եւ անապիտանացեալ ազգն վրաց
յաղագս ոչ ունելոյ փոյթ զայսմանէ: Երրորդ գի եւ ինքն ասպեղէն զգեցցի եւ ոչ
բամբակեղէն կամ վշտեղէն եւ ոչ այլոց թույ տացէ: Չորրորդ զատ եւ առանձին ի
միաբանից ոչ յաղ օթսա կացցէ, եւ ոչ ռաց կերիցէ, այլ ընդ միաբանսն ռամոր-
դեսցի, ի յամենայն աղ օթսան եւ ի ռացկերոյ սեղանատեղսն: Հինգերորդ մի
լիցի առանձին տնտեսումն եւ մարան, եւ մի՛ իմ եւ քո ի մէջ բերիցէ ի ռասարակ
տան, ինքն իրալովէքբ աւելորդօբ բան գռարկաւորն շատացեալ, եւ ռասարակ
անիւանեմ եւ անայլելով մանցեալ կարոտ ռարկաւորին, այլ զամենայն մի լիցի,
եթէ զան Յարանս եթէ շտեմարան, եթէ տնտեսումն եւ եթէ սեղանատումն: Վեցե-
րորդ մի զարդարեալ սիգապայ երիվարօք յխորտոացեալ յորանայցէ, այլ կիսի-
շեօք շրջեսցի, որպէս եւ տեսեալ իսկ եմք զնախնին ասոր մերովք: Եօթներորդ
ոչ ունիցի երկու կամ երեք եւ շորք փայեայ որպէս այժմ լնեմք, այլ միով սուր-
ռանդակա բատակականան որպէս ունին կաթուղիկոսունքն: Ութերորդ նոր զար-
մանն եւ ծիծաղելիս ոչ առնել, այսինքն, թէ բարշել առաջի ընդ օրինի իշխանաց եգակա մէկ, երկու, եւ կամ աւելի եւ պակաս, եւ կապել թիր եւ
դաղարաց, որ կարի ռեռի է ի ռոգետոր իշխանութենէ, զի զեն գինորոութեան
մերոյ ոչ է մարմնաւոր՝ այլ ռոգետոր ընդ առաբելոյ: Իններորդ ոչ պամել մատան
մանկունս զապասատորս առաջ զարդարեալ զգետատիք ի ռայթակոութիւն
տկարամտաց, այլ կատարեալ ռասակա եւ մուրսօք սեւազգետ եւ խոշորա-
ռանդերն ի յամօթ ռակառակորդաց բամբատողաց: Տասներորդ առանց տոիտոց
եւ անվարժից մի՛ տացէ պատիհ Եպիսկոպոսական, եւ իշխանութիւն վարդապետական, բանգի նռքա որ ունին ջան, եւ աշխատասիրութիւն ուսման՝ տեսանելով
զայլս թարգ ջանից եւ աշխատանաց ընկալեալ զպատիհ Եպիսկոպոսութեան եւ
զասոտիճան վարդապետութեան, եւ նռքա յուսաhատեալ խափան լինին ի բարի
յառաջիմոութենէ եւ մնալ ազգս ի մէջ անգիտութեան խաւարի յաղագս աննրան-
րութեան ընդ Արիստոտելի որ աստ, եթէ կամիս բարեկարգութիւն տալ, ընդրեա
զլան ի վարդարէն եւ զվասասակարդ յանջանէն, եւ ընդ իմաստունոյն թէ՝
գիտատ իմասոտումբ ժամանգեցացեն: Մետասաներորդ՝ ոչ ադել պատիիմա ան-
պատողան ի վերայ ուրոիք անայարմար կարգի եւ ասոիճանի, որպէս լնեմք թէ
այս ին մարդոյ մուրուս կորել է, եւ այս ին մարդ ի սին կապեալ, ոչ միանգամ
լնեմք՝ այլ յոլովակի, ուստի՞ ունի օրինակ զայդպիսի անոպայ արարմանց, զայր
եպիսկոպոս առանց ժողովոյ եւ դատաստանի, ի ժամ՝ ռաց կերութեան եւ գինի
ընմպութեան կապեալ ի սին եւ բրածծ տալ առնել առանց սրիկայից եւ ելու-
զակաց եւ յետոյ զմուրունս ռատանել: Բարեպայծմն Կոստանդինեանս երբ առար
զայդ Արիրոսի թեպետ եւ սպաոնաս էր արծաթն, եւ կամ փորձն Թէոդոս աո
ներատոր երբ գործեագ զայդ, եւ կամ Հայրապետն սուրբք երբ օրէնս վարկան եւ
իրաւունք ռամարեցան այդպիսի դատաստանան դատել զեկեղեցական եւ մանաւանդ եպիսկոպոս, որպէս գրէ սուրբն Կիւրեղ Աղեբսանդրաց յաղագս պիծողն
Նեստոոր թէ՝ լուծումն արարաբ զնա յեպիսկոպոսութենէ իրաւամբք ժողովույն:
Չի Մովսէս ռոգետոր տերն երբ արար զայդ եւ կամ լուսաւոր ռոգի Փիլիպպոս
կաթուղիկոսն, Ի՞Դ ամ վարեալ զկաթուղիկոութիւնն երբ եւ կամ ո՞ւմ մուրուս
կորեաց կամ սին կապեաց, ռոյնպէս եւ Յակոբ ռոգետոր Տէրն բսան եւ ռինգ ամ
կացեալ յաթոռն միայն Ոնոփրիոսին եած զայդ պատիմ, ձինն աշխարհ վկայեր
մառու գոլ արժանի, եւ ոչ լոկ պատմոյ, գոր այժմա տարի եւ վես է բանիսն լնեմք

գայղպիսի խայտառակեալ զուր եւ ունայն պատճառաւ, այղպիսի պատիժ քա
ղաքական օրինի եւ դատաստանի է աննկ եւ ոչ եկեղեցական։ Վասն որոյ ոչ
կամիմք զայր եպիսկոպոս կամ վարդապետ թարգ ժողովլդ եւ կանոնաց դատել
կամ պատժել, յորմէ պատճառէ վնաս յոլով ծանանի, զի ժամանակս շար է։
Երկոտասանեներորդ մի՛ փոփոխեցէ գրեմ եւ զվիճակ Եպիսկոպոսաց ըստ Ընա
նութեան բրբիշՕւ եւ շմուելի, որ միՕՕ զմեներալ Եպիսկոպոսաց վիճակն յափռշ
տակեր, իսկ միւս եւ զկեՕղանի Եպիսկոպոսաց. որպէս գրէ քերթողաՒայլն
Մովսէս ի վիպագրութեան իւրում։ Այլ ըստ ուղղիդ կանՕնաց առաքելական եւ
Ֆայրապետատակա իրաքանչիւր Եպիսկոպոս տիրէ լիւրում վիճակին, եւ իրա
քանչիր թէմ լիւրում աթոռոյ կացցէ եւ մատսցէ՝ գոր ի քէ ունի կարզեալ եւ
Ֆատտատեայլ։ Բայց թէ առաջնորդ Եպիսկոպոսն անուղղագործ ունիցի՝ դատես
ցի ըստ իրաւանց կանՕնաց եկեղեցոյ, եւ որպէս արժանն է պատժեսցի, քանզի ի
փոփոխմաՒ եւ ի բաժանմաՒ բազում չարիս ծնեալ է, ծնՕնի եւ ծնանելցՕ է,
ըստ ՏէրունականՕ բանի՝ տուն, քաղաք, եւ թագաւորութիւն բաժանեալ կործա
Օ. եւ զի ամենեցունՕդ է քաջայայտ որ իրաքանչիր աթոռ պասակեալ է ընդ
իւրղ վիճակին, որդ ոչ է պարտ բաժանի ի միմեանց. թէպէտ յետ սրբասէր կա
թողիկոսի Ստեանն Ֆիլիպպոսի, ումանց բաժանումՕ եղեալ է, եւ այն ոչ կանՕ
Օական իրաւամբք՝ այլ յանիրա յարձակմանՕ՝ որդ յայսմֆետէ ոչ կամիմք, եւ ոչ
թողացուցանեմք լինիլ զայն անկարգութիւնՕ։ Եւ ի վերայ այսոր ամենայնի,
աստապատոցի ՄինասՕ արտաքսեցէ եւ Ֆալածեցէ ի սուրբ Աթոռոդ եւ յԱյ
րարատ գաառատ, եւ կորուսցէ ի քինք տեղի իւր, եւ գոր ինչ ստացեալ է եւ ունի՝
խլեցէ ի ձեռացՕ, մուրուս կորելոդ, սին կապելոդ, եւ բրածեծ առնելոդ դա է
արժանի, եւ ոչ այս եւ այլ. Ֆալածեալ կորուսանՕիցէք ձեռագրով որ այլ լերեան
շկրիխէ քարի է, ապա թէ ոչ՝ ՕշմարտիՕ յայոնՕ է, մեք առնեմք արքունի ֆրամա
Օաս, եւ գիտեմք թէ որպէս անկպատմելի, եւ անատելի խայտատակութամբ կորու
սանՕելցո եմք ֆաՖդերձ դատատավարտական պատժիք, քանզի դա եա բազ
դդիմ կաշաոք կորրացուցանՕեր զայս գարշելի այրակերոդ գագանա յաղագս ի
գլուխ Ֆանելոդ զիր չարութեան գործՕ, վասն որոյ ոչ կամիմք այղպիսի բան
սարկու եւ շոգմոդ առն մՕալ ի սուրբ եւ ի ֆոշակաւոր տեղիդ, այլ յանկեան
ուրեք ծակամուտ կացցէ, որպէս եւ արժան իսկ է:

Անա զայս երկոտասան բանք կարզեալք պահանջեմք ի կաթուղիկոսէն,
ով ոք եւ իցէ եւ զայս բանս խնդրանաց եղբայրական սիրով առ ձեզ առաքե
ցաք իբրեւ անդրամբ միմեանց լիՕելոդ ցաւակիցք, եւ դուք տարեալ ցուցէք իրՕ,
եթէ Ֆալանի եւ ընդունի գրով եւ կնքով իրՈdov, եւ վկայութամբ երջանիկ եպիս
կոպոսաց՝ առ մեզ առաքեցէք իբրեւ զայեունիկ անչինք մՕալ առ մեզ. յայն
ժամ եւ մեք սիրով ֆլու ֆայատակութամբ Օնագան ծ լիցուր ԸՕա իրրեւ գլխոյ, եւ
ինքՕ թատագորեցէ յեկեղեցիս մեր որպէս զարեգակՕ, ապա թէ ոչ ընղունՕiği
զասածեալս մեր եւ կամ՝ զրէալքս խոտան Ֆամարեսցի՝ յայնժամ զգրեանս մեր
դարձմուցիք յետս, յայնՕ ֆետո գիտեմք եւ մեք թէ որպէս պարտ իցէ առնել
յամեՒայն կորմանէ անխիոՕ:

Տգեցու տիպա երկու ֆարիր, ի դրան սուրբ ԱմեՖնապիրկչի վանաց Օոր
Ջուղայու, լիսաֆանան քաղաքի, ի թուում կեՖնարարին մեււդ ֆագար վեց ֆարիր
ինՖնունՕ եւ երեք: Եւ ի ֆայոց ֆազար ֆարիր քատասունՕ եւ երկու: ՑամՖնեանՕ
Մայիսի Ա:

Document #17

The Armenian communities of Burwari and Ṗeria declare their
loyalty to the Diocese of New Julfa.[1]

We, the Christian villagers in the districts of Burwari and Ṗeria;
priests, leaders and people at large, declare that, since the arrival of our
ancestors to this country, as we have been told, we have always been
under the jurisdiction of the diocese of All Saviour's monastery of New
Julfa, and have been loyal to the primate of the diocese of New Julfa,
whoever he might be. At present also, we the undersigned priests and
people, do recognise the jurisdiction of All Saviour's monastery and are
loyal to its primate. In testimony of that and with our free will, we put
our seals underneath. Written in August 20, 1142.[2]

The reason for this statement is the following: I [the undersigned]
Melik, appointed *kalantar* by Royal Decree, together with my region,
have been under the jurisdiction of the monastery of Julfa. Whoever the
primate of the monastery of Julfa might be, we, the people of Ṗeria are
loyal to him and do not recognise anybody else. [Seal]

The reason for this statement is the following: I Zaḳaria, appointed
Kalantar by Royal Decree—let me be sacrificed for the King—together
with my region, have been under the jurisdiction of the monastery of
Julfa. Whoever the primate of the monastery of Julfa might be, we the
people of Burwari are loyal to him and do not recognise any other
primate, except the primate occupying his place in the monastery of
Julfa.[3]

---

[1] Fragmented text in AASM (file 30B, doc.2). Printed by L.G. Minasean, *Patmutiwn
P'eriayi Hayeri*, pp. 411-412.

[2] 1693.

[3] The document is signed and sealed by the priests, *kadkhudas* and the people of the
following villages of Burwari and Ṗeria: Villages of Burwari - Čamxɔsu, Ḳavarza,
Anavš,Jašun, Čēšmē Ṗara, Xmsťan, Verin Čarbał, Nerḳin Čarbał, Janxoš, Jłagurk,
Borḳoḳ, Ṗarmišan, Łasumava, Šavrava, Khosrowabad, Šarharun, Dēynov, Gulbahar,
Hmaya, Ṗarčis. Villages of Ṗeria - Mēvrstan, Azgol, Hazarjarib, Mēydanak, Ałča,
Ṗnstan, Boloran, Daškēšan, Verin Khuygan, Sangbaran, Khnkirana, Šahbua,
Šuriškan, Milakert, Ťang Halvayi, Nerḳin Khuygan, Mułan, Sangerd, Bēku, Muḳēli
Geł.

ՀԱՄԱԽՕՍԱԿԱՆ ԲՈՒՐՎԱՐԻԻ ԵԻ
ՓԷՐԻԱՅԻ ՀԱՅՈՑ, 1693

Մեք Բուրվարու եւ Փէրիու գեղօրէից քրիստոնեայք, քահանայք, տանու֊
տէրք եւ ռամարակ ժողովուրդք, չունք որ մեր Ճախնիքն էս երկրիս դախիլ ան ելել
էապէսա դաստուր ելել որ մեք Ձուղայու ամենափրկչի վանքին թէմանք ելել
ովոր Ձուղայու վանքումն առաջնորդ եւել նորա առաջնորդին ըննագանդան
ելել. ըրմի էլ մեք նէրքոյ գրած քահանայք եւ ժողովուրդք սուրբ ամենափրկչին
վանքին թէմանք եւ նորին առաջնորդին ըննագանդ եմք: Էս նէրքեւն որ մեք
մռըելեմք մեր յօժարութեամբ եւ մեզ դարուլայ: Գրեցաւ Քրիստոսի ՌՃԽԲ
Օգոստոսի ամսոյն Ի ումն:

Պատճառ գրոյս այս է եւ Մէլիքս, որ թագաւորի ռաղամօն քաղաք֊
թարեմ, եւ իմ երկրովն Ձուղայու ամենափրկչին վանքին թէմանք ելել, այլ զի
ովոքոր Ձուղայու վանքին առաջնորդայ մեք Փարիու ժողովուրդա նորայ ինա֊
գանդեմք այլ ուրիշ մարդ չեմք ճանաչել: (կնիք)

Պատճառ գրոյս այս է. եւ Ջաքարեւ, որ թաքաւորի ռաղամօւն քաղաք֊
թարեմ, որ ջանա թաքաւորին փտա լինի, եւ իմ յերկրովն Ձուղայու վանքին
թէմանք ելել ովոքոր Ձուղայու վանքին առաջնորդա մեք Բուրվարու ժողովուրդա
նորա առաջնորդութենին ինագանդեմք. այլ ուրիշ առաջնորդ չեմք ճանաչել
դեյոգ Ձուղայու վանք իր տեղի Աստած առաջնորդն: (կնիք)

Document #18

An Open Letter against Kaḱoḻikos Nahapet from the clergy and
lay leadership of New Julfa to the Armenian clergy and laity
around the world.[1]

To all our beloved clergy united in Christ: blessed bishops,
theologian *vardapets*, expiating priests, and all religious members of the
Holy Order, also to pious laymen: princes of gentle origin, *meliks* of
noble families, *tanuterḱ* who judge righteously, prudent merchants, hard
working farmers, skilful craftsmen and to the Armenian people at large,
who are scattered everywhere around the world. Greetings in the name
of Jesus Christ our Lord, from the bishops, *vardapets*, priests and all
servants of the Church in Isfahan, and from *Kalantar* Ḻukas, *dawlaṭawork̈*
and the people at large.

Greetings to you in the name of Jesus Christ. Be informed our
beloved brethren that according to the civil law and human nature, men
should work hard to better their lives. That is a fact which applies not
only to humans, but to animals as well. And if we are making all these
efforts to improve our earthly existence, which is temporal, shouldn't
we then make greater efforts to secure a spiritual life which is eternal?
We can gain that unchanging and eternal favour by strengthening our
faith and following religious orthodoxy.

Our forefathers gave their lives or tormented themselves to
establish the Orthodox faith and the good orders of the Armenian
Church, which were sometimes destroyed and spoiled by feeble leaders,
but which were reestablished by good and truthful men like kaḱoḻikoi
Movsēs and P̌ilippos. Armenian churches were reformed accordingly,
and the country was filled with the knowledge of God. This situation
lasted until the tenth year[2] of the pontificate of Yakob, when it started to
deteriorate daily, and continues to do so until today.

We don't want to tell you how it happened, because it is common
knowledge. Whatever was saved from the locusts, was eaten by
caterpillars under that Nahapet, who, against the will of God and
without being elected by men, occupied the See with bribes and money,

---

[1] Armenian text in AASM (cab. 5, dr. 6, doc. 2).
[2] 1665.

to serve his own ends, not the glory of God. To pursue his ambitions and physical pleasures, he ignored the words and the power of God. Unfearful of God, shameless of men and with his natural ignorance and evil roguery, he justifies the words of Solomon, who says: "honour is not seemly for a fool,"[3] because he will be carried further in his foolishness, as it happened to him. Everybody heard of his evil deeds, and affronting letters were sent to him from everywhere.

Together with our father and Spiritual Lord Stepannos of blessed memory, we wrote precautionary and scolding letters to him several times, but he did not react, the way an amputated limb does not feel the pains caused by cutting and burning. After all those efforts all of us were disgusted when we received your complaints and letter of agreement against him, imploring our help. That is why we rose against him, dismissed and drove him out and in response to your earnest requests we forced our spiritual and benevolent father to be katolikos, because we knew that nobody from among our contemporaries could be compared with him in his strong faith, solid hope, true love, just work and complete honesty, as is evident in his achievements. But the second Cain and Juda [Nahapet], succeeded in having him [Stepanos] tortured and eventually killed. Last year, in Tabriz, without even being tortured or facing hardship, he was ready to apostatize. That son of Satan is the type of man who cannot bear even the slightest pressure. Because of that and because of his vicious nature and ambitions, he renounced his faith before kings and princes and caused the death of such a true servant of Christ and a hard working laborer after making him suffer various kinds of tortures.

Honorable brothers, have you realised what kind of a person was the blessed martyr of Christ, Saint Stepannos the Katolikos? We want such a person to become Katolikos, who is perfect in faith and service, and who will be ready to face even death for the truth and the orders of religion. We do not need bandits and rascals like him [Nahapet], disrespectful of religion and full of evil and abomination. The Persians call such detestable and wicked people, *molhed masab*.[4]

Beloved brothers, we were greatly amazed when you accepted him again, because in your joint letter of agreement, signed and sealed by all *vardapets*, bishops and prelates—which is in our hands—you had called him devil and falcon. He was a falcon then, a corpse full of devils, although he had not yet denounced Christ and not killed the Katolikos. Now, when he has committed those sins and has followed his father,

---

[3] Proverbs, XXVI, 1.
[4] Infidel.

Satan, he has become hospitable and acceptable to you. Alas to the blindness of our minds.

Without taking the results into consideration, we presented a new petition to our *Valey Na'amat*[5] King of Kings - - - -[6] of Divine honour—let the Lord God grant him long life and success in his works—who responded to our pleas by dethroning that evil. These are the good news for the faithful of our Church, because Bēl[7] is overthrown and Dagon[8] exterminated. The troublemaker of the Church is eliminated and the dragon of hell is succumbed. The beast who used to eat, grind and crush the rest under his feet, is now broken backed and defeated for the glory of satan.

We could punish him more severely with the order of - - - - [King of kings], but we were aware of his impatient character: therefore, we let that atheist free, provided that he will get lost. Our elderly father Isahak *Vardapet* will serve as Locum Tenens at the Holy See, until the election of a new Kaťolikos, who will hold the evil [Nahapet] accountable, will take back from him everything he has wasted or lost and only then will the son of perdition be able to get lost and go wherever he chooses to go.

Now, after all those arrangements, you may elect Kaťolikos anybody you like, except from among the monks of Western Armenia and Astapat. Report to us and let the commonly elected person come to kiss the feet of - - - - [King of kings], receive the *hokm*[9] and the *Khelat*,[10] return to the See and be consecrated, as is the natural procedure and as we have indicated in our petition.

We accept Isahak *Vardapet* as our Kaťolikos, provided that Sargis Kafayeči should not enter the Holy See and should not interfere in the plans and the affairs of the Kaťolikos. The rest is up to you. We have more or less presented our intentions. But in addition, we demand from the new Kaťolikos to completely eliminate from the Holy See and our nation the habits of Western Armenians, namely: vestments, gestures, ostentatiousness, love for horses, life style, ordinations with bribes, geographic and administrative changes within dioceses for money and other intolerable disorders which are spread by them. Each diocese should remain intact, as it was established from the very beginning and later approved by Kaťolikoi Movsēs and Ṗilippos, but not by others.[11]

---

[5] Beneficient in Persian.

[6] It was customary not to mention the King's name in such documents.

[7] God of Babylon (Isaiah, XLVI, 1. Jeremiah, L, 2, etc.).

[8] God of Philistines (Judges, XVI, 23, etc.)

[9] Royal Decree of confirmation.

[10] Robe of honour.

[11] The document is not dated. L. G. Minasean has listed it under the year 1695 (See *Diwan S. Amenaṗrkič Vanḱi*, pg. 78). But it is obvious that it was written at least one year after the death of Step'annos J̌ulayeči (January 4, 1698), possibly in 1699.

ԹՈՒՂԹ ԸՆԴԴԷՄ ՆԱՀԱՊԵՏ ԿԱԹՈՂԻԿՈՍԻ, 1699

Սիրելեացդ Սրբազանից ի Քրիստու գումարելոց, երջանիկ եպիսկոպոսաց, Աստուածաբան վարդապետաց, մեղսաքաւից քահանայից եւ բոլոր վիճակաւորաց ուխտի սրբութեան։ Նաեւ աշխարհիկ առանց բարեպաշտիրց, Ազատագարմ իշխանաց, ազնուատոհմ Մելիքներաց, իրաւադատ տանուտերաց, խոհեմ վաճառականաց, աշխատասէր երկրագործաց, իմաստալեզ արհեստաւորաց, միանգամայն ընթանուր ազգաց հայկազունեաց, որք ի սփիուս էք յամենայն տեղիս, ողջոյն ի Քրիստու Յիսու ի Տէր մեր։ Յիսպանեան եղեալ Յեպիսկոպոսաց, վարդապետաց, քահանայից եւ համօրէն ժառանգաւորաց եկեղեցւոյ։ Այլ եւ քաղանթար Ղուկասէ եւ ամենայն դուլվապ թաորաց եւ համօրէն ժողովրդականաց միշտ տերամբ խնդալ։

Եւ ընդ քրիստոսապարգեւ ողջունիս գիտութիւն լիցի սիրելեացդ եւ հարազատացդ։ Քանզի կարդ եւ օրէն է քաղաքական օրինաց, եւ մանաւանդ համօրէն ծննդոց Ադամայ որ ամենեքեան ի կենցաղումն անդուլ վարանմամբ եւ անհանգիստ երկսամբք գոն գործեալ չանան, զի թերեւս ճնարել մարթասցին ստանալ կենցաղոզուս շահաւետութիւն եւ որպէս ասացաք ոչ միայն ի բանականս, այլ եւ յանբրան տեսանի այսպիսի իրողութեան հայթայթան։ Չի եթէ առ մարմնաւորս այսքան գտուանի յօժարութիւն երկրասիրութեան, որ անգատորն է եւ մանաւոր, քանի՞ օն առաւել պարտիմք չանան եւ ճնարել յազագս ճոգեւորին որ բոլորն է եւ յաւիտենական։ Եւ զի՞նչ իւիք արդեօք կարեմք ստանալ զայն բարի որ անկոխիխն է եւ մշտնչենաւոր, եթէ ոչ հաւատով հաստատութեամբ եւ կրօնից ուղղութեամբ, որով վասն մեղ ճարքն եւ մաճու շահ ճագնեցան նախնիքն միշտել հաստատեցին գուղդափատութիւն հաւատով եւ գրարեձեւութիւն կարգաց եւ կրօնից Հայաստանան եկեղեցւոյ, որ թէպէտ երբեմն երբեմն բայբայել եւ խախարել է ձեռամբ թուլամորբից առաջնորդաց, սակայն ի ձենճ բարի առանց եւ ճշմարտասիրաց, ուղղեալ եւ հաստատեալ է, որպէս ի վերջին աւուրս սրբազան ճայրապետութ Մովսեսի եւ Փիլիպպոսի թէ որպէս պայծառացման եկեղեցիք հաստարանանց եւ նորոգեզան բարեկարգութքն եւ ամենայն բարեզարդութքն ըստ այլմ, թէ լցաւ երկիր գիտութեամբ Տեառն։ Եւ այս միշտչեւ ի տաս ամն Յակոբ կաթողիկոսին, զոր յայնմ ճետէ սկսա քայրայի եւ անկարգանաւ օր աւուր միշտել ի ժամանակս յայս։ Եւ թէ ո՞վ եւ յորմէ՞ եղեւ լոււթեամբ պատմեսցի։

Քանզի ամենեցուն է քաջայայտ, զի որ մնաց ի մարախոյ եկեր թրթուր, որպէս եւ յաւուրս նանճապետիդ այն որ թարգ ճաճնութեան Աստուծոյ եւ ընդրութեան մարդկան, անձնամբ առեալ պատմի եւ ոչ լԱստուծոյ, եւ դարձեալ կաչառանօք եւ մամնայի եւ ոչ ի փառս Աստուծ, յազագս փատամնյութեան եւ ճեշտութեան մարմնոյ եւ ախտից, եմուտ ի յայն գերագոյն աստճանն, ոչ գիտելով զգիրս եւ զգօրութիւն Աստուծ, մանաւանդ անեղկիդ լԱստուծ եւ անպատկատ ի մարդկան, լաւել ի վերալ իր բնական տգիտութեան եւ անզգամութեան զշարութիւն, ըստ իմաստունն թէ ոչ է պատի յարգոյ անզգամին զի առաւել եւս վարի անզգամութեամբ, որպէս եւ դմա պատաճեցաւ։ Չի ճնչեցոյց գլուր չարութեան իրոյ յականճս ամենեցուն, որպէս եւ երջանիկ ճարք մերոյ Ստեփանոսին ճողեւոր սիրրի յոլով անգամ թուղ զգուշութեան եւ սասատի գրեցաք եւ դա ոչինչ զգաց, ըստ Ընանութիւն ճիստեալ անդանմոյ որ ոչինչ իմանա զճատուումն եւ զխասումն, որմէ ձանձրացաք դուք եւ մեք, միշտել ի ձէնչ եկն առ մեզ բողոք եւ մանսար, տիճա աղաչանք եւ ողերսանք, յազագս որոյ յոտին կացաք, կորուսաք

եւ արտաքսեցաք զնա եւ ըստ թախանձանաց ձերոց ստիպեցաք հարկիւ զ հոգ-
գելոր եւ գրագմերախտ հայրն մեր լինիլ կաթուղիկոս եւ հայրապետ քանզի գի-
տեաք որ ոչ զոյր նարդեաձս ամանակի լրնթանոր որդիս Արամայ այր համեմատ
ն մա, ըստ հաստատուն քաջութեան, ըստ լուսոյն հաստատութեան, ըստ սիրոյն
ճշմարտութեան, ըստ գործոյն ուղղութեան, եւ ըստ առաքինութեան լրութեան,
որպէս եւ յարդեանցն իսկ յայտնի եղեւ, որ երկրորդ Կայենդ եւ Ցուդայդ որպիսի˚
դանն տանջանօք եւ չարչարանօք տուատ սպանանել, գոր յանցեալ ամին ինքն
ի դավրէժ քաղց տանջանաց եւ նեղութեան կամեր ուրանալ:

Այդպիսի որ է զատակդ սատանայի, որ ինքն մէկ պակաս խոսք տանելով
չունի կարողութին, վասն որոյ ուրացաւ զհաատունն առաջի թագաւորաց եւ իշխանաց, լաղագս ախտի եւ փառամոլութեան, եւ զայնպիսի ճշմարիտ ծառայ
Քրիստոսի եւ բրտնաջան մ յակ, զանազան եւ պէսպէս տանջանօք ետ ի
սպանունմ˚:

Ծանեայք արդեո˚ք ով պատուականք թէ որպիսի որ էր երանեալ Նանա-
տակն Քրիստոս Սուրբն Ստեփաննոս երջանիկ կաթուղիկոսն: Այնպիսի այր կամիմք լինիլ կաթուղիկոս, որ նովին հաստատով եւ գործով իցէ կատարեալ որ մինչեւ ի մա մատից վասն ճշմարտութեան եւ կրոնից կարգաց, եւ ոչ այդպիսի
այր ելուզակ եւ սրիկայ ի մանկութենէ լցեալ ամենայն չարութեամբ եւ գարշու-
թեամբ, եւ արտաքոյ ամենայն դէնի եւ պաշտամանն, զոր պարսիկք մլիութ մա-
սասպ անեն այդպիսի առ պղծոյ եւ չարագործի:

Զարմանք մեծ կալաւ զմեզ սիրելիք, թէ որպէ˚ս վերստին ընդունիցիք
դուք զդա, զի դեւ եւ փալկ անուանեալ էիք ի հասարակ մանսարումն ձեր
որ կա այժմ ի ձեռս մեր, բյուր վարդապետավ, եպիսկոպոսավ եւ առաջնորդաց
թողով եւ կնքով: Եթե յայնժամն փալկն էր, այսինքն դի˚ լցեալ դիոբ, որ տա-
կալին չեր ուրացող Քրիստոսի եւ հայրապետուական, այժմ զայն ետս յալել, եղեւ
կամարար հողի իրոլ սատանայի, եղեւ ձեզ ասպնջական եւ ընդունելի: Աւա˚դ
կուրութեան մաց մերոց:

Բայց արդ˚ զի˚ անչ եւ իցէ, կրկին արգ արարք Մեծապատիս Արքայից Ար-
քայիս մերոյ վելիննամատ **** որ եւ տացէ ամենաթագաւորն Աստուած իրն եր-
կարութին կենաց եւ յաջողութին գործող, լուաս հայցուածոց մերոց, եւ արար
զպիղծն զայն մանզուլ: Անա աւետիս լուսաւորչածին որդւոյս, քանզի անկա
բել, եւ կործանեցաւ դագոն, բարձաւ խոխվարարն եկեղեցլոյ, եւ ընկեննաւ վի-
չաակ անդրնդին, զագանն որ մւտեր եւ մանրեր եւ զմանգեալն ւն ունն հար-
կաներ, ողնաբեկ եղեաւ սատակեցաւ ի փատս ամենամայի: Քանզի կարեքաբ
առաւել եւս յաւելով պատութսս դմին հրաանա **** բայց գիտեք զանճամբեր
բարս դորին վասն այն տուաք թոյլ անձիթ: Սիայն այս լինի որ դա կորնչի:

Ծերունի հայրն մեր Իսանակ վարդապետն տեղպասեն ննտի յարտն, մինչեւ նոր կաթուղիկոս հաստատեցի եւ զնմարն պանանջեցէ ի պդձոյն, վատ-
նեալն եւ կորուսեալն առցէ, եւ ապա ուր կամիցի կորիցէ որդիս կորստեան,
աւերից եկեղեցլոյ: Եւ արդ լետ սրրին այսպէս լինելլոյ զո˚վ կամիք ընտրեցէք
լինիլ կաթուղիկոս, բաց ի հոումեցոց ի յատտապատոց սեաազխաց, այլ զով
կամիք եւ ընտրէք, զեկյցէք եւ մեզ, եւ ապա հասարակաց ընտրութեամբ, ելեալ
եկեցցէ առ ուտա **** եւ արասցէ փայրուս եւ առցէ հութ եւ խիլայ, եւ ապա
դարձցի լարթող եւ ձեռնադրեցի որպէս սովորութին է բնական: Քանզի եւ մեր
այսպէս եմք արգ արարեալ: Իսկ մերս կողմանէ, Իսանակ վարդապետն ընդունելի է մեզ լինիլ կաթուղիկոս: Բայց այսու պայմանաւ որ քաֆայեցի Սարգիսն
մի մտցէ լարթոնն, եւ ի մէչ խորիրրող եւ մասլանաթ կաթուղիկոսիս, եւ այլն
դուք գիտեք: Քանզի դիտաւորութին մեր այս էր գոր ծանուցաք փորք ի շատէ:

Եւ ի վերայ այսր ամենայնի, նոր կաթուղիկոսն զայս պանանչեմք մաղ-
թելով զի զնոննմեցոց գործճէ, արարրք, զգքանշն, շարժանումբ, պերգասիրութին,
ձեւասիրութին, ննտեըն եւ յանենն, կաչառօք ձեռնադրութին եւ մամոնայի
թէմ եւ առաջնորդ փոխփոխելն եւ զայլ անեերելի անկարգութին որ ի ննցունջ

ընծիդեցաւ, բոլորովիմբ աննետ առնել յաթոռոյն եւ յազգէս, այլ իրաքանչիր թէմ եւ վիճակ այնմ աթոռոյ եղիցի, որպէս եւ յառաջագոյն կարգեալն է, եւ յետոյ ի Մովսէս եւ ի Փիլիպպոս կաթողիկոսացն եւս, եւ ոչ այլոց:

Document #19

The Decree of Shah 'Abbas II, forbidding the Catholics to build churches in New Julfa.[1]

[The Seal of Shah 'Abbas II]

This high order is issued to inform Muhammad, the *Vazir* in charge of Armenian and other religious minorities' affairs, that previously We had responded favourably to the request of the representative of His Royal Majesty the King of France, to allow the Francs build the church they intend to build, in the town of Julfa, near the Capital City of Isfahan. But now, the Armenian *ra'yats*[2] who reside in the Capital have presented petitions, arguing that the construction of such a church may cause divisions among the *ra'yats* and result in their affiliation with the French infidels. At this time we order that the construction of the said church be stopped. This order should be followed even after the return of the French envoy from the land of the infidels.

Rabi Al-Awal, 1064.[3]

---

[1] Persian text in AASM (cab 6, file 41, doc. 47).
[2] Subjects.
[3] Jan. 20-Feb. 18, 1654.

فرمان شاه عباس ثانی صفوی
سال ۱۶۵۴م.

مُهر
بندهٔ شاه ولایت عباس ۱۰۵۲

حکم جهانمطاع شد آنکه شرافت و وزارت و رفعت پناه آصفی بیان محال رعیت ارامنه و غیره بداند که قبل ازین حسب الاستدعا ایلچی پادشاه والاجاه فرنگ مقرر فرموده بودیم که فرنگیان کلیسیایی که اراده داشته باشند در جولاه دارالسلطنهٔ اصفهان احداث نمایند و در ینوقت رعایای ارامنه ساکن دارالسلطنهٔ مزبور بعرض رسانیدند که احداث کلیسیای مزبور باعث تفرقهٔ رعایا و رفتن ایشان بالکاء فرنگست بنابراین ساختن کلیسیای مزبور را درینوقت موقوف فرمودیم که بعد از مراجعت ایلچی مزبور از الکاء فرنگ آنچه مقرر فرمائیم بعمل آورند

تحریراً فی شهر ربیع الثانی سنه ۱۰۶۴

Document #20

The letter of Kaťoḷikos Ałekśandr to Movsēs, Bishop of New
Julfa, against the Catholic missionaries in Tabriz.[1]

From Kaťoḷikos Ałekśandr, with love in the Holy Spirit and
greetings in Christ. Be informed beloved and spiritual brother Movsēs
Vardapet that with the grace of the Lord and your brotherly prayers, we
arrived safely in Tabriz on August 2 and found the city in turmoil and
confusion, because the accursed and wicked Catholics had persecuted
the Orthodox faithful even more severely than Diocletian[2] and
Maximian.[3] They have imposed a collateral on the priests to prevent
them from preaching against the Francs in the churches, so that they
may not anathematize the wicked Leo, who is already anathematized by
God, the Angels and all the Saints.

In the same manner they have imposed a bond of fifty *tomans* on
laymen, who slander the Francs and prevent their fellow Armenians
from visiting the houses of the Francs. They are able to impose all kinds
of new laws on the Armenians.

We sent Bējanbek to *Jahnšin*[4] to ask him why was he ignoring our
one thousand and two hundred years old order? He replied as follows:
"I do not exchange the dog of an Armenian with one thousand Francs. I
also know that they have paid some gold to obtain that *eltezam*.[5] I can do
nothing against the order. Bring me a new order and I will hang them
along with dogs."

Now it is your turn to act bravely for the sake of the Orthodox faith.
Make the efforts and I will provide the funds. Act in such a way that the
enemies of truth may not rejoice. As I wrote to you from Kuškar,[6] you
must obtain such an order—signed and sealed by the Shah—that
whenever an Armenian is proved to be Catholic, the local judge should

---

[1] Armenian text in AASM (cab. 5, dr. 3, doc. 26).
[2] Emperor of Rome (284-305).
[3] Co-Emperor of Rome (286-305).
[4] *Janeshin*? Vice governor.
[5] Recognizance.
[6] A village north of Urmiya. The letter written in Kuškar is dated July 16, 1706.
(AASM, cab. 5, dr. 3, doc. 29).

give him a warning, declare his conversion invalid, make him pay fines and punish him. If the Judge fails to do all these, he will be disobeying the King's order.

All the Catholic missionaries in Iran do not have their own Franc communities. They are here to convert the Armenians; they have already converted twenty persons in Tabriz and have sent them to Europe. Last year they even sent a woman, the daughter of a nobleman. Where these people live is not my concern. But we must obtain an order to prevent them from living in Tabriz. Only in that case will this evil schism be eliminated and you will be greatly rewarded by God. Be well.

Written on August 7.[7] Today I will continue my travel. We will celebrate the feast of Holy Virgin's Assumption at the Surb *Virap*.[8] Goodbye and live in peace. Written in my own hand.

---

[7] 1706.

[8] The Holy Pit near Artašat, where St. Gregory the Illuminator was imprisoned.

ՆԱՄԱԿ ԱՂԷՔՍԱՆԴՐ ԿԱԹՈՂԻԿՈՍԻ, 1706
(կնիք)

Ի Տէր Աղէքսանդր կաթուղիկոսէ սիրով սուրբ հոգւոյն եւ քրիստոսական ողջունիւ, ծանիր սիրելի հոգի եւ հոգհացեալ եղբայր Մովսէս վարդապետ, զի աՀա շնորհիւ Տեառն եւ աղօթիւք հարազատիդ յամենայնէ անփորձ եւ անկնաս յամենայնՆ Օգոստոսի Բ. մտաք ի Թարվէզ եւ գտաք զքաղաքս այլայլեալ եւ վրդովեալ։ Քանզի անիծեալ շունն լեւոնականքն յարուցեալ էին հալածանս ի վերայ ողղափառացն առաւել քան գղիոկղետիհանոսին եւ մաքսիմիհանոսին։ Չի քահանայիցն ըլթգամ էին առեալ թէ ի մէջ եկեղեցւոյն ֆռանկի վատ չաստէ։ Դիտաւորութիւն այն թէ շան պոռ լեւոնն չնգովեն, որ Նգովեալն է յԱստուծոյ, ի հրեշտակաց եւ յամենայն սրբոց։ Նմանապէս եւ յաշխարհականաց Ծ թուման ըլթգամ թէ ֆռանկաց վատ չաստէ, անցա տուն գնացողն չարգելուք։ Ինչ օրէնք կամին առնեն հայոց։ Եւ մեք գրէժան բէկն առաքեցաք առ ՋանՆշինն թէ այդ ինչ ճանապարհ է որ մեր Ռ եւ ԲՃ տարէն կարգն կու խափանես։ Ջայս էր տրուեալ պատասխանի, թէ ես հայի շունն չեմ տալ Ռ ֆռանկ առնուլ։ Ապա գիտեմ որ մէկ քանի ոսկի են տուած այդ ըլթգամն գրած։ Եսչ եմ կարող Ռբմէն դուրս բան առնել։ Դուք մէկ հուրմ բերէք, ես զՆրա շան ձեռ կալխեմ։

Այսուհետեւ շան եւ շանում բեզ է հասեալ ժամանակ արիութեան։ Ի փառս ողղափառ հաւատոյ, շանք ի բէն եւ դրամն յինէն։ Այնպէս արա որ թոշ-Նամիքն ամչութեան մի կարդասցէն վաշ վաշ։ Որպէս եւ խուշքատու գրեցի, մէկ այլնպէս ոադյան լինի, թէ Շահին դալամնովկամն, ինչ հայի վերայ ֆռանկնութիւն սապիդ լինի, տեղոյն Ռեքիմն թամքին, ասայ, չատիմէն եւ սիասարն առնէ։ Թէ չառնէ, խային է թագատրին հրամանին եւ դարձեալ թէ ինչ տեղ իրանայ երկ-րումն պատրի է Ֆնտած ֆռանկ ժողովուրդ չունի։ Միայն այս է պատճառն որ հայերն բաղրան անեն, որպէս որ Թարվէզոյ մինչեւ Ի հոգի բաղրան են արա-րած ողորկած ֆռանկուսան։ Միչ գի հեռու կին այլ են ողորկած, որ է աղդ աղջիկն։ Թէ ինչ տեղ անտին, գլխներն քարն, միայն հուրմ լինի որ Թարվէզ այլ մին բաղ պատրի չՆատէ։ Թէ որ այսպէս լինի, բոլորովիմ անհետ կու լինի չար աղանձն։

Սորին վարձատրութիւն քո անկշռելի լինի առաջի Աստուծոյ, հաւատամ յԱստուծած։ Ողջ լեր։ ՅՕգոստոսի Է գրեցաւ եւ յայսմաւուր եղայ։ Աստուծով վերափոխման տօնն ի Սուրբ Վիրապն եմք կատարելոյ։ Կրկին կացէք բարեաւ եւ մնացէք խաղաղութեամբ։ Ձեռամբ իմով գրեցի։

Document #21

Petition of Kaťołikos Ałekśandr to Shah-Quli *Khan*, against the
Catholic Missionary activities among the Armenians.[1]

Honorable, glorified and illustrious lord, Prince of Princes - - - -.
This is to inform and petition your lordship and sovereignty that our
first and last request from you will be the following: Let the Armenians
be Armenian and the Francs be Franc.[2] The Francs want to preserve
their identity and convert the Armenians. We do not accept that. We do
not want to see the King's subjects become Franc, like the twenty six
persons from Tabriz, priests and laymen who went to the country of the
Francs and did not return. It is thirty years now since they became
Franc.

Now we ask your Highness for an order and decree, indicating that
the Armenians should remain Armenian and the Francs should remain
Franc. The Armenians should not go to the Church of the Francs and
they should not be allowed to send their children to their schools. If they
do, they should be considered guilty and the local judge should punish
them. We must receive that order, which we will keep and use against
all concerned.

We will be grateful if you show us mercy; otherwise, respond to our
pleas once and for all, saying: "Let the subjects of the King of Kings
become Franc." Our lives and rights are in your hands.

May the Lord of Lords and the King of Kings make you and your
state's rule stable and glorious for many years to come, Amen.

Again, if you do not concern yourself with this matter and do not
issue the order, all the Armenians may become Franc. We beg Your
Honorable Lordship to have mercy upon your subjects and let this
danger of conversion be eliminated. May God strengthen your rule and
grant you long life, Amen.

This petition was written at the Holy See of Ējmiacin by the servant
of this Holy place, Kaťołikos Ałekśandr, in the year 1156.[3]

---

[1] Armenian text in AASM (cab. 1, file 7).
[2] Literally means French. Here it refers to Western Catholics in general.
[3] 1707.

ԱՂԵՐՍ ԱՂԵՔՍԱՆԴՐ ԿԱԹՈՂԻԿՈՍԻ, 1707

Շահ Ղուլի Խանիդ

Իշխանաշուք, փառաւորեալ, պերճապատիւ, պայազատ եւ իշխանազուն իշխանաց իշխան **** գիտութիւն եւ արդ լիցի մեծապատիւ տերութեան եւ իշխանութեան քո: Աha մեր խնդիրքն առաջին եւ միջին եւ վերջին այս է. որ հայն հայ լինի եւ ֆրանկն ֆրանկ լինի: Բայց ֆրանկայ կամքն այս է որ ֆրանկն ֆրանկ լինի, հայն եւս ֆրանկ լինի: Բայց մեք ոչ կամիմք այսպէս: Չուզեմք որ **** ռահարն ֆրանկ լինի, ինչպէս որ թարվիզու ԻՋ մարդ գնացել են ֆրանկկրատան այլ յետ չեն եկած, թէ քահանայ եւ թէ աշխարհական: Աha լ ամ է ֆրանկ են դարձել տեղն:

Այժմս մեր խնդիրքն այս է ի մեծութենէդ, որ մեկ հուքմ եւ ռադամ լինի թէ հայն հայ կենայ եւ ֆրանկն ֆրանկ: Հայն ֆրանկի ժամ չգնայ, եւ տղա կարդալու չտայ: Հարկայ անէն, սահակ թասխիր լինի, տեղին ռէքիմն թամբէն անէ: Այս հուքմս մեր ձեռս գայ որ պահեմք ամէնուն չողապն տամք: Թէ շաֆաղաթ կու լինի, բարի է, ապա թէ ոչ մի անգամ մեզ չողապ լինի թէ թողէք **** ռահարն ֆրանկ դառնայ, ումարն ախտիարն ձեր է:

Տէրն տերանց եւ թագաւոր թագաւորաց պահեսցէ հաստատուն գիշխանութիւնդ քո, եւ հայրենեաց քոց, երկար ամանակա ճոխասիան պայծառութեամբ, Ամէն:

Դարձեալ երէ այս ֆրանկաց բանին վերահասու չլինիս եւ հուքմն չուդարկես, հայքն ամէն ֆրանկ կու լինի: Աղաչեմ մեծապատիւ տերութենէդ, որ ռահարիդ ողորմիս, այս ֆրանկութիւն վերանայ: Աստուած **** եւ քո հրամանանցդ ղօլվարն եւ ումարն գիադայ անէ, Ամէն:

Գրեցաւ արգայա ի սուրբ Աթոռս Էջմիածին, ի սրրին սպասատոր Աղեքսանդր կաթուղիկոսէ: ՌՃվՉ թուին, ի դրան Սրբոյ Էջմիածնի:

Document #22

The Decree of Shah sultan Husayn, forbidding the Catholic
Missionary Activities among the Armenians.[1]

[The position of His Majesty's Sacred Seal]

A high order is issued.

At this time, the chief of the Christians, Ałek'sandr, *Kalife* of *Uč
Kilisa*, petitioned us based on the Royal Decree issued in the month of
Rabi' Al-Thani, 1122,[2] according to which the *Amirs*, the *Hakems* and the
Vazirs of Iran must not allow anyone from among the Francs and
Catholic missionaries to intervene in the religious affairs of the
Armenians, to convert them or to bring the children and the youth to
their churches and schools, to educate them in their own manner, to
marry their women, to build churches and purchase land and property
in their areas in order to convert the Armenians to their religion
[Catholicism] and cause them hardship.

However, at this time, the Catholics living in Tabriz have obtained a
decree, issued in *Rabi' Al-Awal*, 1123,[3] which allows them to continue in
converting the Armenians as they use to do before. They have petitioned
the Honorable *Beglarbegi*'s deputy of that city, and have already forced
twenty five people put up a bond of fifty *tomans* each, to make sure that
they will not prevent those Armenians, who go to the houses and the
churches of the Catholics. This situation which has created divisions
among the Armenians is contrary to Our high order.

They [the Armenians] have asked a new order to be issued
concerning these matters, so that the above mentioned missionaries will
behave according to the new Royal Order. The new order will have to
guarantee that the missionaries will not create similar situations, will
not cause trouble to the Armenians and will return the above mentioned
amounts—which are fixed by bonds—to the Armenians.

---

[1] Persian text in AASM (cab. 6, file 41, doc. 94).
[2] May 31-June 28, 1710.
[3] April 9-May 8, 1712.

Thus, because the behaviour of the above mentioned Francs towards the Armenians is against the sacred *Sharia't* law,[4] We hereby issue a decree ordering that the Honorable Governors, *Beglarbegis*, *Vazirs*, *Darughas*[5] and the leaders of Iran implement all the terms of the previously issued decree, and in all circumstances act accordingly. No one should be allowed to disobey this Royal Decree. From now on they should not allow the Catholic missionaries and the Francs to cause trouble among the Armenians, to mislead and convert them to the religion of the Franks and forcefully and contrary to their wish teach their children the Armenian language.

Whenever Catholic missionaries and Francs living in Iran, particularly in the Royal Capital of Isfahan, Tabriz, Gurǰistan,[6] Ganja, Qarabagh, Shirvan, *Chukhur-i Sa'd* and Hamadan do commit such offences and whenever the above mentioned *Khalife* [Ałeksandr] or *Khalife* Movsēs and other monks or priests of the Armenians are informed about those offences, Catholics should not be allowed to intervene in the religious affairs of the Armenians or to mislead their children and youth and convert them to the religion of Francs and they should let them in every aspect, act according to their religion and tradition. Nobody should prevent them from being governed by their own laws. In that respect, everybody should extend assistance to the Armenians and not permit some Armenians—who have converted to Catholicism—to go to Catholic churches and associate with the Catholics. All transgressors should be punished and prevented from acting against these orders. In this matter, they should absolutely do their utmost and not be remissive in their duty.

Written in *Shawwal*, 1124.[7]

---

[4] The book of Islamic law.
[5] Officials entrusted with the task of guarding towns and maintaining the civil order. (See *Tadhkirat Al-Muluk*, pg. 82).
[6] Georgia.
[7] November 2-30, 1712.

بسم الله الرحمن الرحیم

اینکه چون در یوقت قدیم ... اسکندریه ... قرح کلیسیا ... بعرض ... متقلبات ...

شهر ربیع الثانی ۱۱۳۲ شرف صدور یافته ... احکام و وزراء و عمال ممالک محروسه ... خرج ...

و مذهبشان ... طائفه ارامنه با مذهب خود تربیت و جبال جوانان را کلیسیا ... در کلیسیا ... و نظارت ...

و بازاریان ... موصلت ... و در اماکن ایشان کلیسیا ... ساخته ملک خانه خریداران و دخوی سلوک کنند ...

ارامنه تفرقه ... در زحمت کمال زینه ... و در یوقت بادریان ... سکنه دارالسلطنه ... تاریخ شهر ربیع الاول ۱۱۳۲

به با بطریقه به قدر این بار ... ارامنه سلوک می نمایه ... و دنباب ... کفر سیاکانکاه ... عرض و جمع ...

کرفته از هریک ... جماعت و توان الترام با ... عمایه در مانع ... ارامنه چنانها و کلیسیا ... بادریان ...

تفرقه ارامنه و خلاف فرمان مطاع ... حادثه ... انکید ... این جواب بوده ... بادریان مزبور ...

از مضمون و مدلول آن ... نوزده و مرتکب امور مذکور ... و مرحمت کمال ایشان زینه و التزام و جمع نمود ...

باشند ... داده شود ... بر این ... تکلیف مزبور و قریان ... ارامنه خلاف شریعت عزت ... مقرر فرمودند و ملک ...

امراء عظام و حکام و وزراء و دارو عمال و کلام و مقصدیان ... و رایا و ممالک محروسه ... مضبوط ...

به قبل از این ... اینها جبل در شهر مزبور از مضمون و مدلول آنکه عمل و انحراف نوزده و در ... با این اظهار ...

احد را ... نمودند ... مضمون ... از آنچه مطاعه ... مزبور ... مذهبند و کذار ... در خرج کلیسیا فتح ...

فرمایند مراحم احوال ارامنه مذکور ... اطفائیان ... تکلیف فرقها ... مذهب فرقها کبیر و عدم رضا ...

نمایند و هرکاه ... بادریان و فرقیان ... در محمل محروسه ... در دارالسلطنه اصفهان و بنادر و کذار ...

و جهور ... و همدان ... کفر ... و مرتکب امور مزبور و هیشه ... و عهد المسیحیه را ... و طایفه موسی ...

ارامنه ... عهد ... جان ... منع ... محافظت ... کذار ... به سعو ... جمع الوجوه دون ... این و آئین ...

اعذر و تکلیف مذهب فرقه ... و کذار ... و در باره ارامنه تقدیم زینه و کذار ...

از طریقه خود نفی و در بین ابواب ... و در ها ... قریه ... بادریان و کلیسیا بادریان روند و با ایشان نهریش زینه و هرکاه جهان خلاف امور مزبور عهد ...

و در بین ابواب قدیم و ابقای تمام ... این ... نوزده ... محمد امین ... شهر

فرمان شاه سلطان حسین صفوی
سال ۱۷۱۲ م.
موضع مُهر مهر آثار

حکم جهانمطاع شد آنکه چون درینوقت عمدة المسیحیه آلکسندر خلیفه اوچ کلیسیا بعرض رسانید که قبلزین بر طبق عرض مشارالیه پروانچهٔ اشرف شهر ربیع الثانی سنه ۱۱۲۴ شرف صدور یافته که امرا وحکام و وزرا وعمّال ممالک محروسه من بعد نگذارند که احدی از فرنگیان و پادریان دخل در دین و مذهب ایشان نموده جماعت ارامنه را بمذهب خود ترغیب نمایند و اطفال وجهال ایشانرا به کلیسیا و مکتبخانهٔ خود برند و بطریقهٔ خود درس وتعلیم دهند و با زنان ایشان مواصلت نمایند ودر اماکن ایشان کلیسیا ساخته ملک و خانه خریداری نمایند و نحوی سلوک کنند که باعث تبدیل مذهب ارامنه بفرنگی شود و مزاحمت بحال رسانند و درینوقت پادریان سکنهٔ دارالسلطنهٔ تبریز رقمی بتاریخ ربیع الاول سنه ۱۱۲۴ صادر نموده اند که باز بطریقی که قبل ازین با ارامنه سلوک می‌نموده‌اند سلوک نمائید بنایب عالیجاه بیگلربیگی الکاء مزبور عرض و بیست و پنجنفر از ارامنه را گرفته از هر یک مبلغ پنجاه تومان التزام بازیافت نموده‌اند که مانع تردد ارامنه بخانها و کلیسیاهای پا دریان بشوند و امر مزبور تفرقگی ارامنه و خلاف فرمان مطاع است و استدعای رقم تأکید درین ابواب نمود که پادریان مزبوره بنحوی که پروانچهٔ اشرف صادر شده عمل و از مضمون و مدلول آن تخلف نورزند و مرتکب امور مذکوره نشده مزاحمت بحال ایشان نرسانند و التزامی که بشرح فوق (از) ارامنه گرفته، شده بایشان پس داده شود بنابرین چون تکالیف مزبوره فرنگیان بارامنه خلاف شریعت غرامت مقرّر فرمودیم که ولات و بیگلر بیگیاه و امراء عظام و حکام و وزرا و داروغگان و عمّال کرام ومتصدیان و مباشرین امور دیوانی ممالک محروسه در هر باب مضمون پروانچه مطاعیه را که قبل ازین درین ابواب صادر شده اجری نموده از مضمون و مدلول آن عدول و انحراف نورزند و در هر باب از آنقرار بعمل آورند واحدی را نیز مجال تمرّد و تخلّف از مضمون پروانچهٔ مطاعه مزبوره ندهند و نگذارند که من بعد بخلافشرع اطهر احدی از پا دریان و فرنگیان مزاحم احوال ارامنهٔ مذکوره شده اطفال ایشانرا اغوی و تکلیف بمذهب فرنگی یا بجبر وعدم رضا اراده ترویج زبان ارامنه نمایند و هرگاه پادریان و فرنگیانی که در ممالک محروسه بتخصیص در دارالسلطنهٔ اصفهان و تبریز وگرجستان وگنجه و قراباغ و شیروان وچخور سعد وهمدان سکنی دارند مرتکب امور مزبوره میشده باشند وعمدة المسیحیه مشارالیه وخلیفه موسس و سایر خلیفگان وکشیشان ارامنهٔ ممالک

محروسه بایشان اعلام نمایند ممانعت نموده نگذارند که بهیچوجه من الوجوه دخل در دین و آئین ارامنه نموده اطفال و جهال ایشانرا اغوی و تکلیف بمذهب فرنگی نمایند و گذارند که ایشان در هر باب موافق دین و آئین خود عمل نمایند و احدی ایشانرا مانع از طریقه خود نشود و درین ابواب امداد و اعانت حسابی درباره ارامنه بتقدیم رسانند و نگذارند که چند نفری از ارامنه که درینوقت فرنگی شده‌اند بنماز و کلیسیای پادریها روند و با ایشان آمیزش نمایند و هرگاه احدی بخلاف امر مزبور عمل نماید او را تنبیه نمایند و درین ابواب قدغن و اهتمام تمام لازم دانسته مسامحه و اهمال نورزند

تحریراً فی شهر شوال المبارک سنه ۱۱۲۴

The Armenian Churches of New Julfa and Isfahan

Existing churches in New Julfa

Dedication	Date of construction or earliest reference	Location
1. Surb Amenaṗrkič Vanḱ	1664	Mec Mēydan
2. Surb Yakob Chapel	1606	Mec Mēydan
3. Surb Gēworg (Xojenč)	1610*	Ṗokr Mēydan
4. Surb Astuacacin	1613	Mec Mēydan
5. Surb Steṗanos	1614	Yakobjan
6. Surb Yovhannēs Mkrtič	1621	Čarsu
7. Surb Katarineanč nunnery	1623	Čarsu
8. Surb Betłehēm	1628	Mec Mēydan
9. Surb Nikołayos	1630	Łaragel
10. Surb Grigor Lusaworič	1633	Ṗokr Mēydan
11. Surb Sargis or Ohanavanḱ	1659	Erewan
12. Surb Minas or Surb Lusaworič	1663	Tawriz
13. Surb Nersēs or Surb Aweteač	1666	Gawrabad (Ḱočer)

Destroyed or ruined churches in New Julfa

14. Surb Nazarēt	1611	Mec Mēydan
15. Surb Yakob Muratenč (Xiara Gmbēt)	1632	Mec Mēydan
16. Surb Yovhannēs Šahvelenč	1658*	Marnan
17. Surb Astuacacin	1658*	Dawlatabad
18. Surb Yakob Bałařay	1666	Erewan
19. Surb Tovma (Zangov Žam)	1695	Ṗokr Mēydan
20. Surb Hogi	?	Mec Mēydan
21. Surb Astuacacin	?	Gask
22. Surb Minas	?	Gask
23. Surb Anania Ařakeal	?	Łeynun
24. Surb Astuacacin Šafrazeanč	?	Marnan

Churches in Isfahan totally destroyed in the 17th century

Dedication	Date of construction or earliest reference	Location
25. Surb Yovhannēs Mkrtič	1609*	?
26. Surb Hreštakapet	1609*	?
27. Surb Yakob	1609*	?
28. Surb Sargis	1609*	?
29. Surb Yaruťiwn	1617*	?
30. Surb Astuacacin	1617*	Ṫorskan
31. Surb Amenapṙkič	1634*	Ṫorskan
32. Surb Astuacacin	1643*	Šaxasoron
33. Surb Grigor Lusaworič	1660*	Govdēh Zayenderud
34. Surb Grigor Lusaworič	?	Ṫorskan
35. Surb Beťlehēm	?	Šamsabad

---

* The dates with asterics mark the earliest reference to the churches in question. The references are mostly found in manuscript colophons. See Hakobyan V., ŽĒ Dari Hišatakaranner, vol. I., pp. 349, 360-1, 621, vol. II, pp. 400, 452, 562, 623, 711, vol. III, pp. 91, 845-6, 959.

Chronology of the 17th and early 18th Century Katołikoi of Ējmiacin and Primates of New Julfa

Katołikoi		Primates	
Dawit Vałaršapatći	1584-1624?	Mesrop Jułayeći	1608?-23
Melkiset Garneći co-adjutor	1593-1626	Xačatur Kesaraći	1623-29
Awetis co-adjutor	1601?-23	Połos Tiwrikeći	1629-30
Srapion Urhayeći co-adjutor	1603-6	Zakaria *Vardapet*	1630-1
Sahak Garneći co-adjutor	1623-7	Xačatur Kesaraći	1631-46
Movsēs Siwneći	1629-32	Dawit Jułayeći	1652-83
Pilippos Ałbakeći	1633-55	Stepanos Jułayeći	1683-96
Yakob Jułayeći	1655-80	Aleksandr Jułayeći	1698-1706
Ełiazar Ayntapći	1681-91	Movsēs Jułayeći	1706-24
Nahapet Edesaći	1691-1705		
Stepanos Jułayeći	1696-7		
Ałeksandr Jułayeći	1706-14		
Astuacatur Hamadanći	1715-25		

Chronology of New Julfa Kalantars[1]

Safar, son of *Khwaja* Xačik	1605-1618
Nazar, brother of Safar	1618-1636
Sarfraz, son of Nazar	1636-1656
Haykaz, brother of Sarfraz	1656-1660?
Astuacadur Mirifenč	1671
Ałapiri, converted to Islam	1671
Abraham,	1673?
Awetis,	1683
Łukas,	1687
Awet, converted to Islam	1691
Łukas (possibly the former Kalantar), son of Petros	1692-1703?
Awet,	1703?-1705
Yarufiwn, son of Grigor	1705 - 1707
Stepanos Musabekenč, son of Ałapiri	1707 - 1708
Zakʻarē, son of Kirakos	1709-1719?
Xačik, killed by the Afghans	1719? -1722
Ohannēs	1727

---

[1] Based on published sources and manuscript colophons, Š.L. Xačikyan has compiled a partial list of New Julfa *Kalantars*. See *Nor Jułayi Hay Vačarakanutyunə ew Nra Arevtratntesakan Kaperə Rusastani Het XVII-XVIII Darerum;*, Erevan, 1988, pg. 30. During my research, I was able to discover six additional names in the archives of the All Savior's Monastery and compile the present list of New Julfa *Kalantars* in the Safavid period.

BIBLIOGRAPHY

I. SOURCES

A. Archives of All Saviour's Monastery

1. Royal Decrees (Cab. 6, file #41)

Shah 'Abbas I, concerning the settlement of Armenians in the suburb of Isfahan, 1606. #6.

Shah 'Abbas I, to build a cathedral in New Julfa, with the sacred stones of Ějmiacin, 1614, #7.

Shah 'Abbas I, granting royal lands to the Armenians, 1619. #8.

Shah 'Abbas II, concerning the taxes paid by the Armenians, 1651. #45.

Shah 'Abbas II, forbidding the Catholics to build a church in New Julfa, 1654. #47.

Shah 'Abbas II, confirming the election of Katołikos Yakob Ĵułayeći, 1658. #53.

Shah Sulayman, forbidding Persian officials to intervene in the internal religious affairs of the Armenians, 1669. #63.

Shah Sultan Husayn, sending Katołikos Nahapet into exile, 1696. #78.

Shah Sultan Husayn, replacing Katołikos Nahapet by Bishop Stepanos of New Julfa, 1696. #79.

Shah Sultan Husayn, confirming the election of Movsēs, bishop of New Julfa, 1708. #87.

Shah Sultan Husayn, forbidding the Catholic missionary activities, 1712. #94.

2. Encyclicals and letters of the Katołikoi of Ějmiacin (Cab. 5, dr. 3, file #27d, and Cab. 2, file #99).

Encyclical of Katołikos Pilipos to communities of Iran introducing his legate, 1641.

Letter of Katołikos Pilipos to Yakobĵan, concerning a loan given to Yovhannēs *Vardapet*, 1646-7.

Encyclical of Katołikos Pilipos to the diocese of New Julfa, appointing Dawit, bishop of New Julfa, 1652. #1.

Letter of Katołikos Pilipos to Yakobĵan, concerning the activities of Father Paul Piromali, 1653, #2.

Letter of Kaťołikos Ṗilipos to Yakobǰan, seeking assistance against local Persian officials, 1653, #3.

Letter of Yakob *Vardapet* (J̌ułayeči), Locum Tenens of Ēǰmiacin to *Khwaja* Safar, confirming the receipt of a will, 1651.

Encyclical of Kaťołikos Yakob to the churches of Burwari and Ṗeria, declaring them as a separate diocese, 1659. #5.

Encyclical of Kaťołikos Yakob, restoring the administrative jurisdiction of the diocese of New Julfa over the neighbouring districts, 1660. #6.

Encyclical of Kaťołikos Yakob, appointing Isahak *Vardapet* bishop of Geandiman and J̌łaxor, 1663. #8.

Letter of Kaťołikos Yakob to *Khwaja* Yakobǰan, seeking assistance to settle certain matters with Persian officials, 1670?

The confirmation of a loan taken by Kaťołikos Yakob from a certain Yovhannēs, 1675.

Encyclical of Kaťołikos Ełiazar, delegating Steṗanos *Vardapet* and *Kalantar* Awetis to obtain official orders against the debtors of the late Kaťołikos Yakob, 1683. #10.

Encyclical of Kaťołikos Ełiazar, bestowing upon Movsēs J̌ułayeči the title of *Vardapet*, 1686. #11.

Encyclical of Kaťołikos Ełiazar, restoring the jurisdiction of the diocese of New Julfa over neighbouring districts, 1689. #12.

Letter of Kaťołikos Ełiazar to Bishop Steṗanos of New Julfa, condemning the rebellious behaviour of Yovhan *Vardapet*, 1689.

Letter of Minas *Vardapet* (Astapatči) to Movsēs *Vardapet* J̌ułayeči, requesting the payment for goods purchased by the Kaťołikate of Ēǰmiacin, 1691.

Encyclical of Kaťołikos Nahapet, dividing the diocese of New Julfa and appointing Yovhan *Vardapet*, primate of certain districts, 1693? #14.

Letter of Kaťołikos Nahapet to Yovhan *Vardapet*, advising him to reconcile with Steṗanos, the bishop of New Julfa, 1695. #15.

Letter of Kaťołikos Nahapet to Yovhan *Vardapet*, threatening to punish him for his rebellious behaviour, 1695. #16.

Encyclical of Kaťołikos Nahapet reappointing Yovhan *Vardapet*, primate of Erewan, Tawriz, Dašt and other districts, 1697. #19.

Letter of Kaťołikos Nahapet to *Paron* Petros, asking him to suport Yovhan *Vardapet*, 1698, #9.

Letter of Kaťołikos Nahapet to *Kalantar* Zaḱum, asking support for Yovhan *Vardapet*, 1698. #22.

Letter of Kaťołikos Nahapet, authorising a certain Sahak *Agha* to collect taxes and donations on behalf of Ēǰmiacin, 1704.

Encyclical of Kaťołikos Nahapet to *Paron* Setała and *Paron* Safraz, asking their cooperation for the collection of taxes from New Julfa, 1705. #24.

Ktak, last will of Stepanos Julayeci, 1695.

Letter of Katolikos Stepanos to Aleksandr, Dawit and Movsēs *Vardapets*, written from Prison, 1697.

Letter of Katolikos Stepanos to Dawit and Movsēs *Vardapets* and *Varpet* Kostand, written from prison, 1697. #18.

Letter of authorisation from Katolikos Stepanos to Aleksandr *Vardapet*, to raise 2000 *tomans* for his release from prison, 1697.

List of items taken from Katolikos Stepanos by the *khan* of Erevan, 1697.

Letter of Katolikos Aleksandr to Stepanos and Esayi *Vardapets* in India, describing the circumstances of his election, 1706. #27.

Letter of authorisation from Katolikos Aleksandr to Movsēs *Vardapet*, for the settlement of his personal accounts, 1706.

Letter of Katolikos Aleksandr to Movsēs *Vardapet*, describing his plans to establish order in Ejmiacin, 1706.

Letter of Katolikos Aleksandr to Movsēs and Yovhan *Vardapets*, for the settlement of the administrative conflict in New Julfa, 1706.

Letter of Katolikos Aleksandr to Yovhan *Vardapet*, ordering him to submit to the authority of Movsēs *Vardapet*, 1706.

Letter of Katolikos Aleksandr to Movsēs *Vardapet*, reporting on the Catholic missionary activities in Tabriz, 1706.

Letter of Katolikos Aleksandr to Movsēs *Vardapet*, suggesting to obtain an official order against the Catholic missionaries, 1706.

A petittion by Katolikos Aleksandr to Shah Quli *Khan* of Tabriz, against the Catholic missionaries, 1707.

Letter from Katolikos Aleksandr to Astuacatur *Vardapet*, against the Catholic missionaries in Constantinople, 1707.

Letter from Katolikos Aleksandr to the monks of All Saviour's monastery, advising them to cooperate with the newly elected primate, Movsēs *Vardapet*, 1707. #31.

Letter from Katolikos Aleksandr to a group of *Khwajas* in New Julfa, describing his arrival in Ejmiacin and his reception by the *Khan* of Erevan, 1707, #30.

Letter from Katolikos Aleksandr to Movsēs *Vardapet*, concerning the wills of two deceased Armenian merchants, 1708, #37.

Letter from Katolikos Aleksandr to Movsēs *Vardapet*, confirming the receipt of official documents, 1709, #44.

Letter from Katolikos Aleksandr to Movsēs *Vardapet*, providing detailed information on his economic reforms in Ejmiacin, 1713, #50.

Letter from Katolikos Aleksandr to Movsēs *Vardapet*, concerning the debts of churches, 1713, #51.

Letter from Katolikos Aleksandr to Movsēs *Vardapet*, requesting an official order against Persian officials who enter Ejmiacin and spend weeks in the monastery, 1714, #54.

Letter from Kaťołikos Astuacatur to Movsēs *Vardapet*, concerning the activities of Armenian monks in Aleppo and certain events in Jerusalem, 1715.

Letter of Kaťołikos Astuacatur to *Khwaja* Grigor, concerning the unjust claims of a Muslim official, 171. #57.

Letter of Kaťołikos Astuacatur to Movsēs *Vardapet*, reporting on the economic situation of Ējmiacin and the church affairs in Constantinople and Jerusalem, 1718. #58.

Letter of Kaťołikos Astuacatur to Movsēs *Vardapet*, requesting financial contributions, 1719.

Letter of Kaťołikos Astuacatur to *Khwaja* Safraz, reporting on the financial difficulties of Ējmiacin, 1719. #59.

3. Miscellaneous Documents:

Letter from Patriarch Yovhannēs (Kolot) of Constantinople to Movsēs *Vardapet*, concerning the election of Yakob (Šťayakir) *Vardapet* for the patriarchal see of Jerusalem, 1720?

Letter from Dawiť and Steṗanos *Vardapets* to the community of Hamadan appointing Tēr Manuēl as senior pastor (Awagerēč), 1683.

Letter of Yovhan *Vardapet* to the communities of Ḱali and Alinjan, complaining against the monks of New Julfa, 1698.

Letter of Movsēs *Vardapet*, to the priests of St. Gregory the Illuminator church appointing a certain *Paron* Steṗanos as trustee (eresṗox) of the church, 1715.

Circular letter of Movsēs *Vardapet*, ordering the churches to raise funds for the benefit of the poor, 1715.

Letter of Movsēs *Vardapet*, to the priests of St. Stephens church, appointing a certain *Paron* Grigor as trustee of the church, 1718.

A petition by the people of Ṗeria and Burwari, declaring their loyalty to the diocese of New Julfa, 1693.

A petition by the people of Geandiman and Burwari, declaring their loyalty to the diocese of New Julfa, 1697.

An open letter from the clergy and lay leadership of New Julfa, expressing their opposition to Kaťołikos Nahapet, 1698.

Letter from the clergy and lay leadership of the diocese of Ayrarat to the religious community of New Julfa, expressing their regrets for the martyrdom of Kaťołikos Steṗanos and appealing for peace and conciliation, 1698.

A petition by the religious community of Ējmiacin to Kaťołikos Nahapet, to divide the diocese of New Julfa between Yovhan and Ałeḱsandr *Vardapets*, 1698?

A statement from the clergy and lay leadership of Agulis region, expressing their support to Kaťołikos Nahapet, 1701.

Letter from Mesrop, Minas and a number of other *vardapets* to the religious community of New Julfa, expressing opposition to Kaťolikos Nahapet, 1705.

A joint declaration of the clergy of New Julfa, against all those who convert to Catholicism, 1706.

Dašanč Ťułť (letter of agreement) against all schismatic Armenians who betray their church and join other churches, 1721.

List of taxes imposed on the Armenian churches of New Julfa, Ṗeria and Burwari, 1675.

Financial accounts related to Ějmiacin, 1719.

Accounts of New Julfa churches, 1712.

Inventory of the Church of Shiraz, 1717.

B. Patriarchal Archives at the Matenadaran of Erevan

Encyclical of Kaťolikos Yakob Ĵułayeči, dividing the diocese of New Julfa and appointing Yovhan, bishop of the newly created diocese, 1675. File #244, doc. #359.

C. Archives of Caro Owen Minasian at UCLA

The Decree of Shah Sultan Husayn, forbidding the catholic missionary activities among the Armenians, 1710.

D. Armenian Printed Sources

Abraham Ercwanči, *Patmuťiwn Paterazmačn* 1721-1736 (History of the Wars), Venice, 1977.

Ałaneanč G. (ed.), *Diwan Hayoč Patmuťean*, (Archives of Armenian History), vols. I-X, Tbilisi, 1893-1912.

Ałekšandr Ĵułayeči, *Girḱ Atenakan or Asi Vičabanakan* (Book of Discourse or Polemics), New Julfa, 1687.

_____, *Kondak Ktakaranač Tearn Ałekšandri Ĵułayečwoy Kaťułikosi Amenayn Hayoč*, (Testimonial Encyclical of Ałekšandr Ĵułayeči Kaťołikos of All Armenians), *Azgaser Araratean*, Calcutta, 1848, #12, pp. 91-95.

_____, *Lettre D'Alexandre, Catholicos D'Arménie, Au Patriarche de Rome Clément (XI), Au Sujet de la Conduite Blamable des Missionnaires Qui, par une Injustice Criante, Jettent le Trouble Parmi les Agneaux Innocents de la Sainte Église D'Arménie*, Ayvazoski G. (tr.), *Maseač Aławni*, 1856, pp. 115-123.

_____, *Ťułťḱ ař Klement ŽA Pap*, (Letters to Pope Clement XI),

Galēmk̄earean G. (pub.), *Handēs Amsorya*, 1914, pp. 532-62.

_____, *Tuttk̄ Rusastani Petros Kaysrin*, (Letter to Tsar Peter of Russia), Hovhannisyan A.G., *Hay-Rus Orientać̄iayi Cagman Xndirǝ* (The Origin of Armeno-Russian Orientation), Ēĵmiacin, 1921, Appendix, pp. XIII-XV.

Aṙak̄el Dawrižeći, *Girk̄ Patmuk̄eanć̄*, (Book of History), Amsterdam, 1669.

_____, *Patmuṫiwn Aṙak̄el Vardapeti Dawrižeć̄woy*, (History of Aṙak̄el Vardapet Dawrižeći), Vaḷaršapat, 1896.

Aristakēs Lastivertć̄i, *Patmuṫiwn Aristakisi Lastivertć̄woy*, (History of Aristakēs of Lastivert), Erevan, 1963.

Augustin Baĵeći, "Itinéraire du très Révérend Frère Augustin Badjetzi, Evêque Arménien de Nakhidchevan de l'Ordre de Frères Prêcheurs à Travers l'Europe", M. Brosset (tr.), *Journal Asiatique*, 1837, pp. 209-45.

Datastanagirk̄ Astraxani Hayoć̄ (Book of Code of the Armenian community of Astrakhan), Poḷosyan F.G. (ed.), Erevan, 1967.

Girk̄ Žoḷovacoy Ǝnddem Erkabnakać̄, (A collection against the Dyophysites), New Julfa, 1687.

Grigor Daranaḷći, *Žamanakagruṫiwn Grigor Vardapeti Kamaḷeć̄woy Kam Daranaḷć̄woy*, (Chronicle of Grigor Vardapet Daranaḷći or Kamaḷeći), Jerusalem, 1915.

Hakobyan V., Hovhanissyan A., *ŽĒ Dari Hayeren Jeṙgreri Hišatakaranner*, (XVIIth century colophons of Armenian Manuscripts), vols. I-III, Erevan, 1977-84.

Haranć̄ Vark̄, (Lives of Church Fathers), New Julfa, 1641.

Hovhannes Tēr Davṫyan Ĵulayeć̄u Hašvetumarǝ, (The account Book of Hovhannēs Tēr Davṫyan Ĵulayeći), Xačikyan L.S., P̄ap̄azyan H.D. (eds.), Erevan, 1984.

Kanonagirk̄ Hayoć̄ (The Armenian Book of Canons), V. Hakobyan (ed.), vol. I-II, Erevan, 1964-71.

Kirakos Ganjakeći, *Patmuṫiwn Hayoć̄,* (History of Armenia), Erevan, 1961.

Mahser (Petition) from the Armenians of Constantinople to Kaṫolikos Aḷek̄sandr, *K̄runk Hayoć̄ Ašxarhi*, 1863, pp. 663-83.

Manr Žamanakagrutyunner, (Minor Chronicles), V. Hakobyan (ed.), vols. I-II, Erevan, 1951-6.

"Martiros Di Aṙak̄eli Žamanakagruṫyunǝ" (The Chronicle of Martiros Di Aṙak̄el), Abrahamyan A. (publ.), *Gitakan Nyuṫeri Žoḷowacu*, #1 (1941), pp. 93-100.

Matṫeos Urhayeći, *Patmuṫiwn,* (History), Jerusalem, 1869.

Minasean L. G., *Ć̄uč̄ak Jeragrać̄ Nor Ĵulayi S. Amenap̄rkč̄ean Vanać̄ Ṫangarani*, (Catalogue of Manuscripts of All Saviour's Monastery of New Julfa), vol. II, Vienna, 1972.

_____, *Nor Ĵulayi Gerezmanatunǝ*, (The Cemetery of New Julfa), New Julfa, 1985.

_____, *Nor Ĵulayi Tparann U Ir Tpagrač Grḱerᵊ*, (The Printing House of New Julfa and its Publications), New Julfa, 1972.

Movsēs Bĵnedi, *Yalags Kargi Kaᵗuᵗikos Jernadrutean*, (The Order of Election-Consecration of the Kat´olikos), New Julfa, 1693.

Movsēs Xorenadi, *Patmuᵗiwn Hayoc´*, (History of Armenia), Venice, 1865.

Mxit´ar Goš, *Girḱ Datastani*, (Book of Code), X.T. T´orosyan (ed.), Erevan, 1975.

Oskan Erewandi, "Patmut´iwn Kenac´ Oskanay Erewandwoy Tpagroli Groys ew Ayloz" (Biography of Oskan *Vardapet* Erewandi, Publisher of the Present Book and Others), in Aŕaḱel Dawriẑedi, *Girḱ Patmuᵗeanᵈ*, Amsterdam, 1669, pp. 629-38.

Oskanyan N., Korkotyan Ḱ, Savalyan A., *Hay Girḱᵊ 1512-1800 Tᵥakannerin*, (The Armenian Printed Books in the Years 1512-1800), Erevan, 1988.

P´awstos Buzand, *Patmuᵗiwn Hayoc´*, (History of Armenia), Venice 1933.

Petros Di Sarkis Gilanentz, *The Chronicle of Petros di Sarkis Gilanentz Concerning the Afghan Invasion of Persia in 1722*, Caro O. Minassian (tr.), Lisbon, 1959.

Samuel Anedi, *Hawaḱmunḱi Groc´ Patmagrac´*, (Collections from the Books of Historians), Valarŝapat, 1893.

Simēon Erewandi, *Ĵambr* (Archives), Valarŝapat, 1873.

_____, *Simēon Katᵒlikosi Yiŝatakaranᵊ* (The Memoirs of Katᵒlikos Simeon), in *Diwan Hayoc´ Patmuᵗean*, G. Alaneanᵈ (ed.), Book A-B, Tbilisi, 1893.

Simēon Ĵulayedi, *Namak aŕ Oskan Erewandi*. "Letter to Oskan Erewandi", *Bazmavep*, 1967, #6-8, pp. 131-33.

Stepˊanos Daštedi, *Norayayt Talasac´ Me Stepˊanos Daštedi*, (Stepˊanos Daštedi, a Newly discovered Poet), Simonean S. (publ.), Beirut, 1981.

Stepˊanos Erec´, *Patmuᵗiwn*, (History), Ms. #654. All Saviour's Monstery of New Julfa.

Tēr Awelisean S., *Cˊucˊak Jeragrac´ Nor Ĵulayi S. Amenapˊrkčean Vanac´ T´angarani*, (Catalogue of Manuscripts of All Saviour's Monastery of New Julfa), vol. I, Vienna, 1970.

Vŕtanēs Ḱertol, "*Ḣnddem Patkeramartic´*", (Treatise Against the Iconoclasts), E. Durean, *Usumnasiruᵗiwnḱ ew Ḱnnadatuᵗiwnḱ* (Studies and Criticisms), Jerusalem, 1935, pp. 299-308.

Xacˊatur Ĵulayedi, *Patmuᵗiwn Parsic´*, (History of Persia), Valarŝapat, 1905.

Xacˇikyan L. S., *ŽD Dari Hayeren Jeragreri Hiŝatakaranner*, (XIVth Century Colophons of Armenian Manuscripts), Erevan, 1950.

_____, *ŽE Dari Hayeren Jeragreri Hiŝatakaranner*, (XVth Century Colophons of Armenian Manuscripts), vols. I-III, Erevan, 1951-6.

Yakob Ĵulayedi, "Ktak Yakobay Katᵒlikosi Ĵulayecˊwoy", (The Will of Katᵒlikos Yakob Ĵulayedi), *Patma-Banasirakan Handes*, 1966, #4, pp. 173-86.

Yovhannēs Makuedi, "Olb Hayastaneac´ Aŝxarhi yErewanay ev Ĵulayu", (Lamentation for Armenia, From Erevan to Julfa), P. M. Xacˇatryan,

Hay Miǰnadaryan Patmakan Otber, Erevan, 1969, pp. 274-94.

Yovhannēs Mrk̕uz, *Girk̕ Hamarot Vasn Iskapes Čšmarit Hawatoy - Dawanu n̄wn Hayoč ev Neracu n̄wn Anutlič*, also entitled in Latin as *Symbolum Armeniorum et Introductio de Di Directam*, New Julfa, 1688.

_____, *Girk̕ Patmutean Arareal I Norn J̌utayu Srboy Amenap̕rkči Gerahraš Vani Miaban Yovhannēs Čgnazgeač Vardapetin Vičabanu n̄wn aṙ Šah Slemann Parsič*, Calcutta, 1797.

Zak̕aria Aguleču Oragrut̕una, (The Journal of Zak̕aria Aguleči), Erevan, 1938.

Zak̕aria Sarkawag K̕anak̕erči, *Patmagru n̄wn* (Historiography), Vałaršapat, 1870.

E. Western Travelers' Accounts, Catholic Missionary Reports, Persian and Ottoman Sources.

Anon, *A Chronicle of the Carmelites in Persia, and the Papal Mission of the XVIIth and XVIIIth Centuries*, vols. I-II, London, 1939.

Bedik P., *Cehil Sutun*, Vienna, 1678.

Bruyn, Cornelis de. *A New and More Correct Translation than has hitherto appeared in public, of Mr. Cornelius Le Brun's Travels into Muscovy, Persia, and Divers Parts of the East Indies; containing an Accurate Description of all such Articles as one most remarkable in each of these different countries, and most worthy the Attention of the Curious Reader...*, London, 1759.

Chardin, Jean. *Voyages du Chevalier Chardin, en Perse, et autres Lieux de l'Orient. Enrichis de Figures en Taille-douce, qui representent les Antiquités et les choses remarquables du Païs. Nouvelle Edition, Augmentée du Couronnement de Soliman III. et d'un grand nombre de passages tirés du Manuscript de l'Auteur, qui ne se trouvent point dans les Editions Précédentes*, vol. I-IV, Amsterdam, 1735.

_____, Sir John Chardin's Travels in Persia, New York, 1988.

Clement XI, Pope. "Letter to Kat̕otikos Ałek̕sandr," G. Galemk̕earean (tr.), *Handēs Amsoreay*, 1914, pp. 553-55.

Della Valle, Pietro. *Les Fameux Voyages de Pietro Della Valle, Gentil-home romain, surnommé l'illustre voyageur; avec un denombrement tres-exact des choses les plus curieuses, et les plus remarquables qu'il a veues dans la Turquie, l'Egypte, la Palestine, la Perse, et les Indes Orientales, et que les Autheurs qui en ont cy devant écrit, n'ont jamais observées; Le tout écrit en forme de Lettres, addressées au Sieur Schipano son plus intime Amy*, Paris, 1663.

Deslandes, André Daulier. *Les Beautez de la Perse, ou la Description de ce qu'il y a de plus curieux dans ce Royaume, enrichie de la carte du païs, et de plusieurs Estompes designées sur les lieux...* Paris, 1673.

_____, *The Beuties of Persia*, Sir A.T. Wilson (tr.), London, 1926.

Du Mans, Raphael. *Estat de la Perse en 1660*. Paris, 1890.

Evlia Čelēbi, *Travels*, A.X. Safrastyan (tr.), Erevan, 1967.

Fleuriau (de Armenoville), Thomas Charles. *Estat Present de l'Armenie, tant pour le Temporal que pour le Spirituel. Avec une description du pays et des Mœurs de ceux qui l'habitent*, Paris, 1694.

Fryer, John M.D., *A New Account of East India and Persia, being Nine years' Travels, 1672-1681*. vols. I-III, London, 1909-15.

Gabriel de Chinon, *Relations Nouvelles du Levant; ou Traités de la Religion, du Gouvernement, et des coûtumes des Perses, des Arméniens, et des Gaures. Avec une description particulière de l'établissement, et des progrès qui y font les missionaires, et diverses disputes qu'ils ont eu avec les orientaux*, Lyon, 1671.

Galanus, Clement, *Conciliationis Ecclesiae Armenae Cum Romana ex Ipsis Armenorum Patrum & Doctorum Testimoniis, in duas Pontes, Historialem & Controversialem divise*, vols. I-III, Rome 1650-61.

Godreau, Abbé Martin, *Relation d'une Mission Faite Nouvellement par Monseigneur l'Archevesque d'Ancyre a Ispahan en Perse pour la Reunion des Arméniens à l'Eglise Catholique*, Paris, 1702.

Gouvea, Antonio de. *Relation des Grandes Guerres et Victoires Obtenues par le Roy de Perse Cha Abbas Contre les Empereurs de Turquie Mahomet et Achmet son fils. En suite du Voyage de Quelques Religieux de l'Ordre des Hermites de S. Augustin Envoyez en Perse par le Roy Catholique dom Philippe Second Roy de Portugal*, Rouen, 1646.

Hakobyan H. (tr.) *Ułegruťyunner* (Travel Accounts), vol. I, Erevan, 1932.

Herbert, Sir Thomas. *Some Years Travels into Parts of Africa and Asia the Great. Describing more Particularly the Empires of Persia and Industan: Interwoven with such remarkable occurances as hapened in those parts during these later times...*, London, 1677.

Krusinski, Tadeusz Juda. *The History of the Late Revolutions of Persia: Taken from the Memoirs of Father Krusinski, Procurator of the Jesuits at Ispahan; who lived Twenty Years in that Country...*, London, 1729.

Machault, Jacques de. "History of Mission of the Fathers of the Society of Jesus, Established in Persia by the Reverend Father Alexander of Rhodes", Sir Arnold Wilson (tr.), *Bulletin of the School of Oriental Studies*, 1925, #4, pp. 675-706.

Monshi, Eskandar Beg. *History of Shah 'Abbas the Great*, R.M. Savory (tr.), vols. I-II, Colorado, 1978.

Olearius, Adam. *The Voyages and Travels of the Ambassador from the Duke of Holstein, to the Great Duke of Muscovy, and the King of Persia. Begun in the Year MDCXXXIII and finished in MDCXXXIX.*

Containing a Complete History of Muscovy, Tartary, Persia and other Adjacent Countries..., London, 1662.

Papazyan H. D., *Matenadarani Parskeren Hrovartaknerə* (The Persian Decrees in the Collection of *Matenadaran*), vol. I, Books I-II, Erevan, 1956-9.

Rabbath, Antoine S.J., *Documents Inédits pour Servir à l'Histoire du Christianisme en Orient (XVI-XIX Siècles)*, vols. I-II, Paris, 1907-10.

Rhodes (Alexander) of Viet Nam, *The Travels and Missions of Father Alexander de Rhodes in China and other Kingdoms of the Orient*, S. Hertz (tr.), Maryland, 1966.

Safrastyan A.X. (tr. & ed.), *Türkakan Albyurnerə Hayastani, Hayeri ev Andrkovkasi Myus Žolovurdneri Masin*, (The Turkish Sources on Armenia, the Armenians and other Peoples of Transcaucasia), vol. I, Erevan, 1961.

Sherley, Sir Anthony. *Sir Anthony Sherley His Relation of His Travels into Persia. The Dangers and Distresses, which befell him in his passage, both by sea and land, and his strange and unexpected deliverances. His Magnificent Entertainement in Persia, his Honorable Employment there-hence, as Embassadour to the Princes of Christendome, the cause of his disapointment therein, with his advice to his brother Sir Robert Sherley. Also a true Relation of the great Magnificence, Valour, Prudence, Justice, Temperance, and other manifold Vertues of Abas, now King of Persia, with his great conquests, whereby he hath inlarged his Dominions*, London, 1613.

Silva Y Figueroa, D. Garcia de. *L'ambassade de D. Garcias de Silva Figueroa en Perse, Contenant la politique de ce grand empire, les mœurs du Roy Schach Abbas, & Une Relation exacte de tous les lieux de Perse & des Indes, où cet Ambassadeur a esté l'espace de huit annés qu'il y a demeure*, Paris, 1667.

Struys, Jan Janszoon. *The Voiages and Travels of John Struys through Italy, Greece, Muscovy, Tartary, Media, Persia, East-India, Japan, and other countries of Europe, Africa and Asia: containing Remarks and Observations upon the Manners, Religion, Politics, Customs and Laws of the Inhabitants, and a Description of their several Cities, Towns, Ports, and places of strength...*, London 1684.

Tadkirat Al-Muluk: A manual of Safavid Administration, V. Minorsky (tr. & ed.), Cambridge, 1943.

Tavernier, John Baptista. *The Six Travels of John Baptista Tavernier, Baron of Aubonne, through Turkey and Persia to the Indies, during the space of Forty Years...*, London, 1684.

_____, *Les Six Voyages en Turquie et en Perse*, Paris, 1930.

Thevenot, Jean de. *The Travels of Monsieur de Thevenot into the Levant...*, vols. I-III, London 1687.

Tournefort, Joseph Pitton de. *A voyage into the Levant: Perfomed by the command of the late French King. Containing the Ancient and Modern State of the Islands of the Archipelago; as also of Constantinople, the coasts of the Black Sea, Armenia, Georgia, the Frontiers of Persia, and Asia Minor. With plans of the Principle towns and places of Note; an Account of the Genius, Manners, Trade, and Religion of the Respective People inhabiting those parts...*, London 1741.

Villotte, Jacques S.J., *Meknu ńwn Dawanu ťean Uťłapari Hawatoy*, also entitled in Latin as *Explanation Professionis Fidei Orthodoxae*, Rome 1711.

_____,*Turquie, en Perse, en Arménie, en Arabie, et en Barbarie*, Paris, 1730.

II. LITERATURE

Abrahamyan A., *Hamarot Urvagic Hay Gałťavayreri Patmuťyan* (A Brief Survey of the History of Diaspora Armenian Communities), vol. I, Erevan, 1964.

Ačaŕyan H., *Hayoč Anjnanunneri Baŕaran* (Dictionary of Armenian Personal Names), vol. I-V, Beirut, 1972.

Akinean N., "*Movsēs G. Taťewa či Kaťołikos*" (Kaťołikos Movsēs Taťewači), *Handēs Amsoreay*, 1933, pp. 161-209, 385-414, 513-533; 1934, pp. 1-27, 235-259, 481-533.

Ałanean V., *Nor Ĵu łayi Ekełe či Srbate ťiner* (Churches and Sanctuaries of New Julfa), New Julfa, 1927.

Ališan Ł., *Ayrarat*, Venice 1890.

_____, *Sisakan*, Venice 1893.

_____, *Kameni č*, Venice, 1896.

_____, *Hayapatum* (History of Armenia), Venice, 1901.

Alpoyačean A., *Patmu ńwn Hay Dpro či* (History of Armenian Education), vol. I, Cairo, 1946.

_____, *Patmu ńwn Hay Gałťakanu ťean*, (History of Armenian Migration), vol. III, Cairo, 1961.

Amatuni G., *Oskan Erewan či ew ir Žamanak ǝ* (Oskan Erewanči and his Time), Venice, 1975.

Anasyan Y. S., *Haykakan Matenagitu ťyun*, (Armenian Bibliography), vol. I, Erevan, 1959.

Aťaḱelean H., *Parskastani Hayer ǝ, Nran č An čeal ǝ, Nerkan ew Apagan* (The Armenians of Persia: Their Past, Present and Future), Vienna, 1911.

Aťaḱelyan A.G. *Hay Žołovrdi Mtawor M šakoy ń Zarga čman Patmu ńw n* (History of the Intellectual-cultural Development of the Armenian People), vol. III, Erevan, 1975.

Aŕakelean V.D., "Aŕakel Dawrižeći", *Patma-Banasirakan Handes*, 1970, #3, pp. 33-45.

Ashjian M. (ed.), *Album, All Saviour's Cathedral. New Julfa - Isfahan*, Tehran, 1975.

Atamian A., *The Archdiocese of Naxjewan in the Seventeenth Century*, unpublished Ph.D. dissertation, Columbia University, 1984.

Avdalbegyan Ť., "Anhayt Ałandavorner Hayoć Meĵ Žz U ŽĒ Darerum" (Unknown Heretics Among the Armenians in XVI-XVII Centuries), *Hayagitakan Hetazotuťyunner* (Armenian Studies), Erevan, 1969, pp. 193-211.

_____, "Bahran U Myulkə XVII ew XVIII Darerum" (Bahra and Mulk in XVII-XVIII Centuries), ibid, pp. 414-40.

_____, "Sectes Arméniennes Ignorées du XVIe et XVIIe Siècles," *Revue des Etudes Arméniennes*, N.S., #1, 1964, pp. 299-319.

Ayvazovski G., "Lettre du Catholicos Alexandre Ier au Pape Clément XI," *Maseać Aławni*, 1856, pp. 110-114.

Ayvazyan A., *Ĵuła* (Julfa), Erevan, 1984.

_____, *Naxiĵewani Patma-Čartarapetakan Yušarjannerə* (Historical Architectural Monuments of Naxčawan), Erevan, 1978.

Baghdiantz McCabe I., *The Armenian Merchants of New Julfa: Some Aspects of their International Trade in the Late Seventeenth Century*, Unpublished Ph.D. dissertation, Columbia University, 1993.

Barbier de Meynard C., *Dictionnaire Géographique, Historique et Littéraire de la Perse et des Contrées Adjacentes*, Amsterdam, 1970.

Basil A., *Armenian Settlements in India*, Calcutta, 1969.

Bayani K., *Les Relations de l'Iran avec l'Europe Occidentale à l'Epoque Safavide*, Paris, 1937.

Bayburdyan A.V., "XVII Darum Arevelyan Hayastanum Kaŕolik Missionerneri Gorcuneuťyan Patmuťyunić" (From the History of the Seventeenth Century Catholic Missionary Activities in Eastern Armenia), *Patma-Banasirakan Handes*, 1989, #2, pp. 147-157.

_____, "Karmelyanneri Miabanuťyan Misionerneri Gorcuneuťyunn Iranahayuťyan Šrĵanum (XVII D.)," (The Activities of Carmelite Missionaries Among the Armenians of Iran in the XVII Century), *Lraber*, 1988, #11, pp. 51-61.

Bayburdyan V.A., "Nor Ĵułayi Haykakan Gałuťe ew Kaŕolik Missionerneri Kazmakerpuťyunnerə" (The Armenian Community of New Julfa and the Catholic Missionary Orders), *Tełekagir*, 1964, #9.

_____, "Nor Ĵułayi Vačaŕakanuťyunə ev Arewmtaewropakan Kapitali Tntesakan Egsṕansian Iranum" (The Trade of New Julfa and the Economic Expansion of Western European Capital in Iran), *Patmabanasirakan Handes*, Erevan, 1966, #3, pp. 215-20.

Bellan L.L., *Chah Abbas, Sa Vie, Son Histoire*, Paris, 1932.

Blunt W., *Ispahan, Perle de la Perse*, R. Latone (tr.), Paris, 1967.

Boase T.S.R., "A Seventeenth Century Typological Cycle of Paintings in the Armenian Cathedral of Julfa," *Journal of Warburg and Courtland Institutes*, vol. XIII, #3-4, 1950, pp. 323-7.

Bournoutian G., "The Armenian Community of Isfahan in the Seventeenth Century," *The Armenian Review*, vol. XXIV, #4, (Winter, 1971), pp. 27-45, vol. XXV, #1, (Spring, 1972), pp. 33-50.

Čamčean M., *Patmu ťiwn Hayoč* (History of Armenia), vol. III, Venice, 1786.

Carswell J., *New Julfa: the Armenian Churches and Other Buildings*, Oxford, 1968.

_____, "New Julfa and the Safavid Image of the Armenians," *The Armenian Image in History and the Literature*, R.G. Hovhannessian (ed.), Malibu, 1981, pp. 83-104.

Cash W.W., "The Anglican Church in Persia: Anglican Missionary Attempts in the Colony of Orthodox Armenians in Julfa," *The Muslim World*, #XX (1930), pp. 45-49.

Cook M.A., (ed.), *A History of the Ottoman Empire to 1730*, Cambridge, 1976.

Coste P., *Monuments Modernes de la Perse*, Paris, 1867.

Danełyan L.G., "Hayeri Bŕnagałŕn Iran 17rd Darum" (The Forced Migration of the Armenians to Iran in the Seventeenth Century), *Lraber*, 1969, #8, pp. 63-75.

De Borgomale H.L.R., *Coins, Medals and Seals of the Shahs of Iran, 1500-1941*, Hartford, 1945.

Der Nersessian S., *Armenia and Byzantine Empire*, Cambridge, 1947.

_____, Mekhitarian A., *Armenian Miniatures from Isfahan*, Brussels, 1984.

Edgarean A., *Irani Čarmahal Gawaŕə* (The District of Čhar Mahal in Iran), Tehran, 1963.

Eganyan H.M., "Hołayin Rentan Žamanakakič Iranakan Gyułum" (The Land Tenure in Modern Iranian Village), *Arevelagitakan Žołovacu*, vol. I, Erevan, 1960, pp. 39-75.

_____, "Iranum Vakfayin Hołatiruťyan Instituti Patmuťiwnič" (From the History of the Institution of Vaqf Lands in Iran), *Arevelagitakan Žołovacu*, vol. II, Erevan, 1964, pp. 193-215.

Encyclopaedia Iranica, E. Yarshater (ed.), vol. V, California, 1992.

Encyclopaedia of Islam, M.T. Houtsma and Sir T.W. Arnold (eds.), vols. 1-4, Leiden, 1908-38.

Eremean A., "Nkarič Minasi Keanḱi ev Stełcagorcuťean Himnakan Gcerə" (The Basic Characteristics of the Life and Art of Painter Minas), *Anahit*, 1938, May-August.

_____, "Noragiwt Ějer Nor Jułayi Ormnankarčuťiwnič", (New Pages from the History of Wall Paintings of New Julfa), *Anahit*, 1939, Jan-March, pp. 24-32.

_____, *Nor Jula* (New Julfa), New Julfa, 1919.

_____, *Nor Ĵuḷayi 17rd Dari Ormnankarčakan Yušarjanə* (The Seventeenth Century Monumental Painting of New Julfa), New York, 1944.

_____, *Spahani Ṗeria Gawaṙə* (The District of Ṗeria in Isfahan), New Julfa, 1919.

Fattal A., *Le Status Légal des Non-Musulmans en Pays d'Islam*, Beirut, 1958.

Ferrier R.W., "The Agreement of the East India Company with the Armenian Nation, 22nd June, 1688," *Revue des Etudes Arméniennes*, N.S., VII (1970), pp. 427-43.

_____, "The Armenians and the East Company in Persia," *Economic History Review*, N.S., I (1973), pp. 38-62.

_____, "The European Diplomacy of Shah Abbas I and the First Persian Embassy to England," *Iran*, XI (1973), pp. 75-92.

Frangean Ē., *Atrpatakan*, Tbilisi, 1905.

Frazee C.A., "The Catholic Missions to Azerbaijan and Nakhichevan," *Diakonia*, vol. 9 (1974), #3, pp. 251-60.

_____, *Catholics and Sultans*, Cambridge, 1983.

Freeman-Grenville G.S.P., *The Muslim and Christian Calendars*, London, 1963.

Galēmḱearean G., "Yovakim V. Ĵuḷayeči Arḱepiskopos Ējmiacni (1666-1720)," Handēs Amsoreay, 1914, pp. 532-540.

Ghougassian V., "Steṗanos Kaṫoḷikos Ĵuḷayeči," *Hask Hayakitakan Hanes*, N.S., vol. II-III, pp. 313-44.

Goroyeanč N.Y., *Parskastani Hayerə* (The Armenians of Persia), Tehran, 1968.

Gregorian V., "Minorities of Isfahan: The Armenian Community of Isfahan 1587-1722," (Studies on Isfahan, Part II), *Iranian Studies*, vol. VII, #3-4, (Summer-Autumn, 1974), pp. 652-80.

Gulbenkian R.B., *Hay-Portugalakan Haraberuṫyunner* (Armeno-Portugese Relations), Erevan, 1968.

_____, "Philippe de Zagly, Marchand Arménien de Julfa, et l'Etablissement du Commerce en Courlande en 1696," *Revue des Etudes Arméniennes*, N.S., VII (1970), pp. 361-426.

_____, "Rapports Entre Augustiniens et Dominicains Portugais avec les Dominicains Arméniens au XVIIe Siècles," *Römische Quartalschrift für Christliche Alterumskunde und Kirchengescichte*, 70 (1975), pp. 79-99.

Gušakean Ṫ., *Hndkahayk* (Armenians of India), Jerusalem, 1941.

Haig T.W., "Graves of Europeans in the Armenian Cemetery at Isfahan," *Journal of the Royal Asiatic Society of Great Britain*, 1919, pp. 321-52.

Hakobyan T.H., "Hayeri Payḱare Kaṫolikakan Misionerneri Asimilyatorakan Jgtumneri Dem Iranum (XVII-XVIII D.D.)," (The struggle of the Armenians Against the Assimilation Tendencies of the Catholic

Missionaries in Iran. XVII-XVIII C.C.),*Arewelagitakan Žołovacu*, vol. I, Erevan, 1960, pp. 266-284.

Hananean J.G., "Nor Jułayi Bnakčutiwnə Skisbič mincew Mer Orerə" (The Population of New Julfa from the Beginning to our Own Days), *Nor Azdarar*, Calcutta, 1951, pp. 10-15.

Hay Žołovrdi Patmutyun (History of the Armenian People), A Publication of the ASSR Academy of Sciences, vol. IV, Erevan, 1972.

Hewsen R.H., "The Meliks of Eastern Armenia," *Revue des Etudes Arméniennes*, N.S., vol. IX (1972), pp. 285-329.

Hovannessian A., "Petros di Sargis Gilanentz: Notes Biographiques et Historiques," *Revue des Etudes Arméniennes*, N.S., I (1964), pp. 217-32.

Hovhannisyan A., *Drvagner Hay Azatagrakan Mtki Patmutyan* (Episodes from the History of the Armenian Liberation Ideology), vol. II, Erevan, 1959.

Irazek Y., *Patmutiwn Hndkahay Tpagrutean* (History of the Armenian Printing in India), V. Ghougassian (ed.), Antelias, 1986.

Jackson P. (ed.), *The Cambridge History of Iran*, vol. VI, Cambridge, 1986.

Kanonadrutiwn Parska-Hndkastani Temi Hayoč Azgayin Sahmanadrutean (By-Laws of the Armenian Diocese of Iran and India), New Julfa, 1909.

Karapetian K., *Isfahan, New Julfa: The Houses of the Armenians*, Part I, Rome 1974.

Kevonian K., "Marchants Arméniens au XVII Siècle, A Propos d'un Livre Arménien publié à Amsterdam en 1699," *Cahiers du Monde Russe et Soviétique*, XVI (2), Avril-Juin, 1975.

Kevorkian R.H., "La Diplomatie Arménienne Entre l'Europe et la Perse au temps de Louis XIV," *Arménie Entre Orient et Occident*, Paris, 1996, pp. 188-195.

_____, "Le Négoce International des Arméniens au XVIIe Siècle," *Arménie Entre Orient et Occident*, Paris, 1996, pp. 142-151.

_____, "Livres Missionaire et Enseignement Catholique Chez les Arméniens 1583-1700," *Revue des Etudes Arméniennes*, N.S., Tome XVI, Paris, 1982, pp. 589-599.

Kiwrdean Y., *Yakob Katołikos Jułayeči*, Antelias, 1965.

Lambton A.K.S., *Landlord and Peasant in Persia: A Study of Land Tenure and Land Revenue Administration*, London, 1969.

Łazaryan M., *Hay Kerparvestə XVII-XVIII Darerum* (The Armenian Painting Art in the XVII-XVIII Centuries), Erevan, 1974.

Leo, *Haykakan Tpagrutiwn* (The Armenian Printing), vol. I, Tbilisi, 1902.

_____, *Hayoč Patmutyun* (History of Armenia), vol. III, Book I, Erevan, 1969.

_____, *Xojayakan Kapitalə yev Nra Kałakakan-Hasarakakan Derə Hayeri Mej* (The Merchant Capital and its Socio-political Role among the Armenians), Erevan, 1934.

Levonyan G., "Hovhannēs V., Mrkuz," *Ējmiacin*, 1944, #1, pp. 29-34.
Lewis B., "Some English Travellers in the East," *Middle Eastern Studies*, IV, 3 (April, 1968), pp. 296-315.
Lockhart L., *The Fall of the Safavi Dynasty and the Afghan Occupation of Persia*, Cambridge, 1958.
Manandyan H.A., "Nyuter Hin Hayastani Tntesakan Kyanki Patmutyan" (materials on the Economic History of Ancient Armenia), *Erker* (Works), vol. IV, Erevan, 1981, pp. 134-170.
_____, *The Trade and Cities of Armenia in Relation to Ancient World Trade*, N. Garsoïan (tr.), Lisbon, 1965.
Manoukian A. & A. (eds.), Documents of Armenian Architecture #21: *Nor Djulfa*, Venice, 1992.
Mateosyan A., "Čanaparhaćoyć Julayeći Petrosi Ordi Yakobi" (Itinerary of Petros Julayeći Son of Yakob), *Bamber Matenadarani*, #8, Erevan, 1967, pp. 285-90.
Meinardus O., "The Last Judgement in the Armenian Churches of New Julfa," *Oriens Christianus*, Wiesbaden, vol. 55 (1971), pp. 182-94.
Minasean L.G., *Diwan N. Julayi S. Amenaprkič Vanki 1600-1900* (Archives of All Saviour's Monastery of New Julfa, 1600-1900), New Julfa, 1976. A revised and enlarged second edition: *Diwan S. Amenaprkič Vanki 1600-1960* (Archives of All Saviour's Monastery 1600-1960), New Julfa, 1983.
_____, *Nor Julayi Gerezmanatuna* (The Cemetary of New Julfa), New Julfa, 1985.
_____, *Patmagir Stepanos Ereć* (The Historian Stepanos Ereć), Tehran, 1956.
_____, *Patmutiwn Periayi Hayeri* (History of the Armenians of Peria), Antelias, 1971.
_____, *Spahani Hayoć Temi Arajnordnera* (The Primates of the Armenian Diocese of Isfahan), New Julfa, 1996.
_____, Xoja Awetik ew Amenaprkič Vanki Tačari Nkarazarduma" (*Khwaja* Awetik and the decoration of the Cathedral of All Saviour's Monastery), *Hask*, 1971, January, pp. 20-23.
Minorsky V. (tr. & ed.), *Tadkirat Al-Muluk: A Manual of Safavid Administration*, Cambridge, 1943.
Mirzoyan H.Ł., *Simeon Julayeći*, Erevan, 1971.
Msereanć Z., *Hayoć Katolikosać Tłtakćutiwnk Hromay Paperi Het* (The Correspondence of the Armenian Katolikoi with the Popes of Rome), *Paros*, 1873, #2, p. 3-28.
Najaryan H., *Turk-Iranakan Haraberutyunnera XVI Darum U XVII Dari Arajin Kesin ev Hayastana* (The Turkish-Iranian Relations in the XVIth and the First half of the XVIIth Century and Armenia), Erevan, 1961.
Nasr H., "Religion in Safavid Persia," *Iranian Studies*, vol. VII, Winter-Spring 1979, #1-2, pp. 271-86.

Ormanean M., *Azgapatum* (National History), vols. I-III, Beirut, 1960.

P̌ap̌azyan Y., "Arewtrakan Čanaparhneri Paštpanuťyunə Sefean Petuťyunum XVII Darum" (The Security of Trade Roads in the Seventeenth Century Safavid Kingdom), *Patma-Banasirakan Handes*, 1986, #4, pp. 156-62.

_____, "Rayaťneri Irawakan Azatuťean Harčə Arewelean Hayastanum 16-18rd Darerum ew Šah Sulťan Husēyni Hrovartakə" (The Issue of the Legal Freedom of the *Ra'iya* in Eastern Armenia in the 16-18th Centuries and the Decree of Shah Sultan Husayn), *Ejer Hay žołovrdi Patmuťyan ew Banasiruťean*, Erevan, 1971, pp. 127-36.

_____, Sefyan Irani Asimilyatorakan Ḱałaḱakanutyan Harči Šurjə (On the Issue of the Safavid Policy of Assimilation), *Banber Matenadarani*, #3, (1956), pp. 85-100.

Petrosean P., *Nor Ĵułayi Naxkin Hay Bnakičneri Keankʿə* (The Life of the Old Armenian Inhabitants of New Julfa), New Julfa, 1974.

Ra'in I., *Iraniane Armani* (The Iranian Armenians), Tehran, 1970.

Sahab A. (ed.), *Atlas of Ancient and Historical Maps of Iran*, Tehran, 1976.

Sarkissian K., *The Armenian Christian Tradition in Iran*, New Julfa, 1975.

Savory R.M., *Iran Under the Safavids*, Cambridge, 1980.

Sefeanč M.Y., "Haykaban Vardapet Mi Yisusean" (An Armenist Jesuit Priest), *Bazmavep*, 1922, pp. 326-8, 354-7, 1923, pp. 3-5.

Seth M.J., *Armenians in India*, Calcutta, 1937.

_____, "I Širakay ČHndiks Kam Cagumn Ĵułayečwoč ew Hndkahayoč" (From Širak to India: The Origin of the Armenians of Julfa and India), *Parskahay Tarečoyč*, vol. I, Tehran, 1927, pp. 169-175.

Siassi A.A., *La Perse au Contact de l'Occident*, Paris, 1931.

Sykes P., *A History of Persia*, vol. II, London, 1951.

Tadjirian E., Karapetian M., "Les Voies de Transit du Commerce Arménien en Moscovie aux XVIIe et XVIIIe Siècles," *Arménie Entre Orient et Occident*, Paris, 1996, pp. 157-161.

Tałiadean M., *Patmuťiwn Parsič* (History of Persia), vol. I, Calcutta, 1846.

_____, *Čanaparhorduťiwn I Hays* (Travel in Armenia), vol. I, Calcutta, 1847.

_____, *Ułegruťyunner* (Travel Accounts), Erevan, 1975.

Ter Petrosian L., *Ancient Armenian Translations*, G. Maksoudian (tr.), New York, 1992.

Tēr Yovhaneanč Y., *Patmuťiwn Nor Ĵułayu or yAspahan* (History of New Julfa-Isfahan), vols. I-II, New Julfa, 1980-1.

Ťerzean M., *Yakob D. Ĵułayeči*, Beirut, 1956.

Thierry J. M., Donabedian P., *Armenian Art*, France, 1989.

Ťorosyan H., "Ekełečakan Hołatiruťyunə ev Vanakan Kalvacatirakan Tntesuťyunn Arevelyan Hayastanum (XVI-XVII D.D.)," (The Church Lands and Land Related Monastic Economy in the Eastern Armenia in the XVI-XVII C.C.), *Lraber*, 1981, #10, pp. 80-89.

Tournebize F.S.J., "Les Frères Uniteurs," *Revue de L'Orient Chrétien*, 1920, pp. 145-61, 249-79.

Vadala R., *Le Golfe Persique*, Paris, 1920.

Van Rooy S., "Armenian Merchant Habits as Mirrored in 17-18th Century Amsterdam Documents," *Revue des Etudes Arméniennes*, N.S., III (1966), pp. 347-57.

Vartoogian J.C., *The Image of Armenia and European Travel Accounts of the 17th Century*, Unpublished Ph.D. Dissertation, Columbia University, 1974.

Waterfield R.E., *Christians in Persia*, U.S.A. 1973.

Welch A., *Shah 'Abbas and the Arts of Isfahan*, New York, 1973.

Wilson sir Arnold T., *A Bibliography of Persia*, Oxford, 1930.

Xačikyan L.S., "The Ledger of the Merchant Hovhannes Joughayetsi" *Journal of the Asiatic Society*, vol. VIII, #3, (1966), pp. 153-66.

_____, "Le Registre d'un Marchant Arménien en Perse et Inde et au Tibet (1682-1693)," *Annales: Economies, Sociétés, Civilisations*, vol. XXII (1967), pp. 231-78.

Xačikyan Š.L., "1667t̀. Hay-Rusakan Aṙewtrakan Paymanagirə ew Nor Ĵuɫai Inḱnavar Marminnerə" (Armeno-Russian Trade Agreement of 1667 and the Autonomous bodies of New Julfa), *Haykazean Hayagitakan Handēs*, vol. VIII, Beirut, 1980, pp. 259-287.

_____, "Les Livres de Comptes des Négociants Arméniens des XVIIᵉ et XVIIIᵉ Siècles," Arménie Entre Orient et Occident, Paris, 1996, pp. 152-156.

_____, *Nor Ĵuɫayi Hay Vačaṙakanutyunə ev Nra Aṙevtra-tntesakan Kaperə Rusastani Het XVII-XVIII Darerum* (The Armenian Merchants of New Julfa and their Trade and Economic Ties with Russia in XVII-XVIII Centuries), Erevan, 1988.

_____, *Šahvelu Ordi Sarhadi Hašvematyanə* (The Account Book of Sarhad, son of Šahveli), Erevan, 1994.

Zēḱiean P.L., "Xoĵa Safar Šah Abasi Despan Venetiki Meĵ" (*Khwaja* Safar Ambassador of Shah 'Abbas in Venice), *Patma-Banasirakan Handes*, 1983, #1, pp. 105-16.

Zulalyan M.K., *Ĵalalineri Šaržumə ev Hay Žoɫowrdi Vičakə Osmanyan Kaysrutyan Meĵ* (The Jalali Movement and the Condition of the Armenian People in the Ottoman Empire), Erevan, 1966.

INDEX